Magna Charta Barons
and their
American Descendants

"There is no transaction in the ancient part of our English history more interesting and important than the rise and progress, the gradual mutation and final establishment of the Charter of Liberties."—WILLIAM BLACKSTONE.

"It is called Magna Charta, not that it is great in quantity, but in respect of the great importance and weightiness of the matter."—EDWARD COKE.

"Perhaps there is no event of the history of England which is more popularly remembered and referred to, than the Granting of the Great Charter of King John."—RICHARD THOMSON.

The Magna Charta Barons and their American Descendants together with the Pedigrees of the Founders of the Order of Runnemede deduced from the Sureties for the Enforcement of the Statutes of the Magna Charta of King John

By

Charles H. Browning

Member of the American Historical Association, American Authors
Guild, etc.; Editor of "Americans of Royal Descent"

JANAWAY PUBLISHING
Santa Maria, California

> **Notice**
>
> In many older books, foxing (or discoloration) occurs and, in some instances, print lightens with wear and age. Reprinted books, such as this, often duplicate these flaws, notwithstanding efforts to reduce or eliminate them. The pages of this reprint have been digitally enhanced and, where possible, the flaws eliminated in order to provide clarity of content and a pleasant reading experience.

The Magna Charta Barons and Their American Descendants
With the Pedigrees of the Founders of the Order of Runnemede
Deduced from the Sureties for the Enforcement of the Statutes of the
Magna Charta of King John

Copyright © 1898, Charles H. Browning

Originally published:
Philadelphia
1898

Reprinted by:

Janaway Publishing, Inc.
732 Kelsey Ct.
Santa Maria, California 93454
(805) 925-1038
www.JanawayGenealogy.com

2016

ISBN: 978-1-59641-381-8

Made in the United States of America

Table of Contents

	PAGE
THE STORY OF THE MAGNA CHARTA OF KING JOHN	9
THE MAGNA CHARTA OF KING JOHN	30
DESCRIPTION OF THE MAGNA CHARTA	45
RUNNEMEDE	51
LISTS OF THE MAGNA CHARTA BARONS	56
Barons in arms for the Charter.	
Barons loyal to King John.	
Barons appointed Sureties.	
RELATIONSHIP OF THE MAGNA CHARTA SURETIES	61
MEMOIRS OF THE MAGNA CHARTA SURETIES	69
AMERICANS DESCENDED FROM THE SURETIES	133
FOUNDERS OF THE ORDER OF RUNNEMEDE	187

The Story of the Magna Charta

of

King John

The Story of the Magna Charta

AS this is rather a book of the genealogies of the most prominent of the English Barons who procured the great Charter of Liberty from King John than an essay on the Magna Charta itself, it is deemed only necessary to state briefly the popular grounds on which the Magna Charta of King John, it seems most probable, was demanded, and the apparent methods by which it was finally gained and confirmed, and to give an idea of the manner in which the Barons acted, according to the monkish chroniclers of the time. Those who desire to go more deeply into the history and trace the rise, fluctuating progress, and permanent conclusion of this great instrument can find such information given with great minuteness in the essays of Sir William Blackstone, Sir Edward Coke, John Richard Green, Richard Thomson, William Chadwick, and others, based on the meagre information given in Roger de Wendover's "Flowers of History," from which this outline of the accepted facts and few details connected with the Magna Charta has been rewritten, for it must occupy a history of no trivial extent to show all the circumstances and events concerning it.

Historians, basing their knowledge or deductions on the few prejudiced chroniclers of the Plantagenet period, differ in the details of the century of great and minor events leading up to and causing the final insurrection of the Barons; but in the main they agree that these were efforts to give the Anglo-Norman, or English nation, a certain constitution. Therefore, the uprising of the Barons in 1214–15 may be termed the culmination of desire for a tangible form of government. The spirit of enlightenment was upon them, and their eyes were wide open to the abuse of kingly power, and the outcome was the Magna Charta, the first great public act of the English nation after it realized its own identity.

In the century since the conquest of England the descendants of the conquerors had learned that the laws of the conquered, instituted by equity, had been supplanted by only the old-time arbitrary will of the Norman kings, and, although they had never enjoyed the blessings of a constitutional monarchy, they had, by association with those who in a measure had, come to see their virtues, or, at least, those of the code of Saxon laws, as formed by the Confessor. Therefore, from the conquest of England there had been a struggle between those who sought to enforce the feudal exactions which the Normans had learned and been accustomed to in France, and those who attempted to resist the innovations and to hold to old Saxon customs. At first it was a contest between the monarch, with his Norman following on one side, and the Saxon population, the conquered race, on the other. But when the leading Norman Barons had been won over to the Saxon ideas, to gain the restoration or adoption of these statutes became the endeavor of these Anglo-Norman peers. Each sovereign, from William the Conqueror to Richard the Lion-Hearted, had been earnestly entreated to grant their renewal; but if promises were made, they were evaded. Only once did a sovereign, Henry I., the lawyer, in 1100, concede a limited charter for rectifying the most glaring abuses transplanted into England, but it was never enforced and was soon forgotten.

THE STORY OF THE MAGNA CHARTA

The ascent of John to the throne on Ascension Day, in 1199, was apparently pleasing to the majority of the English Barons and the people generally, as his succession sprang out of a national choice as well as regal inheritance, but it was claimed he was handicapped from the start by a few discontented ecclesiastics, who were sufficiently influential to make his reign an exceedingly troublesome one to the end. In his coronation oath John swore that, bad laws being destroyed, he would substitute good ones, and exercise true justice in the kingdom of England. Therefore, early in his troublous reign, the propriety of a grant of fixed laws was the question of the day, and was championed by Robert Fitz-Walter, Saher de Quincey, and Eustace de Vesci, and these, on the part of the other Barons, kept at the king, persistently requesting him to give it. Therefore, to conciliate them, and to gain, if possible, a cessation, or at least a respite, from their importunities, John, like his predecessors, promised a restoration of those liberties the Barons, and very probably "the people," though they had no voice in the matter, so earnestly desired,—a confirmation of the charter of rights and liberties granted by his great-grandfather, Henry I., and the renewal or adoption of the Anglo-Saxon code.

This promise, made at the beginning of the new reign, gave the Barons some hope for their performance. But the Barons were in error in their judgment, for, seen in the light of subsequent events, John, probably naturally selfish, was particularly jealous and solicitous of his royal prerogatives, which he was certain would be curtailed by the articles of the proposed charter.

In the first years of his reign, John was so unfortunate as to lose his great Duchy of Normandy to Philip of France, and, while but few of the English Barons had holdings at the time in that country, consequently the pride of the nation was offended, so that the dissatisfaction with their king suddenly became general among his subjects. Whatever unpleasant opinions we may form of John's private character and public actions, based upon sketches of him which have been transmitted to us by the monks of his day, we must admit that he was attentive to the work of administration, quick to discern the difficulties of his position, and inexhaustible in the resources with which he met them, and the charge of incapacity against him cannot be sustained.

Upon his return to England after the loss of Normandy, in 1204, John's whole energies were bent to recover his lost dominions; but at the very outset he discovered the spirit of national freedom which had sprung up in England during his absence, and his project was thwarted by his chief councillors, Primate Hubert Walter representing the Church and William Marshall, Sr., the peerage. John at once braced himself to a struggle which he felt was coming. An unexpected chance to strengthen his position came with the sudden death of the primate. He brought about the election, to fill the vacancy, of one whom he could deal with and trust, but an opposition candidate had been defeated, and, as the election had to be ratified by the Pope, both claimants appealed to Rome, and the Pope quashed both elections and commanded the English monks to elect Cardinal Stephen Langton, then a stranger to England, to the archiepiscopal see of Canterbury and Primate of England, which was done. The decision was a startling one to King John, for it revealed the Pope's power and ambitions. It was at once a usurpation of the rights of the Church and of the crown. John immediately protested and then resisted, but Langton was consecrated primate in June, 1207, by the Pope, who threatened the realm with interdict if the cardinal was excluded from his see, as John had refused to recognize him. But the Pope found John hard to control. He replied by a counter-threat that the interdict would be followed by the banishment of the clergy. Pope Innocent considered himself and his high office insulted, and, as he was not a man to draw back from his purpose, the interdict he had threatened fell upon England in March, 1207-8. To John's impiety and rebellion against the authority of the Church can be attributed the picture of his shameless character and wickedness drawn by the priests, the only "historians" of those days whose works have come down to us, and who were the only "authorities" followed by modern biographers until the recent printing of the national records of the thirteenth and fourteenth centuries made them generally accessible, and many of the important statements of the monks regarding King John were refuted by his official records.

After a year, John giving no sign of yielding to his authority, the Pope excommunicated him personally, but this only increased his opposition and defiance, and the result was that the Church changed its attitude and became the ally of the Barons in their struggle for betterment of the laws and the curtailment of the powers of the king, for the acts of Rome after the confirmation of the Magna Charta show clearly that Pope Innocent III. was in fact never very hostile to English freedom. Here we get the best impression of the king. He stood alone, with his nobles estranged from him and the Church against him. His strength seemed utterly unbroken. He was unconquered, standing at bay, defiant alike to his Barons as to the Church. So years passed by and John was as unyielding and as unmindful of his promise, virtually to curtail his own authority, as had been any Norman predecessor on the English throne, and instead greatly increased the royal levies and other burdens.

The Barons began to lose patience with him and then to

devise ways to force him to keep his promise. They systematized their procedure, and, by the spring of the year 1213, they had become so organized and powerful that the king was almost alone in his glory and almost powerless, but still obstinate, and was driven to desperation, as a war was pending between England and France. At this juncture, when he summoned the Barons to his aid, at mid-Lent, 1213, they refused to attend him to defend the kingdom,—first, because he had not kept his promise to them in regard to the Charter, and, secondly, because he was an excommunicated man and his kingdom was still under the papal interdict for having banished his ecclesiastics,—Cardinal Stephen Langton, Archbishop of Canterbury, and his monks,—who failed to respond to his will in 1207.

Upon this John made what has been termed by some a bold and statesman-like move, but others claim it was the Pope's doing, for, as spiritual head of Christendom, he could remove an excommunicated ruler from his throne who, by the law of the Church, had ceased to be a Christian, and take crown to himself, or confer it on one of his selection. However, the facts are, John recalled his banished prelates and Barons, and petitioned the Pope to remove his excommunication and the interdict he had brought upon his kingdom; the price of this being that he assign, grant, and convey his entire kingdom and revenues to the Pope, and to receive back and hold his inheritance as "vicegerent," or tenant-in-chief of the realm, under the Church of Rome, at a nominal annual rental of seven hundred marks for England and three hundred marks for Ireland. This bargain being concluded, the transfer of the crown of England was made by contract, dated May 13, 1213.*

---

* Because of this particular transaction between King John and Pope Innocent III., it is argued that John then became only a tenant-in-chief or freeholder—a vassal—of the Church of Rome, and paid rent to it for his tenement,

By this transaction, a political measure, the success of which was immediate and complete, John protected his kingdom from French invasion, as it was then "Church property," and the faithful were strictly forbidden to trespass,—a scheme of defence which was pursued by England for one hundred and fifty years. But the interdict was not removed until June 29, 1214, by solemn ceremony at the cathedral church of St. Paul, London, it having remained as a security for John's fulfilling the terms of his agreement with the Pope, and John was not formally absolved from his excommunication until at Winchester, July 16, 1214. Upon this occasion he took a solemn oath, before Cardinal Langton, that the good laws of his ancestors, and especially those of Edward the Confessor, should be recalled and the evil ones destroyed, and that his subjects should receive justice, according to the upright decrees of his court, before the coming Easter.

Thus was John freed from excommunication and the interdict tardily removed; but, as he had sworn "that all corporations and private persons whom the interdict had damaged should receive full restitution of all which had been taken away," this delay was only disagreeable. But with freedom from ecclesiastic outlawry vanished all of John's promises, and he supposed that his Barons would not renew the struggle for the liberties of the Magna Charta. This hope was futile.

The Barons finding that, while the country was then in a

England, and that all his landowning or landholding subjects, Earls and Barons included, were only undertenants or copy-holders, according to feudal laws, and that this fact broke the letters-patent of the nobility, and consequently the baronage ceased to be peers of the realm when John transferred his crown to the Pope. And, further, that since Barons were only, in feudal law, copy-holders, they had no right to legislate at Runnemede or elsewhere, and consequently the Magna Charta granted by King John was invalid in title and worthless as a legal document.

comparatively prosperous state, abuses and excessive taxes were unabated. Secret meetings were held throughout England by the Barons and their following, and their grievances made common property, and all united in a firm determination not to give the king a single man for another proposed invasion of France and an effort to recover Normandy. At this time the strongest opposition to John's martial plans was among his northern Barons. The great houses of de Lacie, de Vesci, de Percy, de Ros, and others, were thoroughly English, and had no interest, excepting by tradition, in Normandy, and took a most decided attitude of opposition to his schemes. Furious at this revolt, John was preparing to march the royal army against the northern Barons, when he was dissuaded from this revengeful determination by his Justiciary, John Fitz-Geoffrey, who was secretly friendly to the Barons' cause, aided by the primate, Stephen Langton, also in sympathy with the Barons, who counselled the king to compel the northern Barons to obey him by process of law.

By this time the Barons saw clearly that John was only temporizing with them in the matter of the Charter, so a general assembly of the peers and ecclesiastics was convened at St. Paul's Church, London, on August 25, 1214, when Archbishop Langton presided and addressed them, bringing to mind the oath made by the king on the occasion of the removal of his excommunication, and then presented to the convention an original copy of the Charter granted by Henry I., which he asked them to support and accept as a base for needed reforms, that the long-lost liberties of England might be restored. This copy of the instrument was addressed by King Henry "to Hugh de Boclande, Justiciary of England, and all his faithful subjects, as well French as English, in Hertfordshire, greeting," and was witnessed by " Maurice, Bishop of London, William, Bishop-elect of Winchester, Gerard of Hereford, Earl Henry, Earl Simon, Earl Walter Gifford, Robert de Montfort, Roger Bigod, and many others." The contents of this instrument, which had not only never been enforced, but of which all trace had been lost, was, after some changes, acceptable and incorporated in the draft of the Magna Charta. The assembly of Barons then took solemn oath in a body to defend their liberties with their lives, all feeling that the covenant then made would eternally reflect honor on their names.

This was the conclusion of the first formal meeting of the Barons for securing, by force if necessary, the king's consent to the Magna Charta. From that moment the baronage was no longer drawn together in secret conspiracies by a sense of common wrong, or a vague longing for common deliverance; they had openly united in a definite claim of national freedom and national law. But many were the difficulties they had to encounter before such a conclusion of their efforts was reached, and the liberties of Magna Charta formed the only ostensible motive under which they continued to act together.

The report of this meeting was taken by Langton to the king, then with his army at Northampton, and it was then that he and the justiciary persuaded the king to go to law rather than war with the northern Barons. John now became much alarmed and applied to the Pope, as a tributary, for aid. This gave His Holiness an opportunity he desired. He sent his legate at once to fully secure the Church's sovereignty in England by receiving an additional act of submission from John. All the legate's demands were conceded, but he declined to interfere with the Barons, though John so requested him. This was, in fact, a second resignation of the crown by John to the Pope, and, in behalf of the Barons, Archbishop Langton entered a protest against the proceeding. Spiritual aid was all the benefit John derived from Rome, and excommunications were showered on the Barons and ecclesiastics of England, who were in opposition to the king and, therefore, to the Pope.

The year 1214 continued to pass away without any appearance of the liberties of the Magna Charta being instituted or the old laws being recalled. John's object in meeting the Barons' claim by delay appears to have been the hope that a victory over the French, as at this juncture he had again carried war into their land, would turn their minds to foreign from domestic affairs; but again he was defeated and his return forced on the crisis to which events had so long been drifting, for this last defeat gave strength to the opposition party at home, and the open resistance of the northern Barons encouraged the others. So on November 20, 1214, a second convention of the Barons and prelates was called to take place in the abbey church of Bury St. Edmunds, in County Suffolk, the object of which was to take into consideration the most effective methods for obtaining their demands and for compelling John to keep his promise.

Archbishop Langton again presided. He read again the Charter of Henry I., and also a rough draft of the Charter desired, and, after some amendments, it was agreed to, the proceedings being very formal. Before adjournment the Barons confessed themselves annoyed and irritated in the extreme by the procrastinations of the king, and called on the presiding prelate to witness their solemn oath, which was in effect that the king should immediately grant and confirm the laws and liberties they desired by a charter under his seal, or that they would withdraw themselves from his fealty until they should gain the satisfaction they desired.

At length it was agreed that after the ensuing Christmas, in 1214, they should go to the king in a body to demand the confirmation of their liberties, and that in the mean time they should provide themselves with horses and arms, so that if the king should endeavor to depart from his oath, put them off again with promises, or refuse their requests altogether, they would instantly, by capturing his castles, compel him to satisfy their demands. Then the Barons returned to their respective homes.

This engagement was kept, and January 6, 1214-15, a large delegation of the Barons appeared, fully mailed and armed, before the king at the New Temple, in London, and in distinct and resolute terms made known the wishes of the peers, and demanded the confirmation of the liberties and laws of King Edward and of Henry I. John was much concerned with their impetuosity and surprised at their military array.

But all the Barons could get out of the king was that, as it was a great and difficult thing which they asked, he must have a respite until the end of or after Easter, April 19, 1215, for its consideration, and then, if it were in his opinion proper, they should receive full satisfaction, as he had promised in his oath of July 16 previous. This was an old story to the Barons, and the most impetuous were for keeping their oath made at St. Edmund's Bury; but, on the matter being canvassed, it was decided to give the king his wish, but to demand sureties for his promises. So John nominated Langton, the Archbishop of Canterbury, the Bishop of Ely, and William Marshall, Earl of Pembroke, who were accepted, when these Barons returned to their homes.

Here, then, at last, was a certain day assigned, when all hoped the civil contentions between the king and his subjects would finally terminate. But John, during the period yet allowed him, endeavored by various means to fortify himself against the conclusion, so long procrastinated. To circumvent the Barons, he caused the oath of allegiance to be again administered to all his subjects and the nobles to renew homage to him, assumed the cross in order to secure personal shelter under ecclesiastic protection, and yielded to the English prelates alone some of the liberties they contended for.

Notwithstanding all these precautions, the king did not strengthen his position. Easter, April 19, arrived, and, according to their promise,—they always fulfilled their promises to John,—the Barons assembled with a large, well-equipped army, in which there were upward of two thousand knights, at the town of Stamford, in Lincolnshire, Easter week, to receive the ratification of John's promises. The king was, however, they learned, awaiting their coming at Oxford; therefore, on Monday, April 27, the Barons marched and encamped at Brockley, in Northamptonshire, about fifteen miles from Oxford. Upon receiving a report of their numbers and situation, the king thought it best for him not to attend in person any conference with them, but deputed William Marshall, Sr., Earl of Pembroke, and the Archbishop of Canterbury, two of his sureties, to go to them in his behalf and to demand a further description of those laws and liberties which the Barons demanded, although he had repeatedly been informed of them.

However, a schedule of the desired Charter was delivered to the royal messengers, who were really their friends at court, with the positive assurances that if the king still refused to confirm it, under his seal, the Barons were resolved at once to break through all the ties which had hitherto withheld them, and force his lingering consent by seizing upon his fortresses. John, upon receiving this reply, was much agitated, and declared that it was the Barons' wish to deprive him of his kingdom, but that his consent should never be yielded to liberties which would involve his prerogative in slavery.

The Barons were well aware, by such a reply, which the royal messengers brought to them, that time would effect but little in their behalf, and that force alone could prosper their faltering cause. Accordingly they prepared to execute those resolutions which their message to the king had already premised. In pursuance of their intentions they consulted together and unanimously elected Robert Fitz-Walter, one of their number, their leader or general, under the title of "Marshal of God and the Holy Church."

Without any declaration of war or further warning, the Barons proceeded to carry their threat into execution. On May 5 they solemnly threw off their allegiance at Wallingford. Their first aggressive move was to lay siege to the castle of Northampton. Here, however, meeting with no success after fifteen days' siege, as they had not prepared battering-engines, the baronial army, after the loss of the standard-bearer of Robert Fitz-Walter by a shot, withdrew to Bedford, where the castle, on demand, was yielded to them by William de Beauchamp, its owner.

Whilst the Barons were thus openly proceeding, a secret plan of operations was also carrying on with the principal citizens of London, including the mayor, who had agreed to deliver up to them one of the gates of the city. Accordingly, by forced marches in the night, going through Ware, in Hertfordshire, the Barons arrived at London at daybreak, Sunday, May 24, and entered the city at Aldgate, without any tumult, whilst the inhabitants were at church. The Barons, having thus got into the city, placed their own guards in charge of each of the gates, and then arranged all matters in the city at will, for the rich citizens were favorable to them and the poor ones were afraid to murmur against them, and took security from the citizens.

Exeter and Lincoln followed the lead of London and surrendered to detachments of the baronial army; promises of aid came from Scotland and Wales, and the northern Barons marched hastily, under the leadership of Eustace de Vesci, to join the others in the capital.

King John at the time of the capture of London by the Barons was at Windsor, near the city, and was wholly ignorant, it is presumed, of this hostile move of the Barons and of their intention to besiege his strongest fortress, the Tower of London. It appears from his Itinerary, made up from his dated official documents, that John continued at Windsor till June 3, and then went to Odiham, and was at Winchester until the 8th, and from there went to Merton, in Surrey, and was back again at Odiham on the 9th, whence he returned to Windsor, where he had his head-quarters during the meetings with the Barons at Runnemede until June 26, when he went to Winchester, where he remained until July.

The advantages the Barons had now gained were made use of by them to gather to themselves as many as possible of the Barons who had retained their allegiance to the king, and those others who had up to this remained neutral. So, while preparations for the siege of the Tower were being made, circular letters were sent to the nearest, demanding their assistance in the interests of the Magna Charta, and assuring them of the heaviest vengeance on their estates and castles if they refused. The result was that the neutral peers, with their armed followers, joined the baronial army, and some of John's friends left his cause, deeming it hopeless.

John's situation was now trying in the extreme. Virtually powerless, with nearly his whole baronage and subjects of all degrees in arms against him, the pleas of the exchequer and of the sheriff's courts stopped through the realm because there was no one to make a valuation for the king, he surrendered almost without striking a blow in defence. He sent from Winchester, on June 7, William Marshall, Earl of Pembroke, as a royal messenger to the Barons in the city to declare his readiness to accede to their demands, and expressed his willingness that an early period be assigned for the conclusion and ratification of the Magna Charta. The Barons returned for answer, by the Earl of Pembroke, that they would wait upon him with the Charter on Tuesday, June 9, outside of the city, on what was known as Council Meadow, or Runnemede, on the bank of the river Thames. John issued his writ of safe-conduct to the Barons, dated June 8, at Merton, and they at once withdrew their army from the city and encamped upon this meadow to await him. But that night John sent a messenger deferring the meeting till the Monday following. So the Barons again had to await his pleasure.

On Trinity Monday, June 15 (O.S.), King John came out from the city, attended by Langton and Marshall and a few supporters, and occupied the royal tent on Runnemede. He was astonished at the baronial array, and saw it would be folly to retract or temporize again. The chief Barons went into the royal tent. Preliminaries having been arranged and carried out, ceremony was dispensed with and the business was quickly and firmly arranged. The engrossed copy of the Magna Charta was read over by the Earl of Pembroke to the king and compared with the schedule and articles already submitted to John, and spread before him for his final act. There was almost breathless silence in the royal tent and in the great multitude without whilst the king confirmed the Magna Charta by a solemn oath and placed his seal to the precious instrument, June 15, 1215, in the seventeenth year of his reign, and then was heard, even to London, a great shout of victory.

The original schedule of the principal liberties contained in the Magna Charta, preparatory to the final settlement of the more perfect instrument, was also sealed in a manner similar to the charter itself. The original Magna Charta was copied and the Great Seal of England, or the king's seal, attached to it and sent to all the cathedrals in the kingdom.

King John now left the Barons' camp and returned to Windsor, while the Barons proceeded to the election of twenty-five of their number whose duty it should be to enforce the observance of all which the Magna Charta contained. Those who were intrusted with this authority were certainly some of the most celebrated men of their time, both with regard to descent, to valor, and to intellectual endowments.

The next day it had been the intention of the Barons to break camp and return home, but some one raised the question of security. It was true, he said, that they had got the Charter from John, but what real and substantial security for his performance of the articles of the Charter had they? Therefore a covenant was drawn up giving the Barons custody of the city and Tower of London till August 15 ensuing, and afterwards until the Charter should be carried into execution, and the king was sent for and again came to Runnemede and complied with the request of the Barons and sealed and delivered the Covenant on June 19, four days after the confirming of the Magna Charta. On this day John also delivered to the twenty-five sureties their writs, or letters of election, as they were called, addressed by the king to the sheriffs, etc., in the various counties of England. These gave the status of the sureties, indicated their authority, and provided for the election of twelve knights of the shire in each county who should have power to rectify the laws and customs of their respective counties and be responsible to the surety under whose care the county was.

Before disbanding the major part of their army, the

Barons resolved to have a tournament in celebration of their victory. But evidently this carried with it some risk, as Robert Fitz-Walter issued an order to William d'Albini, commander in the city of London, to be very vigilant to keep possession of the city, as he had heard of an effort intended to be made to take possession of it for the king. On taking this precaution, Fitz-Walter issued an invitation to all his companions, saying, "We enjoin and earnestly beseech you to come to the tournament [June 29] near London, in Staines' Wood, and at the town of Hounslow, well provided with horses and arms, that you may there obtain honor. Whoever performs well there will receive a bear, which a lady will send to the tournament. Farewell."

Holinshead states: "Great reiosing was made for this conclusion of peace betwixt the kinge and his Barons, the people iudging that God had toutched the king's heart and mollified it, wherby happie daies were come for the relame of England, as though it had beene deliuered out of bondage of Aegypt, but were much deceiued, for the kinge hauing condescended to make such grant of liberties, farre contrarie to his mind, was right sorrowfull in his hearte." The final acts immediately connected with the Runnemede proceedings were John's writs dated at Runnemede, June 23, dismissing his foreign troops, and one dated Winchester, June 27, for causing all persons to swear obedience to the twenty-five sureties.

The Barons were still suspicious of John, and, although they held London, they thought it advisable to secure Rochester Castle, and sent William d'Albini to take possession of it as a garrison. But as this was a matter outside of his agreement with the Barons, John sent his royal troops to retake it, which they did only after a siege of three months, starving the garrison into capitulating, and d'Albini was imprisoned in Corfe Castle. Why the Barons did not go from London to the aid of d'Albini is one of the mysteries of the foggy historical atmosphere of these times.

After the final adjournment of the Barons, John did all that he could to make the Charter a dead-letter. He prevailed on the Pope to annul the Magna Charta and to suspend Langton by bull dated September 24, and to excommunicate thirty-one of the Barons therein named, which bull was dated December 16, 1215. The excommunicated were: "Those citizens of London who have been the chief promoters of the aforesaid crime and Robert Fitz-Walter, Saher, Earl of Winchester, R[obert] de Quincey, his son, G[eoffrey] de Mandeville, and William his brother, Robert [*sic*], Earl of Clare, and G[ilbert], his son, H[umphrey], Earl of Hereford, R[ichard] de Percy, Eustace de Vesci, John [de Lacie], Constable of Chester, William de Mowbray, William d'Albini, W[illiam], his son, R[obert] de Ros, and William, his son, P[eter] de Brus, R[oger] de Cressy, John, his son, Ralph Fitz-Robert, R[oger], Earl Bigod, H[ugh], his son, Robert de Vere, Fulk Fitz-Warren, W[illiam] Malet, W[illiam] de Montacute, W[illiam] Fitz-Marshall, William de Beauchamp, S[imon] de Kime, R[oger] de Mont Begon, and Nicholas de Stuteville, and also several others expressed in the decree by name as guilty."

John also again imported hired continental soldiers and committed disgraceful devastations on the Barons' English estates, and, to revenge and protect themselves, the Barons offered the crown of England to the Dauphin of France (subsequently King Louis VIII.), upon condition of his supplying them with an army to defeat John and his hirelings.

In spite of papal wrath, the Dauphin landed with an army in England, May 21, 1216, entered London, and was conducted by the Barons to St. Paul's, where he received their homage and took an oath to govern them in the manner they desired. The baronial cause was now attended with rapid success, whilst that of John declined in proportion. It seemed as if all England, and even Scotland, declared in favor of Louis and the Barons. His few loyal Barons deserted John to Louis, and his foreign troops left him and returned home. John, after this, was unfortunate in the field, and died, after a few days' illness, at Newark Castle, October 19, 1216, in the forty-ninth year of his age, and his body was deposited in Worcester Cathedral.

In a week, on October 27, a few days after John's body had been deposited in the cathedral with befitting ceremonies, the ecclesiastics and Barons friendly to the deceased king were again convened here by the Pope's legate, and arranged for the coronation of John's successor, his eldest son, Henry, then only ten years old. On the following morning the lad was crowned in this cathedral, and after this function, William Marshall, Sr., Earl of Pembroke, was appointed Protector of the realm during the nonage of the young king.

Almost immediately the Protector proceeded to attempt to rid the country of the cause for a divided baronage and to win the dissatisfied back to their allegiance. He recruited the royal army, and called upon all Englishmen to join the royal standard in a campaign against the French, who had gained a foothold in England. Some of the sureties for the Magna Charta—conspicuously William de Fortibus, William d'Albini, William Marshall, Jr., Roger de Montbegon, Richard de Percy, and Robert de Ros—joined the royal standard again, but the majority still remained loyal to the cause of the Charta (de Mandeville, de Vesci, and Roger de Mowbray were dead, and de Laci was in the Holy Land), as, as yet, no assurance had been given that it would be confirmed by the new king. In the spring the Protector started out to hunt up the Dauphin's army, and eventually chased it into the city of Lincoln, which he gallantly took by storm, killing the French commander, the Count de Perche, and completely annihilating his army, on May 19, 1217, when the sureties Saher de Quincey, Henry de Bohun, Robert Fitz-Walter, Richard de Montfichet, William de Mowbray, and Gilbert de Clare were taken prisoners. Immediately afterwards the Protector took possession of London, when terms were agreed upon allowing the Dauphin to take his soldiers honorably to France, and ratified on Runnemede meadow. Subsequently the Magna Charta, with amendments, was confirmed by the king and a general amnesty extended to all who had been in arms in its interest.

This is the story briefly told of the Magna Charta of King John up to the time of Henry III. A great many of its stipulations refer to feudal exactions, now so long obsolete that the restraints on them cease to be intelligible and not particularly interesting to non-professional readers; but its stipulations on the supremacy of fixed principles of the law over the will and power of a monarch and its establishment of a common law, with trial by jury, has endeared it to multitudes of English-speaking people, Sir Edward Coke writing of it: "As the gold-finer will not out of the dust, threads, or shreds of gold let pass the least crum, in respect of the excellence of the metal, so ought not the learned reader to let pass any syllable of This Law in respect of the excellence of the matter." King John's Great Charter has the most conspicuous place in the history of all English charters, not only from its comparative completeness and that it was exacted by his Barons in arms, and was not, therefore, a concession carelessly conceded and readily forgotten, but because this is the only charter which provided securities for its observance. In all subsequent charters and grants there was no clause similar to Section 69, the omission probably being occasioned by a conviction that the provision was derogatory to the rights of the crown. However, the circumstances under which this Charter was forced from the king, and the uncertainty of John's promises, probably justified the appointment of overseers, especially, too, as this was to be a general change of old customs all over England.

The clause in the Charter stating that if the complaints of the Barons were not redressed within forty days after they had petitioned the king, it should become their duty to levy war upon him, aided by the whole nation, was, in the opinion of nearly all critics of the Magna Charta of King John, most crafty and unlawful, and amounted to a permission to commit a species of high treason under the pretence of reforming the laws, so it was omitted in succeeding charters from its positive illegality. After the king had left Runnemede he renewed this command, adding that those who were unwilling to swear allegiance and assist the Barons against the king would be compelled, by his command, to do so! This command was given in a formal writ, dated at Winchester, June 27, 1215.

The Magna Charta of King John

[Translated from the original copy preserved in the archives of Lincoln Cathedral.]

JOHN, by the Grace of God, King of England, Lord of Ireland, Duke of Normandy and Aquitaine, and Earl of Anjou, to his Archbishops, Bishops, Abbots, Earls, Barons, Justiciaries, Foresters, Sheriffs, Governors, Officers, and to all Bailiffs, and his faithful Subjects, Greeting!

Know ye, that We, in the presence of God, and for the salvation of our own soul, and of the souls of all our ancestors, and of our heirs, to the honor of God, and the exaltation of the Holy Church and amendment of our Kingdom, by the counsel of our venerable fathers, Stephen, Archbishop of Canterbury, Primate of all England, and Cardinal of the Holy Roman Church; Henry, Archbishop of Dublin; William, of London, Peter, of Winchester, Joceline, of Bath and Glastonbury, Hugh, of Lincoln, Walter, of Worcester, William, of Coventry, and Benedict, of Rochester, Bishops; Master Pandulph, our Lord the Pope's Subdeacon and familiar; Brother Almeric, Master of the Knights Templar in England, and of these noble persons, William Mareschal, Earl of Pembroke; William, Earl of Salisbury; William, Earl of Warren; William, Earl of Arundel; Alan de Galloway, Constable of Scotland; Warin Fitzgerald, Hubert de Burgh, Seneschal of Poictou; Peter Fitz-Herbert, Hugh de Nevil, Matthew Fitz-Herbert, Thomas Basset, Alan Basset, Philip de Albiniac, Robert de Roppel, John Mareschal, John Fitz-Hugh, and others, our liegemen, have in the first place granted to GOD, and by this our present Charter, have confirmed, for us and our heirs forever:

That the English Church shall be free and shall have her whole rights and liberties inviolable; and we will this to be observed in such manner, that it may appear from thence, that the freedom of elections, which is reputed most requisite to the English Church, which we granted, and by our Charter confirmed, and obtained the Confirmation of the same, from our Lord, Pope Innocent the Third, before the rupture between us and our Barons, was of our own free will; which Charter we shall observe, and we will it to be observed with good faith, by our heirs for ever.

We have also granted to all the Freemen of our Kingdom, for us and our heirs for ever, all the underwritten Liberties, to be enjoyed and held by them, and by their heirs, from us and from our heirs:

I. If any of our Earls or Barons, or others who hold of us in chief by military service, shall die, and at his death his heir shall be of full age, and shall owe a relief, he shall have his inheritance by the ancient relief; that is to say: the heir or heirs of an Earl, a whole Earl's Barony, for one hundred pounds; the heir or heirs of a Baron, for a whole Barony, by one hundred pounds; the heir or heirs of a Knight, for a whole Knight's Fee, by one hundred shillings at most; and he who owes less, shall give less, according to the ancient custom of fees.

But if the heir of any such be under age, and in wardship, when he comes to age he shall have his inheritance without relief and without fine.

The warden of the land of such heir, who shall be under age, shall not take from the lands of the heir any but reasonable issues, and reasonable customs, and reasonable services, and that without destruction and waste of the men or goods.

And if we commit the custody of any such lands to a Sheriff, or any other person who is bound to us for the issues of them, and he shall make destruction or waste upon the ward-lands, we will recover damages for him, and the lands shall be committed to two lawful and discreete men of that fee, who shall answer for the issues to us, or to him to whom we have assigned them.

And if we shall give or sell to any one the custody on any such lands, and he shall make destruction or waste upon them, he shall lose the custody, and it shall be committed to two lawful and discreete men of that fee, who shall answer to us in like manner as it is said before.

But the warden, as long as he hath the custody of the lands, shall keep up and maintain the houses, parks, warrens, ponds, mills, and other things belonging to them, out of their issues, and shall restore to the heir, when he comes of full age, his whole estate, provided with ploughs and other implements of husbandry, according as the time of Wainage shall require, and the issues of the lands can reasonably afford.

Heirs shall be married without disparagement, so that before the marriage be contracted, it shall be notified to the relations of the heir by consanguinity.

II. A widow, after the death of her husband, shall immediately, and without difficulty, have her marriage and her inheritance; nor shall she give any thing for her dower, or for her marriage, or for her inheritance, which her husband and she held at the day of his death; and she may remain in her husband's house forty days after his death, within which time her dower shall be assigned.

No widow shall be distrained to marry herself while she is willing to live without a husband; but yet she shall give security that she will not marry herself without our consent, if she hold of us, or without the consent of the lord of whom she does hold, if she hold of another.

III. Neither we, nor our Bailiffs, will seize any lands, or rent, for any debt, while the chattels of the debtor are sufficient for the payment of the debt; nor shall the sureties of the debtor be distrained, while the principal debtor is able to pay the debt. And if the principal debtor fail in payment of the debt, not having wherewith to discharge it, the sureties shall answer for the debt; and if they be willing, they shall have the lands and rents of the debtor, until satisfaction be made to them for the debt which they had before paid for him unless the principal debtor can show himself acquited thereof against the said sureties.

IV. If any one hath borrowed any thing from the Jews, more or less, and die before that debt be paid, the debt shall pay no interest so long as the heir shall be under age, of whomsoever he may hold; and if that debt shall fall into our hands, we will not take any thing except the chattel contained in the bond.

And if any one shall die indebted to the Jews, his wife shall have her dower and shall pay nothing of that debt; and if children of the deceased shall remain who are under age, necessaries shall be provided for them, according to the tenement which belongs to the deceased; and out of the residue the debt shall be paid, saving the rights of the lords [*of whom the lands are held*]. In like manner let it be with debts owing others than Jews.

V. No scutage, nor aid shall be imposed in our kingdom, unless by common council of our kingdom; excepting to redeem our person; to make our eldest son a knight, and to marry our eldest daughter once; and not for these [*causes*] unless a reasonable aid shall be demanded. In like manner let it be concerning the aids of the City of London.

The City of London shall have its ancient liberties, and its free customs, as well by land as by water. Furthermore we will and grant that all other Cities, and Burghs, and Towns, and Ports shall have their liberties and free customs. And also to have the common council of the kingdom, to assess and aid, otherwise than in the three cases aforesaid.

For the assessing of scutages, we will cause to be summoned the Archbishops, Bishops, Abbots, Earls, and great Barons, individually, by our letters. And besides, we will cause to be summoned, in general, by our Sheriffs and Bailiffs, all those who hold of us in chief, at a certain day, that is to say, at a distance of forty days [*before their meeting*], at the least, and to a certain place; and in all the letters of summons we will express the cause of the summons. And the summons being thus made, the business shall proceed on the day appointed, according to the counsel of those who shall be present, although all who had been summoned have not come.

We will not give leave to any one, for the future, to take an aid of his own free-men, except for redeeming his own body, and for making his eldest son a knight, and for marrying once his eldest daughter, and not that unless it be a reasonable aid.

VI. No one shall be distrained to do more service for a Knight's Fee, nor for any other free tenement, than what is due from thence.

VII. Common Pleas shall not follow our court, but shall be held in some certain place.

Trials upon writs of *Novel Disseisin*, of *Mort d'Ancestre*, and *Darrien Presentment* shall not be taken but in their proper counties, and in this manner:—we, or our Chief Justiciary, if we are out of the kingdom, will send two Justiciaries into each county, four times in the year, who, with four Knights of each county, chosen by the county, shall hold the aforesaid assizes, within the county, on the day and at the place appointed. And if the aforesaid assizes cannot be taken on the day of the county-court, let as many knights and freeholders, of those who were present at the county-court, remain behind, as shall be sufficient to do justice, according to the great, or less importance of the business.

VIII. A freeman shall not be amerced for a small offence, but only according to the degree of the offence, and for a great crime, according to the magnitude of the crime, saving his contenement; a Merchant shall be amerced in the same manner, saving his merchandise; and a villain shall be amerced after the same manner, saving to him his Wainage, if he shall fall into our mercy. And none of the aforesaid amerciaments shall be assessed but by the oath of honest men of the neighborhood. Earls and Barons shall not be amerced but by their peers, and that only according to the degree of their delinquency. No Clerk shall be amerced for his lay-tenement, but according to the manner of the others as aforesaid, and not according to the quantity of his ecclesiastical benefice.

IX. Neither a town, nor any person, shall be distrained to build bridges, or embankments, excepting those which anciently, and of right, are bound to do it.

X. No Sheriff, Constable, Coroners, nor other of our Bailiffs, shall hold pleas of our crown.

XI. All Counties and Hundreds, Trethings, and Wapentakes shall be at the ancient rent, without any increase, excepting in our Demesne-manors.

XII. If any one holding of us a lay-fee, dies, and the Sheriff or our Bailiff shall show our letters-patent of summons concerning the debt which the deceased owed to us, it shall be lawful for the Sheriff, or our Bailiff, to attach and register the chattels of the deceased, found upon his lay-fee, to the amount of that debt, by the view of lawful men, so that nothing shall be removed from thence until our debt be paid to us; and the rest shall be left to the executors to fulfil the will of the deceased; and if nothing be owing to us by him, all the chattels shall fall to the deceased saving to his wife and children their reasonable shares.

XIII. If any freeman shall die intestate, his chattels shall be distributed by the hands of his nearest relations and friends, by the view of the Church, saving to every one the debts which the deceased owed.

XIV. No Constable, nor Bailiff of ours, shall take the corn, or other goods, of any one without instantly paying him money for them, unless he can obtain respite from payment by the free will of the seller.

XV. No Constable shall distrain any Knight to give money for castle-guard, if he be willing to perform it in his own person, or by another able man, if he cannot perform it himself, for a reasonable cause. And if we have carried, or sent him into the army, he shall be excused from castle-guard, according to the time that he shall be in the army by our command.

XVI. No Sheriff, nor Bailiff of ours, nor any other person shall take the horses, or carts of any freeman, for the purpose of carriage, without the consent of the said freeman.

XVII. Neither we, nor our Bailiffs, will take another man's wood, for our castles, or other uses, unless by consent of him to whom the wood belongs.

XVIII. We will not retain the lands of those who have been convicted of felony, excepting for one year and one day, and then they shall be given up to the lord of the fee.

XIX. All wears for the future shall be quite removed out of the Thames and the Medway, and through all England, excepting upon the sea-coast.

XX. The writ which is called Præcipe, for the future shall not be granted to any one of any tenement, by which a freeman may lose his cause.

XXI. There shall be one measure of wine throughout all our kingdom, and one measure of ale, and one measure of corn, namely, the quarter of London, and one breadth of dyed cloth, and of russets, and of halberjects, namely, two ells within the lists. Also it shall be the same with weights as with measures.

XXII. Nothing shall be given, or taken for the future for the Writs of Inquisition for life or limb; but it shall be given without charge, and not denied.

XXIII. If any hold of us by Fee-Farm, or Socage, or Burgage, and hold land of another by Military Service, we will not have the wardship of the heir, nor of his lands, which are of the fee of another, on account of that Fee-Farm, or Socage, or Burgage; nor will we have the custody of the Fee-Farm, Socage or Burgage, unless the Fee-Farm owe Military Service. We will not have the wardship of the heir, nor of the lands of any one, which he holds of another by Military Service, on account of any Petty Sergeantry which he holds of us, by the service of giving us daggers or arrows or the like.

XXIV. No Bailiff, for the future, shall put any man to his oath, upon his simple affirmation, without credible witnesses produced for that purpose.

XXV. No freeman shall be seized, or imprisoned, or dispossessed, or outlawed, or in any way destroyed; nor will we condemn him, nor will we commit him to prison, excepting by the legal judgment of his peers, or by the laws of the land.

XXVI. To none will we sell; to none will we deny; to none will we delay right or justice.

XXVII. All Merchants shall have safety and security in

coming into England, and going out of England, and in staying and in travelling through England, as well by land as by water, to buy and sell, without any unjust exactions, according to ancient rights and customs, excepting in the time of war, and if they be of a country at war against us. And if such are found in our land at the beginning of a war, they shall be apprehended without injury of their bodies and goods, until it be known to us, or to our Chief Justiciary, how the Merchants of our country are treated who are found in the country at war against us; and if ours be in safety there, the others shall be in safety in our land.

XXVIII. It shall be lawful to any person, for the future, to go out of our kingdom, and to return, safely and securely, by land or by water, saving his allegiance to us, unless it be in time of war, for some short space, for the common good of the kingdom; excepting prisoners and outlaws, according to the laws of the land, and of the people of the nation at war against us, and Merchants, who shall be treated as it is said above.

XXIX. If any hold of any escheat, as of the Honor of Wallingford, Nottingham, Boulogne, Lancaster, or of other escheats which are in our land, and are Baronies, and shall die, his heir shall not give any other relief, nor do any other service to us, than he should have done to the Baron, if that Barony had been in the hands of the Baron; and we will hold it in the same manner that the Baron held it.

XXX. Men who dwell without the Forest, shall not come, for the future, before our Justiciaries of the Forest on a common summons, unless they be parties in the plea or sureties for some person or persons who are attached for the Forest.

XXXI. We will not make Justiciaries, Constables, Sheriffs, or Bailiffs, excepting of such as know the laws of the realm, and are well disposed to observe them.

XXXII. All Barons who have founded Abbeys, which they hold by charters from the Kings of England, or by ancient tenure, shall have the custody of them when they become vacant, as they ought to have.

XXXIII. All Forests, which have been made in our time, shall be immediately disafforested; and it shall be so done with Water-banks, which have been taken, or fenced-in by us during our reign.

All evil customs of Forests and Warrens, and of Foresters and Warreners, Sheriffs and their officers, Water-banks and their keepers, shall be immediately inquired into by twelve Knights of the same county, upon oath, who shall be elected by good-men of the same county; and within forty days after the inquisition is made, they shall be altogether destroyed by them never to be restored; provided that this be notified to us before it be done, or to our Justiciary, if we be not in England.

XXXIV. We will immediately restore all hostages and charters, which have been delivered to us by the English, in security of the peace and of their faithful service.

XXXV. We will remove from their bailiwicks the relations of Gerard d'Athyes, so that, for the future, they shall have no bailiwick in England, [*also*] Engelard de Cygony, Andrew, Peter and Gyone de Chancell, Gyone de Cygony, Geoffrey de Martin, and his brothers, Philip Mark, and his brothers, and Geoffrey, his nephew, and all their followers. And immediately after the conclusion of the peace, we will remove out of the kingdom all foreign knights, cross-bow men, and stipendiary soldiers, who have come with horses and arms to the molestation of the kingdom.

XXXVI. If any one hath been disseised, or dispossessed by us, without a legal verdict of his peers, of his lands, castles, liberties, or rights, we will immediately restore these things to him; and if any dispute shall arise on this head, then it shall be determined by a verdict of the twenty-five Barons, of whom mention is made below, for the security of the peace. Concerning all those things of which any one hath been disseised, or dispossessed, without legal verdict of his peers, by King Henry, our father, or King Richard, our brother, which we have in our hand, or others hold with our warrants, we shall have respite, until the common term of the Croisaders, excepting those concerning which a plea has been moved, or an inquisition taken, by our precept, before our taking the Cross; but as soon as we shall return from our expedition, or if, by chance, we should not go upon our expedition, we will immediately do complete justice therein.

The same respite will we have, and the same justice shall be done, concerning the disafforestation of the forests, or the forests which remain to be disafforested, which Henry, our father, or Richard, our brother, have afforested; and [*the same*] concerning the wardship of lands which are in another's fee, but the wardship of which we have hitherto had, occasioned by any of our fees held by Military Service; and for the abbeys founded in any other fee than our own, in which the Lord of the fee hath claimed a right; and when we shall have returned, or if we shall stay from our expedition, we shall immediately do complete justice in all these pleas.

XXXVII. No man shall be apprehended, or imprisoned on the appeal of a woman, for the death of any other man than her husband.

XXXVIII. All fines that have been made by us unjustly, or contrary to the laws of the realm; and all amerciaments that have been imposed unjustly, or contrary to the laws of the realm, shall be wholly remitted, or ordered by the verdict of the twenty-five Barons, of whom mention is made below, for the security of the peace, or by the verdict of the greater part of them, together with the aforesaid Stephen, Archbishop of Canterbury, if he can be present, and others whom he may think fit to bring with him; and if he cannot be present, the business shall proceed, notwithstanding, without him, but so, that if one, or more, of the aforesaid twenty-five Barons have a similar plea, let them be removed from that particular trial, and others elected and sworn by the residue of the same twenty-five, be substituted in their room, only for that trial.

XXXIX. If we have disseised, or dispossessed any Welshmen of their lands, or liberties, or other things, without a legal verdict of their peers, in England, or in Wales, they shall be immediately restored to them; and if any dispute shall arise upon this head, then let it be determined in the Marches by the verdict of their peers: for a tenement of England, according to the law of England; for a tenement of Wales, according to the law of Wales; for a tenement of the Marches, according to the law of the Marches. The Welsh shall do the same to us and to our subjects. Also concerning those things of which any Welshman hath been disseised, or dispossessed without the legal verdict of his peers, by King Henry, our father, or King Richard, our brother, which we have in hand, or others hold with our warrant, we shall have respite, until the common term of the Croisaders, excepting for those concerning which a plea hath been moved, or an inquisition made, by our precept, before our taking the Cross. But as soon as we shall return from our expedition, or if, by chance, we should not go upon our expedition, we shall immediately do complete justice therein, according to the laws of Wales, and the parts thereof. We will immediately deliver up the son of Llewellyn and all the hostages of Wales, and release them from their engagements which were made with us, for the security of the peace.

XL. We shall do to Alexander, king of Scotland, concerning the restoration of his sisters and hostages, and his liberties and rights, according to the form in which we act to our other Barons of England, unless it ought to be otherwise by the charters which we have from his father, William, the late king of Scotland; and this shall be by the verdict of his peers in our court.

All these customs and liberties aforesaid, which we have granted to be held in our kingdom, for so much of it as belongs to us, all our subjects, as well clergy as laity, shall observe towards their tenants as far as concerns them.

Since we have granted all these things aforesaid, for GOD, and for the amendment of our kingdom, and for the better extinguishing of the discord which has arisen between us and our Barons, we, being desirous that these things should possess entire and unshaken stability forever, give and grant to them the security underwritten; namely, that the Barons may elect twenty-five Barons of the kingdom, whom they please, who shall, with their whole power, observe, keep and cause to be observed, the peace and liberties which we have granted to them, and have confirmed by this, our present Charter, in this manner: that is to say, if we, or our Justiciary, or our Bailiffs, or any of our officers, shall have injured any one in anything, or shall have violated any article of the peace or security, and the injury shall have been shown to four of the aforesaid twenty-five Barons, the said four Barons shall come to us, or to our Justiciary, if we be out of the kingdom, and making known to us, the excess committed, petition that we cause that excess to be redressed without delay.

And if we shall not have redressed the excess, or, if we have been out of the kingdom, our Justiciary shall not have redressed it within the term of forty days, computing from the time when it shall have been made known to us, or to our Justiciary, if we have been out of the kingdom, the aforesaid four Barons shall lay that cause before the residue of the twenty-five Barons, and they, the twenty-five Barons, with the community of the whole land, shall distress and harass us by all the means in which they are able; that is to say, by the taking of our castles, land, and possessions, and by [*any*] other means in their power until the excess shall have been redressed, according to their verdict; saving [*harmless*] our person and [*the persons*] of our Queen and children; and when it hath been redressed, they shall behave to us as they have done before.

Whoever of our land pleaseth, may swear that he will obey the commands of the aforesaid twenty-five Barons, in accomplishing all the things aforesaid, and that with them he will harass us to the utmost of his power; and we will publicly and freely give leave to every one to swear who is willing to swear; and we will never forbid any to swear. But all those of our land, who, of themselves, and of their own accord, are unwilling to swear to the twenty-five Barons, to distress and harass us [*together*] with them, we will compel them by our command, to swear as aforesaid.

If any one of the twenty-five Barons shall die, or remove out of the land, or in any other way shall be prevented from executing the things above said, they who remain of the twenty-five Barons shall elect another in his place, according to their own pleasure, who shall be sworn in the same manner as the rest.

In all those things which are appointed to be done by these twenty-five Barons, if it happen that all the twenty-five have been present, and have differed in their opinions about anything; or if some of them who had been summoned, would not, or could not be present, that which the greater part of those who were present, shall have provided and decreed, shall be held as firm and as valid as if all the twenty-five had agreed in it.

The aforesaid twenty-five [*Barons*] shall swear, that they will faithfully observe, and with all their power, cause to be observed, all the things mentioned above.

We will obtain nothing from any one, by ourselves, nor by another, by which any of these concessions and liberties may be revoked, or diminished. And if any such thing shall have been obtained, let it be void and null; and we will never use it, neither by ourselves, nor by another.

We have fully remitted and pardoned to all men, all the ill-will, rancour, and resentments, which have arisen between us and our subjects, both clergy and laity, from the commencement of the discord. Moreover, we have fully remitted to all the clergy and laity, and, as far as belongs to us, have fully pardoned all transgressions committed by occasion of the said discord, from Easter, in the sixteenth year of our reign, until the conclusion of the peace. And, moreover, we have caused to be made to them testimonial-letters of the Lord Stephen, Archbishop of Canterbury, the Lord Henry, Archbishop of Dublin, and of the aforesaid Bishops, and of Master Pandulph, concerning this security and the aforesaid concessions.

Wherefore our will is, and we firmly command that the Church of England be free, and that the men in our kingdom have and hold the aforesaid liberties, rights and concessions, well and in peace, freely and quietly, fully and entirely, to them and their heirs, of us and our heirs, in all things and places, for ever as is aforesaid.

It is also sworn, both on our part, and on that of the Barons, that all the aforesaid shall be observed in good faith, and without any evil intention.

Witnessed by the above, and many others.

Given by our hand in the meadow which is called Runnemede, between Windsor and Staines, this fifteenth day of June, in the seventeenth year of our reign.

[SEAL]

The Magna Charta Described

THE following descriptions of the series of English Charters of Liberties, which are now extant in any form, granted before and immediately after the time of King John, have been compiled from authentic sources, with the intent of giving a general idea of their appearance. A compilation of the preserved fragments of the ancient Anglo-Saxon Statutes can be found in Dr. Wilkins's "Leges Anglo-Saxonicæ."

The first separate Charter, properly so called, issued for the restoration of the early Common Law of England, was the one granted about A.D. 1100 by King Henry I., which was the foundation of King John's Magna Charta and all Charters of Liberties that succeeded. Of this Charter, entitled "The Institutions of King Henry," the earliest text appears now to be preserved in the ancient manuscript, in the Chartulary at Rochester, entitled "Textus Roffensis," compiled by the bishop of that see, between 1116 and 1125.

Stephen, Earl of Blois, the successor to Henry I., when he took his coronation oath, December 26, 1135, made the terms of it almost equivalent to a Charter of Liberties, and subsequently, in the first year of his reign, secured the liberties, principally ecclesiastical, which he had promised by two proper instruments. One of these interesting relics of English history is preserved in the archives of Exeter Cathedral, with part of the Great Seal still remaining attached to it. The parchment containing it measures ten and five-eighths by four and seven-eighths inches. The seal of King Stephen is attached to a thin cord, and the Latin script is comprised in nineteen lines of a small kind of Norman running-hand, with numerous contractions.

King Stephen violated every article in this Charter, which caused his Barons to revolt from their allegiance, forfeit their estates, and the whole realm become involved in a civil war for the remainder of his reign. The other Charter of Liberties granted by this sovereign was very brief, also written in Latin, without date, and is preserved in an ancient entry in the Cottonian MSS.

King Henry II. made no promises concerning charters and liberties which had so much involved his predecessors. To restore tranquillity to his kingdom, he convened the National Assembly at Wallingford, when it was decreed that the ancient laws of England should be restored, and he also confirmed the Charter of his grandfather, Henry I., a copy of which confirmation is preserved in the Red Book of the Exchequer. In 1175, Henry II. again confirmed the common laws of King Edward the Confessor, after which all great proceedings upon the Charters of Liberties were suspended until the time of King John, since the Barons were too much occupied with foreign wars in the reign of Richard I.

In the second year of his reign commenced the disputes between King John and the clergy, which in 1207 laid the whole kingdom under an interdict, and lasted till in 1214, when it terminated in the resignation of his crown to the Pope and the granting of his first Charter, giving an absolute freedom in the choice of prelates for England. This Charter was " Given at the New Temple, by the hand of Master Robert de Marsh, our Chancellor, the 21st day of November," and was witnessed by Peter de Rupibus, William Marshall, Sr., William de Warren, Ralph de Meschines, Saher de Quincey, Geoffrey de Mandeville, William de

THE MAGNA CHARTA DESCRIBED 47

Ferrers, William de Briwere, Warine Fitz-Gerald, William de Cantilupe, Hugh de Nevill, Roger de Vere, and William de Huntingfield. An ancient copy of this Charter is preserved in the Register-books in the archives of Canterbury Cathedral. The Pope confirmed this Charter March 30, 1215.

An undoubted original of the articles or rough draught of the Magna Charta containing the heads of the statutes incorporated into the Magna Charta of King John, with a fragment of the Great Seal in brown wax still suspended to the lower part by a parchment label, is preserved in the Library of the British Museum. It is pasted on muslin and preserved beneath a frame and glass in the room containing the Royal Library, No. VII. These articles are in Latin, written on a skin of parchment, eighty-nine inches long, and measure ten and three-quarters inches in breadth by twenty-one and one-half inches in length, inclusive of the fold for receiving the label. The seal is considerably damaged, but the script is well preserved, excepting some letters which have been worn out by the creases in the parchment. The character is a very small Norman running-hand, with many contractions, generally the same throughout the whole, though some parts appear to have been added some short time subsequent to the rest, in a more hasty hand, as if done upon more mature deliberation.

It is believed that the original of the Magna Charta, that which was first actually drawn into form, and upon which King John placed his seal at the meadow of Runnemede, the original whence all the perfect copies were made for distribution throughout the realm, is the one preserved in the Cottonian Library in the British Museum, because of its deficiency in several words and sentences which are added for insertion beneath the instrument, while the other few copies extant have not this probable proof of originality.

This celebrated instrument is written in Latin on a skin of parchment, now measuring fourteen and one-half inches in breadth by twenty and one-half inches in length, including the fold for the label. It was very much shrivelled and mutilated, and the seal reduced to almost a shapeless mass, by a fire which took place at Westminster, October 23, 1731. It is a curious circumstance that the passages of the Magna Charta which remain the most legible are the two most famous sections in the whole instrument, which would alone have procured it the title of the Great Charter. These are Sections XXV. and XXVI.

The whole Charter, the character in which it is written being nearly similar to that of the preliminary articles, consists of eighty-six lines, including one of the additions, which are referred to by asterisks, to be inserted in four different places. This mutilated, original Magna Charta is exhibited in a frame, under glass, and its preservation is considered one of the most remarkable instances of the recovery of ancient manuscripts. One of the provisions of the treaty of peace concluded between Henry III. and Louis, the Dauphin, was dated at the Lambeth Palace, and contained the provision that Louis should restore to the king certain public records and the Magna Charta granted by King John, which were in the possession of him and the English Barons. These writings were deposited in the archbishop's palace after the compact was concluded, and remained forgotten in the archives until in 1640, when, on December 18, William Laud, Archbishop of Canterbury, was brought to the bar of the House of Lords. Apprehending the termination of the trial, Dr. Laud sent Dr. John Warner, the Bishop of Rochester, to Lambeth, to go over his papers and destroy or secrete all which were compromising. Dr. Warner carried away the Magna Charta with the mass of the archbishop's manuscripts he desired to secrete. This quaint document was discovered and appropriated by the executor of Dr. Warner, and, through the hands of his son's executor, Colonel Lee, passed into the appreciative hands of Bishop Burnet, the historian, by whom it was transmitted to the museum.

It is not known how many copies of the Magna Charta were made for distribution throughout the various shires, but to this fact and the Anglo-Saxon custom of registering and preserving important writings in religious houses is due the preservation of several original copies in the archives of the English cathedrals. A well-preserved copy is in the Lincoln Cathedral, carefully written in a small Norman running-hand, with many contractions, with the added words in their proper places. The whole instrument occupies fifty-four lines and measures seventeen and one-eighth by seventeen and one-half inches, exclusive of the fold for the label, and is a fair example probably of the copies distributed in the summer of 1215. Another original copy of the Magna Charta is in the archives of the Salisbury Cathedral, and another is in the Cottonian Collection, British Museum. It measures seventeen inches by twenty-one inches, and the script is written on the length of the parchment, the character being similar, however, to that of the other copies, occupying fifty-two lines.

There is no original copy extant of the Covenant of Security given by King John to the Barons. The only ancient record of it is on the Close Roll of the seventeenth of John, in the Tower of London. The next in importance of this series of instruments is the First Great Charter of Henry III., dated at Bristol, November 12, 1216, and is preserved in the archives of Durham Cathedral. The copy of the Second Great Charter of Henry III. is in the Bodleian Library, at Oxford, and in appearance resembles the others, with Cardinal Gaulo's seal in white wax and William Marshall's in green. All of the other original Charters of Henry III. and of Edward I. have also been preserved by the English government.

These ancient original Charters are generally written in Latin across the shortest way of the parchment, without paragraphs, and bore no signatures, although it is a popular notion that the Magna Charta of King John was signed by him and witnessed by the signatures or seals of certain Barons. There are no appearances of signatures on the original Magna Charta, nor on any of the orignal copies of it, and the words of the Charter—*Data per manum nostram*—only signify that the instrument was given by the king's hand, as a confirmation of his own act. In simply placing his seal on the Magna Charta, the king followed only the common law maxim that sealing was sufficient to authenticate a deed, though it was essential that it should be delivered before witnesses, whence the expression in the Magna Charta,—*Testibus supradictis, et multis aliis.* Therefore King John's seal was the only one attached to the instrument, and he did not sign it, nor did any Baron sign or attach his seal to it. The seal which John used on the Magna Charta was accidentally lost, with all his treasure, in a whirlpool when crossing the washes of Lincoln from Crosskeys to Fosdyke, October 12, 1216, only a week before his death. For two years after this the only seal used on public or royal documents was that of the Protector, William Marshall.

Runnemede

THE famous meadow or plain upon which the Barons encamped, and where King John sealed and delivered to them the long-desired Magna Charta, is situate on the southwest bank of the river Thames, between Staines and Windsor, in the hundred of Godley, or Chertsey, in the county of Surrey.

> "Here was that Charter seal'd, wherein the Crown,
> All marks of arbitrary pow'r lays down;
> Tyrant and Slave, those names of hate and fear,
> The happier style of King and Subject bear—
> Happy when both to the same centre move,
> When Kings give Liberty, and Subjects Love."

Thus does the poet, Sir John Denham, in his poem entitled "Cooper's Hill," an eminence which bounds the prospect to the west of Runnemede, allude to this historic spot.

The origin of the name of this celebrated meadow has not been distinctly traced, and this probably accounts for its varied spelling: Runimed in the original Latin Magna Charta, Runnemede in the popular translations of it, varied to Runemed, Runemeid, Rendmed, Redmede, Runnymede, Runni-mede, Runney Mead, Rennemed, and even Rumney Mead. Conjecture is that it was derived from the Saxon words *Rune*, signifying *Council*, and *Mede*, or *Mædewe*, Mead, or Meadow. The vulgar name given to this historic spot is Running Mead, from the running of horses here, or the race-course, or from the river running beside it. It also has been called Council Mead or Meadow.

This field proper—a triangular slip of meadow about a mile long—contains about one hundred and sixty acres of pasture-land, and adjoins two other large meadows, called Long Mead, on the west, and Yard Mead, on the southeast; but there is no doubt that the whole of the bottom or level was all in one field at the time of the sealing and delivering of the Magna Charta. Between Runnemede and the Thames River is a raised causeway, constructed at the cost of a patriotic merchant of London, Thomas de Henford, in the reign of Henry III., and since carefully maintained as a barrier against the river floods. It is a portion of the manor of Egham, and, although belonging to the crown, Runnemede is part freehold and part copy-hold, and tithe free. It is let at from twenty to thirty shillings per acre, to generally a dozen persons, who have the sole use of it from March to the middle of August, when it becomes common to all the parish of Egham, which then turns on it all the cattle for pasturage. The last week in August it is enclosed for public horse-races, when the so-called Egham races are run on a good two-mile track, which take place on the last Tuesday in August and the following two days, and this is the only annual celebration on this historic mead, but the events of 1215 are recalled by the racing for the "Magna Charta," "Runnemede," and "King John" stakes. From time immemorial it would seem that this mead has been appropriated to horse-racing, and in early times to stag-hunting.

It has been several times in contemplation to erect a column on Runnemede as a perpetual memorial of the great historic event which took place here in 1215; but, either from insufficient means or a reproachful deficiency of

English sentimental patriotism, no effectual steps have been taken to accomplish that desirable object.

The poet Mark Akenside, about the middle of the last century, composed the following lines as an appropriate inscription for the panel of such a monument:

> "Thou who the verdant plain dost traverse here,
> Whilst Thames among the willows from thy view
> Retires, O Stranger! stay thee, and the scene
> Around contemplate well. This is the place
> Where England's ancient Barons, clad in arms
> And stern with conquest, from their tyrant King
> (Then rendered tame), did challenge and secure
> The Charter of thy freedom. Pass not on
> Till thou hast bless'd their memory, and paid
> Those thanks which God appointed the reward
> Of Public Virtue. And if chance thy home
> Salute then with an honour'd Father's name,
> Go, call thy Sons;—instruct them what a debt
> They owe their ancestors; and make them swear
> To pay it, by transmitting down intire
> Those sacred rights to which themselves were born."

There has been a tradition current in modern times that the Magna Charta was sealed on an eyot, or small island, in the Thames, adjacent to Runnemede, and not in the mead itself; but this is easily disproved by the closing passage of the original Charter, which expressly states that it was "given by our own hand, in the Meadow which is called Runnemede, between Windsor and Staines."

The opinion is sometimes expressed that the treaty was negotiated on the island, and the Charter itself sealed in the meadow. Aubrey's "History of Surrey" says, "On the back side of Egham, northwards, lies Rumney-Mead, towards the Thames; in which meadow was sealed Magna Charta. In this flat of meadow which is long, extending westward by the River side, are several enclosures, but doubtless then it lay all open. The meadow called Rumney-Mead lies between Long-Mead and a mead abutting on Humber Lane. They say one of the armies lay in Long Mead, and the other in the aforesaid meadow, next Egham. The tradition is, that the Treaty was in an Eight, over against Yard-mead, which is Rumney-mead, and the Great Charter was settled here."

The only person particularly interested in having this island, which contains about fifteen hundred acres of land, as the scene of the sealing of the Magna Charta, is its owner, or lessee, as there is a unique lodge on the island fitted up as a refreshment-room, and "Charta Island" is noted principally for this among the pleasure-seekers and sight-seers. This "Memorial Lodge," as the inscription on a stone slab informs the visitor, was erected in 1834, by George S. Harcourt, of Ankerwyke House, lord of the manor, and then high sheriff of Buckinghamshire, in which county Charter Island is situated. Though certainly the island was not the place where John granted the Magna Charta, it could easily have derived its appellation from having been historically connected with the events of that era, for, according to Matthew Paris's statements, in his "History of England," of the events of this time, the treaty between Henry III. and the Dauphin of France, whereby the foreign auxiliaries, both of the deceased king, John, and of the Barons, were constrained to quit the country, was finally settled "near the town of Staines, in a certain Island by the river Thames." "There King Henry, with the legate and great marshal and many others, on the one part, and Louis, with the Barons and others associated with him, on the other part, by the grace of God, settled the terms of peace, on the 3d of the ides of September, 1217." There is a tradition that the Barons often held consultations in a great hall beneath Reygate Castle, in County Surrey, near to Runnemede, which was one of the seats of the Warrens, ancient Earls of Surrey. At the time of the baronial uprising it was held by an Earl of Warren and Surrey who was more friendly to King John than to the Barons. Although he was frightened by the Barons into taking up arms against the king, his name appears on John's part in the opening passage of the Magna Charta. As the Barons seized his Castle of Reygate to keep him with them, it is possible they may have used it, and particularly the great hall.

The Magna Charta Barons

SOME of the Barons and Knights in arms to procure the Magna Charta from King John:

Odonel d'Albini,
Philip d'Albini,
William d'Albini,
William d'Albini, Jr.,
Robert d'Arcie,
Norman d'Arcy,
Reginald d'Argentine,
William d'Aquillon,
Thomas d'Astley,
William de Badlesmere,
Walter de Beauchamp,
William de Beauchamp,
William de Beaumont,
John Beke,
Robert de Berkeley,
Peter de Bermingham,
Roger Bertram,
Hugh Bigod,
Roger Bigod,
Osbert de Bobi,
Henry de Bohun,
Ralph le Boteler,
Robert le Boteler,
William le Boteler,
R—— de Brackele,
Henry de Braibrock,
William de Braose,
Baldwin Bretel,
Peter de Brus,
Bertram de Bulemer,
Robert Bulkeley,
Ralph de Camois,
William de Cantilupe,
Simeon de Cauci,
Hugh de Charneles,
Robert de Charun,
Gilbert de Clare,
Richard de Clare,
John de Clavering,
Walter de Clifford,
Henry de Cobeham,
Robert de Coleville,
William de Coleville,
John de Cressie,
Roger de Cressie,
Hamon Crevequer,
Ralph de Cromwell,
Oliver Deincourt,
Gilbert Delaval,
Walter de Dunstanville,
W—— d'Einford,
Richard Engaine,
J—— de Fereby,
Biset de Fersi,
John Fitz-Alan,
Osbert Fitz-Alan,
Peter Fitz-John,
Philip Fitz-John,

THE MAGNA CHARTA BARONS

Roger Fitz-Pain,
Gilbert Fitz-Reinfride,
John Fitz-Robert,
Ralph Fitz-Robert,
Robert Fitz-Walter,
Fulke Fitz-Warrine,
William Fitz-William,
Walter Foliot,
William de Fortibus,
Gilbert de Gant,
Maurice de Gant,
Richard Giffard,
Hugh de Gournay,
Robert de Gresley,
Osbert Gyfford,
William de Hardell,
Humphrey de Hastang,
William de Hastings,
Giles de Hersi,
Gervase de Hobregge,
W—— de Hobregge,
John de Humet,
William de Huntingfield,
William de Keynes (Kayneto),
Simon de Kyme,
John de Lacie,
Simon Langton,
William de Lanvallei,
Roger de Leiburne,
Adam de Lincoln,
Henry Lovell,
Richard de Lucie,
Geoffrey de Luterel,
William Malet,
John Maltravers,
Geoffrey de Mandeville,
William de Mandeville,
R—— de Mandeville,
Robert de Marmion,
Robert de Marmyon,
William de Marmyon,
William Marshall, Jr.,
William de Mauduit,

Geoffrey de Meantune,
Giles de Melun,
Roger de Merley,
William de Mersbray,
William de Montacute,
Roger de Montbegon,
Richard de Montfichet,
Peter de Montfort,
Simon de Montfort,
Roger de Mowbray,
William de Mowbray,
Thomas de Multon,
Thomas de Mulutune (Muletan),
Eustace de Nevill,
Walter de Norton,
Geoffrey de Norwich,
Henry d'Oyly,
Hugh Paganel,
Adam Painel,
William Pantulf,
Richard de Percy,
Robert de Pincheni,
Hugh de Playz,
Adam de Port,
Michael de Poynings,
Hugh de Poyntz,
Nicholas de Poyntz,
Alex. de Puinter (Puintune),
Robert de Quincey,
Saire de Quincey,
Robert de Ros (Roos),
William de Ros (Roos),
Geoffrey de Say,
Roger de Somerville,
Almaric de Spencer,
Hugh de Spencer,
Thurstan de Spencer,
William de Studham,
Nicholas de Stuteville,
Alex. de Sutune (Sutton),
Roger St. John,
William St. John,
Roger de St. Philibert,

58 THE MAGNA CHARTA BARONS

Richard Talbot,
Hugh Thacun,
Walter de Tibetot,
William de Todeni (Tuintuna),
Ralph de Toni,
Richard d'Umfraville,
Theobald de Valoines,
Oliver de Vaux,

Ranulph de Vaux,
Robert de Vaux,
Nicholas de Verdon,
Robert de Vere,
Eustace de Vesci,
Ralph de Willoughby,
W—— de Wymes (Wymiss).

Some of the Barons and Knights in arms on the part of King John, or in sympathy with him:

Richard Affenvast,
William Agorlun,
Philip d'Albini,
William d'Albini,
Henry d'Alditheley,
Bernard de Baliol,
Hugh de Baliol,
Richard de Banks,
Alan Basset,
Thomas Basset,
John de Bassingebourne,
Warine de Bassingebourne,
Andrew de Beauchamp,
Hugh de Beauchamp,
Ranulph Blundeville,
Thomas Botterel,
Robert de Braybrook,
Fowke de Breant (Brent),
Henry de Brentfield,
Fulke de Briwere,
William de Briwere,
Hubert de Burgh,
Geoffrey de Buteville,
Oliver de Buteville,
Gerald de Camville,
William de Cirent,
Henry de Cornhill,
John de Courci,
Geoffrey de Cracombe,
Robert d'Eivill,
Thomas d'Erdington,

—— Faulkes,
William de Ferrers,
Roger Fitz-Bernard,
Henry Fitz-Count,
Warren Fitz-Gerald,
Warren Fitz-Gilbert,
Matthew Fitz-Herbert,
Peter Fitz-Herbert,
John Fitz-Hugh,
Ralph Fitz-Nicholas,
Gerard de Furnival,
Alan de Galloway,
Roger (Robert) de Gaugi,
William Gernon,
Walter de Godarville,
Richard de Grey,
Thomas Hardington,
Ralph de la Hay,
Roger Huscari,
Robert d'Iver,
Brian de l'Isle,
Bogo de Knovill,
Geoffrey de Lacie,
Walter de Lacie,
Alured de Lincoln,
William Longespee,
Geoffrey de Lucie,
Philip Marcy,
Richard de Marisco,
Robert Marsh,
John Marshall,

Richard Marshall,
William Marshall, Sr.,
Peter de Maulei,
Ralph Meschines,
John de Monmouth,
Hugh de Mortimer,
Robert de Mortimer,
Roger de Mortimer,
R—— Musgard,
Robert de Nereford,
Hugh de Nevill,
Robert de Newburg,
Ralph de Normanville,
Robert Oldbridge,
William Parc,
William de Percy,
Robert de Pierrepont,
Robert Pinkey,
William Plantagenet,
Henry de Pont Omar,
Engerus de Pratest,
William de Redvers,
William de Rokeland,
Robert de Ropele (Roppel),
Nicholas de St. Philibert,
Almeric de St. Mauro,
Jordan de Sackville,
Stephen de Segrave,
Nicholas de Stapleton,
John le Strange,
John le Strange, Jr.,
Henry de Tibetot,
Ralph le Tyris,
Philip d'Ulecote (Olcott),
Alberic de Vere,
Ivo de Vipount,
Robert de Vipount,
William de Wortham,
Roger de Zucha, (Zouche).

The Sureties for the Observance of the Magna Charta.

* William d'Albini, lord of Belvoir Castle, *d.* 1236.
* Hugh le Bigod, Earl of Norfolk, *d.* 1225.
* Roger le Bigod, Earl of Norfolk, *d.* 1220.
* Henry de Bohun, Earl of Hereford, *d.* 1220.
* Gilbert de Clare, Earl of Hertford and Gloucester, *d.* 1229.
* Richard de Clare, Earl of Hertford and Gloucester, *d.* 1262.
* John Fitz-Robert, lord of Warkworth and Clavering, *d.* 1240.
* Robert Fitz-Walter, lord of Dunmow Castle, *d.* 1234.
  William de Fortibus, Earl of Albemarle, *d.* 1241.   His only child *d. s. p.*
  William de Hardell, mayor of the city of London.   *Issue?*
* William de Huntingfield, sheriff of Norfolk and Suffolk shires, *d.* 1256.
* John de Lacie, Earl of Lincoln, *d.* 1240.
* William de Lanvallei, governor of Colchester Castle, 1217.
* William Malet, sheriff of Somerset and Dorset shires, *d.* 1224.
  Geoffrey de Mandeville, Earl of Essex, *k. s. p.* 1216.
  William Marshall, Jr., Earl of Pembroke, *d. s. p.* 1231.
  Richard de Montfichet, justice of the king's forests, *d. s. p.* 1258.
  Roger de Mowbray, *d. s. p.* 1218.
* William de Mowbray, governor of York Castle, *d.* 1223.
  Richard de Percy, *d. s. p.* 1244.
* Saher de Quincey, Earl of Winchester, *d.* 1219.
* Robert de Roos, lord of Hamelake Castle, *d.* 1226.
* Geoffrey de Say, *d.* 1230.
* Robert de Vere, Earl of Oxford, *d.* 1221.
* Eustace de Vesci, *k.* 1216.

---

* These eighteen of the twenty-five Sureties are lineal ancestors of the founders of the Order of Runnemede. Of the remainder, five died without issue; one, de Fortibus, had no grandchildren, and of the other, de Hardell, it is not known that he had issue.

Relationship of the Sureties

WILLIAM D'ALBINI.—He was a grandson of the mother of No. 8 by her second husband. His granddaughter was the wife of a grandson of No. 22. A cousin was the wife of No. 19, and she was a cousin of No. 8.

2. HUGH BIGOD.—He was the son of No. 3. His granddaughter married the half-brother of the wife of No. 4. This granddaughter's husband was also the half-brother of No. 15. His grandmother was the aunt of No. 24. He was a cousin of No. 24. His wife was a sister of No. 16, and a sister of the wife of No. 5. His wife's maternal great-grandfather was a brother of a grandfather of No. 6.

3. ROGER BIGOD.—He was the father of No. 2. His mother was the aunt of No. 24. His daughter was the wife of a brother of No. 24.

4. HENRY DE BOHUN.—His wife was a sister of No. 15, and her half-brother married a granddaughter of No. 2. His son's wife was a granddaughter of the aunt of the wife of the son of No. 9. His son married a granddaughter of the sister of the father of the wife of the son of No. 9. His grandson's mother-in-law was a sister of No. 16, whose great-grandfather's brother was the grandfather of No. 6, the father of No. 5. His grandson was the son-in-

law of a sister of No. 16. His son's wife was a cousin of the wife of the son of No. 9. His son-in-law was a nephew of the mother of No. 20. His granddaughter was a sister-in-law of No. 16. His son-in-law was a cousin of No. 20.

5. GILBERT DE CLARE.—He was a son of No. 6. His son's wife was a daughter of No. 12. He was a cousin of No. 8. His wife was a sister of No. 16, and also of the wife of No. 2, and her maternal great-grandfather was a brother of the grandfather of No. 5. His great-grandaunt was the wife of the great-grandfather of No. 17.

6. RICHARD DE CLARE.—He was father of No. 5. His paternal great-grandfather and the paternal grandfather of No. 8 were brothers. He was a cousin of Nos. 8, 19, and 20. His ancestor, the first Earl of Clare's daughter, was the wife of the great-grandfather of No. 17. His grandfather's granddaughter was the mother of No. 20. His father's sister was the wife of No. 19. His wife was a sister of No. 15. His grandfather and the maternal grandfather of No. 16 were brothers. His great-aunt married an ancestor of No. 17. His father's cousin's widow was the mother of No. 21. His wife's brother married a sister of the father-in-law of No. 21. His brother-in-law married the aunt of the wife of No. 21. His paternal grandfather was a brother of the paternal great-grandfather of No. 16. He was a cousin of No. 16. His wife's maternal grandfather was a brother of the paternal great-grandmother of No. 16. His ancestor, the first Earl of Clare's wife, was of the same family as that of the wife of No. 24. His maternal grandmother's brother was grandfather of the wife of the son of No. 21. His granddaughter was the wife of a grandson of No. 19. His paternal grandfather was a brother of the paternal grandmother of No. 24. His aunt

RELATIONSHIP OF THE SURETIES

was the mother of No. 26. His granddaughter married a grandnephew of No. 26. His mother's second husband was a cousin of No. 1. His grandfather's brother was the maternal great-grandfather of the wife of No. 2; of the mother-in-law of No. 25; of the son-in-law of No. 13; and of the second husband of a granddaughter of No. 21.

7. JOHN FITZ-ROBERT.—He was a cousin of No. 25, and of No. 12. His wife and the wife of No. 25 were cousins.

8. ROBERT FITZ-WALTER.—He was a cousin of Nos. 5 and 6. His paternal grandfather and the paternal great-grandfather of No. 6 were brothers. He was related by marriage to No. 9. His mother's second husband was the grandfather of No. 1. His paternal grandmother had as second husband the father of No. 21. He was a cousin of No. 15. His grandmother's nephew was a cousin of No. 21, and the husband of an aunt of the wife of No. 25.

9. WILLIAM DE FORTIBUS.—His son married a daughter of the brother of the great-grandmother of the daughter-in-law of No. 4. His wife was a sister of No. 17. His sister was the first wife of No. 16. His mother was the widow of a nephew of the grandmother of No. 23, and this nephew's first wife was a daughter of No. 8. His aunt was the second wife of No. 16.

10. WILLIAM DE HARDELL.—He does not seem to have been related by blood or intermarriage to any of the Sureties.

11. WILLIAM DE HUNTINGFIELD.—He does not seem to have been related by blood or intermarriage to any of the Sureties. His great-grandfather held the manor of Hunt-

ingfield, in Suffolk, as the undertenant of Robert Malet, the father or grandfather of No. 14.

12. JOHN DE LACIE.—His daughter was the wife of a son of No. 5. His second wife was a daughter of the son of No. 21. His mother was the half-sister of the paternal grandmother of No. 23. His paternal grandmother was a great-aunt of No. 15. His maternal grandfather's first wife—the great-grandmother of No. 23—was the sister of the paternal grandfather of No. 24. His widow married a brother of No. 16, a cousin of Nos. 5 and 6.

13. WILLIAM DE LANVALLEI.—His wife and the wife of No. 14 were cousins. His daughter's father-in-law's third wife was the widow of No. 15, and his fourth wife was a sister of the wives of Nos. 22 and 25. His daughter was the second wife of a brother of No. 16. His son-in-law was a great-grandson of the brother of the grandfather of No. 6, whose wife's grandfather was a brother of the great-grandmother of the son-in-law of No. 13.

14. WILLIAM MALET.—His wife was a cousin of the wife of No. 13. See under No. 11.

15. GEOFFREY DE MANDEVILLE.—He died without issue. His wife was a sister of the wife of No. 6, and their maternal grandfather's sister was the wife of a granduncle of No. 6. He was a cousin of No. 23. His sister was the wife of No. 4. His half-brother married a granddaughter of No. 2. His great-aunt was the paternal grandmother of Nos. 12 and 23. His wife's brother married a sister of the father-in-law of No. 21. His wife's brother's wife's sister married a son of the brother of the mother of No. 21 (nephew of the mother of No. 21), who was also the nephew of the grandmother of No. 8. His maternal great-

grandmother was a sister of the grandfather of No. 24. His grandfather was also the grandfather of No. 23. His wife's maternal grandfather was the brother of the maternal great-grandmother of No. 16.

16. WILLIAM MARSHALL, JR.—He died without issue. One of his sisters was the mother-in-law of a grandson of No. 4; another was the wife of No. 5; another was the wife of No. 2; another was the mother-in-law of No. 25, and her husband's second wife was a granddaughter of No. 21. He was a cousin of No. 6. One of his brothers married a granddaughter of No. 4; another married, first, a sister of the wives of Nos. 22 and 25, and married, secondly, a daughter of No. 13; another married the widow of No 12, who was the granddaughter of No. 21. His first wife was a sister of No. 9, and his second wife was a daughter of King John. His step-mother was the aunt of No. 9. His mother's grandfather and the grandfather of No. 6 were brothers. His paternal great-grandfather was a brother of the paternal great-grandfather of No. 6. His paternal great-grandmother was a sister of the maternal grandfather of the wife of No. 6, and the wife of No. 15.

17. RICHARD DE MONTFICHET.—He died without issue. His sister was the wife of No. 9. His father's grandfather married a daughter of the first Earl of Clare, ancestor of Nos. 5 and 6. His sister was the mother-in-law of No. 24, and an ancestor married a great-aunt of No. 6.

18. ROGER DE MONTBEGON.—He died without issue. He deserted the Barons soon after being made a Surety, and No. 26 was substituted for him. He does not seem to have been related by blood or intermarriage with the other Sureties.

19. WILLIAM DE MOWBRAY.—His mother was a sister of the father of No. 6. His wife was a cousin of No. 1. His grandson married a granddaughter of No. 6. His youngest brother, No. 26, was substituted for No. 18.

20. RICHARD DE PERCY.—He died without issue. His mother was a granddaughter of the grandfather of No. 6. His mother was a cousin of No. 6, and also aunt of a son-in-law of No. 4.

21. SAHER DE QUINCEY.—His granddaughter was the second wife of No. 12, and she married, secondly, a brother of No. 16. His son's wife's grandfather was a brother of the maternal grandmother of No. 6. His mother was the widow of a cousin of Nos. 5 and 6, and the paternal grandmother of No. 8. His daughter married a son of No. 24. His wife's aunt was the sister-in-law of the wives of Nos. 6 and 15. His cousin (mother's brother's son, also nephew of the grandmother of No. 8, and cousin of No. 25) married a sister-in-law of the wives of Nos. 6 and 15. His granddaughter's second husband was a great-grandson of a brother of the grandfather of No. 6, whose wife was a sister of the wife of No. 15.

22. ROBERT DE ROOS.—His grandson married a granddaughter of No. 1. His wife was a daughter of the father of the wife of No. 25, and a sister-in-law of No. 16.

23. GEOFFREY DE SAY.—He was a cousin of No. 15. His grandfather was the grandfather of No. 15. He was related by marriage to No. 9. His paternal grandmother's half-sister was the mother of No. 12. His paternal grandmother was a great-aunt of No. 15

24. ROBERT DE VERE.—His wife was a niece of No. 17, and was of the family of the first Earl of Clare, ancestor of Nos. 5 and 6. His paternal grandfather's sister—great-aunt—was the first wife of the maternal grandfather of No. 12. His son's wife was a daughter of No. 21. His paternal grandmother was a sister of the paternal grandfather of No. 6. His brother married a daughter of No. 3. His father's sister was the mother of No. 3, and the grandmother of No. 2. His paternal grandfather's sister married, secondly, the great-grandfather of No. 15.

25. EUSTACE DE VESCI.—He was a cousin of No. 7. His wife was the daughter of the father of the wife of No. 22, and the sister of the son-in-law of No. 16. His wife's aunt married a cousin of Nos. 8 and 21. His mother-in-law was the great-granddaughter of the brother of the grandfather of No. 6. His wife's sister's husband was a great-grandson of the brother of the grandfather of No. 6.

26. ROGER DE MOWBRAY.—He was substituted for No. 18. He was a brother of No. 19, and his mother was an aunt of No. 6. His sister-in-law was a cousin of No. 1.

Biographies
of the
Sureties for the Observance
of
The Magna Charta

Biographies of the Sureties

WILLIAM D'ALBINI

THIS Surety was descended from Robert de Todeni, feudal lord of Belvoir Castle, in Lincolnshire, possessed of eighty lordships at the time of the General Survey, who d. 1088. His eldest son by his wife, Adela:

WILLIAM D'ALBINI-BRITO, lord of Belvoir Castle, was a gallant commander in the war in Normandy, and d. 1155, having issue by his wife, Maud, widow of Robert, son of Richard Fitz-Gilbert de Clare:

WILLIAM D'ALBINI-MESCHINES, the Briton, lord of Belvoir Castle, a Baron by tenure, d. 1167, who was the father of

WILLIAM D'ALBINI, lord of Belvoir Castle, third feudal Baron. When his father died he was in ward to King Henry II., and, in 1194, he was in the army of Richard I. in Normandy. In the following year he was constituted sheriff of the counties of Warwick and Leicester, and also held the same office for those of Rutland, Bedford, and Buckingham, between 1196 and 1199. Upon the accession of John to the throne he received several valuable grants, being already wealthy. In 1201, when the Barons refused to attend King John into France, he demanded that their castles should be given up to him as security for their allegiance, beginning with William d'Albini, of whom he claimed Belvoir Castle, instead of which he gave him his son, William, as a hostage.

He appears to have remained longer faithful to the king, as well as more moderate in his opposition to him, than most of the Barons, and did not join the insurgents until he could no longer with safety either remain neutral or adhere to the king, for so late as January, 1214-15, he was one of King John's commissioners appointed for the safe-conduct of such as were travelling to his court, at Northampton. After he joined the Barons he entered with great spirit into their cause, and was elected one of the Sureties for the observance of the Magna Charta, and was excommunicated; but after having gained their point, he was looked upon with suspicion because he did not attend the grand tournament, on June 29, to celebrate the victory, and it was not until after other Barons had alarmed him, that he fortified his castle at Belvoir, and joined them at London. But the sequel proves their suspicions were not well grounded. He was placed as governor of Rochester Castle, when, though he found it so utterly destitute of provisions as almost to induce his men to abandon it, he recruited and held it until famine, weakness, and watching obliged them to surrender to the king. The siege having lasted three months, and being attended with considerable loss, King John ordered that all the nobles in the castle should be hanged; but this sentence being resolutely opposed by his chief councillors, William d'Albini and his son Odonel, with several other Barons, were committed to the custody of Peter de Mauley, and sent prisoners to Corfe and Nottingham Castles. Whilst d'Albini remained at Corfe, the king marched on Christmas morning, 1216, from Nottingham to Langar, near Belvoir Castle, and sent a summons to surrender. Upon this, Nicholas d'Albini, one of the Baron's sons and a clerk in orders, delivered the keys to the king, asking only that his father should be mercifully treated. The fortress was then committed to the custody of Geoffrey and Oliver de Buteville. His liberty was gained only by William d'Albini paying a fine to the king of six thousand marks (four thousand pounds), the sum being raised from his own lands by his wife, on their being delivered to her for that express purpose. After King John's death, though he submitted himself to King Henry III., he was forced to give his wife and son Nicholas as hostages for his allegiance; but in 1217 he was one of the king's commanders at the battle of Lincoln. ·He *d.* at Offington, May 1, 1236, and his body was buried at Newstead, and his heart under the wall, opposite the high-altar, at Belvoir.

William d'Albini *m.* first, Margery, daughter of Odonel d'Umfraville, and had by her:

WILLIAM D'ALBINI, of Belvoir, *d. s. p. m.* 1285. *Issue.*
ROBERT D'ALBINI.
NICHOLAS D'ALBINI.

He *m.* secondly, Agatha, daughter and coheiress of William de Trusbut.

Arms.—*Gules; a Lion rampant, Or, armed and langued Azure.*

HUGH BIGOD

An account of this Baron's ancestors is given with that of his father. He was the eldest son and heir of Roger Bigod, one of the celebrated twenty-five Sureties for the observance of the Magna Charta, and took part from the beginning in the Barons' Magna Charta proceedings, and was, with his father, elected one of the Sureties for this instrument. There are few particulars of this Baron's life extant, for he enjoyed the title of Earl of Norfolk, and his father's estates and honors, to which he succeeded in 5 Henry III., 1220–21, but a few years, as he died 9 Henry III., 1224–5.

He *m*. Maud, her first husband, eldest daughter and co-heiress of William le Mareschal, or Marshall, by his wife Isabel de Clare, only child and heiress of Richard the Strongbow, second Earl of Pembroke, who had been under the guardianship of King Henry II., and was given in marriage to William Marshall by King Richard the Lion-Hearted, in 1189, before his coronation, and with her he acquired the earldom of Pembroke, and in this rank bore the royal sceptre at the coronation of Richard I. He was brother and heir-male of John, Baron Marshall, hereditary marshal of the king's household, who bore the great golden spurs of the king at the coronation of Richard I., and shortly *d. s. p.*

William Marshall first appears in English history as a supporter of Prince Henry, the rebellious son of Henry II. This prince, upon his death-bed, delivered to his most confidential friend, William Marshall, his cross, to convey to Jerusalem, which commission, however, he personally never fulfilled, as he shortly afterwards married the great heiress, became Earl of Pembroke, and was left at home by Richard Cœur de Lion, when he set out on his journey to the Holy Land, as one of the assistants in the government of the realm during his absence. Upon the decease of his brother John, in 1199, he became lord marshal to King John, and on the day of John's coronation he was invested with the sword of the earldom of Pembroke, being then confirmed in the possession of the said inheritance, and was shortly afterwards appointed high sheriff of the counties of Sussex and Gloucester. In a few years he had grants from King John of Goderich Castle, in County Hereford, and of the whole province of Leinster, in Ireland. Being in such high favor with the king, he was a strenuous supporter of the royal interests upon the breaking out of the baronial insurrection, and was deputed by the king, with the Archbishop of Canterbury, to ascertain the grievances and demands of the Barons, while his eldest son, William, was a supporter of the baronial cause and was elected one of the twenty-five Sureties for the observance of the Magna Charta. At the demise of King John, the Earl of Pembroke was so powerful that he prevailed upon the Barons to appoint a day for the coronation of Henry III., to whom he was constituted guardian, by the Barons who had remained firm in their allegiance. Subsequently he took up arms in the royal cause, and, after achieving a victory over the Barons, at Lincoln, proceeded to London, then held by the Barons, and invested the city, both by land and water, and reduced it to extremity for want of provisions. He was the most eminent statesman and soldier of his time, and was also distinguished for his piety and attachment to the Church. He had five sons, by the heiress of Clare, who each succeeded in his lands and honors, and all died without issue, when all his honors became extinct and his great inheritance devolved upon his five daughters. Lady Maud, wife of Hugh Bigod, obtained as her share the homestead-manor of Hempsted-Marshall, in Berks, with the office of marshal of England, which was inherited by her son, Roger Bigod, fourth Earl of Norfolk, and surrendered to the crown by her grandson Roger, fifth Earl. The Earl of Pembroke had as his second wife, Alice, daughter of Baldwin de Bethune, Earl of Albemarle, *m.* in 1203.

Richard de Clare, aforesaid, surnamed the Strongbow, was the eldest son of Gilbert de Clare (brother of Richard de Clare, first Earl of Hertford), who, having license from the king to enjoy all the lands he should win by his sword in Wales, brought Caerdiganshire under subjection, erected strong castles, and, in 1138, was created Earl of Pembroke by King Stephen. Richard the Strongbow procured for himself a conspicuous place in history by the leading part he took in the subjugation of Ireland, and his romantic marriage with Princess Eva, daughter of Dermot Macmurcha, last king of the province of Leinster, with whom he had in dower a great part of the realm. He was constituted Justiciary of Ireland by King Henry II., and, dying in April, 1176, was buried in the chapter-house at Gloucester, leaving issue an only daughter and heiress, Isabella, who married, as above, William Marshall.

Hugh Bigod and his wife, Lady Maud Marshall, had issue:
ROGER BIGOD, fourth Earl of Norfolk, *d. s. p.*

HUGH BIGOD, an eminent lawyer, appointed Justiciary of England, by the Barons, in 1257. He *m.* first, Joane, daughter of Robert Burnet, and had two sons,—Roger, who succeeded his uncle as Earl of Norfolk, and John. He *m.* secondly, Joan Stuteville, a widow, but had no issue by her.

RALPH BIGOD, *m.* Berta de Furnival, and had an only daughter, Isabel, who *m.* first, Gilbert de Lacie, and *m.* secondly, John Fitz-Geoffrey.

Arms.—*Gules ; a Lion passant, Or.*

ROGER BIGOD

ROGER BIGOD, or le Bigot, a feudal Baron, the first of this great family that settled in England, was in the Conqueror's time possessed of six lordships in Essex and one hundred and seventeen in Suffolk. Adhering to the party that took up arms against William Rufus, he fortified the castle of Norwich, and wasted the country around. At the accession of Henry I., being a witness of the king's laws and stanch in his interests, he obtained gifts of land from the crown, and was lord high steward in right of his wife. In 1103 he and his wife founded the abbey of Whetford, in Norfolk, where he was buried in 1107, 7 Henry I. He *m.* before 1103, Adeliza, or Alice, who survived him, daughter of Hugh Grentemaisnil, lord of Hinckley, Ashby-Legers, County Northampton, lord high steward of England, *d. s. p. m.* 1098, by his wife Adelhyde, *d.* 1091, daughter of the Count de Beaumont, and had :

HUGH BIGOD, second son, who succeeded his elder brother, William, accidentally drowned *s. p.* with the king's children, 20 Henry I., as steward of the household to Henry I. He was mainly instrumental in raising Stephen, Earl of Boulogne, to the throne, upon the decease of Henry I., and was rewarded by him with the earldom of East Angles, or Norfolk, about 1140. He was steadfast and faithful in his allegiance to King Stephen through the difficulties which beset that monarch, and gallantly defended Ipswich Castle against the Empress Maud and her son, but was finally obliged to surrender for want of timely relief. That he was a wealthy and powerful noble is evident from his certifying his knight's fees to be one hundred and sixty in 12 Henry II. He evidently enjoyed royal favor, as he was recreated Earl of Norfolk by Henry II., and obtained a grant of the office of lord high steward of the kingdom, which his father had held.

Notwithstanding these and other equally substantial marks of the king's liberality, the Earl of Norfolk arrayed himself under the banner of Robert, Earl of Leicester, in the insurrection incited by that nobleman in favor of the king's son, 19 Henry II. His part in this rebellion cost him the loss of his strongest castles and the heavy fine of one thousand marks, over six hundred and sixty-six pounds. After this he made a pilgrimage to the Holy Land, and died 23 Henry II., 1177. He had by his first wife, Juliana, sister of Alberic de Vere, created, 1135, Earl of Oxford, great high chamberlain of England, and daughter of Alberic, second Baron de Vere, of Kensington, appointed by Henry I. great high chamberlain of England, by his wife Adeliza, daughter of Gilbert de Clare, of Tonebruge, Kent, and his wife Adeliza, daughter of Hugh, Count de Clermont:

ROGER BIGOD, eldest son, who succeeded as second Earl of Norfolk, and was reconstituted in his earldom and the office of lord high steward by Richard I. upon his accession, by charter dated November 27, 1189, and also obtained at this time restitution of some manors his father had forfeited, with grants of others, and the confirmation of all demesnes he held. He was appointed, 1189, by King Richard one of the ambassadors from him to Philip of France, for obtaining aid towards the recovery of the Holy Land. Upon the return of King Richard from his captivity in Germany, the Earl assisted at a great council held by the king at Nottingham, 1194, and at this monarch's second coronation his lordship was one of the four earls that had the honor of carrying the silken canopy over the monarch's head.

In 1200 the Earl of Norfolk was sent by King John as

one of his messengers to summon William, King of Scotland, to do homage to him in Parliament at Lincoln, and subsequently attended King John into Poictou, and on his return was won over to their cause by the Barons and became one of the strongest advocates of the Charter of Liberty, and was elected one of the Sureties for the observance of this great instrument, for which he was excommunicated by Pope Innocent III. He *d*. 5 Henry III., 1220-21, having had issue by his wife Isabella, daughter of Hameline Plantagenet, *d*. 1202, fifth Earl of Surrey, in right of his wife, *m*. 1163-4, Isabella, *d*. 1199, widow of Willam de Blois, *d. s. p*. 1160, a natural son of King Stephen (Hameline Plantagenet, *b*. before 1151, was a natural son of Geoffrey, Count of Anjou), and daughter and heiress of William, third Earl of Warren and Surrey, *d. s. p. m.* 1148 (by his wife Alice, or Adela de Talvas, or Talvace, *d*. 1174, daughter of William, Count of Alençon and Ponthieu, by his second wife, Alix, widow of Bertrand, Count de Tripoli, and daughter of Eudes, Duke of Burgundy, a crusader, *d*. 1102, a great-grandson of ROBERT THE PIOUS, KING OF FRANCE), son of William, second Earl of Warren and Surrey, and his wife Isabel, or Elizabeth de Vermandois, daughter of Hugh the Great, son of HENRY I., KING OF FRANCE:

HUGH BIGOD, third Earl of Norfolk.

WILLIAM BIGOD, *m*. Margaret, daughter of Robert de Sutton.

THOMAS BIGOD.

MARGERY, wife of William de Hastings. *Issue*.

ADELIZA, wife of Alberic de Vere, Earl of Oxford; *d. s. p.*

MARY, wife of Ralph Fitz-Robert, of Middlehams.

Arms.—*Gules; a Lion passant, Or*, are the arms generally attributed to this Surety, but there is evidence that *Or, a Cross Gules*, more properly describes the arms he bore.

HENRY DE BOHUN

HUMPHREY DE BOHUN, a kinsman and companion in arms of the Conqueror, generally known as "Humphrey with the Beard," was the founder of the House of Bohun in England. He does not seem to have profited much through his alleged relationship to the Conqueror, as at the General Survey he possessed only one lordship, Taterford, in Norfolk, in which he was succeeded by his son:

HUMPHREY DE BOHUN, who, in contradistinction to his father, or because of the wealth his wife brought him, or because of his conquest of so wealthy a lady, was surnamed the Great. He *m.*, by command of King Stephen, Maud, only daughter of Edward d'Evereux, lord of Salisbury, or Saresbury, sheriff of Wiltshire, who owned manors in eight counties, and had:

HUMPHREY DE BOHUN, eldest son and heir, who was steward and sewer to King Henry I. At the instigation of his father-in-law he espoused the cause of the Empress Maud and her son against King Stephen, and so faithfully maintained his allegiance that the Empress, by her especial charter, granted him the office of steward and sewer, in both Normandy and England. In 20 Henry II. he accompanied Richard de Lacie, Justiciary of England, into Scotland, with an army, to waste the country; and was one of the witnesses to the accord made by William of Scotland and Henry of England, as to the subjection of Scotland to the crown of England.

This feudal Baron *m.* Margery, daughter and coheiress of Milo de Gloucester, first Earl of Hereford, lord high constable of England, whose charter was the earliest of express

BIOGRAPHIES OF THE SURETIES 81

creation, the patent being dated in 1140, and, dying April 6, 1187, had issue:

HUMPHREY DE BOHUN, who was Earl of Hereford and lord high constable of England, in right of his mother. He *m.* Margaret, daughter of Henry, Earl of Huntingdon and Northumberland, *d. v. p* 1152 (and widow of Conale Petit, Earl of Brittany and Richmond, and sister of William the Lion, king of Scots), eldest son of DAVID I., KING OF SCOTS, by his wife, Matilda, widow of Simon de St. Liz, and daughter of Waltheof, Earl of Northumberland and Northampton, beheaded in 1075, and his wife, a niece of William the Conqueror. Lady Margaret's mother, *m.* 1139, *d.* 1178, was Ada de Warren, daughter of William, second Earl of Surrey (by his wife, Isabel, or Elizabeth, *d.* 1131, widow of Robert, Earl of Mellent, and daughter of Hugh the Great, Count de Vermandois, son of HENRY I., KING OF FRANCE), the son of William de Warren, Earl of Surrey, by his wife, Gundreda, the reputed daughter of William the Conqueror, or the daughter of his consort, Queen Maud, or Matilda, of Flanders, by Gherbod, advocate of the Abbey of St. Bestin, at St. Omer, before her marriage to William of Normandy. Humphrey de Bohun and Lady Margaret had:

HENRY DE BOHUN, eldest son and heir, who in reality was the first Earl of Hereford of this family, being so created by charter of King John, dated April 28, 1199; but the office of lord high constable he inherited. As he took prominent part with the Barons against the king, his lands were sequestered, but he received them again at the sealing of the Magna Charta. He was elected one of the celebrated twenty-five Sureties for the observance of the Magna Charta, and having been excommunicated by the Pope, with the other Barons, he did not return to his allegiance on the decease of King John, but was one of the commanders in the army of Louis, the Dauphin, at the battle of Lincoln, and was taken prisoner. After this defeat he joined Saher de Quincey, and others, in a pilgrimage to the Holy Land, and *d.* on the passage, June 1, 1220, 4 Henry III. His body was brought home and buried in the chapter-house of Llanthony Abbey, in Gloucestershire.

He *m.* Maud, daughter of Geoffrey Fitz-Piers, Baron de Mandeville, created, in 1199, Earl of Essex, Justiciary of England, *d.* 1212, and eventually heiress of her brother, William de Mandeville, last Earl of Essex of that family, by whom he acquired the honor of Essex and many extensive lordships, and sister of Geoffrey de Mandeville, one of the celebrated twenty-five Magna Charta Sureties, and had:

HUMPHREY DE BOHUN, second Earl of Hereford and Essex.

MARGARET, wife of Waleran de Newburgh, fourth Earl of Warwick.

RALPH DE BOHUN.

Arms.—*Azure; a Bend Argent, between two Cottises and six Lions rampant, Or.*

GILBERT DE CLARE

An account of the ancestry of this Baron is given in the sketch of his father, Richard de Clare. He was granted some Welsh lordships in 1210–11 by King John, and fortified the castle of Buelth, in Wales, but shortly afterwards, with his father, took up arms with the Barons against the king in the interests of civil and religious liberty, and was elected one of the celebrated Sureties for the Magna Charta, and was excommunicated. He was one of the Barons still opposing the arbitrary proceedings of the crown, who championed Louis, the Dauphin, fought at Lincoln under the baronial banner, and was taken prisoner by the Earl of Pembroke, the Protector of England, and sent to Gloucester, but soon afterwards made his peace and married one of the five daughters, and coheiresses of her five brothers, of the Protector. After the decease of his father, in 1218, he became the fifth Earl of Hertford, and after the decease, in 1219, of Geoffrey de Mandeville, Earl of Essex, the second husband of Isabel, the divorced wife of King John, sister of his mother, Lady Amicia, daughters and coheiresses of William, Earl of Gloucester, he became, in right of his aunt and his mother, Earl of Gloucester.

He m. Isabel Marshall, one of the daughters and eventually coheiresses of William, Earl of Pembroke, Protector of England, by his first wife, Isabel de Clare, and dying in 1229, 14 Henry III., at Penros, in Brittany, was buried in the choir of Tewkesbury Abbey, having issue by Lady Isabel, who after his decease m. Richard, Earl of Cornwall, brother of King Henry III.':

RICHARD DE CLARE, Earl of Hertford and Gloucester. He

was in his minority at the death of his father, and his wardship was granted to the celebrated Hubert de Burgh, Earl of Kent, Justiciary of England, whose daughter Margaret, to the great displeasure of King Henry III., he afterwards clandestinely married, but from whom he was probably divorced, as the king married him the next year to Maud, daughter of John de Lacie, Earl of Lincoln, in consideration whereof the Earl of Lincoln paid to the crown five thousand marks and remitted a debt of two thousand more. This Richard de Clare was a very distinguished personage in the reign of Henry III., and was one of the noblemen present in Westminster Hall, 40 Henry III., when Boniface, Archbishop of Canterbury, pronounced a solemn curse from the altar against all those who should thenceforth violate the Magna Charta.

The other children of Gilbert de Clare, the Surety, were:
WILLIAM DE CLARE.
GILBERT DE CLARE.
AMICIA, wife of Baldwin de Redvers, Earl of Devon; *d. s. p.*
AGNES DE CLARE.
ISABEL, wife of Robert de Brus, Earl of Annandale. *Issue.*
Arms.—*Or; three Chevrons, Gules.*

RICHARD DE CLARE

RICHARD FITZ-GILBERT was the founder of the House of Clare in England. He accompanied William the Conqueror into England, and participated in the spoils of conquest, and obtained extensive possessions in the new and old dominions of his royal leader and kinsman. He was the eldest son of Gislebert, surnamed Crispin, Count of Eu, or Ewe, Earl of Brion, in Normandy, in right of his wife, sister and heiress of the Earl of Brion, and by inheritance from his father, Geoffrey (or Godfrey), Earl or Count of Eu and Brion, or Bryomy, a natural son of Richard I., Sanspeur, third Duke of Normandy, *d.* 986, ancestor of William the Conqueror.

In 6 William I., Richard was joined, under the designation of Ricardus de Benefacta, with William de Warren, Earl of Surrey, in the great office of Justiciary of England, with whom in three years afterwards he was in arms against the rebellious Barons, the Earl of Hereford, and the Earl of Norfolk and Suffolk. At the time of the General Survey of England he was designated as Ricardus de Tonebruge, from his seat at Tonebruge (now Tunbridge), in Kent, which town and castle he had obtained from the Archbishop of Canterbury, in lieu of the castle of Brion, at which time he is recorded as possessed of thirty-eight lordships in Surrey, thirty-five in Essex, three in Cambridgeshire, ninety-five in Suffolk, and some in Wilts and Devon. One of these lordships was that of Clare, on the borders of and in Suffolk, which subsequently becoming his chief seat, he came to be styled Richard de Clare, and his descendants known as Earls of Clare, although never so created. He fell in a skirmish with the Welsh, having issue by his wife Rohese, or Rohais, daughter of Walter Giffard, first Earl of Buckingham, son of Osborne de Bolebec and his wife Aveline, sister of Gunnora, wife of Richard I., third Duke of Normandy, great-grandmother of William the Conqueror. Walter Giffard was distinguished for gallant action in the battle of Hastings. He assisted in making the General Survey of England, and is recorded as the owner of one hundred and seven lordships in the kingdom. He was the commander of the army of William Rufus, in Normandy, in 1089, and in 1102 sided with Robert Curthose against Henry I., and died in this year.

GILBERT DE TONEBRUGE, eldest son of Robert Fitz-Gilbert, inherited all his father's English estates. He appears to have joined in the rebellion against King William Rufus, and lost his castle of Tonebruge, and, dying shortly afterwards, a munificent benefactor of the church, left issue by his wife, Adeliza, daughter of Hugh, first Count de Clermont, by his wife Margaret, daughter of Hildwin IV., Count de Montdider and de Rouci, by his wife Adela, or Alexandria, Countess de Rouci, whose mother, Beatrix, was a daughter of Ranigerus, or Rynerius V., Count of Hainault, 977, and his wife, the Princess Havide, or Hedewige, daugher of HUGH CAPET, KING OF THE FRANKS, 987, by his wife Adela, or Alisa, daughter of William, Duke of Aquitaine and Adelheid, daughter of OTTO I., EMPEROR OF SAXONY. Of this distinguished ancestry was

RICHARD DE CLARE, eldest son and heir of Gilbert de Tonebruge. He was known as the Earl of Hertford, as well as Earl of Clare, and invaded Wales and became lord of vast possessions there by power of his sword, but finally was slain in a skirmish with a few Welshmen, 1139. He had issue by his wife Alice, or Adeliza, daughter of Ranulph de Meschines, Viscount Bayeux, in Normandy, third Earl of

Chester, *d.* 1228 (by his wife Lucia, daughter of Algar, Saxon Earl of Mercia, and widow of Roger de Romera), whose mother was Maud de Abrincis, sister of the celebrated Hugh Lupus, Earl of Chester.

ROGER DE CLARE, second son of the above, succeeded his brother Gilbert, who *d. s. p.* 1151, as third Earl of Hertford and "Earl of Clare." In 3 Henry II. he obtained permission from the king to own all lands in Wales which he could win, marched into Caerdigan, and captured and fortified the castles there. Six years afterwards he was summoned by the celebrated Thomas à Becket, to Westminster, in order to do homage to this prelate for his castle of Tonebruge, which had been restored to his father, but, at the command of King Henry, he refused, alleging that, holding it by military service, it belonged rather to the crown than to the Church. This earl, who, from his munificence to the church and his numerous acts of piety, was called the "good Earl of Hertford," *d.* in 1173, having issue by his wife Maud, daughter of James de St. Hillary, or Sidonis, who *m.* secondly, William d'Albini, Earl of Arundel:

* RICHARD DE CLARE, fourth Earl of Hertford and sixth Earl of Clare. In 7 Richard I. he gave a thousand marks to the king for livery of the lands of his mother's inheritance, with his proportion of those some time belonging to Giffard, Earl of Buckingham. His name appears in the covenant made between King John and the Barons, and as he did not die until "the 3d of the Calends of December in the yeare after Christ 1218,"—December 30, 1218,—and there being no other prominent man of his name, it is very likely that he was the Surety named. He was buried either at Clare, or in the middle of the choir of the priory of Tunbridge, which he founded. He had issue by his wife Amicia, sister of King John's divorced wife, and second daughter and coheiress of William, second Earl of Gloucester,

d. s. p. m. 1183 (by his wife Mabel, daughter of Robert-bossu de Bellomont, or Beaumont, second Earl of Leicester, *d.* 1167, a stanch adherent of Henry I. and of the interests of Henry II., upon whose accession to the throne he was constituted Justiciary of England), son of Robert the Consul, Earl of Mellent, who was created, in 1109, Earl of Gloucester, a natural son of King Henry I. by Elizabeth de Bellomont, daughter of Robert, Earl of Mellent, created, in 1103, Earl of Leicester, and his wife Isabel (or Elizabeth) de Vermandois, daughter of Hugh Magnus, a son of HENRY I., KING OF FRANCE. Richard de Clare had by his wife, Lady Amicia:

GILBERT DE CLARE, Earl of Hertford and Gloucester.
JOAN, *m.* Rhys-gryd, lord of Yestradtywy. *Issue.*
MAUD, or MATILDA DE CLARE.

The arms usually assigned to this earl are *Or; three Chevrons, Gules*, but in Cook's Baronage, Harleian collection, there is the addition of *an Escutcheon of Pretence, Argent, charged with a Canton, Gules.*

JOHN FITZ-ROBERT

The founder of the family in England from which this Surety sprung, was EUSTACE FITZ-JOHN (the nephew and heir of Serlo de Burgh, the founder of Knaresborough Castle), one of the most powerful and influential of the northern feudal Barons, and a favorite of King Henry I. He *m.* first, the heiress of the de Vescis, of Alnwick, and had a son William, founder of the House of de Vesci, and *m.* secondly, Lady Agnes, daughter and heiress of William Fitz-Nigel, Baron of Halton and constable of Chester, and had:

RICHARD FITZ-EUSTACE, Baron of Halton and constable of Chester, who *m.* Lady Albreda Lizures, a half-sister of Robert de Lacy, and had:

ROGER FITZ-RICHARD, third and youngest son, who was granted by Henry II. the lordship of Warkworth, in Northumberland, who had by his wife, Lady Alianore, daughter of Henry of Essex, Baron of Raleigh:

ROBERT FITZ-ROGER, only son. Upon the accession of King John he obtained a confirmation of the castle and manor of Warkworth, and of the manors of Clavering, in Essex, and Eure, in Buckinghamshire, to hold by service of one knight's fee each. He was thrice high sheriff of each of the counties of Northumberland, Norfolk, and Suffolk. In the early proceedings of the Barons in the matter of the Magna Charta, this rich Baron, although indebted to King John for immense territorial possessions, took sides with the Barons; but under apprehension of confiscation and other visitations of royal vengeance, he was induced to return to his allegiance.

He *m.* Lady Margaret, only child and heiress of William

de Cheney, Baron of Horsford, County Norfolk, and, dying in 1240, was succeeded by his only son:

JOHN FITZ-ROBERT. In the fourteenth year of his reign King John ratified to this Baron the grants of the manors of Warkworth and Clavering. At the time of meeting of the Barons at Bury St. Edmunds, this Baron was still loyal to King John, and was, with John Marshall, joint governor of the castles of Norwich and Oxford; but subsequently joining in the insurrection, and, taking such a prominent part that he was chosen one of the twenty-five Sureties for the observance of the Magna Charta, his lands were seized by the king, and confiscated. Returning to his allegiance in the next reign, his castles and vast estates were restored to him, and he was constituted by Henry III. high sheriff of County Northumberland and governor of New Castle-upon-Tyne. This Baron, who never appears to have received any summons to Parliament, his barony being held by tenure, dying in the same year his father did, 1240, had issue, by his wife, Lady Ada de Baliol, probably daughter of Hugh de Baliol, lord of Biwell and Hiche, who was on John's side in the baronial insurrection, and did him good service in the North:

ROGER FITZ-JOHN, lord of Warkworth and Clavering, *d.* 1249. *Issue.*

HUGH D'EURE, lord of Eure, Buckinghamshire. *Issue.*

ROBERT, ancestor of the Eure family of Axholm, Lincolnshire. *Issue.*

Arms.—*Or; two Chevrons, Gules.*

ROBERT FITZ-WALTER

ROBERT FITZ-RICHARD, fifth son of RICHARD FITZ-GILBERT, lord of Clare, in Suffolk, Justiciary of England, 1073, being steward to King Henry I., obtained from that monarch the barony of Dunmow, in Essex, forfeited by William Baynard, as also the honor of Baynard Castle, in the city of London, and, dying about 1134, he had issue by his wife, Maud, Lady of Bradham, reputed daughter of Simon de St. Liz, first Earl of Huntingdon:

WALTER FITZ-ROBERT, lord of Dunmow, eldest son. In the controversy between the Earl of Moreton, brother of King Richard I., and the Bishop of Ely, governor of the realm during the king's absence in the Holy Land, Walter adhered to the bishop, and was given the custody of the Castle of Eye, in Suffolk. He *m.* first, Maud, daughter of Richard de Lucie, with whom he had the lordship of Disce, in Norfolk, and *m.* secondly, Margaret de Bohun, and, dying in 1198, was succeeded by his eldest son, by his first wife, who *d.* in 1140, who was a sister of Geoffrey de Lucie, Bishop of Winchester:

ROBERT FITZ-WALTER, lord of Dunmow, leader of the Barons who secured the Magna Charta from King John, and styled Marshal of the Army of God and the Holy Church. The first public act recorded of this subsequently important Baron, who was castellan and standard-bearer of the city of London, conveys at first a bad impression of him. It is recorded that "in 5 John (1203) Robert Fitz-Walter, being trusted, together with Saier de Quincey, to keep the castle of Ruil, in France, delivered it up to the king of that realm so soon as he came before it with an army." This appears to imply not less of disloyalty than of cowardice; but a short time proved to which of these motives it was to be assigned. At that time the Barons, not only those at home but those abroad, were preparing to try to compel King John to keep his promises in the matter of the proposed statutes, and several conspiracies to this end were discovered, wherein Robert Fitz-Walter was materially concerned. On the discovery of his treasonable practices, Fitz-Walter, with his wife and children, sought an asylum in France; but in the following year, 1213, his friends persuaded him to return home, and with the other Barons he was reconciled to King John. But this friendship was only of short duration, for shortly it was again discovered that he was still plotting against the king in the interests of reform in the government, so his residence in London, the Castle of Baynard, was, in consequence, entirely destroyed, and the hatred between John and Fitz-Walter was violent in the greatest degree. Tradition has assigned a disgraceful act on the part of King John as the principal cause of this, which was no less than an attempt to procure Fitz-Walter's daughter, Maud, for one of his concubines. But whether this is truth or fiction, Fitz-Walter's opposition seemed to be dominated by the desire for the Magna Charta, and his feelings and conduct were engulfed in the agitated sea of history which opened at this period.

To endeavor to win him over to his side, King John pretended to admire Fitz-Walter's skill, prowess, and valor in a tournament, which took place in Normandy, before the courts of the kings of England and France, and, making this an excuse, restored to him the whole of his forfeited estates and permitted him to repair his destroyed fortresses, and constituted him governor of Hertford Castle, 1214-15. But Fitz-Walter's heart was still in the cause of the Barons, and he was soon again in open opposition to the king. His lands were again seized, which course effectually secured him to the discontented Barons and the people. The active spirit of Fitz-Walter made him a desirable leader to their party, and he was selected as one of the commissioners to treat of a composure of differences at a meeting at Erith Church, to which he had letters of safe-conduct, and subsequently he was formally elected their leader under the title of "Marshal of God and the Holy Church in England." To relate his subsequent connection with the efforts to procure the Magna Charta, of which he was one of the twenty-five celebrated Sureties, would be to repeat the story of this period.

After the granting of the Magna Charta, when King John endeavored to elude his promises, Fitz-Walter was one of the committee of the baronial party which went to France to invite the Dauphin to accept the throne of England, and on this prince's coming he, with William de Mandeville and William de Huntingfield, reduced the counties of Essex and Suffolk to the authority of the Dauphin. Upon the accession of Henry III., Fitz-Walter, then a prisoner, with the majority of the Barons, finding the Dauphin a useless political factor, dropped him, and returned to their allegiance, and engaged to ship him back to France. However, as the civil conflict was renewed, we find Fitz-Walter again in arms. One of the haughty and ambitious spirits yet unconquered by the king was Saher de Quincey. He would not yield the castle of Mountsorrel, in Leicestershire. When William Marshall, the Protector, proceeded with part of the royal army to besiege it, de Quincey called on his fellow-Sureties to assist him. They raised a force of about twenty thousand armed men and placed themselves under the leadership of the Dauphin, and Fitz-Walter appears as one of his principal generals. The two armies met and fought the battle of Lincoln, the royal army being victorious, and Fitz-Walter was once more made prisoner along with de Quincey. But, in 1218, he was allowed to assume the cross and join a crusade, when he took part in the famous siege of Damietta, returned home and died a peaceful death in 1234, and was buried before the high-altar of Dunmow Priory. Notwithstanding his enmity to Kings John and Henry III., and the frequent confiscations of his property, Fitz-Walter died possessed of an extensive estate.

Robert Fitz-Walter *m.* first, Gunora, daughter and heiress of Robert, second Baron de Valoinies, by his wife, Roesia, daughter of William, fifth feudal Baron le Blount, or Blund, and *m.* secondly, Roese, who survived him, but whose surname has not been preserved. By his first wife he had:

Sir Walter Fitz-Walter, eldest son and successor, *d.* 1257-8. *Issue.*

Christiana, second wife of William de Mandeville, Earl of Essex, *d. s. p.* 1190. She *m.* secondly, Raymond de Burgh.

Maud or Matilda Fitz-Walter, *d.* young and *unm.*, whom it is alleged King John tried to procure as his concubine, and failing in which he caused her to be poisoned. She was buried on the south side of the choir of Dunmow Priory. See Gough's "Sepulchral Monuments." The persecution and romantic death of this young lady has been worked up into many plays, poems, and popular tales, her name appearing under that of "Matilda the Fair;" "Malkin," or "Maid Marian, the Queen of the May;" the Sherwood Forest mistress of "Robin Hood," or Robert, Earl of Huntingdon.

Arms.—*Or ; a Fesse between two Chevrons, Gules.*

WILLIAM DE FORTIBUS

This Baron had his most distinguished ancestry on his mother's side. She was Hawyse, widow of William de Mandeville, Earl of Essex and Earl of Albemarle, *jure uxoris*, who *d. s. p.* 1190, and daughter and coheiress of William le Grosse, third Earl of Albemarle and Earl of York, a person of great note in the period in which he lived. In 1138 he defeated the Scots under King David at North Allerton, when they had invaded England and claimed Northumberland, and for his gallantry upon this occasion he was rewarded with the earldom of York. He *d.* 1179, leaving issue by his wife Cicily, daughter of William Fitz-Duncan (nephew of Malcom III., King of Scots) by his wife Alice, daughter of Robert de Romely, lord of Skipton, in Craven, etc.: Hawyse, who *m.* secondly, William de Fortibus, who was Earl of Albemarle, in right of his wife, and was constituted by Richard Cœur de Lion one of the admirals of the fleet in which this king soon afterwards sailed towards Jerusalem. De Fortibus *d.* in 1194, having had by Hawyse a son, William, who was the youngest of the Sureties for the Magna Charta, and his widow *m.* thirdly, Baldwine de Bertune, Earl of the Isle of Wight, who *d. s. p.* 1212.

WILLIAM DE FORTIBUS became of age in 1214–15, when King John confirmed to him all the lands which accrued to him by inheritance from his mother, and he succeeded in her right as Earl of Albemarle, or Aumerle, in Normandy. He arrayed himself on the side of the Barons in their contentions with King John, and was one of the celebrated twenty-five chosen to enforce the observance of the Magna Charta, but he subsequently deserted the Barons and joined King

John in his expedition into the north, so marked by spoil and rapine. For his services the king granted him all the lands belonging to his sister Alice, then wife of William Marshall, Jr., and constituted him, in 1218, governor of the castles of Rockingham, in Northamptonshire, Sauvey, in Leicestershire, and Botham, in Lincolnshire, with strict command to destroy all the houses, parks, and possessions of those Barons who were in arms against the king. In the reign of Henry III. this nobleman fought under the royal banner at the battle of Lincoln, and shared largely in the spoils of victory. He was subsequently alternately for and against the king. His rapacious personal excursions being opposed by the king, his submission was procured only by excommunication. In 1230 he was one of the commanders of the royal troops in Normandy, and in 1241, having set out on a pilgrimage to the Holy Land, he died on the Mediterranean Sea, March 29. He *m.* Aveline, sister and coheiress of Richard, Baron de Montfichet, one of the twenty-five Sureties for the Magna Charta, and was succeeded by his only son :

WILLIAM DE FORTIBUS, Earl of Albemarle, whose only child, Lady Aveline, Countess of Holderness and Countess of Devon and the Isle of Wight, *m.* as his first wife, Edmund Plantagenet, a son of King Henry III., and *d. s. p.*

Arms.—*Argent; a Chief, Gules.*

WILLIAM DE HARDELL

But very little is known of the antecedents of this Surety, nor, in fact, of himself. He was the mayor of the city of London (the first mayor by popular election of the citizens) at the time of the insurrection of the Barons, and very likely induced the citizens to deliver up one of the gates of the city, Aldgate, to the Barons, through which they entered the city, Sunday morning, May 24, 1215, while the people were at mass, and, for the part he took in subsequent proceedings, was elected one of the Sureties for the observance of the Magna Charta. There is no evidence that he was even a feudal Baron, and, being a civil officer of so early a period, there is some doubt as to his arms. He served as sheriff of the city of London, in 1207. It is not known that he had descendants. For several years, *temp.* Henry III., Richard, or Ralph, Hardell, a draper, was mayor of London. He may have been a descendant, but his arms were different. A William Hardell was clerk of the wardrobe to Henry III. in 1245–6, and a John Hardell was elected in 1246–7, on the king's writ, to be keeper of the die of the mint of London. A family of this surname held many estates in County Essex, in 1284–5. His surname is sometimes given as Hadel.

Arms.—*Vert; a Fesse flory and counterflory, Or.*

WILLIAM DE HUNTINGFIELD

ROGER DE HUNTINGFIELD, who held the manor of Huntingfield, in County Suffolk, as undertenant, *temp.* Henry I., of Robert Malet, was apparently first to assume this surname, and was the founder of this family. His son, WILLIAM DE HUNTINGFIELD, *d.* 1 Henry II., 1155, having a son and successor, ROGER DE HUNTINGFIELD, whose eldest son:

WILLIAM DE HUNTINGFIELD, was one of the celebrated twenty-five Sureties. In 5 John, 1203-4, he was constable of Devon Castle, and took the usual oath of office before the king, and delivered his son to the Earl of Arundel and his daughter to the Earl of Ferrers, as hostages for his good faith. Five years after this he was one of the itinerant justices, at Lincoln, and some time was high sheriff of Norfolk and Suffolk, until the end of 1213-14, 15 John. He was governor of Sauvey Castle, in Leicestershire, when he joined the cause of the Barons in arms against King John, and, having been elected one of the twenty-five to govern the kingdom, was excommunicated by the Pope, and his lands given to Nicholas de Haya. He seems partly to have returned to his allegiance, since, in 1216, King John restored to him the manor of Clayford, in Hants. But he does not seem to have been thoroughly reconstructed to the satisfaction of the Protector, Earl of Pembroke, as his possessions in several counties were transferred to John Marshall, but they were probably restored at the general amnesty.

Very likely the cause of the Protector's severity towards this baron was that he was one of those who plotted to have the Dauphin come to England, and after his landing was very active in reducing the counties of Essex and Suffolk to his authority.   He was one of the witnesses to the Charter King John granted in 1214, allowing free ecclesiastical elections throughout England.   His brother Roger's possessions were all seized into the king's hands during the interdict, and subsequently were granted to William.

William de Huntingfield *d.* 41 Henry III., 1256-7, having issue by his wife, Alice de St. Liz:

ROGER DE HUNTINGFIELD, *d.* 1257. *Issue.*

ALICE, who married twice, but the name of her first husband has not been preserved. Her father paid a fine of "six fair Norway Goshawks," 15 John, to the king, for liberty to marry Alice, his daughter, then a widow, to Richard de Solers.

Arms.—*Or; on a Fesse, Gules, three Plates.*

JOHN DE LACIE

The widow, Albreda, whose surname has not been preserved, of Henry, feudal Baron de Lacie, of Pontefract Castle, Yorkshire, *temp*. Henry II., *m*. secondly, Eudo de Lisours, and had by him an only daughter and heiress, Albreda, who *m*. first, Richard Fitz-Eustace, lord of Halton and constable of Chester, and had by him a son and heir:

JOHN DE LACIE, who inherited the baronies of Halton and Pontefract, with the constableship of Chester, and assumed the surname de Lacie. He *d*. in the Holy Land, 1179, having issue by his wife, Alice de Vere:

ROGER DE LACIE, lord of Halton and Pontefract and constable of Chester. In 1192 he assisted at the siege of Açon, under Richard the Lion-Hearted, and shared in the subsequent triumphs of this chivalrous monarch. At the accession of John he was a person of great eminence, and was one of the noblemen who escorted William of Scotland to Lincoln to confer with King John, and the next year he was present, also at Lincoln, when David of Scotland did homage and fealty to King John. Receiving word that the Earl of Chester, who had invaded Wales, was forced to take refuge in Rothelan Castle, where he was closely besieged by the Welsh, as constable, Roger de Lacie collected all the men of all descriptions attending a public fair at Chester, and marched to his relief, and upon their approach the Welshmen fled. For this timely service the Earl of Chester conferred upon de Lacie and his heirs the patronage of all minstrels in those parts, as many of the rescuing force were simply minstrels, musicians, and actors, which patronage the constable transferred to his steward, Dutton, and his heirs, and it was long enjoyed by them.

He *d.* in 1211, having issue by his wife Alice, daughter of Geoffrey, third Baron Mandeville, hereditary sheriff of London and Middlesex, and sheriff of Hertfordshire, created Earl of Essex by King Stephen, by his first wife, whose name has not been preserved:

JOHN DE LACIE, Baron of Halton and hereditary constable of Chester, who, in 15 John, undertook the payment of seven thousand marks (four thousand six hundred and sixty-six pounds) in the space of four years, for livery of the lands of his inheritance, and to be discharged of all his father's debts, further obliging himself by oath, that in case he should ever swerve from his allegiance all his possessions should devolve upon the crown; promising also that he would not marry without the king's license. By this agreement it was arranged that the king should retain the castles of Pontefract and Dunnington, and that de Lacie should pay him rent for their use. This was a hard bargain, and it is not surprising that shortly afterwards he joined the baronial standard as one of the earliest who took up arms, and was elected one of the Sureties for the observance of the Magna Charta. He was also appointed to see that the new statutes were properly carried into effect and observed in the counties of York and Nottingham, and was, of course, excommunicated by the Pope. Upon the accession of Henry III. he joined a party of noblemen and made a pilgrimage to the Holy Land, and did good service at the siege of Damietta.

During the dispute between Henry III. and Richard, lord marshal, John de Lacie remained attached to the king, probably because of his gratitude, as this monarch had created him, by charter dated November 23, 1232, Earl of Lincoln, with remainder to the heirs of his body, by his wife Margaret, in whose right only he had previously enjoyed the title. In 1237 the Earl was one of those appointed to prohibit Otto, the Pope's legate, from establishing anything derogatory to the king's crown and dignity, in the great council of English prelates, and was deputed with the marshal to protect the legate as he went to and from the council. In this year, and in 1240, he had a grant of the sheriffalty of Chester, and was made governor of Chester and Beeston Castle. He *d.* July 22, 1240, and was buried in the Cistercian Abbey of Stanlaw, in the county of Chester.

John de Lacie, Earl of Lincoln, *m.* first, Alice, daughter of Gilbert d'Aquila, but had no issue by her. He *m.* secondly, after his marked gallantry at the siege of Damietta, Margaret, the only daughter and heiress of Robert de Quincey, a fellow-crusader, who died in the Holy Land, eldest son of Saier de Quincey, Earl of Winchester, one of the twenty-five Sureties for the Magna Charta. Her mother was Hawyse, a sister and coheiress of Ranulph de Meschines, fourth Earl of Chester and Lincoln, and daughter of Hugh, third Earl of Chester. Earl Ranulph, by a formal charter, granted the earldom of Lincoln to said Hawyse, so that she could be a countess and that her heirs might enjoy the earldom, which grant was confirmed by the king, and at the especial request of the Countess of Lincoln, John de Lacie, her son-in-law, was created Earl of Lincoln, in 1232. John, Earl of Lincoln, had by Lady Margaret, who survived him, and *m.* secondly, William Marshall, Earl of Pembroke:

EDMUND DE LACIE, second Earl of Lincoln, *d.* 1257. He is called the second Earl, although the title was never attributed to him in any charter, by reason that he died before his mother, through whom the dignity came. Dugdale states that he married, in 1247, "an outlandish lady from the parts of Savoy, brought over purposely for him by Peter de Savoy, uncle to the queen, which occasioned much dis content amongst the nobles of England." This lady was Alice, daughter of the Marquess of Saluces, in Italy, and a cousin of the queen.

MAUD, wife of Richard de Clare, Earl of Gloucester. John, Earl of Lincoln, was promised the marriage of his eldest daughter to Richard de Clare, in the event of the king not marrying him to a daughter of the Earl of March, and for this grant he engaged to pay five thousand marks. This agreement, having been made without the consent of the Barons, excited considerable dissatisfaction, especially in the elder de Clare.

DAUGHTER, name unknown. She and her sister, after their father's death, were removed to Windsor and educated with the king's daughters.

Arms.—*Or ; a Lion rampant, Purpure.*

WILLIAM DE LANVALLEI

This Baron was the son of WILLIAM DE LANVALLEI, feudal lord of Hallingbury and Stanway, in County Essex, who d. 12 John, 1210-11, and whose estates do not appear to have been of any very considerable extent, since his widow paid only two hundred marks (£133-6-8) for their delivery.

WILLIAM DE LANVALLEI, the younger, in 17 John, 1215-16, was governor of Colchester Castle when he joined the insurgent Barons, who constituted him one of the twenty-five elected to govern the kingdom, and he was likewise a party to that Covenant which yielded to them the city and Tower of London. He appears to have been reconciled to Henry III. at the great treaty in 1217, but there are no further particulars extant concerning him.

In 14 John, 1212-13, Alan Basset, of Wycombe, who is named in the Magna Charta as one of the king's liegemen, and also the same in the first Charter of Henry III., dated November 12, 1216, gave the king two hundred marks and "an excellent palfry," that his daughter might marry William de Lanvallei, who was also to be discharged of his relief upon doing his homage. The issue of this marriage was an only daughter and heiress:

HAWISE, wife of John de Burgh. *Issue.*

Arms.—*Gules; a Lion passant, Or.*

WILLIAM DE MALET

This Surety was the son of ROBERT DE MALET, feudal lord of the honors of Eye and Huntingfield, in Suffolk, Great Chamberlain of England, *temp.* Henry I., who was "banished and disinherited," and who was probably the son or grandson of William de Malet, one of the commanders in William of Normandy's army of invasion, and appointed governor of York Castle, who was probably the brother of King Harold's wife.

WILLIAM DE MALET appears to be first mentioned as a minor, in 1194, in an expedition then made into Normandy, and in the ensuing year he had delivery of his inheritance. His estates, including the principal one, Curry-Malet, in Somersetshire, were held by the service of twenty knights' fees. In 1210-14 he was sheriff of Somerset and Dorset shires, when he joined the Barons in their insurrection. His lands in four counties were thereupon confiscated and given to Hugh de Vivonia, his son-in-law, and Thomas Basset, his father-in-law, and he was excommunicated by Pope Innocent, having become one of the Sureties for the observance of the Magna Charta. He was also fined two thousand marks, but which was not paid till after his decease, when one thousand marks were remitted, being found due to him for military service to King John in Poictou.

William de Malet *d.* 9 Henry III., 1224-5, having issue by his wife, who predeceased him, daughter of Thomas Basset, who was a son, or grandson, of Ralph Basset, who was constituted Justiciary of England by Henry II., and introduced into the kingdom many salutary laws, especially that of frank-pledge:

WILLIAM DE MALET, eldest son, *d. s. p.*, *v. p.* His sisters were his heirs.

HUGH DE FICHETT, *d. v. p.* *Issue.*

MABEL, wife of Hugh de Vivonia, or Vyvon. *Issue.* Her son, William de Vyvon, *m.* Maud, widow of William de Kyme, and daughter of William de Ferrers, seventh earl of Derby, and his wife, Sybil, a daughter of William Marshall, the Protector, Earl of Pembroke, and sister of William Marshall, the Surety, and had issue:

HAWISE (Hawyse, Helewise, Heloise), who *m.* first, Robert de Muscegros, and had Sir Robert de Muscegros, who had John, father of Sir Robert, of Charlton, in Somerset, whose daughter Hawyse *m.* John de Ferrers, of Chartley, a grandson of William, seventh earl of Derby, whose wife was a granddaughter of Saher de Quincey, the Surety, and *m.* secondly, Hugh de Pointz. *Issue.*

Arms.—*Gules; a Lion rampant, Or, debruised with a Bendlet, Ermine.*

GEOFFREY DE MANDEVILLE

GEOFFREY DE MAGNAVILLE, or de Magna Villa, of Normandy, was among the companions of the Duke of Normandy when he invaded and conquered England, and obtained as his share of the spoils of conquest many valuable manors in a dozen counties, and seated himself at Waldene, He was constituted constable of the Tower of London for life, and at his decease was succeeded by his son:

WILLIAM DE MANDEVILLE, who had by his wife Margaret, only daughter and heiress of Eudo, dapifer or steward to King William, a daughter, BEATRIX DE MANDEVILLE (see below), and GEOFFREY DE MANDEVILLE, who in 5 Stephen had livery of his inheritance, and was advanced by special charter by King Stephen from the degree of baron by tenure to the dignity of Earl of Essex, in order to secure his services. But the Empress Maud, by a more ample charter, allured him to her party, confirming to him whatsoever his ancestors had owned or enjoyed, particularly the Tower of London, with the castle under it, to strengthen and fortify at his pleasure, and bestowed upon him the hereditary sheriffalty of London and Middlesex and of Hertfordshire, and the lands and office of Eudo le Dapifer, and numerous other valuable immunities. As soon as King Stephen heard of this he seized the earl and made him disgorge everything conferred upon him, or inherited, to regain his liberty. Wherefore, the earl and his brother-in-law, William de Say, in revenge, raided the king's property and churches whenever they could. At last, being publicly excommunicated for his many outrages, he besieged Burwell Castle, in Kent, and was mortally wounded. This noble outlaw *m.* Rohesia, daughter of Alberic de Vere, Earl of Oxford, Chief Justice of England, and had WILLIAM DE MANDEVILLE, third son, who succeeded as third Earl of Essex, and *d. s. p.* in 1190, when the earldom expired and the lordship and estates devolved upon his aunt:

BEATRIX DE MANDEVILLE, who *m.* first, Hugh Talbot, from whom she was divorced, and *m.* secondly, William de Say, and had by him:

WILLIAM DE SAY, eldest son, who *d. v. p., s. p. m.*, left two daughters, Maud de Bocland, or Buckland, and

BEATRIX DE SAY, who *m.* as his first wife, Geoffrey Fitz-Piers, Baron de Mandeville, *jure uxoris*, made Justiciary of England by King Richard, and created, in 1199, Earl of Essex by King John, *d.* 1212, and had:

GEOFFREY DE MANDEVILLE, who in 15 John had livery of his lands of his inheritance, and the same year, 1213, bearing the title of Earl of Essex, the king married him, upon payment of twenty thousand marks, to Isabel, Countess of Gloucester, third daughter and coheiress of William, second Earl of Gloucester, which Isabel had first been married to King John himself, but was repudiated on account of consanguinity, both being great-grandchildren of King Henry I., and for want of issue. In right of his wife, Geoffrey became Earl of Gloucester, and was put in possession of all the liberties belonging to the earldom. He was one of the wealthiest of the Barons opposed to King John, and as he adhered to them he was excommunicated by the Pope. He was elected as one of the Sureties for the observance of the Magna Charta, but only lived a short time, as, in 1216, he was mortally wounded at a tournament in London, and was interred in the priory of the Holy Trinity, in the suburbs of the city.

He died without issue, and was succeeded by his brother, William de Mandeville, who also espoused the cause of the

Barons, and maintained it even after the decease of King John, being one of those who then assisted Louis, of France, in the seige of Berkhamstead Castle, occupied by the king's forces. He *d. s. p.* 1227, when the earldom of Essex devolved upon his sister, Maud de Bohun, Countess of Hereford, while the lands which he inherited passed to his halfbrother, John Fitz-Geoffrey Fitz-Piers, sheriff of Yorkshire, whose wife was Isabel Bigod.

Arms.—*Quarterly Or and Gules; an Escarbuncle, Sable.*

WILLIAM MARSHALL, JR.

An account of this Baron's ancestry has been given in the sketch of Hugh Bigod. He was the eldest son, and was commonly called the younger "Comes Mareschal, Jun.," to distinguish him from his father, the famous Protector of the kingdom, and was as strenuous a supporter of the baronial cause as his father was of the royal interests, and was elected one of the celebrated Sureties to make his father and King John observe the Magna Charta, and was excommunicated by the Pope. Upon the death of King John, the Protector procured the consent of the Barons to the coronation of young Henry, requiring the allegiance of the Barons, including his son, William, Jr., who, for making his peace, received a grant of the lands of Saher de Quincey, David le Scot, William de Mowbray, and Gilbert de Gant, who refused to lay down their arms against the king, with the fees of all such as held of them and adhered to the rebellious Barons. In 1223–4 he returned from Ireland and gained a great victory over Prince Llewellyn and the Welsh, who had taken in his absence two of his castles, and was made governor of the castles of Caerdigan and Caermarthen, and, in 1230, captain-general of all the king's forces in Bretagne.

The third Earl of Pembroke died in 1231, very wealthy, but had no issue by his two wives, Alice, daughter of Baldwin de Bertune, Earl of Albemarle, and Princess Alianore Plantagenet, who survived him, sister of King Henry III. and daughter of King John. He was buried near his father, in the New Temple Church, London, April 14.

Arms.—*Parted per pale Or and Vert; a Lion rampant, Gules, armed and langued, Azure.*

ROGER DE MONTBEGON

But little is known of the family of this Baron. He was the successor of Adam de Monte Begonis, whose principal lands were in Lincolnshire, and was apparently the son of this Adam, by his wife, Maud Fitz-Swaine.

During the imprisonment of Richard I. in Germany Roger de Montbegon seems to have favored Prince John's designs on the throne, since he was one of those who held out the castle of Nottingham against the Bishop of Durham, then vicegerent of the kingdom; but when the king, on his return, advanced to besiege that fortress, he came out and submitted himself, without firing an arrow, and, in 1197–8, paid five hundred marks to be reconciled to King Richard, and have restoration of his lands, which had been seized for his rebellion.

In the Barons' proceedings to procure the Charter of Liberty from King John, he evidently took some prominent part, as he was elected one of the twenty-five Sureties for the observance of the Magna Charta, and was one of the parties to the Covenant for surrendering the city and Tower of London into the hands of the Barons, although several lordships were granted or confirmed to him by King John, even so late as 1215–16. However, there is no reason to doubt his original loyalty to the cause of the Barons, for when he took up arms against the king, his possessions were seized and given to Oliver d'Albini, whilst he himself was excommunicated, with the other Barons, by the Pope. He deserted the Barons, nevertheless, before the Magna Charta was confirmed a year, and Roger de Mowbray was substituted for him in the committee of Sureties. He became reconciled to Henry III., and in 1219–20 his lands were again confirmed to him.

Roger de Montbegon *d.* 10 Henry III., 1225–6, and was succeeded by his cousin, Henry de Montbegon, having had no issue by his wife Olivia, *m.* about 1200, widow of Robert de St. John. This surname is variously written. In the ancient list of Securities for the Magna Charta, in the Harleian MSS., it is de Mumbezon, while Matthew Paris writes it de Montbegon and Mount Begon, and in the Covenant he seems properly called de Monte Begonis.

Arms.—*Paly of six, Argent and Gules; fourteen Roundles in Orle, counterchanged.*

RICHARD DE MONTFICHET

This Baron was the son of RICHARD DE MONTFICHET, who was forester of Essex and keeper of the king's houses at Havering and elsewhere in the forests of Essex, and who *d.* 5 John, 1203-4.

Richard de Montfichet was under age at the time of his father's death, and his wardship was committed to Roger de Lacie, constable of Chester. As he did not become of age until in the spring of 1215, his first public act appears to have been joining the baronial party in arms against the king, and for some reason not evident he was chosen as one of the twenty-five Sureties for the observance of the Magna Charta and to govern the realm. The next year he went with Robert Fitz-Walter into France, to solicit aid, and continued one of the most enthusiastic of the Barons until he was taken prisoner at Lincoln. Even after he was released he attended the tournament at Blithe, 7 Henry III., contrary to the king's prohibition, for which his lands were seized. He subsequently made peace with the king, and was, in 1236-7, constituted justice of the king's forests for nineteen counties of England, and, in 1241-2, was made sheriff of Essex and governor of Hertford Castle.

RICHARD DE MONTFICHET never married, and died, without issue, after 1258, and his lands were divided between his three sisters.

Arms.—*Gules; three Chevrons, Or.*

ROGER DE MOWBRAY

This Baron was a younger brother of William de Mowbray, also one of the Sureties, and was elected as a substitute for Roger de Montbegon, who deserted the Barons in less than a year after his election as one of the original Sureties for the observance of the Magna Charta.

Roger de Mowbray died 2 Henry III., 1217-18, unmarried, when his elder brother, William, succeeded to his estate, paying proper relief therefor.

The armorial ensigns of Roger de Mowbray are extant in the south aisle of Westminster Abbey, as he was one of its benefactors.

Arms.—*Gules; a Lion rampant, Argent.*

WILLIAM DE MOWBRAY

ROGER D'ALBINI was the father, by his wife, a sister of Robert de Mowbray, Earl of Northumberland, of two distinguished sons,—William "Pincerna Henrici Regis Anglorum," the king's butler, ancestor of the ancient Earls of Arundel, and

SIR NIGEL D'ALBINI, who came to England with the Conqueror, and obtained several extensive lordships after the victory at Hastings. In the reign of Rufus, he was bow-bearer to the king, and was knighted by Henry I., who conferred many grants and favors upon him, and so attached him to the interests of his sovereign that he served him faithfully in his cause against Robert Curthose, his brother, whom he captured and delivered over to King Henry, for which he had further rich grants of confiscated manors. For distinguished military services in Normandy he was remunerated by a royal grant of the forfeited lands and castles of his maternal uncle, Robert de Mowbray, Earl of Northumberland, both in Normandy and in England, with the castle of Bayeux. These grants made him the possessor of two hundred and forty knights' fees, and consequently one of the most influential Barons of his time. He died at an advanced age, and was buried with his ancestors in the Abbey of Bec, in Normandy.

Sir Nigel d'Albini *m.* first, his aunt, Maud, daughter of Richard d'Aquila, by papal dispensation, her husband, Robert de Mowbray, aforesaid, being then alive, but in prison for rebellion. From her, by whom he had no issue, he was separated by the Pope on account of consanguinity and the scandal the marriage caused. He *m.* secondly, in 1118, Gundreda, daughter of Gerald, or Gerard, de Gournay, *d.* 1096, by his wife, Edith, daughter of William de Warren, first Earl of Surrey, *d.* 1088, and his wife, Gundreda, alleged daughter of Matilda, Queen Consort of King William the Conqueror, and had by this lady:

ROGER DE MOWBRAY, eldest son, who, succeeding to the lands of Mumbray, or Mowbray, assumed by royal command the surname of Mowbray. When he was not yet of age he was one of the chief commanders in the celebrated Battle of the Standard, with the Scots, in 1138; and adhering to King Stephen, in his contest with the Empress Maud, he was taken prisoner with the king at the battle of Lincoln. In 1148 he accompanied Louis VII. of France to the Holy Land and acquired great renown. He was afterwards involved in the rebellion of Prince Henry against King Henry II., and lost some of his castles. Subsequently his grants to the Church were munificent and his religious enthusiasm so fervent that he again assumed the cross and went to the Holy Land, where he was captured, but was redeemed by the Knights Templars. Dying soon afterwards in the East, he was buried at Sures. Some historians state he died in England and was buried in the Abbey of Riland.

He *m.* Alice daughter of Gilbert de Gant, or Gaunt, of Folkingham, a companion of the Conqueror, son of Baldwin VI., eighth Earl of Flanders and Artois, by his wife, Richildis, Countess of Hainault and Namur, and had:

NIGEL DE MOWBRAY, who, like his father, was a crusader, and died on his pilgrimage, 1192–3. He *m.* Mabel, daughter of Roger, Earl of Clare and Hertford, and had:

WILLIAM DE MOWBRAY, eldest son, who was of age in 1194–5, and next year, or 6 Richard I., when a scutage was levied for the king's ransom, he was one of the securities for its payment. He was early embittered against King

John by being compelled by him to surrender the barony of Frontebœuf, which Henry I. had conferred on his great-grandfather, Nigel d'Albini, to a descendant of the original owner. This was probably because de Mowbray, upon the accession of King John, was tardy in pledging his allegiance, and at length only swore fealty upon condition that "the king should render to every man his right." At the breaking out of the baronial war he was governor of York Castle, and it is not surprising that he at once sided with the Barons against King John, and was one of the most forward of them. He was elected one of the Sureties for the Magna Charta, and was a party to the Covenant for holding the city and Tower of London, and one of those whom Pope Innocent III. excommunicated by name. He still continued in arms after the decease of King John, and was in the battle of Lincoln, and taken prisoner there, when his lands were confiscated and bestowed upon William Marshall, Jr., but he was subsequently allowed to redeem them. After this he attached himself to Henry III., and was with him at the siege of Bitham Castle, in Lincolnshire, and, dying 1223-4 (about 8 Henry III.), in the Isle of Axholme, was buried in the Abbey of Newburgh, in Yorkshire.

He *m*. Agnes d'Albini, daughter of William, Earl of Arundel and Sussex, and had:

NIGEL DE MOWBRAY, *d. s. p.* 1228.
ROGER DE MOWBRAY, *d.* 1266. *Issue.*
Arms.—*Gules; a Lion rampant, Argent.*

RICHARD DE PERCY

WILLIAM DE PERCY, who accompanied William of Normandy into England in 1066, was distinguished with the designation "Alsgernons," with the whiskers. He received a barony from the Conqueror, and refounded the Abbey of St. Hilda, in Yorkshire. He accompanied Duke Robert in the first crusade, and died in 1096-7, at Mountjoy, near Jerusalem, having issue by his wife, Emma de Port, of a Saxon family, whose lands were among those bestowed upon him by the Conqueror, "he wedded hyr that was very heire to them, in discharging of his conscience":

ALAN DE PERCY, eldest son and heir to his father's feudal rights, was surnamed the "Great Alan," but why, it is not apparent. He *m.* Emma, daughter of Gilbert de Gaunt, son of Baldwin VI., Count of Flanders and Artois, and a nephew of Maud, queen consort of King William I. of England, and had:

WILLIAM DE PERCY, third feudal Baron of this family, who *m.* Alice, daughter of Richard Fitz-Gilbert de Clare, Justiciary of England, and had by her:

LADY AGNES DE PERCY, second daughter, and sole heiress on the death of her sister Maud, wife of William de Plesset, Earl of Warwick, in 1204-5. She *m.* Josceline, Count of Louvaine and Brabant, fourth Baron de Percy, in right of his wife, who was the brother of Queen Adelicia, second wife of Henry I. of England, and son of Godfrey-barbatus, Duke of Nether Lorraine, Count of Brabant and Lother, *d.* 1140, a descendant of the Emperor Charlemagne. "The ancient arms of Hainault this Lord Josceline retained, and gave his children the surname of Percie," by agreement with the heiress of Percy, by whom he had:

RICHARD DE PERCY, second and youngest son, who, after the decease without issue of his aunt, Countess of Warwick, entered, by the king's advice and his mother's license, into her share of the Percy inheritance, and soon received the major part of his mother's, and continued for the balance of his life at the head of the family and enjoyed all its baronial rights. He was one of the first of the powerful feudal lords who took up arms against King John in the cause of a constitutional government, and, having a principal hand in extorting the great charter of English freedom, was chosen one of the twenty-five Sureties to see that it was duly observed, and was excommunicated by Pope Innocent III. He was appointed by the Barons, with Robert de Ros, a Surety, and Peter de Brus, or Bruce, to subject Yorkshire to the allegiance of the Dauphin of France. He became reconciled to Henry III., as in 1218 he was in arms for this monarch. He *d. s. p.* about 1244, and was succeeded by his nephew, William de Percy, *d.* 1245.

Arms.—*Or; a Lion rampant, Azure.*

SAHER DE QUINCEY

The pedigree of this distinguished Baron is brief and modest, beginning only with his father:

SAIER DE QUINCEY, who had a grant from Henry II. of the manor of Bushby, Northamptonshire. He *m.* Maud de St. Liz, probably a daughter of Simon de St. Liz, a noble Norman, who was created Earl of Northampton and Huntingdon, and his wife Maud, daughter and coheiress of Waltheof, first Earl of Northampton and Northumberland, who, conspiring against the Normans, was beheaded, in 1075, at Winchester, although his wife was a niece of the Conqueror. Waltheof was the son of Syward, the celebrated Saxon Earl of Northumberland.

SAHER DE QUINCEY, a son of the aforesaid, was one of the Barons present at Lincoln when William the Lion, of Scotland, did homage to the English monarch. He subsequently obtained large grants and immunities from King John, and was created Earl of Winchester before 1210, having been in 1203 governor of the castle of Ruil, in Normandy. He was one of the first Barons to contend for the Charter of Liberty, and is credited with having rewritten it from the Charter of Henry I. and the Saxon code, and, opposing the king's concession to the Pope's legate, had the bitter hatred of King John, and was very active in the conferences between the Barons and the king. But though the king made him, in 1215, governor of Mountsorell Castle, he was one of the Barons to whom the city and Tower of London were resigned, and elected one of the twenty-five Barons who were to enforce the Magna Charta and govern the kingdom, being excommunicated with the other Barons in the following year.

He was sent, with Robert Fitz-Walter, by the other Barons to invite the Dauphin of France to assume the crown of England, and even after the death of King John he kept a strong garrison in Mountsorell Castle, on behalf of Prince Louis. The fortress being besieged and nearly captured by a division of the troops of Henry III., the Earl of Winchester and Prince Louis gathered a large force in London, and, having raised the siege, marched to Lincoln, then also surrounded by the king's army. In the general battle which followed, the Barons were defeated, being greatly outnumbered, and Saher de Quincey, with numerous others, was made prisoner and his estates forfeited. In the following October his immense estates were restored upon his submission.

In 1218 the Earl of Winchester went with the Earls of Chester and Arundel to the Holy Land, where he assisted at the siege of Damietta, 1219, and died in the same year in his progress towards Jerusalem. He *m.* before 6 John, 1204, Margaret, youngest sister and coheiress of Robert Fitz-Parnell, last Earl of Leicester, by whom he acquired a very considerable inheritance, and daughter of Robert-blanchmains de Bellomont, or Beaumont, third Earl of Leicester, lord high steward of England, *d.* 1196 (and his wife, *m.* 1167, Petronella, daughter of Hugh de Grentemaisnil, lord high steward of England, *d. s. p. m.* 1098), son of Robert-bossu, second Earl of Leicester, Justiciary of England, *d.* 1168, by his wife Aurelia, or Amicia, daughter of Ralph de Gauder, Earl of Norfolk, Suffolk, and Cambridge, who forfeited in 1074.

Saher, or Saier, or Saerus (his singular Christian name was probably a corruption from the Hebrew *Zair*, affliction; or of the Saxon *Segher*, a conqueror) de Quincey, Earl of Winchester, had issue by Lady Margaret:

ROBERT DE QUINCEY, who *d.* in the Holy Land, having

issue by his wife Hawyse, daughter of Hugh de Keveliock (or Bohun), Powys, Wales, fifth Earl Palatine of Chester, *d.* 1181, and his wife, Bertred, daughter of Simon, Earl of Evereux, in Normandy, an only daughter, Margaret, wife of John de Lacie, Earl of Lincoln, one of the celebrated twenty-five Magna Charta Sureties.

ROGER DE QUINCEY, second son, who had livery of his father's lands, although his elder brother was alive in the Holy Land, and succeeded to the earldom of Winchester, and in right of his first wife, daughter of Alan, lord of Galloway, became lord high constable of Scotland. By this lady he had only three daughters,—Margaret, wife of William de Ferrers, Earl of Derby; Elizabeth, wife of Alexander Comyn, Scotch Earl of Buchan; and Ela, wife of Alan, Baron le Zouche, of Ashby. Earl Roger *m.* secondly, Maud, daughter of Humphrey de Bohun, Earl of Hereford, and widow of Anselme le Mareschall, Earl of Pembroke, and *m.* thirdly, Alianore, daughter of William de Ferrers, Earl of Derby, and widow of William, Baron de Vaux, who survived him, and *m.* Roger de Leybourne. Dugdale states that Earl Roger had a fourth daughter, but by which wife it is unknown, named Isabella, with whom a contract of marriage was made by John, son of Hugh de Nevill, for his son Hugh. His lordship *d.* 1264, when the earldom became extinct, and his great landed possessions devolved upon his daughters, as coheiresses.

ROBERT DE QUINCEY, the younger, third son, who *m.* Helene, daughter of Llewellwyn, Prince of North Wales, and widow of John le Scot, Earl of Huntingdon, and had three daughters,—Anne, a nun; Joane, wife of Humphrey de Bohun, the younger; and Margaret (or Hawise), wife of Baldwin Wake.

Arms.—*Argent; a Fesse,. Azure, and a File of eleven points, Gules.*

ROBERT DE ROS

PETER DE ROS, or Roos, feudal Baron of the lordship of Roos, in Holderness, *temp.* Henry I., is the first authenticated ancestor of this Surety. He *m.* Adeline, one of the sisters and coheirs of Walter d'Espec, lord of the manor of Helmeslac (Hamlake), or Helmesly, in the North Riding of Yorkshire, and had:

ROBERT DE ROS, lord of Hamlake, who was a munificent benefactor to the Knights Templars. He *d.* about 1160, having issue by his wife, Sybil de Valoines (who after his decease *m.* Ralph d'Albini):

EVERARD DE ROS, Lord of Hamlake, who seems to have been very wealthy, as in 1176 he paid the then very large sum of five hundred and twenty-six pounds as a fine for his lands, and other large amounts subsequently. He *m.* Rose, one of the daughters and coheiress of William de Trusbut, lord of Wartre, in Holderness, East Riding, 1139, and, dying in 1186, had:

ROBERT DE ROS, of Furfan, fourth Baron Ros, of Hamlake, *b.* 1177, who, 2 Richard I., 1190–91, paid a thousand marks fine for livery of his lands, although only thirteen years old. In 8 Richard he, being with the king in Normandy, was arrested, 1197, for what offence it does not appear, he was not yet twenty-one, and committed to the custody of Hugh de Chaumont, but Chaumont trusting his prisoner to William de Spiney, the latter allowed him to escape out of the castle of Bonville. King Richard thereupon hanged Spiney and collected a fine of twelve hundred marks—eight hundred pounds—from Ros's guardian as the price of his continued freedom.

Upon the accession of King John, this monarch, to conciliate him, gave Ros the whole barony of his great-grandmother's father, Walter d'Espec, to enjoy in as large and ample a manner as Espec ever held it. Soon afterwards he was deputed one of those to escort William the Lion, King of Scotland, into England, to swear fealty to King John. About 14 John, Robert de Ros assumed the habit of a monk, whereupon the custody of all his lands and Castle Werke, in Northumberland, were committed to Philip d'Ulcote, or Olcott, but he did not long continue a recluse, as in about a year, 1212-15, he was executing the office of high sheriff of County Cumberland.

At the commencement of the struggle of the Barons for a constitutional government, this feudal Baron at first sided with King John, and in consequence obtained some valuable grants from the crown, and was made governor of Carlisle; but he was subsequently won over by the Barons and became one of the celebrated twenty-five appointed to enforce the observance of the Magna Charta, the county of Northumberland being placed under his supervision. He returned to his allegiance in the reign of Henry III., for in 1217-18 his manors were restored to him, and although he was a witness to the Great and the Forest Charters of 1224, he seems to have been in favor with that prince.

He erected the castles of Helmesley, or Hamlake, in Yorkshire, and of Werke, in Northumberland, and was a member of the Order of the Knights Templars. He *d.* 11 Henry III., 1226-7, and was buried "in his proper habit" in the church of the New Temple, at London, where his tomb is yet extant. His effigy is described by Gough, in "Sepulchral Monuments," as "the most elegant of all the figures in the Temple Church, representing a comely young knight in mail, and a flowing mantle with a kind of cowl; his hair neatly curled at the sides, his crown appears shaved. His hands are elevated in a praying posture, and on his left arm is a short pointed shield, charged with three water-bougets. He has on his left side a long sword, and the armor of his legs, which are crossed, has a ridge or seam up the front, continued over the knee, and forming a kind of garter below the knee. At his feet is a lion, and the whole figure measures six feet two inches." See, also, Stothard's "Monumental Effigies."

ROBERT DE ROS *m.* Isabel, a natural daughter of William the Lion, King of Scotland, and had by her:

WILLIAM DE ROS, lord of Hamlake Castle, *d.* 1258. *Issue.*
ROBERT DE ROS, lord of Werke Castle. *Issue.*
Arms.—*Gules; three Water-Bougets, Argent.*

GEOFFREY DE SAY

The authentic pedigree of this Baron begins with his grandfather,

WILLIAM DE SAY, who *m.* Beatrix, the divorced wife of Hugh Talbot, and only daughter of William de Magnaville, or Mandeville, and his wife Margaret, only daughter and heiress of Eudo, steward for Normandy to King William the Conqueror, and had:

GEOFFREY DE SAY, second son. He was one of the Barons chosen to proceed with William de Longchamp, Bishop of Ely, chancellor of England, with the ransom for King Richard I. He *m.* Lettice, sister and eventually heiress of Walkeline Maminot, and, dying in 1214, had:

GEOFFREY DE SAY, eldest son, who had delivery of the estates of his inheritance, both by father and mother, 16 John, for which he paid four thousand marks, proving him to have been wealthy. He early joined the baronial cause, and was elected one of the Sureties for the observance of the Magna Charta, and his extensive lands and possessions in ten counties were confiscated and given to Peter de Crohun, or Crohim, but, returning to his allegiance in the next reign, after the expulsion of the Dauphin, he had full restitution. He died in Gascoigne, August 24, 14 Henry III., 1230.

He *m.* Alice, daughter and coheiress of John de Cayneto, or Caineto, or Cheyney, or Cheney, as the name is variously given, and had:

WILLIAM DE SAY, *d.* 1272. *Issue.*

Arms.—*Quarterly Or and Gules.*

ROBERT DE VERE

ALBERIC DE VERE, son of ALPHONSO, COUNT DE GHISNES, was the founder of this celebrated family in England, and at the time of the General Survey of England possessed numerous lordships in different shires and had his principal residence at his castle at Hedingham, in Essex. In the latter end of his days he assumed the cowl, and died, in 1088, a monk, and was buried in the church of Colne Priory, which he founded. He *m.* Beatrix, daughter of Henry, Castellan of Bourbourg, and was succeeded by

ALBERIC DE VERE, eldest son, who, being in high favor with King Henry I., was constituted by him lord high chamberlain of the kingdom, to hold the same in fee to himself and his heirs. In 5 Stephen, while a joint sheriff with Richard Basset, Justiciary of England, of several counties, he was slain in a popular tumult at London, 1140, having issue by his wife, Adeliza de Clare, sister of Richard Fitz-Gilbert, first Earl of Hertford:

AUBREY DE VERE, eldest son. For his fidelity to the Empress Maud, he was confirmed by her in the lord chamberlainship and all his father's possessions. He was given also the choice of several earldoms, and selected that of Oxford, and was so created by Henry II. He *m.* first, Eufamia de Cantilupe, by whom he had no issue, and *m.* secondly, Lucia, daughter and heiress of William, third Baron d'Abrancis, of Folkestone, in Kent, and had:

ROBERT DE VERE, third Earl of Oxford, second son and heir to his brother Aubrey, *d. s. p.* 1214, who was reputed one of the "evil councillors" of King John. Earl Robert, although lord great chamberlain of the kingdom, pursued a different course in politics from that of his elder brother, and was one of the principal Barons in arms against King John, and was elected one of the Sureties for the observance of the Magna Charta, a party to that Covenant which resigned to the Barons the custody of the city and Tower of London, and one of those excommunicated by the Pope. In the beginning of the reign of Henry III., having made his peace with that young monarch after the battle of Lincoln, he was received into his favor, and was, in 1220–21, appointed one of the judges in the Court of King's Bench, but died a few months afterwards, and was buried in the priory of Hatfield, Broad Oak, in Essex.

Robert, Earl of Oxford, *m.* Isabel, sister and heiress of Walter de Bolebec, and daughter of Hugh, second Baron de Bolebec, who *d.* 1261, and had issue:

HUGH DE VERE, fourth Earl of Oxford. *Issue.*

SIR HENRY DE VERE, of Great Addington, County Northampton. *Issue.*

ISABEL, wife of Sir John Courtenay, Knt.

Arms.—*Quarterly Gules and Or; in the dexter canton, a Mullett, Argent.*

EUSTACE DE VESCI

YVO DE VESCI, a valiant knight in the Conqueror's train, was rewarded for his distinguished services by King William bestowing upon him as his wife a rich heiress, Ada, or Alda, only child of William Tyson, Saxon Lord of Alnwick, in Northumberland, and lord of Malton, Yorkshire, whose father, Gilbert Tyson, was slain at the battle of Hastings, fighting under the Anglo-Saxon banner. The only issue of this marriage was another heiress:

BEATRIX DE VESCI, who *m.* as his first wife, Eustacius Fitz-John de Burgo, lord of Knaresborough, in Yorkshire, who was the nephew and heir of Serlo de Burgh, who erected Knaresborough Castle, and the son of John-monoculus, a great feudal Baron, and friend of Henry I., who gave him great grants of land and the governorship of Bamburgh Castle, in Northumberland; but he was deprived of the latter by King Stephen, although his wife, Magdalen, was the king's aunt. John-with-one-eye was the son of Eustacius de Burgo, brother of Harlowen de Burgo, whose wife was the mother of William the Conqueror, and son of John de Burgo, Earl of Comyn and Baron of Tonsburgh (Tourborough), in Normandy, general of the Norman duke's forces and governor of his chief towns, hence the family name de Burgo, or Burgh. The heiress Beatrix had by her husband, Eustace Fitz-John-monoculus:

WILLIAM DE BURGH DE VESCI, eldest son, who inherited many manors and was high sheriff of Northumberland and of Lancashire. He assisted in repelling an invasion of the Scots, and captured their king in the battle of Alnwick, and, dying in 1184, left issue by his wife Burga, sister and heiress of Robert de Stuteville, lord of Knaresborough, and daughter of William, fourth Baron de Stuteville, *d.* 1203:

EUSTACE DE VESCI, who became of age in 1190, and paid two thousand three hundred marks, nearly fifteen hundred and thirty-two pounds for delivery of his lands and leave to marry. In 1199 he was sent by King John as one of the ambassadors to King William the Lion, of Scotland, whose daughter he had married, but shortly he became intimately connected with the rise and progress of the baronial insurrections. In 1212 he and Robert Fitz-Walter, upon being required to give security for their faithful allegiance, fled to Scotland. His English possessions were seized and his castle of Alnwick was ordered to be destroyed. This and King John's incontinence and vitiating reputation so embittered de Vesci that he became the most inveterate of the king's enemies and a principal leader in the insurrection, and took a prominent part in all their conventions, and was elected one of the twenty-five Sureties for the observance of the Magna Charta. He was one of the Barons to whom the city and Tower of London were committed; was excommunicated, and was one of those who urged the Dauphin to come to England. In attending his brother-in-law, Alexander, king of the Scots, to welcome Prince Louis, and to do him homage for that kingdon, in 1216, they passed by Bernard Castle, which displayed the royal banner. Approaching too near to see if it could be captured, de Vesci was mortally wounded by one of the garrison. He *m.* Margaret, a natural daughter of King William the Lion, of Scotland, and sister of the wife of King Alexander, and had issue:

WILLIAM DE VESCI, eldest son and successor. *Issue.*

ISABEL, wife of William de Welles, of Gremesby. *Issue.*

Arms.—*Gules; a Cross Patonce, Argent.*

Pedigrees of Americans
descended from
The Sureties for the Observance
of the
Magna Charta of King John

Descendants of Magna Charta Barons

PEDIGREE I

HENRY DE BOHUN, a Magna Charta Surety, had:
  HUMPHREY DE BOHUN, Earl of Hereford and Essex, *d.* 1274, who had:
HUMPHREY DE BOHUN, eldest son, *d. v. p.*, who had:
HUMPHREY DE BOHUN, Earl of Hereford and Essex, *d.* 1297, who had:
HUMPHREY DE BOHUN, Earl of Hereford and Essex, *k.* 1321, who had:
MARGARET DE BOHUN, *m.* Hugh de Courtenay, K.G., Earl of Devon, and had:
ELIZABETH DE COURTENAY, *m.* Sir Andrew Luttrell, of Chilton, and had:
SIR HUGH LUTTRELL, lord of Dunster Castle, Somerset, who had:
ELIZABETH LUTTRELL, *m.* John Stratton, of Weston-sur-Mare, and had:
ELIZABETH STRATTON, *m.* John Andrews, of Stoke, Suffolk, and had:
ELIZABETH ANDREWS, *m.* Thomas de Wyndsore, of Stamwell, and had:
SIR ANDREWS DE WYNDSORE, of Stamwell and Bardsley, 1474–1543, who had:
EDITH WYNDSORE, *m.* George Ludlowe, of Hill Deverill, *d.* 1580, and had:
THOMAS LUDLOWE, of Dinton and Baycliffe, *d.* 1607, who had:
GABRIEL LUDLOW, 1587–1639, an attorney-at-law, who had:
SARAH LUDLOW, *d.* before 1669, who *m.* before 1663, as his third wife, Col. John Carter, of Virginia, member of the Virginia House of Burgesses, 1643–58, and of the Governor's Council, 1668, *d.* June 10, 1669, and had issue.

PEDIGREE II

HENRY DE BOHUN, a Magna Charta Surety, had:
  HUMPHREY DE BOHUN, Earl of Hereford and Essex, *d.* 1274, who had:
HUMPHREY DE BOHUN, eldest son, *d. v. p.*, who had:
HUMPHREY DE BOHUN, Earl of Hereford and Essex, *d.* 1297, who had:
HUMPHREY DE BOHUN, Earl of Hereford and Essex, *k.* 1321, who had:
MARGARET DE BOHUN, *m.* Hugh de Courtenay, K.G., Earl of Devon, and had:
ELIZABETH COURTENAY, *m.* Sir Andrew Luttrell, of Chilton, and had:

134   THE MAGNA CHARTA BARONS

Sir Hugh Luttrell, lord of Dunster Castle, Somerset, who had:
Elizabeth Luttrell, *m.* John Stratton, of Weston-sur-Mare, and had:
Elizabeth Stratton, *m.* John Andrews, of Stoke, Suffolk, and had:
Elizabeth Andrews, *m.* Thomas de Wyndsore, of Stamwell, and had:
Sir Andrews de Wyndsore, of Stamwell and Bardsley, *d.* 1543, who had:
Eleanor de Wyndsore, *m.* Sir Edward Nevill, of Aldington, *d.* 1538, and had:
Sir Henry Nevill, of Billingbere, Berks, third son, *d.* 1593, who had:
Sir Henry Nevill, of Mafield, Sussex, *d.* 1615, who had:
Catherine Nevill, *m.* Sir Richard Brooke, of Norton, *d.* 1632, and had:
Anne Brooke, *m.* Edward Hyde, of Hyde, Chester, *d.* 1669, and had:
Robert Hyde, of Hyde and Norbury, Chester, 1642–1670, who had:
Edward Hyde, of Hyde, only son, *d.* in Carolina, who had:
Anne Hyde, *m.* George Clarke, Jr., of Swanswick, Somerset, *d.* 1760, and had:
Edward Clarke, second son, 1716–1776, who had:
George Hyde Clarke, of Hyde, Chester, 1742–1824, who had:
George Clarke, of "Hyde Hall," Otsego County, N. Y., *b.* April 28, 1768, *d.* Nov. 4, 1835. He *m.* first, Sept. 4, 1793, Eliza, dau. of Gen. George Rochford, R.A., of Bellefield, Westmeath, Ireland, and *m.* secondly, Aug. 14, 1844, Anne Carey, widow of Richard Cooper, of Cooperstown, N. Y. Issue by both wives.

PEDIGREE III

Henry de Bohun, a Magna Charta Surety, had:
Humphrey de Bohun, Earl of Hereford and Essex, *d.* 1274, who had:
Alice de Bohun, *m.* Ralph de Toni, of Flamstead, *d.* 1264, and had:
Alice de Toni, *m.* Walter de Beauchamp, of Powyke, *d.* 1306, and had:
Giles de Beauchamp, of Alcester and Powyke, third son, who had:
Roger de Beauchamp, of Bletsho, Bedford, second son, *d.* 1379, who had:
Roger de Beauchamp, of Bletsho and Lydiard-Tregoze, who had:
Sir John de Beauchamp, of Bletsho, *d.* 1413, who had:
Margaret de Beauchamp, *m.* Sir Oliver St. John, of Penmark, and had:
John St. John, K.B., of Bletsho, who had:
Sir John St. John, of Bletsho, Bedfordshire, who had:
Sir John St. John, of Bletsho, who had:
Oliver St. John, first Baron St. John, of Bletsho, 1559, who had:
Thomas St. John, who had:
Oliver St. John, M.P., of Caysho, Bedfordshire, who had:
Elizabeth St. John, *b.* 1605, *d.* 1677. She *m.* Aug. 6, 1629, as his second wife, Rev. Samuel Whiting, *b.* 1597, at Boston, Lincolnshire. They came to New England in 1636, and settled at Lynn, Mass., where he *d.* 1679. *Issue.*

DESCENDANTS OF MAGNA CHARTA BARONS 135

PEDIGREE IV

ROGER BIGOD, a Magna Charta Surety, had:
HUGH BIGOD, a Magna Charta Surety, who had:
SIR RALPH BIGOD, third son, who had:
ISABEL BIGOD, *m.* John Fitz-Geoffrey, Justiciary of Ireland, 1246, and had:
JOHN FITZ-JOHN, Justiciary of Ireland, *d.* 1258, who had:
MAUD FITZ-JOHN, *m.* William de Beauchamp, Earl of Warwick, and had:
GUY DE BEAUCHAMP, Earl of Warwick, *d.* 1315, who had:
THOMAS DE BEAUCHAMP, K.G., Earl of Warwick, *d.* 1369, who had:
PHILIPPA DE BEAUCHAMP, *m.* Hugh, K.G., Earl of Stafford, and had:
MARGARET STAFFORD, *m.* Ralph Nevill, Earl of Westmoreland, and had:
RALPH DE NEVILL, of Oversley, who had:
JOHN DE NEVILL, of Wymersley, York, *d.* 1482, who had:
JOAN DE NEVILL, *m.* Sir William Gascoigne, and had:
SIR WILLIAM GASCOIGNE, of Gawthorpe, York, who had:
DOROTHY GASCOIGNE, *m.* Sir Ninian de Markenfield, and had:
ALICE MARKENFIELD, *m.* Robert Mauleverer, and had:
DOROTHY MAULEVERER, *m.* John Kaye, of Woodsome, and had:
ROBERT KAYE, of Woodsome, York, 1612, who had:
GRACE KAYE, *m.* Sir Richard Saltonstall, of Huntwick, and had:
RICHARD SALTONSTALL, *b.* at Woodsome, York, 1610, came to Massachusetts in 1630, with his father, one of the original patentees of Massachusetts Bay Colony, 1628, and also of Connecticut. He resided at Ipswich, and served as deputy and assistant, and, dying at Hulme, England, April 29, 1694, had issue by his wife, Muriel Gurdon.

PEDIGREE V

ROGER BIGOD, a Magna Charta Surety, had:
HUGH BIGOD, a Magna Charta Surety, who had:
SIR RALPH BIGOD, Knt., third son, who had:
ISABEL BIGOD, *m.* John Fitz-Geoffrey, Chief Justice of Ireland, 1246, and had:
JOHN FITZ-JOHN, Chief Justice of Ireland, *d.* 1258, who had:
MAUD FITZ-JOHN, *m.* William de Beauchamp, Earl of Warwick, and had:
GUY DE BEAUCHAMP, Earl of Warwick, *d.* 1315, who had:
THOMAS DE BEAUCHAMP, K.G., Earl of Warwick, *d.* 1369, who had:
JOAN DE BEAUCHAMP, *m.* Ralph Basset, K.B., of Drayton, and had:
JANE BASSET, *m.* John de Stourton, of Preston, *d.* 1364, and had:

WILLIAM DE STOURTON, steward of Wales, 1402, who had:
SIR JOHN DE STOURTON, Baron Stourton, *d.* 1462, who had:
WILLIAM DE STOURTON, second Baron Stourton, *d.* 1478, who had:
JOAN STOURTON, *m.* Tristram Fauntleroy, of Mitchell's Marsh, *d.* 1539, and had:
JOHN FAUNTLEROY, of Crandall, Hampshire, *d.* 1598, who had:
WILLIAM FAUNTLEROY, of Crandall, *d.* 1625, who had:
JOHN FAUNTLEROY, of Crandall, only son, *b.* 1588, *m.* 1609, *d.* 1644, who had:
COL. MOORE FAUNTLEROY, second son, who came to Virginia before 1643, and became a large land-owner in the colony, member of the House of Burgesses, 1644–1659, justice of old Rappahannock County. He *m.* first, in England, Dec. 26, 1639, Dorothy, dau. of Thomas Colle, of Liss, Hampshire, and *m.* secondly, in Virginia, 1648, Mary Hill. *Issue.*

PEDIGREE VI

RICHARD DE CLARE, a Magna Charta Surety, had:
GILBERT DE CLARE, a Magna Charta Surety, who had:
ISABEL DE CLARE, *m.* Robert Bruce, Earl of Annandale, and had:
ROBERT BRUCE, Earl of Annandale and Carrick, who had:
MARY BRUCE, *m.* first, Sir Neil Campbell, of Lochow, and had:
SIR COLIN CAMPBELL, of Lochow, *d.* 1340, who had:
SIR ARCHIBALD CAMPBELL, of Lochow, who had:
SIR COLIN CAMPBELL, of Lochow, who had:
SIR DUNCAN CAMPBELL, first Lord Campbell, *d.* 1453, who had:
SIR COLIN CAMPBELL, of Glenurchy, *d.* 1478, who had:
SIR DUNCAN CAMPBELL, of Glenurchy, *k.* 1513, who had:
ANNABELLA CAMPBELL, *m.* Alexander Napier, *k.* 1547, and had:
SIR ARCHIBALD NAPIER, of Merchieston, *d.* 1608, who had:
JOHN NAPIER, of Merchieston, 1550–1617, who had:
ADAM NAPIER, of Blackstown, Renfrew, fifth son, who had:
—— NAPIER, *m.* William Craik, of Arbigland, and had:
ADAM CRAIK, of Arbigland, Dumfrieshire, who had:
WILLIAM CRAIK, of Arbigland, Dumfrieshire, who had:
DR. JAMES CRAIK, 1730–1814, who came to Virginia in 1750, and was surgeon-general of the Continental army. He *m.* Nov. 23, 1760, Mariana, dau. of Charles Ewell, of Prince William County, Va. *Issue.*

PEDIGREE VII

RICHARD DE CLARE, a Magna Charta Surety, had :
GILBERT DE CLARE, a Magna Charta Surety, who had :
ISABEL DE CLARE, *m.* Robert Bruce, Earl of Annandale, and had :
ROBERT BRUCE, Earl of Annandale and Carrick, *d.* 1304, who had :
MARY BRUCE, *m.* secondly, Sir Alexander Fraser, *k.* 1332, and had :
SIR JOHN FRASER, of Aberbothnot, who had :
MARGARET FRASER, *m.* Sir William Keith, the marshal, and had :
ELIZABETH KEITH, *m.* Sir Adam de Gordon, of Huntly, *k.* 1402, and had :
ELIZABETH GORDON, *m.* Alexander de Seton, and had :
ALEXANDER DE SETON DE GORDON, Earl of Huntly, *d.* 1470, who had :
GEORGE DE GORDON, second Earl of Huntly, *d.* 1501, who had :
ALEXANDER DE GORDON, third Earl of Huntly, *d.* 1534, who had :
JOHN DE GORDON, eldest son, *d. v. p.* 1517, who had :
GEORGE DE GORDON, fourth Earl of Huntly, *k.* 1562, who had :
JEAN GORDON, *m.* Alexander Gordon, Earl of Sutherland, *d.* 1594, and had :
SIR ROBERT GORDON, Bart., of Gordonstown, *d.* 1656, who had :
CATHERINE GORDON, *m.* Col. David Barclay, of Ury, *d.* 1681, and had :
ROBERT BARCLAY, of Ury, governor of East Jersey, 1682, *d.* 1690, who had :
JEAN BARCLAY, *m.* ALEXANDER FORBES, of Auchorties, and had :
CHRISTIANA FORBES, *m.* William Penn, 3d, of London, and had :
CHRISTIANA GULIELMA PENN, *m.* Peter Gaskell, of Bath, and had :
PETER PENN-GASKELL, of Philadelphia, Pa., who had issue by his wife, Elizabeth Edwards, of Montgomery County, Pa.

PEDIGREE VIII

RICHARD DE CLARE, a Magna Charta Surety, had :
GILBERT DE CLARE, a Magna Charta Surety, who had :
ISABEL DE CLARE, *m.* Robert Bruce, Earl of Annandale, and had :
ROBERT BRUCE, Earl of Annandale and Carrick, *d.* 1304, who had :
ROBERT BRUCE, KING OF SCOTLAND, who had :
MARGERY BRUCE, *m.* Walter, high steward of Scotland, and had :
ROBERT II., KING OF SCOTLAND, who had :
ROBERT III., KING OF SCOTLAND, who had :
MARY STUART, *m.* Sir William Graeme, of Kincardine, *d.* 1424, and had :
WILLIAM GRAEME, third son, who had :
MATTHEW GRAEME, of Garvock, Perth, who had :

ARCHIBALD GRAEME, of Garvock, *k.* at Flodden, 1513, who had:
JOHN GRAEME, of Garvock, who had:
JOHN GRAEME, purchased Balgowan, Perth, in 1584, second son, who had:
JOHN GRAEME, of Balgowan, eldest son, *d.* 1635, who had:
THOMAS GRAEME, of Balgowan, *m.* 1671, who had:
THOMAS GRAEME, M.D., fifth son, *b.* Oct. 20, 1688; came to Pennsylvania in 1717; was member of the Governor's Council, 1725; justice of the Supreme Court of Pennsylvania, 1731; *d.* at Graeme Park, Montgomery County, Pa., Sept. 4, 1772. He *m.* Nov. 12, 1719, Anne, *d.* 1765, dau. of Robert Digges, of Philadelphia. *Issue.*

PEDIGREE IX

RICHARD DE CLARE, a Magna Charta Surety, had:
GILBERT DE CLARE, a Magna Charta Surety, who had:
ISABEL DE CLARE, *m.* Robert Bruce, Earl of Annandale, and had:
ROBERT BRUCE, Earl of Annandale and Carrick, *d.* 1304, who had:
ROBERT BRUCE, KING OF SCOTLAND, who had:
MARGERY BRUCE, *m.* Walter, high steward of Scotland, and had:
ROBERT II., KING OF SCOTLAND, who had:
ROBERT STEWART, Duke of Albany, *d.* 1419, who had:
MURDOCH STEWART, second Duke of Albany, *k.* 1425, who had:
SIR JAMES STEWART, the rebel, fourth son, *d.* 1451, who had:
WALTER STEWART, of Morphies, Kincardine, sixth son, who had:
ANDREW STEWART, second son, succeeded as Lord Evandale, 1502, who had:
ANDREW STEWART, last Lord Evandale, first Lord Ochiltree, *d.* 1548, who had:
ANDREW STEWART, second Lord Ochiltree, who had:
MARGARET STEWART, *m.* Rev. John Knox, the Reformer, and had:
ELIZABETH KNOX, *m.* Rev. John Welch, of Ayr, and had:
—— WELCH, *m.* Rev. James Witherspoon, of Yester parish, and had:
REV. JOHN WITHERSPOON, D.D., LL.D., *b.* Feb. 5, 1722; came to America to take the presidency of the College of New Jersey, at Princeton; member of the Continental Congress, and a signer of the Declaration of Independence. He was twice *m.*, and had issue.

PEDIGREE X

RICHARD DE CLARE, a Magna Charta Surety, had:
GILBERT DE CLARE, a Magna Charta Surety, who had:
ISABEL DE CLARE, m. Robert Bruce, Earl of Annandale, and had:
ROBERT BRUCE, Earl of Annandale and Carrick, d. 1304, who had:
ROBERT BRUCE, KING OF SCOTLAND, who had:
MARGERY BRUCE, m. Walter, high steward of Scotland, and had:
ROBERT II., KING OF SCOTLAND, who had:
ROBERT STUART, Duke of Albany, Earl of Fife, etc., who had:
MARJORY STUART, m. Sir Duncan, Lord Campbell, of Lochow, and had:
SIR COLIN CAMPBELL, of Glenurchy, third son, 1400–1478, who had:
MARIOT CAMPBELL, m. William Stuart, of Baldoran, and had:
JOHN STUART, of Glenbucky, second son, who had:
DUNCAN STUART, of Glenbucky, who had:
ALEXANDER STUART, of Glenbucky, who had:
PATRICK STUART, of Glenbucky, who had:
WILLIAM STUART, of Ledcreich and Translarry, Perth, who had:
PATRICK STUART, of Ledcreich, who had:
ALEXANDER STUART, of Ledcreich, who had:
PATRICK STUART, who came with his family to North Carolina, in 1739, with his brother William (who had issue) and others, and, dying at Cheraws, S. C., had issue by his wife, Elizabeth Menzies.

PEDIGREE XI

RICHARD DE CLARE, a Magna Charta Surety, had:
GILBERT DE CLARE, a Magna Charta Surety, who had:
ISABEL DE CLARE, m. Robert Bruce, Earl of Annandale, and had:
ROBERT BRUCE, Earl of Annandale and Carrick, d. 1304, who had:
ROBERT BRUCE, KING OF SCOTLAND, who had:
MARGERY BRUCE, m. Walter, high steward of Scotland, who had:
ROBERT II., KING OF SCOTLAND, who had:
CATHERINE STUART, m. Sir David Lindsay, first Earl of Crawford, and had:
ALEXANDER LINDSAY, second Earl of Crawford, who had:
SIR WALTER LINDSAY, of Edzell, third son, who had:
SIR DAVID LINDSAY, of Edzell, d. 1527, who had:
WALTER LINDSAY, of Edzell, eldest son, k. at Flodden, 1513, who had:
SIR DAVID LINDSAY, of Edzell, d. 1558, who had:

SIR DAVID LINDSAY, of Edzell, *d.* 1610, who had:
MARGARET LINDSAY, *m.* David, Lord Carnegy, Earl of Southesk, and had:
CATHERINE CARNEGY, *m.* Sir John, Lord Stuart, Earl of Traquier, and had:
JOHN STUART, second Earl of Traquier, 1622–1666, who had:
CHARLES STUART, fourth Earl of Traquier, 1659–1741, who had:
JOHN STUART, sixth Earl of Traquier, 1698–1779, who had:
CHRISTIANA STUART, eldest daughter, sister of Charles, seventh Earl of Traquier, who *m.* 1769, Judge Cyrus Griffin, of Williamsburg, Va., member and president of the last Continental Congress, *b.* 1749, *d.* 1810. *Issue.*

PEDIGREE XII

RICHARD DE CLARE, a Magna Charta Surety, had:
GILBERT DE CLARE, a Magna Charta Surety, who had:
ISABEL DE CLARE, *m.* Robert Bruce, Earl of Annandale, *d.* 1295, and had:
ROBERT BRUCE, Earl of Annandale and Carrick, *d.* 1304, who had:
ROBERT BRUCE, KING OF SCOTLAND, who had:
MARGERY BRUCE, *m.* Walter, high steward of Scotland, and had:
ROBERT II., KING OF SCOTLAND, who had:
CATHERINE STUART, *m.* Sir David Lindsay, Earl of Crawford, and had:
MARJORY LINDSAY, *m.* Sir William Douglas, of Lochlevan, and had:
SIR HENRY DOUGLAS, of Lochlevan and Lugton, 1421, who had:
ROBERT DOUGLAS, of Lochlevan and Kincross, *k.* 1513, who had:
SIR ROBERT DOUGLAS, laird of Lochlevan, who had:
THOMAS DOUGLAS, only son, *d. v. p.*, who had:
ELIZABETH DOUGLAS, *m.* Alexander Alexander, of Menstrie, and had:
ANDREW ALEXANDER, of Menstrie, 1545, eldest son, who had:
JOHN ALEXANDER, of Gogar, 1541, second son, who had:
ALEXANDER ALEXANDER, of Millnab, only son, who had:
DAVID ALEXANDER, of Muthill, second son, who had:
JAMES ALEXANDER, second son, 1691–1756. He came to America in 1714, as surveyor-general of East Jersey, was many years a member of the King's Council, and served as attorney-general and auditor-general of New York. He *m.* Mary, *d.* 1760, dau. of John Sprott, of Wigton, and widow of Samuel Prevost. *Issue.*

PEDIGREE XIII

RICHARD DE CLARE, a Magna Charta Surety, had:
GILBERT DE CLARE, a Magna Charta Surety, who had:
ISABEL DE CLARE, *m.* Robert Bruce, Earl of Annandale, and had:
ROBERT BRUCE, Earl of Annandale and Carrick, *d.* 1304, who had:
ROBERT BRUCE, KING OF SCOTLAND, who had:
MARGERY BRUCE, *m.* Walter, high steward of Scotland, and had:
ROBERT II., KING OF SCOTLAND, who had:
MARGARET STUART, *m.* John-mor Macdonnell, lord of the Isles, and had:
JOHN-OGE MACDONNELL, younger son, *d.* 1369, who had:
MARCACH MACDONNELL, of the Glinns, *k.* 1397, who had:
TIRLOUGH-MOR MACDONNELL, of the Glinns, *d.* 1435, who had:
TIRLOUGH-OGE MACDONNELL, of Leinster, Ireland, who had:
DONOUGH MACDONNELL, of Leinster, *k.* 1504, who had:
EOIN CARRACH MACDONNELL, of Leinster, who had:
TIRLOUGH MACDONNELL, of Leinster, who had:
CALVAGH MACDONNELL, of Tennekill, *d.* 1570, who had:
HUGH-BUIDHE MACDONNELL, of Ballycrassel, *d.* 1618, who had:
BRIAN MACDONNELL, younger son, who had:
ALEXANDER MAC DONNELL, constable of Wicklow, 1641, who had:
BRYAN MAC DONNELL, of Arklow, County Wicklow, a lieutenant in King James's Irish army. In 1691 he came to America with his family and settled in Mill Creek Hundred, New Castle County, Del., and, dying in 1707, had issue by his wife, Mary, dau. of John Doyle, of Arklow.

PEDIGREE XIV

RICHARD DE CLARE, a Magna Charta Surety, had:
GILBERT DE CLARE, a Magna Charta Surety, who had:
ISABEL DE CLARE, *m.* Robert de Bruce, Earl of Annandale, and had:
ROBERT DE BRUCE, Earl of Annandale and Carrick, *d.* 1304, who had:
CHRISTIANA BRUCE, *m.* first, Gratney, Earl of Marr, and had:
ELYNE DE MARR, *m.* Sir John Menteth, lord of Arran, *d.* 1357, and had:
CHRISTIANA MENTETH, *m.* Sir Edward Keith, marshal of Scotland, and had:
JANET KEITH, *m.* Thomas Erskine, of Erskine, *d.* 1419, and had:
SIR ROBERT ERSKINE, eighth laird of Erskine, *d.* 1453, who had:
THOMAS ERSKINE, Earl of Marr, *d.* 1494, who had:
MARY ERSKINE, *m.* William Livingston, laird of Kilsyth, and had:

WILLIAM LIVINGSTON, fourth laird of Kilsyth, *d.* 1540, who had:
MARGARET LIVINGSTON, *m.* Gilbert Cunyngham, of Craigends, *k.* 1547, and had:
JAMES CUNYNGHAM, of Arkenyeard, second son, who had:
WILLIAM CUNYNGHAM, of Glengarnock, second son, who had:
RICHARD CUNYNGHAM, of Glengarnock, *m.* Oct. 13, 1654, who had:
ROBERT CUNYNGHAM, *b.* 1669, *d.* St. Christopher's, W. I., 1749, who had:
MARY CUNYNGHAM, 1699–1771, *m.* 1723, Isaac Roberdeau, and had:
DANIEL ROBERDEAU, only son, *b.* Island of St. Christopher, W. I., 1727; removed to Philadelphia, Pa.; was member Pennsylvania Assembly, 1756–60; of the Council of Safety, 1775; general commanding Pennsylvania Line in the Revolutionary War; member of the Continental Congress, 1777–79; *d.* Winchester, Va., Jan. 5, 1795. He *m.* first, Oct. 3, 1761, Mary Bostwick, who *d.* before 1778, and *m.* secondly, Dec. 2, 1778, Jane Milligan. *Issue.*

❧

PEDIGREE XV

RICHARD DE CLARE, a Magna Charta Surety, had:
GILBERT DE CLARE, a Magna Charta Surety, who had:
ISABEL DE CLARE, *m.* Robert Bruce, Earl of Annandale, and had:
ROBERT BRUCE, Earl of Annandale and Carrick, *d.* 1304, who had:
CHRISTIANA BRUCE, *m.* Gratney, eleventh Earl of Marr, and had:
ELYNE DE MARR, *m.* Sir John Menteth, of Arran, *d.* 1357, and had:
CHRISTIANA MENTETH, *m.* Sir Edward Keith, marshal of Scotland, and had:
JANET KEITH, *m.* Thomas Erskine, of Erskine, *d.* 1419, and had:
SIR ROBERT ERSKINE, eighth laird of Erskine, *d.* 1453, who had:
MARGARET ERSKINE, *m.* James Rutherford, of Edgarston, and had:
THOMAS RUTHERFORD, of Edgarston, Roxburghshire, who had:
ROBERT RUTHERFORD, of Edgarston, Roxburghshire, who had:
THOMAS RUTHERFORD, of Edgarston, Roxburghshire, who had:
RICHARD RUTHERFORD, of Edgarston, Roxburghshire, who had:
ROBERT RUTHERFORD, of Edgarston, Roxburghshire, who had:
JOHN RUTHERFORD, of Edgarston, Roxburghshire, who had:
THOMAS RUTHERFORD, of Edgarston, Roxburghshire, who had:
SIR JOHN RUTHERFURD, young son, *m.* 1710, who had:
MAJOR WALTER RUTHERFURD, captain 62d Foot, Dec. 30, 1755, who was stationed in New York, where he *m.*, 1758, as his first wife, Catherine, dau. of James Alexander (Pedigree XII.), and sister of Gen. William Alexander, titular Earl of Stirling, of the Continental army, and had issue by her.

PEDIGREE XVI

RICHARD DE CLARE, a Magna Charta Surety, had:
GILBERT DE CLARE, a Magna Charta Surety, who had:
RICHARD DE CLARE, Earl of Hertford and Gloucester, d. 1262, who had:
GILBERT DE CLARE, Earl of Hertford and Gloucester, d. 1295, who had:
ELIZABETH DE CLARE, m. John de Burgh, and had:
WILLIAM DE BURGH, third Earl of Ulster, 1312–1333, who had:
ELIZABETH DE BURGH, m. Lionel Plantagenet, Duke of Clarence, and had:
PHILIPPA PLANTAGENET, m. Edmund de Mortimer, Earl of March, and had:
ROGER DE MORTIMER, fourth Earl of March, k. 1398, who had:
ANNE MORTIMER, m. Richard Plantagenet, Earl of Cambridge, and had:
RICHARD PLANTAGENET, third Duke of York, the Protector, k. 1460, who had:
GEORGE PLANTAGENET, K.G., Duke of Clarence, k. 1478, who had:
MARGARET PLANTAGENET, Countess of Salisbury, m. Richard Pole, and had:
HENRY POLE, K.B., Lord Montague, k. 1539, who had:
WINIFRED POLE, m. secondly, Thomas Barrington, sheriff of Essex, and had:
SIR FRANCIS BARRINGTON, Bart., M.P., d. 1629, who had:
JOAN BARRINGTON, m. Sir Richard Everard, Bart., and had:
SIR HUGH EVERARD, Bart., second son, 1654–1705, who had:
SIR RICHARD EVERARD, Bart., governor of North Carolina, d. 1732, who had:
SUSAN EVERARD, who m. David Meade, of County Kerry, Ireland, and removed to Nansemond County, Va. *Issue.*

PEDIGREE XVII

RICHARD DE CLARE, a Magna Charta Surety, had:
GILBERT DE CLARE, a Magna Charta Surety, who had:
RICHARD DE CLARE, Earl of Hertford and Gloucester, d. 1262, who had:
GILBERT DE CLARE, Earl of Hertford and Gloucester, d. 1295, who had:
ELIZABETH DE CLARE, m. John de Burgh, and had:
WILLIAM DE BURGH, third Earl of Ulster, 1312–1333, who had:
ELIZABETH DE BURGH, m. Lionel Plantagenet, Duke of Clarence, and had:
PHILIPPA PLANTAGENET, m. Edmund de Mortimer, Earl of March, and had:
ELIZABETH DE MORTIMER, m. Henry de Percy, K.G. ("Hotspur"), and had:
HENRY DE PERCY, K.G., second Earl of Northumberland, k. 1455, who had:
CATHERINE DE PERCY, m. Edmund de Grey, Earl of Kent, d. 1488, and had:
GEORGE DE GREY, second Earl of Kent, d. 1504, who had:
ANTHONY GREY, of Branspeth, second son, who had:

GEORGE GREY, of Branspeth, who had:
REV. ANTHONY GREY, of Burbache, ninth Earl of Kent, *d.* 1643, who had:
HENRY GREY, tenth Earl of Kent, *d.* 1651, who had:
ELIZABETH GREY, *m.* Banastre, third Lord Maynard, *d.* 1717, and had:
DOROTHY MAYNARD, *m.* Sir Robert Hesilrigge, Bart., *d.* 1721, and had:
SIR ARTHUR HESILRIGGE, Bart., of Noseley Hall, *d.* 1763, who had:
SIR ROBERT HESILRIGGE, Bart., of Noseley Hall, who removed to Boston, Mass., and *m.* Sarah, dau. of Nathaniel Waller, of Roxbury, Mass., and had:

    1. HANNAH, *m.* Rev. Thomas Abbot, Roxbury, Mass. *Issue.*
    2. SARAH, *m.* Col. David Henley, Boston, Mass. *Issue.*

PEDIGREE XVIII

RICHARD DE CLARE, a Magna Charta Surety, had:
    GILBERT DE CLARE, a Magna Charta Surety, who had:
ISABEL DE CLARE, *m.* Robert Bruce, fifth Earl of Annandale, and had:
ROBERT BRUCE, Earl of Annandale and Carrick, *d.* 1304, who had:
MARY BRUCE, *m.* first, Sir Neil Campbell, of Lochow, and had:
SIR COLIN CAMPBELL, of Lochow, *d.* 1340, who had:
SIR ARCHIBALD CAMPBELL, of Lochow, who had:
SIR COLIN CAMPBELL, of Lochow, who had:
SIR DUNCAN CAMPBELL, Lord Campbell, of Lochow, who had:
ARCHIBALD CAMPBELL, second son and heir, *d. v. p.*, who had:
SIR COLIN CAMPBELL, first Earl of Argyle, *d.* 1493, who had:
HELEN CAMPBELL, *m.* Hugh Montgomery, first Earl of Eglington, and had:
SIR NEIL MONTGOMERY, of Lainshaw, third son, *k.* 1547, who had:
SIR NEIL MONTGOMERY, of Lainshaw, second son, who had:
SIR NEIL MONTGOMERY, of Lainshaw, *d. ante* 1613, who had:
WILLIAM MONTGOMERY, of Brigend, second son, *d.* 1659, who had:
JOHN MONTGOMERY, of Brigend, *d. ante* 1647, who had:
HUGH MONTGOMERY, of Brigend, 1630–1710, who had:
WILLIAM MONTGOMERY, of Brigend, eldest son, who sold Brigend, in 1692, and removed to Monmouth County, N. J., in 1701, where he purchased from his father-in-law, in 1706, an estate, which he named "Eglington." He *m.* in Scotland, Jan. 8, 1684–5, Isabel, dau. of Robert Burnet, of Lethintie, one of the original proprietors of East Jersey, and had sasine of Bangour upon his contract of marriage, recorded at Ayr, May 28, 1684. *Issue.*

PEDIGREE XIX

RICHARD DE CLARE, a Magna Charta Surety, had :
GILBERT DE CLARE, a Magna Charta Surety, who had :
ISABEL DE CLARE, *m.* Robert Bruce, Earl of Annandale, and had :
CHRISTIANA BRUCE, *m.* Patrick, Earl of Dunbar, *d.* 1298, and had :
PATRICK DUNBAR, eighth Earl of Dunbar, *d.* 1309, who had :
PATRICK DUNBAR, Earl of Dunbar and March, 1285–1369, who had :
AGNES DUNBAR, *m.* James Douglas, of Dalkieth, *d.* 1420, and had :
JANET DOUGLAS, *m.* Sir John Hamilton, of Cadyow, d. 1397, and had :
SIR JAMES HAMILTON, of Cadyow, 1424, who had :
GAVIN HAMILTON, fourth son, Provost at Bothwell, who had :
JOHN HAMILTON, of Orbiston, who had :
GAVIN HAMILTON, of Orbiston and Raplock, *d.* 1540, who had :
JOHN HAMILTON, of Orbiston, *k.* at Langsyde, who had :
MARJORY HAMILTON, *m.* David Dundas, of Duddingston, and had :
GEORGE DUNDAS, of Manor, 1628, younger son, who had :
JOHN DUNDAS, of Manor, who had :
RALPH DUNDAS, of Manor, who had :
JOHN DUNDAS, of Manor, who had :
JAMES DUNDAS, *b.* at Manor, 1734, removed to Philadelphia, Pa., in 1757, where he *d.* in 1788, having issue by his wife, Elizabeth Moore, who *d.* 1789.

PEDIGREE XX

RICHARD DE CLARE, a Magna Charta Surety, had :
GILBERT DE CLARE, a Magna Charta Surety, who had :
ISABEL DE CLARE, *m.* Robert Bruce, Earl of Annandale, *d.* 1295, and had :
ROBERT BRUCE, Earl of Annandale and Carrick, *d.* 1304, who had :
MARY BRUCE, *m.* secondly, Sir Alexander Fraser, *k.* 1332, and had :
SIR JOHN FRASER, of Aberbothnot, who had :
MARGARET FRASER, *m.* Sir William Keith, marshal of Scotland, and had :
ELIZABETH KEITH, *m.* Sir Adam Gordon, of Huntly, *k.* 1402, and had :
ELIZABETH GORDON, *m.* Alexander de Seton, and had :
ALEXANDER DE GORDON, first Earl of Huntly, *d.* 1470, who had :
MARGARET GORDON, *m.* Hugh Rose, of Kilravock, *d.* 1517, and had :
JOHN ROSE, first laird of Bellivat, second son, who had :
JOHN ROSE, second laird of Bellivat, who had :
JOHN ROSE, third laird of Bellivat, who had :

HUGH ROSE, second son, who had :
PATRICK ROSE, eldest son, *d.* 1727, who had :
JOHN ROSE, of Wester Alves, *d. v. p.* 1724, who had :
REV. ROBERT ROSE, third son (brother of Rev. Charles Rose, of Westmoreland County, Va.), *b.* Feb. 12, 1704 ; came to Virginia, 1725 ; was rector of St. Anne's parish, Essex County, 1728–1747, and of Albemarle parish, 1747–1751, *d.* at Richmond, Va., June 30, 1751. He *m.* first, Feb. 23, 1733-4, Mary Tarrent, and *m.* secondly, Nov. 6, 1740, Anne Fitzhugh. *Issue* by each wife.

PEDIGREE XXI

RICHARD DE CLARE, a Magna Charta Surety, had :
GILBERT DE CLARE, a Magna Charta Surety, who had :
ISABEL DE CLARE, *m.* Robert Bruce, Earl of Annandale, and had :
ROBERT BRUCE, Earl of Annandale and Carrick, *d.* 1304, who had :
ISABELLA BRUCE, *m.* Sir Thomas Randolph, of Strathwith, and had :
THOMAS RANDOLPH, created Earl of Moray, 1314, who had :
AGNES RANDOLPH, *m.* Patrick Dunbar, Earl of March, and had :
GEORGE DUNBAR, Earl of Dunbar and March, *d.* 1420, who had :
SIR DAVID DUNBAR, of Cockburn, sixth son, who had :
MARIOTA DUNBAR, *m.* Alexander Lindsay, Earl of Crawford, and had :
SIR WALTER LINDSAY, of Edzell, third son, who had :
SIR DAVID LINDSAY, of Edzell, *d.* 1527, who had :
WALTER LINDSAY, of Edzell, *k.* at Flodden, 1513, who had :
ALEXANDER LINDSAY, second son, who had :
RT. REV. DAVID LINDSAY, Bishop of Ross, 1600, *d.* 1613, who had :
SIR HIEROME LINDSAY, of The Mount, *d.* 1642, who had :
REV. DAVID LINDSAY, of Northumberland County, Va., 1603-1667, who had :
HELEN LINDSAY, only child and sole heiress, according to her father's will, dated April 2, 1667, to which she was executrix, and which she proved in April, 1667. She *m.* Thomas Opie, of Northumberland County, Va. *Issue.*

PEDIGREE XXII

RICHARD DE CLARE, a Magna Charta Surety, had:
GILBERT DE CLARE, a Magna Charta Surety, who had:
ISABEL DE CLARE, *m.* Robert Bruce, Earl of Annandale, and had:
ROBERT BRUCE, Earl of Annandale and Carrick, *d.* 1304, who had:
ISABELLA BRUCE, *m.* Sir Thomas Randolph, of Strathwith, and had:
THOMAS RANDOLPH, created Earl of Moray, 1314, who had:
AGNES RANDOLPH, *m.* Patrick Dunbar, Earl of March, and had:
GEORGE DUNBAR, Earl of Dunbar and March, *d.* 1420, who had:
SIR DAVID DUNBAR, of Cockburn, sixth son, who had:
MARIOTA DUNBAR, *m.* Alexander Lindsay, Earl of Crawford, and had:
SIR WALTER LINDSAY, of Edzell, third son, who had:
SIR DAVID LINDSAY, of Edzell, *d.* 1527, who had:
WALTER LINDSAY, of Edzell, *k.* at Flodden, 1513, who had:
ALEXANDER LINDSAY, second son, who had:
RT. REV. DAVID LINDSAY, Bishop of Ross, 1600, *d.* 1613, who had:
RACHEL LINDSAY, *m.* Archbishop John Spottiswood, *d.* 1639, and had:
SIR ROBERT SPOTTISWOOD, of New Abbey, Kent, *k.* 1646, who had:
ROBERT SPOTSWOOD, M.D., third son, *d.* 1680, who had:
MAJ.-GEN. ALEXANDER SPOTSWOOD, only son, *b.* 1676, *d.* June 7, 1740. He was lieutenant-governor and commander-in-chief of the Virginia Colony, 1710–1723; resided at "Porto Bello," James City County. He *m.*, in 1724, Anne Butler Bryan. *Issue.*

PEDIGREE XXIII

RICHARD DE CLARE, a Magna Charta Surety, had:
GILBERT DE CLARE, a Magna Charta Surety, who had:
ISABEL DE CLARE, *m.* Robert Bruce, Earl of Annandale, and had:
ROBERT BRUCE, Earl of Annandale and Carrick, *d.* 1304, who had:
ISABELLA BRUCE, *m.* Sir Thomas Randolph, of Strathwith, and had:
THOMAS RANDOLPH, created, 1314, Earl of Moray, who had:
AGNES RANDOLPH, *m.* Patrick Dunbar, Earl of March, and had:
AGNES DUNBAR, *m.* James Douglas, of Dalkeith, *d.* 1420, and had:
JANET DOUGLAS, *m.* Sir John Hamilton, of Cadyow, *d.* 1397, and had:
SIR JAMES HAMILTON, of Cadyow, 1424, eldest son, who had:
GAVIN HAMILTON, fourth son, provost at Bothwell, who had:
JOHN HAMILTON, of Orbiston, who had:

GAVIN HAMILTON, of Orbiston, 1512–1540, who had:
JOHN HAMILTON, of Orbiston, *k.* at Langsyde, who had:
MARJORY HAMILTON, *m.* David Dundas, of Duddingston, and had:
JAMES DUNDAS, of Duddingston, Linlithgow, who had:
BETHIA DUNDAS, *m.* James Hume, of Fastcastle, and had:
ISABEL HUME, *m.* Patrick Logan, *b.* Ormiston, 163–, *d.* Bristol, 169–, and had:
JAMES LOGAN, *b.* Lurgan, Ireland, Oct. 20, 1674, who was living in Bristol, England, when his father died, and in 1699 came to Pennsylvania with William Penn, as his secretary, and became chief justice and secretary of the province of Pennsylvania, a member and president of the Provincial Council, and *d.* at "Stenton," Philadelphia County, Dec. 31, 1751. He *m.*, 1714, Sarah Read, of Philadelphia. *Issue.*

PEDIGREE XXIV

RICHARD DE CLARE, a Magna Charta Surety, had:
GILBERT DE CLARE, a Magna Charta Surety, who had:
RICHARD DE CLARE, Earl of Hertford and Gloucester, who had:
THOMAS DE CLARE, governor of London, 1274, who had:
THOMAS DE CLARE, third son, who had:
MAUD DE CLARE, *m.* Robert de Clifford of Appleby, and had:
ROGER DE CLIFFORD, of Appleby, *d.* 1390, who had:
CATHERINE DE CLIFFORD, *m.* Ralph de Greystock, *d.* 1417, and had:
SIR JOHN DE GREYSTOCK, *d.* 1435, who had:
SIR RALPH DE GREYSTOCK, *d.* 1487, who had:
ANNE DE GREYSTOCK, *m.* Sir Thomas Asheton, and had:
MARGARET ASHETON, *m.* Sir William Bothe, *d.* 1520, and had:
GEORGE BOTHE, *d.* 1531, who had:
GEORGE BOTHE, *d.* 1548, who had:
SIR WILLIAM BOTHE, *d.* 1579, who had:
SUSAN BOTHE, *m.* Sir Edward Warren, of Poynton, 1563–1609, and had:
THOMAS WARREN, who was one of the early adventurers to Virginia, and, in 1635, patented land in Charles City County, and represented James City County in the House of Burgesses, 1644, 1658, and 1663, and County Surrey, 1666. He *m.*, 1634–5, first, Susan, widow of Robert Greenleaf, and *m.* secondly, 1654, Elizabeth, widow of Robert Sheppard. *Issue.*

PEDIGREE XXV

RICHARD DE CLARE, a Magna Charta Surety, had:
GILBERT DE CLARE, a Magna Charta Surety, who had:
RICHARD DE CLARE, Earl of Hertford, *d.* 1262, who had:
GILBERT DE CLARE, Earl of Hertford, *d.* 1295, who had:
MARGARET DE CLARE, *m.* Hugh d'Audley, Earl of Gloucester, and had:
MARGARET D'AUDLEY, *m.* Ralph de Stafford, Earl of Stafford, and had:
JOAN DE STAFFORD, *m.* John de Cherleton, lord of Powys, and had:
SIR EDWARD DE CHERLETON, K.G., lord of Powys, *d.* 1420, who had:
JOAN CHERLETON, *m.* John de Grey, K.G., Earl of Tankerville, and had:
SIR HENRY DE GREY, second Earl of Tankerville, *d.* 1449, who had:
ELIZABETH GREY, *m.* Sir Roger Kynaston, *d.* 1517, and had:
HUMPHREY KYNASTON, of Morton, Salop, *d.* 1534, who had:
MARGARET KYNASTON, *m.* John Lloyd, of Dyffryn, and had:
HUMPHREY LLOYD-WYNN, of Dyffryn, Montgomeryshire, who had:
KATHERINE LLOYD, *m.* John Lloyd, of Doloban, *b.* 1575, and had:
CHARLES LLOYD, of Doloban, Montgomeryshire, 1613–1651, who had:
THOMAS LLOYD, *b.* Feb. 17, 1640–1, *d.* Sept. 10, 1694. He was the agent of William Penn in America, and his first deputy governor of the province of Pennsylvania, and was member and president of the Provincial Council. He *m.* first, Sept. 9, 1665, Mary, daughter of Roger (or Gilbert) Jones, of Welshpool, Wales, and had ten children; and *m.* secondly, Patience Gardiner, widow of Robert Story, but no issue by her.

PEDIGREE XXVI

ROBERT FITZ-WALTER, a Magna Charta Surety, had:
WALTER FITZ-WALTER, *d.* 1257, who had:
SIR ROBERT FITZ-WALTER, first Baron by writ, *d.* 1325, who had:
ROBERT FITZ-WALTER, second Baron, *d.* 1328, who had:
JOHN FITZ-WALTER, third Baron, *d.* 1361, who had:
ALICE FITZ-WALTER, *m.* Aubrey de Vere, Earl of Oxford, and had:
RICHARD DE VERE, Earl of Oxford, *d.* 1417, who had:
ROBERT DE VERE, second son, who had:
JOHN DE VERE, only son, who had:
JOHN DE VERE, K.G., fifteenth Earl of Oxford, *d.* 1539, who had:
ANNE DE VERE, *m.* Edmund, first Lord Sheffield, *k.* 1548, and had:
JOHN SHEFFIELD, second Lord Sheffield, of Butterwicke, who had:

ADMIRAL EDMUND SHEFFIELD, K.G., Earl of Mulgrave, *d.* 1646, who had:
FRANCES SHEFFIELD, *m.* Sir Philip Fairfax, of Steeton, and had:
SIR WILLIAM FAIRFAX, of Steeton, Yorkshire, 1610–1692, who had:
ISABELLA FAIRFAX, *m.* Nathaniel Bladen, of Hemsworth, and had:
WILLIAM BLADEN, *b.* Hemsworth, Yorkshire, 1672 ; came to Maryland, and was commissary-general of the province, and *d.* in 1718, having issue by his first wife, Letitia, dau. of Judge Dudley Loftus, vicar-general of Ireland.

PEDIGREE XXVII

WILLIAM DE HUNTINGFIELD, a Magna Charta Surety had:
ROGER DE HUNTINGFIELD, *d.* 1257, who had:
SIR WILLIAM DE HUNTINGFIELD, *d.* 1282, who had:
ROGER DE HUNTINGFIELD, *d.* 1301, who had:
WILLIAM DE HUNTINGFIELD, *d.* 1314, who had:
ALICE DE HUNTINGFIELD, *m.* Sir John de Norwich, *d.* 1361, and had:
CATHERINE DE NORWICH, *m.* William de la Pole, *d.* 1367, and had:
MICHAEL DE LA POLE, K.G., Earl of Suffolk, *d.* 1388, who had:
SIR MICHAEL DE LA POLE, second Earl of Suffolk, *d.* 1415, who had:
SIR THOMAS DE LA POLE, third son, who had:
CATHERINE DE LA POLE, *m.* Sir Miles Stapylton, *d.* 1466, and had:
ELIZABETH STAPYLTON, *m.* Sir William Calthorpe, *d.* 1494, and had:
ELIZABETH CALTHORPE, *m.* Francis Hassylden, of Gilden Morden, and had:
FRANCES HASSYLDEN, *m.* Sir Robert Peyton, of Iselham, *d.* 1550, and had:
ROBERT PEYTON, of Iselham, Cambridgeshire, 1523–1590, who had:
SIR JOHN PEYTON, Knt., Bart., and M.P., of Iselham, *d.* 1616, who had:
SIR EDWARD PEYTON, Knt., Bart., of Iselham, 1578–1656, who had:
THOMAS PEYTON, of Wicken and Rougham, Norfolk, 1616–1687, who had:
MAJOR ROBERT PEYTON, of Gloucester County, Va., *d. s. p. m.*, who had:
ELIZABETH PEYTON, who *m.* in 168–, Col. Peter Beverley, of Gloucester County, Va., a member and speaker of the Virginia House of Burgesses ; surveyor-general and treasurer of the Virginia Colony, and member of the Governor's Council, *d.* 1728. *Issue.*

PEDIGREE XXVIII

JOHN DE LACIE, a Magna Charta Surety, had:
MAUD DE LACIE, *m.* Richard de Clare, Earl of Gloucester, and had:
GILBERT DE CLARE, Earl of Hertford and Gloucester, *d.* 1295, who had:
ELIANORE DE CLARE, *m.* Hugh le Despencer, Jr., *d.* 1326, and had:
EDWARD LE DESPENCER, second son, *d.* 1342, who had:
EDWARD LE DESPENCER, K.G., Baron Spencer, *d.* 1375, who had:
THOMAS LE DESPENCER, Earl of Gloucester, *d.* 1400, who had:
ISABEL DESPENCER, *m.* Richard, Earl of Worcester, and had:
ELIZABETH DE BEAUCHAMP, *m.* Edward Neville, K.G., *d.* 1476, and had:
GEORGE NEVILLE, Baron Abergavenny, *d.* 1492, who had:
GEORGE NEVILLE, K.G., Baron Abergavenny, *d.* 1535, who had:
URSULA NEVILLE, *m.* Sir Warham St. Leger, of Ulcombe, and had:
SIR WARHAM ST. LEGER, of Ulcombe, Kent, *d.* 1631, who had:
URSULA ST. LEGER, *m.* Rev. Daniel Horsmanden, *d.* 1654, and had:
COL. WARHAM HORSMANDEN, of Purleigh Park, Essex, who had:
MARIA HORSMANDEN, *d.* Nov. 9, 1699, who *m.* Col. William Byrd, who came to Virginia in 1674, and *d.* in 1704. *Issue.*

PEDIGREE XXIX

JOHN DE LACIE, a Magna Charta Surety, had:
MAUD DE LACIE, *m.* Richard de Clare, Earl of Hertford, and had:
GILBERT DE CLARE, Earl of Hertford and Gloucester, *d.* 1295, who had:
MARGARET DE CLARE, *m.* Hugh d'Audley, Earl of Gloucester, and had:
MARGARET D'AUDLEY, *m.* Ralph de Stafford, K.G., Earl of Stafford, and had:
JOAN DE STAFFORD, *m.* John de Cherleton, lord of Powys, and had:
SIR EDWARD DE CHERLETON, K.G., lord of Powys, *d.* 1420, who had:
JOAN CHERLETON, *m.* John de Grey, K.G., Earl of Tankerville, and had:
SIR HENRY DE GREY, second Earl of Tankerville, *d.* 1449, who had:
ELIZABETH GREY, *m.* Sir Roger Kynaston, *d.* 1517, and had:
MARY KYNASTON, *m.* Howell ap Ievan, of Ynya-y-Maengwyn, and had:
HUMPHREY AP HOWELL, who had:
ANE, *m.* Griffith ap Howell, of Nannau, Merionethshire, 1541, and had:
JOHN AP GRIFFITH, second son, who had:
LEWIS AP JOHN, who had:
REES AP LEWIS, who had:

ELLIS AP REES, of Bryn Mawr, Merionethshire, who had:
ROWLAND AP ELLIS, *b.* 1650, who came to Pennsylvania in 1686, and settled at Bryn Mawr, Merion Township, Philadelphia (now Montgomery) Co., Pa., where he *d.* in 1726, having issue bearing the surname ELLIS, by his second wife, Margaret, dau. of Robert ap Owen.

PEDIGREE XXX

JOHN DE LACIE, a Magna Charta Surety, had:
MAUD DE LACIE, *m.* Richard de Clare, Earl of Hertford, and had:
GILBERT DE CLARE, Earl of Hertford and Gloucester, *d.* 1295, who had:
ALIANORE DE CLARE, *m.* Hugh le Despencer, Jr., *d.* 1326, and had:
ELIZABETH LE DESPENCER, *m.* Maurice de Berkeley, *d.* 1368, and had:
THOMAS DE BERKELEY, Viscount de Lisle, *d.* 1416, who had:
ELIZABETH BERKELEY, *m.* Richard de Beauchamp, Earl of Warwick, and had:
ALIANORE BEAUCHAMP, *m.* Edmund de Beaufort, Duke of Somerset, and had:
JOAN DE BEAUFORT, *m.* Robert St. Lawrence, Lord Howth, and had:
ANNE ST. LAWRENCE, *m.* Thomas Cusack, of Gerardstown, and had:
ELIZABETH CUSACK, *m.*, 1563, Patrick de la Field, and had:
JOHN DE LA FIELD, who had:
JOHN DE LA FIELD, *m.* 1610, who had:
JOHN DE LA FIELD, *m.* 1636, who had:
JOHN DE LA FIELD, Count of the Holy Roman Empire, 1697, who had:
JOHN DE LA FIELD, Count of the Holy Roman Empire, *b.* 1656, who had:
JOHN DE LA FIELD, *b.* 1692, second son, who had:
JOHN DE LA FIELD, Count of the Holy Roman Empire, 1720-1763, who had:
JOHN DE LA FIELD, of New York City, Count of the Holy Roman Empire, eldest son, *d.* July 3, 1824, having issue by his wife, whom he *m.* in 1784, Anne, *b.* 1766, *d.* 1839, dau. of Joseph Hallett, of New York.

PEDIGREE XXXI

JOHN DE LACIE, a Magna Charta Surety, had:
MAUD DE LACIE, *m.* Richard de Clare, Earl of Hertford, and had:
GILBERT DE CLARE, Earl of Hertford and Gloucester, *d.* 1295, who had:
ALIANORE DE CLARE, *m.* Hugh le Despencer, Jr., *d.* 1326, and had:
EDWARD LE DESPENCER, second son, *d.* 1342, who had:
EDWARD LE DESPENCER, K.G., Baron Despencer, 1336-1375, who had:
THOMAS LE DESPENCER, first Earl of Gloucester, *d.* 1400, who had:

DESCENDANTS OF MAGNA CHARTA BARONS 153

ISABEL SPENCER, *m.* Richard de Beauchamp, Earl of Worcester, and had:
ELIZABETH DE BEAUCHAMP, *m.* Edward Nevill, K.G., *d.* 1476, and had:
SIR GEORGE NEVILL, second Baron Abergavenny, *d.* 1492, who had:
GEORGE NEVILL, K.B., K.G., third Baron Abergavenny, *d.* 1535-6, who had:
URSULA NEVILL, *m.* Sir Warham St. Leger, of Ulcombe, Kent, and had:
ANNE ST. LEGER, *m.* Gen. Thomas Digges, of Digges Court, *d.* 1595, and had:
SIR DUDLEY DIGGES, of Chilham Castle, Kent, *d.* 1638, who had:
EDWARD DIGGES, third son, *b.* 1621; came to Virginia, and was governor of the colony, 1655-58; member of the Governor's Council, 1654-1675; *d.* at his seat, "Bellville," on the York River, Virginia, March 15, 1675-6, having six sons and seven daughters by his wife, Elizabeth Bray.

PEDIGREE XXXII

JOHN DE LACIE, a Magna Charta Surety, had:
MAUD DE LACIE, *m.* Richard de Clare, Earl of Hertford, and had:
GILBERT DE CLARE, Earl of Hertford and Gloucester, *d.* 1295, who had:
ALIANORE DE CLARE, *m.* Hugh le Despencer, Jr., *d.* 1326, and had:
EDWARD LE DESPENCER, second son, *d.* 1342, who had:
EDWARD LE DESPENCER, K.G., Baron Despencer, *d.* 1375, who had:
THOMAS LE DESPENCER, first Earl of Gloucester, *k.* 1400, who had:
ISABEL DESPENCER, *m.* Richard Beauchamp, Earl of Worcester, and had:
ELIZABETH BEAUCHAMP, *m.* Edward Nevill, K.G., *d.* 1476, and had:
SIR GEORGE NEVILL, second Baron Abergavenny, *d.* 1492, who had:
SIR EDWARD NEVILL, of Aldington, third son, *k.* 1538, who had:
CATHERINE NEVILL; *m.* Clement Throckmorton, of Haseley, and had:
CATHERINE THROCKMORTON, *m.* Thomas Harby, of Adston, *d.* 1592, and had:
CATHERINE HARBY, *m.* Dr. Daniel Oxenbridge, of Daventry, *d.* 1642, and had:
REV. JOHN OXENBRIDGE, *b.* at Daventry, Northamptonshire, Jan. 30, 1609-10. He removed to New England, and became pastor of the First Church, Boston, where he *d.* Dec. 28, 1674. *Issue.*

PEDIGREE XXXIII

JOHN DE LACIE, a Magna Charta Surety, had:
MAUD DE LACIE, *m.* Richard de Clare, Earl of Hertford, and had:
GILBERT DE CLARE, Earl of Hertford and Gloucester, *d.* 1295, who had:
ELIZABETH DE CLARE, *m.* John de Burgh, and had:
WILLIAM DE BURGH, third Earl of Ulster, *k.* 1333, who had:
ELIZABETH DE BURGH, *m.* Lionel Plantagenet, Duke of Clarence, and had:

154 THE MAGNA CHARTA BARONS

PHILIPPA PLANTAGENET, *m.* Edmund de Mortimer, Earl of March, and had:
ELIZABETH MORTIMER, *m.* Henry Percy ("Hotspur") *k.* 1403, and had:
HENRY PERCY, K.G., second Earl of Northumberland, *k.* 1455, who had:
HENRY PERCY, K.G., third Earl of Northumberland, *k.* 1461, who had:
HENRY PERCY, K.G., fourth Earl of Northumberland, *k.* 1489, who had:
HENRY ALGERNON PERCY, K.G., fifth Earl of Northumberland, who had:
MARGARET PERCY, *m.* Henry Clifford, K.G., Earl of Cumberland, and had:
CATHERINE CLIFFORD, *m.* Sir Richard Cholmoneley, of Roxby, and had:
SIR HENRY CHOLMONELEY, of Roxby, *d.* 1641, who had:
MARY CHOLMONELEY, *m.* Rev. Henry Fairfax, of Oglethorpe, and had:
HENRY FAIRFAX, fourth Lord Fairfax, of Cameron, *d.* 1688, who had:
HENRY FAIRFAX, of Denton, second son, *d.* 1708, who had:
WILLIAM FAIRFAX, of "Belvoir," in Virginia, fourth son, *b.* 1691, *d.* 1757, president of H. M. Council for Virginia, manager of the Virginia estates of Thomas, sixth Lord Fairfax. He *m.* first, Sarah Walker, and *m.* secondly, Deborah Clark. *Issue.*

PEDIGREE XXXIV

WILLIAM DE LANVALLEI, a Magna Charta Surety, had:
HAWISE DE LANVALLEI, *m.* Sir John de Burgh, and had:
JOHN DE BURGH, Baron Lanvallei, *d.* 1279, who had:
MARGARET DE BURGH, *m.* Richard de Burgh, Earl of Ulster, and had:
ELIZABETH DE BURGH, *m.* Robert I., King of Scots, and had:
MARGARET BRUCE, *m.* William, Earl of Sutherland, and had:
WILLIAM, EARL OF SUTHERLAND, *d.* 1389, who had:
ROBERT, EARL OF SUTHERLAND, *d.* 1442, who had:
ALEXANDER SUTHERLAND, of Dunbeath, third son, who had:
MARJORY SUTHERLAND, *m.* William St. Clair, Earl of Orkney, and had:
WILLIAM ST. CLAIR, second Earl of Caithness, *k.* 1513, who had:
JOHN ST. CLAIR, third Earl of Caithness, *k.* 1529, who had:
GEORGE ST. CLAIR, fourth Earl of Caithness, *d.* 1582, who had:
JOHN ST. CLAIR, Master of Caithness, *d. v. p.*, 1576-7, who had:
SIR JAMES ST. CLAIR, of Murchil and Halcro, 1593, who had:
JAMES ST. CLAIR, of Assery, 1628, and Brawlbin, 1631, who had:
JAMES ST. CLAIR, of Assery, who had:
JAMES ST. CLAIR, of Thurso, *d.* 1713, who had:
WILLIAM ST. CLAIR, of Thurso, 1734, who had:
ARTHUR ST. CLAIR, who came to America in 1758, and became a major-general in the Continental army, *d.* Aug. 31, 1818. He *m.* at Boston, 1760, Phœbe Bayard, of Boston, Mass. *Issue.*

PEDIGREE XXXV

WILLIAM DE LANVALLEI, a Magna Charta Surety, had:
HAWYSE DE LANVALLEI, *m*. Sir John de Burgh, and had:
JOHN DE BURGH, Baron de Lanvallei, *d. s. p. m.* 1279, who had:
MARGARET DE BURGH, *m*. Richard de Burgh, Earl of Ulster, and had:
ELIZABETH DE BURGH, *m*. ROBERT I., KING OF SCOTLAND, and had:
MARGARET BRUCE, *m*. William, Earl of Sutherland, *d*. 1370, and had:
WILLIAM DE SUTHERLAND, fifth Earl of Sutherland, *d*. 1389, who had:
ROBERT DE SUTHERLAND, sixth Earl of Sutherland, *d*. 1442, who had:
ALEXANDER SUTHERLAND, of Dunbeath, third son, who had:
MARJORY SUTHERLAND, *m*. William Sinclair, Earl of Orkney, and had:
MARJORY SINCLAIR, *m*. Andrew Leslie, Master of Rothes, *d*. 1502, and had:
WILLIAM LESLIE, third son, *k*. at Flodden, 1513, who had:
GEORGE LESLIE, third Earl of Rothes, *d*. 1558, who had:
HELEN LESLIE, *m*. Mark Ker, Abbot of Newbottle, *d*. 1584, and had:
MARK KER, Earl of Lothian, *d*. 1609, who had:
JANET KER, *m*. Robert Boyd, Master of Boyd, *d. v. p.*, and had:
JAMES BOYD, eighth Lord Boyd, of Kilmarnock, *d*. 1654, who had:
WILLIAM BOYD, ninth Lord Boyd, Earl of Kilmarnock, *d*. 1692, who had:
ROBERT BOYD, fourth son, *b*. Aug. 6, 1689, *d*. 1761, who had:
JAMES BOYD, *b*. Kilmarnock, May 3, 1732, came to New England in 1756, and resided at Newburyport, Mass., *d*. Sept. 30, 1798. He *m*. first, Aug. 11, 1757, Susanna Coffin, of Newburyport, and *m*. secondly, July 23, 1791, Ann Bulfinch, of Boston, Mass., and had issue by his first wife.

❦

PEDIGREE XXXVI

WILLIAM DE LANVALLEI, a Magna Charta Surety, had:
HAWYSE DE LANVALLEI, *m*. Sir John de Burgh, and had:
JOHN DE BURGH, Baron de Lanvallei, *d. s. p. m.* 1279, who had:
MARGARET DE BURGH, *m*. Richard de Burgh, Earl of Ulster, and had:
ELIZABETH DE BURGH, *m*. ROBERT I., KING OF SCOTLAND, and had:
MARGARET BRUCE, *m*. William, Earl of Sutherland, *d*. 1370, and had:
WILLIAM DE SUTHERLAND, fifth Earl of Sutherland, *d*. 1389, who had:
ROBERT DE SUTHERLAND, sixth Earl of Sutherland, *d*. 1442, who had:
ALEXANDER DE SUTHERLAND, of Dunbeath, third son, who had:
MARJORY SUTHERLAND, *m*. William Sinclair, Earl of Orkney, and had:
MARJORY SINCLAIR, *m*. Andrew Leslie, Master of Rothes, *d*. 1502, and had:

WILLIAM LESLEY, third son, *k.* 1513, who had :
GEORGE LESLEY, third Earl of Rothes, *d.* 1558, who had :
AGNES LESLEY, *m.* William Douglas, sixth Earl of Morton, and had :
AGNES DOUGLAS, *m.* Archibald Campbell, seventh Earl of Argyle, and had :
MARY CAMPBELL, *m.* Robert Montgomery, Jr., of Skelmurle, *d. v. p.*, and had :
SIR ROBERT MONTGOMERY, second Bart., of Skelmurle, *d.* 1684, who had :
MARGARET MONTGOMERY, *m.* Godfrey Macalester, laird of Loup, and had :
JOHN MACALESTER, of Torrisdale Glen and Ardnakill, who had :
MARGARET MACALESTER, *m.* Charles Macquarrie, of Campbelltown, and had :
ISABELLA MACQUARRIE, *m.* Charles Macalester, of Tarbert, *d.* 1797, and had :
CHARLES MACALESTER, *b.* Campbelltown, in Kintyre, 1766 (his father was Master of Campbelltown, and was lost at sea), and removed to Philadelphia, Pa., where he *d.* in 1832, having issue by his wife, Anne Sampson, of Perth.

♣

PEDIGREE XXXVII

WILLIAM DE LANVALLEI, a Magna Charta Surety, had :
HAWYSE DE LANVALLEI, *m.* Sir John de Burgh, and had :
JOHN DE BURGH, Baron of Lanvallei, *d.* 1279, who had :
MARGARET DE BURGH, *m.* Richard de Burgh, Earl of Ulster, and had :
ELIZABETH DE BURGH, *m.* ROBERT I., KING OF SCOTLAND, and had :
MATILDA BRUCE, *m.* Thomas Isaac, and had :
JOAN ISAAC, *m.* John d'Ergadia, lord of Lorn, and had :
ISABEL D'ERGADIA, *m.* Sir John Stuart, of Muermeath, and had :
SIR JAMES STUART, the Black Knight of Lorn, who had :
SIR JOHN STUART, of Lorn, first Earl of Athol, *d.* 1512, who had :
ISABEL STUART, *m.* Alexander Robertson, of Strowan, and had :
JOHN ROBERTSON, of Muirton, second son, who had :
GILBERT ROBERTSON, of Muirton, who had :
DAVID ROBERTSON, of Muirton, who had :
WILLIAM ROBERTSON, of Muirton, who had :
WILLIAM ROBERTSON, of Gladney, who had :
REV. WILLIAM ROBERTSON, of Edinburgh, who had :
JEAN ROBERTSON, *m.* Alexander Henry, of Aberdeen, and had :
JOHN HENRY, who came to the Virginia Colony in 1730, and resided at his seats, "Studley" and "The Retreat," in Hanover County, Va. He *m.*, in Virginia, Sarah, dau. of Isaac Winston, and widow of Col. Syme. *Issue.*

PEDIGREE XXXVIII

WILLIAM DE LANVALLEI, a Magna Charta Surety, had:
HAWYSE DE LANVALLEI, *m.* Sir John de Burgh, and had:
JOHN DE BURGH, Baron of Lanvallei, *d.* 1279, who had:
MARGARET DE BURGH, *m.* Richard de Burgh, Earl of Ulster, and had:
JOAN DE BURGH, *m.* Thomas Fitz-Gerald, Earl of Kildare, and had:
MAURICE FITZ-GERALD, fourth Earl of Kildare, *d.* 1390, who had:
GERALD FITZ-GERALD, fifth Earl of Kildare, *d.* 1410, who had:
JOHN FITZ-GERALD, sixth Earl of Kildare, *d.* 1427, who had:
THOMAS FITZ-GERALD, seventh Earl of Kildare, *d.* 1478, who had:
GERALD FITZ-GERALD, eighth Earl of Kildare, who had:
ELEANOR FITZ-GERALD, *m.* Donald MacCarthy, Prince of Carberry, and had:
JULIA MACCARTHY, *m.* Dermod O'Sullivan, lord of Beare, *k.* 1549, and had:
SIR PHILIP O'SULLIVAN-BEARE, of Ardea Castle, Kerry, who had:
DANIEL O'SULLIVAN-BEARE, of Ardea, Kerry, who had:
PHILIP O'SULLIVAN-BEARE, of Ardea, Kerry, 1650, who had:
DANIEL O'SULLIVAN-BEARE, of Ardea, Kerry, 1675, who had:
OWEN O'SULLIVAN, of Ardea, County Kerry, who had:
MAJOR PHILIP O'SULLIVAN, of Ardea, County Kerry, who had:
JOHN O'SULLIVAN, *b.* Ardea, Kerry, June 17, 1690, came to New England in 1723, and resided and *d.* at Berwick, Me., June 20, 1795, aged 105 years, having issue by his wife, Margaret Browne, of Ardea, *b.* 1714, *d.* 1801.

PEDIGREE XXXIX

WILLIAM DE MALET, a Magna Charta Surety, had:
MABEL MALET, *m.* Hugh de Vivonia, and had:
WILLIAM DE VIVONIA, who had:
CICELY DE VIVONIA, *m.* John de Beauchamp, of Hache, and had:
JOHN DE BEAUCHAMP, first Baron by writ, *d.* 1336, who had:
JOHN DE BEAUCHAMP, second Baron by writ, *d.* 1343, who had:
JOHN DE BEAUCHAMP, third Baron by writ, *d.* 1360, who had:
CICELY DE BEAUCHAMP, *m.* Sir Roger de Seymour, and had:
SIR WILLIAM DE SEYMOUR, of Evenswinden, who had:
ROGER DE SEYMOUR, who had:
SIR JOHN DE SEYMOUR, who had:
JOHN DE SEYMOUR, who had:
JOHN DE SEYMOUR, who had:

SIR JOHN DE SEYMOUR, of Wolf Hall, Wilts, who had:
SIR HENRY DE SEYMOUR, K.B., who had:
JEAN SEYMOUR, *m.* Sir John Rodney, 1557–1612, and had:
WILLIAM RODNEY, of Hantsfield and Bristol, third son, 1610–1699, who had:
WILLIAM RODNEY, *b.* Bristol, 1652; came to Pennsylvania in 1682; resided in Kent County, Del.; member and first Speaker of the Assembly of Delaware; sheriff of Sussex County; a member of Penn's council, 1688. He *d.* April 8, 1708, having issue by his first wife, *m.* in Philadelphia, 1688, Mary, *d.* Dec. 20, 1692, dau. of Thomas and Sarah Hollyman.

PEDIGREE XL

WILLIAM DE MOWBRAY, a Magna Charta Surety, had:
ROGER DE MOWBRAY, second son, *d.* 1266, who had:
ROGER DE MOWBRAY, of the Isle of Axholme, *d.* 1298, who had:
JOHN DE MOWBRAY, of the Isle of Axholme, *d.* 1321, who had:
JOHN DE MOWBRAY, of the Isle of Axholme, *d.* 1361, who had:
JOHN DE MOWBRAY, of the Isle of Axholme, *k.* 1368, who had:
MARGERY MOWBRAY, *m.* John, Baron Welles, of Gainsby, *d.* 1422, and had:
EUDO DE WELLES, eldest son, *d. v. p.*, who had:
SIR LEO DE WELLES, of Gainsby, third Baron by writ, *k.* 1461, who had:
MARGARET WELLES, *m.* Sir Thomas Dymoke, of Scrivelsby, Lincoln, and had:
SIR LIONEL DYMOKE, of Scrivelsby, Lincolnshire, *d.* 1519, who had:
ALICE DYMOKE, *m.* Sir William Skipwith, of Ormsby, and had:
SIR WILLIAM HENRY SKIPWITH, of Prestwould, Leicestershire, who had:
SIR WILLIAM SKIPWITH, of Prestwould, Leicestershire, who had:
SIR WILLIAM SKIPWITH, of Prestwould, a Baronet, Dec. 20, 1622, who had:
SIR GUY SKIPWITH, third Bart., second son, removed to Virginia, who had:
SIR WILLIAM SKIPWITH, fourth Bart., of Virginia, who had:
SIR WILLIAM SKIPWITH, sixth Bart., of "Prestwould," Mecklenburg County, Va., 1707–1764. He *m.* Elizabeth, dau. of John Smith, sheriff of Middlesex County, Va. *Issue.*

PEDIGREE XLI

WILLIAM DE MOWBRAY, a Magna Charta Surety, had:
ROGER DE MOWBRAY, second son, *d.* 1266, who had:
ROGER DE MOWBRAY, of Axholme, first Baron by writ, *d.* 1298, who had:
JOHN DE MOWBRAY, of Axholme, second Baron, *d.* 1321, who had:
JOHN DE MOWBRAY, of Axholme, third Baron, *d.* 1361, who had:
JOHN DE MOWBRAY, of Axholme, fourth Baron, *k.* 1368, who had:
ELEANOR DE MOWBRAY, *m.* Roger, Baron de la Warr, *d.* 1371, and had:
JOAN DE LA WARR, *m.* Sir Thomas, Baron de West, *d.* 1405, and had:
SIR REGINALD DE WEST, second son, Baron de la Warr, *d.* 1451, who had:
SIR RICHARD DE WEST, second Baron de la Warr, 1432–1476, who had:
THOMAS DE WEST, K.G., third Baron de la Warr, *d.* 1524, who had:
SIR GEORGE WEST, second son, *d.* 1538, who had:
SIR WILLIAM WEST, created Lord Delaware, *d.* 1595, who had:
SIR THOMAS WEST, second Lord Delaware, *d.* 1602, who had:
PENELOPE WEST, *m.* Herbert Pelham, of Boston, Lincolnshire, and had:
HERBERT PELHAM, M.P., *b.* 1600, who came to Massachusetts in 1638 (bringing his sister Penelope, *d.* 1702, who *m.*, as his second wife, Richard Bellingham, governor of Massachusetts Colony, 1641, *d.* 1672, and had issue), and became treasurer of Harvard College, 1643; assistant, 1645; *d.* in England in July, 1674. He was twice married, and had issue.

PEDIGREE XLII

WILLIAM DE MOWBRAY, a Magna Charta Surety, had:
ROGER DE MOWBRAY, second son, *d.* 1266, who had:
ROGER DE MOWBRAY, of Axholme, first Baron by writ, *d.* 1298, who had:
JOHN DE MOWBRAY, of Axholme, second Baron, *d.* 1321, who had:
JOHN DE MOWBRAY, of Axholme, third Baron, *d.* 1361, who had:
JOHN DE MOWBRAY, of Axholme, fourth Baron, *k.* 1368, who had:
ELEANOR DE MOWBRAY, *m.* Roger de la Warr, *d.* 1371, and had:
JOAN DE LA WARR, *m.* Sir Thomas, Baron de West, *d.* 1405, and had:
SIR REGINALD DE WEST, Baron de la Warr, second son, *d.* 1451, who had:
SIR RICHARD DE WEST, second Baron de la Warr, 1432–1476, who had:
THOMAS DE WEST, K.G., third Baron de la Warr, *d.* 1524, who had:
SIR GEORGE WEST, second son, *d.* 1538, who had:
SIR WILLIAM WEST, created Lord Delaware, *d.* 1595, who had:
SIR THOMAS WEST, second Lord Delaware, *d.* 1602, who had:
COL. JOHN WEST, *b.* Hampshire, Dec. 14, 1590; B.A. Oxford, Dec. 1, 1613; member of Virginia Council, 1630–59; governor of the Virginia Colony, 1635–7, *d.* 1659. *Issue.*

PEDIGREE XLIII

WILLIAM DE MOWBRAY, a Magna Charta Surety, had :
ROGER DE MOWBRAY, second son, *d.* 1266, who had :
ROGER DE MOWBRAY, of Axholme, first Baron by writ, *d.* 1298, who had :
JOHN DE MOWBRAY, of Axholme, second Baron, *d.* 1321, who had :
JOHN DE MOWBRAY, of Axholme, third Baron, *d.* 1361, who had :
JOHN DE MOWBRAY, of Axholme, fourth Baron, *k.* 1368, who had :
ELEANOR DE MOWBRAY, *m.* Roger de la Warr, *d.* 1371, and had :
JOAN DE LA WARR, *m.* Sir Thomas, Baron de West, *d.* 1405, and had :
SIR REGINALD DE WEST, second son, Baron de la Warr, *d.* 1451, who had :
MARGARET DE WEST, *m.* Thomas, Baron d'Echingham, *d.* 1482, and had :
MARGARET D'ECHINGHAM, *m.* William le Blount, and had :
ELIZABETH LE BLOUNT, *m.* Sir Andrews, Baron Windsor, *d.* 1543, and had :
ELEANOR DE WINDSOR, *m.* Sir Edward Nevill, of Aldington, and had :
CATHERINE NEVILL, *m.* Clement Throckmorton, Haseley, *d.* 1594, and had :
CATHERINE THROCKMORTON, *m.* Thomas Harby, of Adston, *d.* 1592, and had :
CATHERINE HARBY, *m.* Dr. Daniel Oxenbridge, of Daventry, d. 1642, and had :
ELIZABETH OXENBRIDGE, *m.* Caleb Cockercraft, *d.* 1644, and had :
ELIZABETH COCKERCRAFT, *m.* Nathaniel Herring, d. 1678, and had :
OLIVER HERING, who had :
OLIVER HERING, who had :
CAPT. JULINES HERING, of Jamaica, W. I., who had :
MARY HERING, who *m.* Henry Middleton, of Charleston, S. C., governor of South Carolina, U. S. Minister to Russia, son of Arthur Middleton, a signer of the Declaration of Independence. *Issue.*

PEDIGREE XLIV

SAHER DE QUINCEY, a Magna Charta Surety, had :
ROGER DE QUINCEY, second Earl of Winchester, *d.* 1264, who had
ELA DE QUINCEY, *m.* Sir Alan le Zouche, of Ashby, *d.* 1269, and had :
EUDO LE ZOUCHE, second son, *d.* 1285, who had :
WILLIAM LE ZOUCHE, of Haryngworth, first Baron by writ, who had :
EUDO LE ZOUCHE, eldest son, *d. v. p.*, who had :
WILLIAM LE ZOUCHE, of Haryngworth, third Baron, who had :
SIR WILLIAM LE ZOUCHE, of Haryngworth, fourth Baron, who had :
WILLIAM LE ZOUCHE, of Haryngworth, fifth Baron, who had :
WILLIAM LE ZOUCHE, of Haryngworth, sixth Baron, who had :

DESCENDANTS OF MAGNA CHARTA BARONS 161

WILLIAM LE ZOUCHE, of Haryngworth, seventh Baron, who had:
JOHN LE ZOUCHE, of Haryngworth, eighth Baron, who had:
JOAN LE ZOUCHE, *m.* Sir Edward Hungerford, of Heytesbury, and had:
SIR WALTER HUNGERFORD, beheaded in 1541, who had:
SIR ANTHONY HUNGERFORD, of Burton-Ings, Oxford, who had:
LUCY HUNGERFORD, *m.* Edmund Lechmere, of Henley, and had:
THOMAS LECHMERE, who was surveyor-general of customs at Boston, Mass., *d.* June 4, 1765, having issue by his wife, *m.* Nov. 17, 1709, Anne, *d.* 1746, dau. of Wait Still Winthrop, chief justice of Massachusetts, son of Gov. John Winthrop and his second wife.

PEDIGREE XLV

SAHER DE QUINCEY, a Magna Charta Surety, had:
ROGER DE QUINCEY, second Earl of Winchester, *d.* 1264, who had:
MARGARET QUINCEY, *m.* William de Ferrers, Earl of Derby, *d.* 1254, and had:
WILLIAM DE FERRERS, of Groby, second son, *d.* 1287, who had:
ANNE FERRERS, *m.* John de Grey, of Ruthyn, *d.* 1323, and had:
MAUD GREY, *m.* Sir John de Norville, lord of Norton, York, and had:
JOHN DE NORTON, of Sharpenhow, Bedford, who had:
JOHN DE NORTON, of Sharpenhow, Bedford, who had:
RICHARD NORTON, second son, who had:
WILLIAM NORTON, of Sharpenhow, Bedford, who had:
WILLIAM NORTON, of Storford, Hertfordshire, who had:
REV. WILLIAM NORTON, *b.* 1610, who came to New England and resided at Ipswich, Mass., and *d.* April 30, 1694, having issue by his wife, Lucy, dau. of Emanuel Downing and his wife, Lucy, sister of John Winthrop, governor of Massachusetts Colony.

PEDIGREE XLVI

SAHER DE QUINCEY, a Magna Charta Surety, had:
HAWYSE DE QUINCEY, *m.* Hugh de Vere, Earl of Oxford, and had:
ROBERT DE VERE, fifth Earl of Oxford, *d.* 1296, who had:
JOAN DE VERE, *m.* William de Warren, *d. v. p.*, 1286, and had:
ALICE DE WARREN, *m.* Edmund Fitz-Alan, K.B., Earl of Arundel, and had:
RICHARD FITZ-ALAN, K.G., Earl of Arundel and Surrey, *d.* 1375, who had:

RICHARD FITZ-ALAN, K.G., Earl of Arundel and Surrey, *d.* 1398, who had:
ELIZABETH FITZ-ALAN, *m.* thirdly, Sir Robert Goushill, and had:
ELIZABETH GOUSHILL, *m.* Sir Robert Wingfield, of Letheringham, and had:
SIR HENRY WINGFIELD, of Orford, Suffolk, *d.* 1483-4, who had:
SIR ROBERT WINGFIELD, of Orford and Upton, *d.* 1575-6, who had:
ROBERT WINGFIELD, M.P., of Upton, Northants, *d.* 1580, who had:
DOROTHY WINGFIELD, *m.* Adam Claypoole, of Latham, Lincoln, and had:
SIR JOHN CLAYPOOLE, of Narboro', Northants, *m.* 1622, who had:
JAMES CLAYPOOLE, who came to Pennsylvania, June 8, 1683, resided in Philadelphia, and was a prominent merchant-citizen and treasurer of the Free Society of Traders of Pennsylvania, and, dying in 1687, had issue by his wife, Helen Merces, *d.* 1688, whom he *m.* at Bremen, Dec. 12, 1657.

PEDIGREE XLVII

SAHER DE QUINCEY, a Magna Charta Surety, had:
HAWYSE DE QUINCEY, *m.* Hugh de Vere, Earl of Oxford, and had:
ROBERT DE VERE, fifth Earl of Oxford, *d.* 1296, who had:
JOAN DE VERE, *m.* William de Warren, *d. v. p.* 1286, and had:
ALICE DE WARREN, *m.* Edmund Fitz-Alan, K.B., Earl of Arundel, and had:
RICHARD FITZ-ALAN, K.G., Earl of Arundel and Surrey, *d.* 1375, who had:
ALICE FITZ-ALAN, *m.* Thomas de Holland, Earl of Kent, *d.* 1397, and had:
ELIZABETH DE HOLLAND, *m.* Sir John de Nevill, *d. v. p.*, 1423, and had:
SIR JOHN DE NEVILL, *k.* 1461, who had:
RALPH DE NEVILL, third Earl of Westmoreland, *d.* 1498, who had:
RALPH DE NEVILL, Lord Nevill of Hornby, *d. v. p.* 1498, who had:
ANNE NEVILL, *m.* Sir William Conyers, of Pateshull, *d.* 1514, and had:
REGINALD CONYERS, of Wacherlei, Northamptonshire, who had:
RICHARD CONYERS, of Wakerley, 1553, who had:
CHRISTOPHER CONYERS, of Wakerley, who had:
EDWARD CONYERS (CONVERSE), *b.* Wakerley, Jan. 30, 1590, came to New England in 1630, and resided in Charlestown, Mass. He performed the duties of several public offices, and *d.* at Woburn, Mass., in 1663, having issue by his first wife, Jane Clarke, of Theckenham.

PEDIGREE XLVIII

SAHER DE QUINCEY, a Magna Charta Surety, had:
   HAWISE DE QUINCEY, *m.* Hugh de Vere, Earl of Oxford, and had:
ROBERT DE VERE, fifth Earl of Oxford, *d.* 1296, who had:
JOAN DE VERE, *m.* William de Warren, *d. v. p.* 1286, and had:
ALICE DE WARREN, *m.* Edmund Fitz-ALAN, K.B., Earl of Arundel, and had:
RICHARD FITZ-ALAN, K.G., Earl of Arundel and Surrey, *d.* 1375, who had:
ALICE FITZ-ALAN, *m.* Thomas de Holland, Earl of Kent, and had:
MARGARET DE HOLLAND, *m.* John de Beaufort, Earl of Somerset, and had:
JOAN DE BEAUFORT, *m.* James I., King of Scotland, and had:
JANET STEWART, *m.* James Douglas, Earl of Morton, and had:
JANET DOUGLAS, *m.* Patrick Hepburn, Earl of Bothwell, and had:
MARGARET HEPBURN, *m.* John Murray, of Fallahill, and had:
WILLIAM MURRAY, of Stanhope, Peebleshire, who had:
WILLIAM MURRAY, of Stanhope and Romano, 1531, who had:
JOHN MURRAY, of Stanhope and Romano, 1587, who had:
WILLIAM MURRAY, of Stanhope and Romano, who had:
ADAM MURRAY, of Cardow, 1657, who had:
WILLIAM MURRAY, of Cardow, who had:
CHRISTIANA MURRAY, *m.* John Wallace, of Drumellier, 1674-1733, and had:
JOHN WALLACE, *b.* Drumellier, Jan. 7, 1718, removed in 1742 to Somerset County, N. J., where he *d.*, at "Hope Farm," in 1783, having issue by his wife Mary, *d.* 1784, only dau. of Joshua Maddox, of Philadelphia, Pa.

PEDIGREE XLIX

GEOFFREY DE SAY, a Magna Charta Surety, had:
   WILLIAM DE Say, eldest son, *d.* 1272, who had:
WILLIAM DE SAY, eldest son, *d.* 1295, who had:
GEOFFREY DE SAY, eldest son, first Baron by writ, *d.* 1322, who had:
GEOFFREY DE SAY, second Baron by writ, admiral, *d.* 1359, who had:
IDONEA DE SAY, *m.* John, third Baron Clinton, and had:
WILLIAM DE CLINTON, fourth Baron Clinton, who had:
JOHN DE CLINTON, fifth Baron Clinton, who had:
JOHN DE CLINTON, sixth Baron Clinton, who had:
JOHN DE CLINTON, seventh Baron Clinton, who had:
THOMAS DE CLINTON, eighth Baron Clinton, who had:

EDWARD DE CLINTON, ninth Baron, first Earl of Lincoln, *d.* 1584, who had:
HENRY DE CLINTON, K.B., tenth Baron, second Earl of Lincoln, who had:
THOMAS DE CLINTON, eleventh Baron, third Earl of Lincoln, *d.* 1619, who had:
SUSAN CLINTON, who *m.* John Humphrey, *b.* Dorchester, Dorset, *d.* Sandwich, Kent, 1661. They came to New England in 1634, Mr. Humphrey (or Humfrey) being one of the gentlemen to whom the Council of Plymouth, England, sold part of Massachusetts in 1628, and settled at Lynn, when he entered upon his duties as assistant to Gov. John Winthrop, and was a member of the Ancient and Honorable Artillery Company, and, in 1641, appointed commander of the militia. *Issue.*

PEDIGREE L

ROBERT DE VERE, a Magna Charta Surety, had:
HUGH DE VERE, fourth Earl of Oxford, *d.* 1263, who had:
ROBERT DE VERE, fifth Earl of Oxford, *d.* 1296, who had:
JOAN DE VERE, *m.* William de Warren, *d. v. p.*, 1286, and had:
ALICE DE WARREN, *m.* Edmund Fitz-Alan, K.B., Earl of Arundel, and had:
RICHARD FITZ-ALAN, K.G., Earl of Arundel and Surrey, *d.* 1375, who had:
ALICE FITZ-ALAN, *m.* Thomas de Holland, Earl of Kent, *d.* 1397, and had:
MARGARET DE HOLLAND, *m.* John de Beaufort, Earl of Somerset, and had:
EDMUND DE BEAUFORT, K.G., fourth Duke of Somerset, *k.* 1455, who had:
ELEANOR DE BEAUFORT, *m.* Sir Robert Spencer, of Spencer Combe, and had:
MARGARET SPENCER, *m.* Thomas Cary, of Chilton-Folliot, and had:
WILLIAM CARY, second son, esquire to Henry VIII., d. 1528, who had:
CATHERINE CARY, *m.* Francis Knolleys, K.G., 1514-1596, and had:
ANNE KNOLLEYS, *m.* Sir Thomas Leighton, of Feckingham, and had:
THOMAS LEIGHTON, of Feckingham, Wilts, who had:
ANNE LEIGHTON, *m.* Sir John St. John, Bart., of Lidiard-Tregoze, and had:
ANNE ST. JOHN, *m.* Sir Francis Henry Lee, Bart., of Ditchley, and had:
FRANCIS HENRY LEE, of Quarendon, Berks, second son, who had:
EDWARD HENRY LEE, Bart., first Earl of Litchfield, *d.* 1716, who had:
CHARLOTTE LEE, *m.* Benedict Calvert, fifth Lord Baltimore, *d.* 1715, and had:
BENEDICT LEONARD CALVERT, 1700-1751, governor of Maryland, who had:
ELEANOR CALVERT, d. 1814, who *m.* first, Feb. 3, 1774, John Parke Custis, of "Abingdon," in Virginia, *d.* 1781, and *m.* secondly, 1787, Dr. David Steuart, of "Ossian Hall," in Virginia. Issue by both husbands.

PEDIGREE LI

ROBERT DE VERE, a Magna Charta Surety, had:
  HUGH DE VERE, fourth Earl of Oxford, d. 1263, who had:
ROBERT DE VERE, fifth Earl of Oxford, d. 1296, who had:
JOAN DE VERE, m. William de Warren, d. v. p. 1286, and had:
ALICE DE WARREN, m. Edmund Fitz-Alan, K.B., Earl of Arundel, and had:
RICHARD FITZ-ALAN, K.G., Earl of Arundel and Surrey, d. 1375, who had:
ALICE FITZ-ALAN, m. Thomas de Holland, Earl of Kent, and had:
MARGARET DE HOLLAND, m. John de Beaufort, Earl of Somerset, and had:
JOAN DE BEAUFORT, m. secondly, Sir James Stewart, of Lorn, and had:
SIR JOHN STEWART, first Earl of Athol, d. 1512, who had:
ELIZABETH STEWART, m. Andrew, third Lord Gray, and had:
JOAN GRAY, m. Sir Alexander Blair, of Balthyock, and had:
SIR THOMAS BLAIR, of Balthyock, Perthshire, who had:
EUPHEME BLAIR, m. Andrew Scott, of Balweary, and had:
ANDREW SCOTT, of Kirkstyle, who had:
GEORGE SCOTT, of Kirkstyle, who had:
PATRICK SCOTT, of Ancrum, Roxburyshire, who had:
SIR JOHN SCOTT, Bart., of Ancrum, d. 1712, who had:
JOHN SCOTT, third son, who came to New York, and was made a citizen in 1702, and m. the same year, Magdalen, dau. of John Vincent Cooper, of New York. *Issue.*

PEDIGREE LII

ROBERT DE VERE, a Magna Charta Surety, had:
  HUGH DE VERE, fourth Earl of Oxford, d. 1263, who had:
ROBERT DE VERE, fifth Earl of Oxford, d. 1296, who had:
JOAN DE VERE, m. William de Warren, d. v. p. 1286, and had:
ALICE DE WARREN, m. Edmund Fitz-Alan, K.B., Earl of Arundel, and had:
RICHARD FITZ-ALAN, K.G., Earl of Arundel and Surrey, d. 1375, who had:
JOHN FITZ-ALAN, Lord Maltravers, second son, d. 1379, who had:
JOHN FITZ-ALAN, eldest son, d. v. p., who had:
SIR THOMAS FITZ-ALAN, younger son, d. 1485, who had:
ELEANOR FITZ-ALAN, m. Sir Thomas Browne, and had:
SIR GEORGE BROWNE, of Beechworth Castle, Surrey, second son, who had:
SIMON BROWNE, of Browne Hall, Lancastershire, who had:
THOMAS BROWNE, of Brandon, Suffolk, d. 1608, who had:
FRANCIS BROWNE, of Weybird Hall, Suffolk, d. 1626, who had:
WILLIAM BROWNE, b. 1608, who came to Salem, Mass., in 1635, and d. Jan. 25, 1687. He m. first, Mary Youngs, d. 1635, and m. secondly, Sarah, dau. of Samuel Smith, of Yarmouth, Mass. *Issue.*

PEDIGREE LIII

ROBERT DE VERE, a Magna Charta Surety, had :
HUGH DE VERE, fourth Earl of Oxford, *d.* 1263, who had :
ISABEL DE VERE, *m.* John de Courtenay, of Oakhampton, *d.* 1273, and had :
SIR HUGH DE COURTENAY, of Oakhampton, first Baron, *d.* 1291, who had :
EGELINA COURTENAY, *m.* Sir Robert, Baron Scales, K. B., *d.* 1322, and had :
ROBERT DE SCALES, third Baron Scales, *d.* 1369, who had :
ELIZABETH SCALES, *m.* Sir Roger Bigod de Felbrigge, of Norfolk, and had :
SIR SIMON DE FELBRIGGE, K.G., of Colby, *d.* 1442-3, who had :
ALANÆ FELBRIGGE, *m.* Sir William Tyndale, of Dene, *d.* 1426, and had :
SIR THOMAS TYNDALE, of Dene and Redenhall, Norfolk, who had :
SIR WILLIAM TYNDALE, K.B., of Hockwold, Norfolk, *d.* 1496, who had :
SIR JOHN TYNDALE, K.B., of Hockwold, Norfolk, *d.* 1539, who had :
SIR THOMAS TYNDALE, of Hockwold, Norfolk, 1561, who had :
SIR JOHN TYNDALE, D.C.L., of Great Maplestead, Essex, *k.* 1616, who had :
MARGARET TYNDALE, *b.* 1591, who *m.* April 24, 1618, as his third wife, John Winthrop, governor of Massachusetts Colony; and, dying June 14, 1647, had issue by him.

PEDIGREE LIV

RICHARD DE CLARE, a Magna Charta Surety, had :
GILBERT DE CLARE, a Magna Charta Surety, who had :
ISABEL DE CLARE, *m.* Robert Bruce, Earl of Annandale, and had :
ROBERT BRUCE, Earl of Annandale and Carrick, *d.* 1304, who had :
ROBERT BRUCE, KING OF SCOTLAND, who had :
MARGERY BRUCE, *m.* Walter, high steward of Scotland, and had :
ROBERT II., KING OF SCOTLAND, who had :
ROBERT III., KING OF SCOTLAND, who had :
JAMES I., KING OF SCOTLAND, who had :
JANE STUART, *m.* secondly, James, Earl of Morton, and had :
JOHN DOUGLAS, second Earl of Morton, who had :
AGNES DOUGLAS, *m.* Alexander, Lord Livingston, and had :
WILLIAM LIVINGSTON, sixth Lord Livingston, *d.* 1592, who had :
ALEXANDER LIVINGSTON, Earl of Linlithgow, *d.* 1622, who had :
ANNE LIVINGSTON, *m.* Sir Alexander Seton-Montgomery, and had :
HUGH MONTGOMERY, Earl of Eglington, *d.* 1669, who had :
ALEXANDER MONTGOMERY, Earl of Eglington, *d.* 1701, who had :
ALEXANDER MONTGOMERY, Earl of Eglington, *d.* 1729, who had :

DESCENDANTS OF MAGNA CHARTA BARONS

EUPHEMIA MONTGOMERY, *m.* George Lockhart, of Carnwarth, and had:
GEORGE LOCKHART, of Carnwarth, Lanark, who had:
GEN. COUNT JAMES LOCKHART-WISHART, Kt., M.T., who had:
MARIANNA WISHART, *m.* Anthony Aufrère, of Hoverton Hall, and had:
LOUISE ANN MATILDA AUFRÈRE, *d.* Feb. 16, 1868, who *m.* Dec. 8, 1818, George Barclay, of New York City, 1790–1869, a descendant of John Barclay, deputy governor of East (New) Jersey, *d.* 1731. *Issue.*

PEDIGREE LV

EUSTACE DE VESCI, a Magna Charta Surety, had:
WILLIAM DE VESCI, lord of Alnwick, *d.* 1253, who had:
WILLIAM DE VESCI, of Alnwick, first Baron, *d.* 1297, who had:
ISABEL DE VESCI, *m.* William de Welles, of Alford, and had:
ADAM DE WELLES, first Baron, *d.* 1311, who had:
SIR ADAM DE WELLES, third Baron, *d.* 1345, who had:
JOHN DE WELLES, fourth Baron, *d.* 1361, who had:
JOHN DE WELLES, fifth Baron, *d.* 1421, who had:
MARGERY DE WELLES, *m.* Sir Stephen le Scrope, *d.* 1406, and had:
SIR HENRY LE SCROPE, of Masham, third Baron, *k.* 1415, who had:
JOAN LE SCROPE, *m.* Henry Fitz-Hugh, *d.* 1386, and had:
HENRY FITZ-HUGH, K.G., third Baron, *d.* 1424, who had:
SIR WILLIAM FITZ-HUGH, fourth Baron, *d.* 1452, who had:
HENRY FITZ-HUGH, fifth Baron, *d.* 1472, who had:
ELIZABETH FITZ-HUGH, *m.* Sir William Parr, K.G., and had:
WILLIAM, LORD PARR, of Horton, Northampton, *d.* 1546, who had:
ELIZABETH PARR, *m.* Sir Nicholas Woodhull, Knt., and had:
FULKE WOODHULL, of Thenford, Northumberland, who had:
LAWRENCE WOODHULL, of Thenford, Northumberland, who had:
RICHARD WOODHULL, *b.* at Thenford, Sept. 13, 1620; came to America about 1647, and in 1665 purchased 108,000 acres on Long Island, now the site of Brookhaven; *d.* 1690. *Issue.*

THE PEDIGREE OF LADY ANNA VON RYDINGSVÄRD

Richard de Clare, a Magna Charta Surety, Earl of Hertford, d. 1218, m. Amicia, dau. of William, Earl of Gloucester, and had:

Gilbert de Clare, a Magna Charta Surety, Earl of Hertford and Gloucester, d. 1229, m. Isabel, dau. of William Marshall, Earl of Pembroke, and had:

Richard de Clare, Earl of Hertford and Gloucester, d. 1262, m. secondly, Maud, dau. of John de Lacie, Earl of Lincoln, and had:

Thomas de Clare, second son, governor of London, 1274, m. Amy, dau. of Sir Maurice Fitz-Maurice, lord of Kerry, and had:

John de Lacie, a Magna Charta Surety, Earl of Lincoln, d. 1246, m. secondly, Margaret, dau. of Robert de Quincey, and had:

Maud de Lacie.

Robert de Vere, a Magna Charta Surety, Earl of Oxford, d. 1221, m. Isabel, dau. of Hugh de Bolebec, and had:

Hugh de Vere, Earl of Oxford, d. 1263, m. Hawise, dau. of Saher de Quincey, Earl of Winchester, and had:

Saher de Quincey, a Magna Charta Surety, Earl of Winchester, d. 1219, m. Margaret, dau. of Robert de Beaumont, Earl of Leicester, and had:

Hawise de Quincey.

DESCENDANTS OF MAGNA CHARTA BARONS 169

THOMAS DE CLARE, third son, *d. s. p. m.*, who had:

MARGARET DE CLARE, *m.* Bartholomew de Badlesmere, executed in 1322, and had:

MAUD DE BADLESMERE, *m.* John de Vere, Earl of Oxford, *b.* 1360, and had:

MARGARET DE VERE, *m.* secondly, Sir John Devereux, and had:

ROBERT DE VERE, Earl of Oxford, *d.* 1296, *m.* Alice, dau. of Gilbert de Saundford, and had:

ALPHONSUS DE VERE, second son, *d. v. p.*, who *m.* Jane, dau. of Sir Richard Foliot, and had:

JOHN DE VERE, Earl of Oxford.

Roger Bigod, a Magna Charta Surety, Earl of Norfolk, *d.* 1220, *m.* Isabel, dau. of Hameline Plantagenet, Earl of Warren and Surrey, and had:

Hugh Bigod, a Magna Charta Surety, Earl of Norfolk, *d.* 1225, *m.* Maud, dau. of William Marshall, Earl of Pembroke, and had:

SIR RALPH BIGOD, third son, *m.* Berta, dau. of Gerard de Furnival, and had:

ISABEL BIGOD, *m.* first, Gilbert de Lacy, *d. v. p.*, son of Walter de Lacy, lord of Trim, and had:

MAUD DE LACY, *m.* Geoffrey de Genevill, lord of Trim, first Baron by writ, lord of Ludlow Castle, governor of Windsor Castle, 1244, *d.* 1306, and had:

Henry de Bohun, a Magna Charta Surety, Earl of Hereford and Essex, *d.* 1220, *m.* Maud, dau. of Geoffrey Fitz-Piers, Earl of Essex, and had:

HUMPHREY DE BOHUN, Earl of Hereford and Essex, *d.* 1274, *m.* Maud, dau. of Henry d'Eu, and had:

HUMPHREY DE BOHUN, eldest son, *d. v. p.* 1265, *m.* Eleanor, dau. of William de Braose, of Brecknock, and had:

THE PEDIGREE OF LADY ANNA VON RYDINGSVÄRD—*Continued.*

SIR WILLIAM DEVEREUX, *m.* Anne, dau. of Sir John Barre, and had:

HUMPHREY DE BOHUN, Earl of Hereford and Essex. *d.* 1297, *m.* Maud, dau. of Ingelram de Fienes, and had:

PETER DE GENEVILL, second son, *m.* Joan, dau. of Hugh le Brune, Earl of Angoulesme, and had:

HUMPHREY DE BOHUN, Earl of Hereford and Essex, *b.* 1321, *m.* Elizabeth, dau. of Edward I., King of England, and had:

JOAN DE GENEVILL, *m.* Sir Roger de Mortimer, Earl of March, beheaded in 1330, and had:

AGNES DE BOHUN, *m.* Robert de Ferrers, of Chartley, second Baron, *d.* 1350, and had:

BLANCHE DE MORTIMER, *m.* Sir Peter de Grandison, second Baron, *d.* 1358, and had:

JOHN DE FERRERS, of Chartley, third Baron, *d.* 1367, *m.* Elizabeth, dau. of Ralph de Stafford, first Earl of Stafford, and had:

ISABEL DE GRANDISON, *m.* Sir Baldwin de Brugge, in Hereford, and had:

SIR WALTER DEVEREUX, *b.* 1402, *m.* Agnes Crophull, and had:

ROBERT DE FERRERS, of Chartley, fourth Baron, *d.* 1413, *m.* Margaret, dau. of Edward, Baron de Spencer, and had:

SIR JOHN DE BRUGGE, M.P., second son, sheriff of Hertford, 1416, and of Gloucestershire, 1420, who had:

ELIZABETH DEVEREUX, *m.* Sir John Milbourne, and had:

EDMUND DE FERRERS, of Chartley, fifth Baron, *d.* 1436, *m.* Helen, dau. of Thomas de la Roche, lord of Bromwick Castle, Darby, and had:

JOAN DE BRUGGE, *m.* Sir John Baskerville, of Erdisley, Hereford, and had:

DESCENDANTS OF MAGNA CHARTA BARONS 171

WILLIAM DE FERRERS, of Chartley, sixth Baron, *d. s. p. m.* 1450, *m.* Elizabeth, dau. of Sir Hamon Belknap, and had:

SIR RALPH BASKERVILLE, *m.* Anne Blaket, and had:

SIMON MILBOURNE, *m.* Jane, dau. of Sir Ralph Baskerville, of Erdisley, Hereford, and had:

ANNE DE FERRERS, *m.* Sir Walter Devereux, Baron Ferrers, of Chartley, and had:

JANE BASKERVILLE.

BLANCHE MILBOURNE, *m.* James Whitney, of Newport in the marches, and had:

SYBIL DEVEREUX, *m.* Sir James Baskerville, K.B., sheriff of Hereford, and had:

𝕎𝕚𝕝𝕝𝕚𝕒𝕞 𝕕𝕖 𝕃𝕒𝕟𝕧𝕒𝕝𝕝𝕖𝕚, a Magna Charta Surety, *d.* 1217, *m.* a daughter of Alan Basset, and had:

SIR ROBERT WHITNEY, K.B., a magistrate in Gloucestershire, *m.* Margaret Wye, and had:

SIR WALTER BASKERVILLE, K.B., sheriff of Hereford, *m.* Anne vch. Morgan ap Jenkyn ap Philip, of Pencoyd, and had:

HAWISE DE LANVALLEI, *d.* 1275, *m.* Sir John de Burgh, son of Hubert, Earl of Kent, and had:

SIR JAMES BASKERVILLE, *m.* Elizabeth Breynton, and had:

JOHN DE BURGH, of Lanvallei, *d. s. p. m.* 1279, *m.* Cicely, dau. of Hugh de Baliol, and had:

𝕎𝕚𝕝𝕝𝕚𝕒𝕞 𝕄𝕒𝕝𝕖𝕥, a Magna Charta Surety, *m.* a daughter of Thomas Basset, and had:

SIR ROBERT WHITNEY, knighted October 2, 1567, *d.* August 5, 1553, *m.* Sybil, dau. of Sir James Baskerville, and had:

SYBIL BASKERVILLE.

MARGARET DE BURGH, *m.* Richard de Burgh, Earl of Ulster, *d.* 1326, and had:

MABEL MALET, *m.* Hugh de Vivonia, and had:

THE PEDIGREE OF LADY ANNA VON RYDINGSVÄRD—Continued.

Geoffrey de Say, a Magna Charta Surety, d. 1230, m. Alice, dau. of John de Cheney, and had:

John de Burgh, d. 1313, m. Elizabeth, dau. of Gilbert de Clare, Earl of Gloucester, and had:

William de Vivonia, m. Maud, dau. of William de Ferrers, Earl of Derby, and had:

William de Say, governor of Rochester Castle, 1260, d. 1272, who had:

William de Burgh, Earl of Ulster, m. Maud, dau. of Henry Plantagenet, Earl of Lancaster, and had:

Cicely de Vivonia, m. John de Beauchamp, of Hache, Somerset, d. 1283, and had:

William de Say, d. 1295, who had:

Elizabeth de Burgh, m. Lionel Plantagenet, Duke of Clarence, son of Edward III., King of England, and had:

John de Beauchamp, of Hache, first Baron by writ, d. 1336, m. Joan d'Audley, and had:

Geoffrey de Say, first Baron by writ, d. 1322, m. Idonea, dau. of William de Leyburn, and had:

Philippa Plantagenet, m. Edmund de Mortimer, Earl of March, d. 1381, and had:

John de Beauchamp, of Hache, second Baron d. 1343, m. Margaret ——, and had:

Catherine de Say, m. John St. John, third Baron, d. 1349, and had:

Elizabeth de Mortimer, m. Sir Henry Percy, called "Hotspur," k. 1403, and had:

John de Beauchamp, of Hache, third Baron, d. 1361, m. Alice, dau. of Thomas de Beauchamp, Earl of Warwick, and had:

Sir Edward St. John, d. v. f., who m. Anastacia, dau. of William d'Aton, of Vesci, second Baron, and had:

Elizabeth Percy, m. John de Clifford, seventh Baron, d. 1432, and had:

Cicely de Beauchamp, d. 1393, m. first, Sir Roger de St. Maur, and had:

DESCENDANTS OF MAGNA CHARTA BARONS 173

Margaret St. John, *m.* Sir Thomas de Bromflete, of Vesci, sheriff of Yorkshire, *d.* 1431, and had:

Thomas de Clifford, eighth Baron, *b.* 1454, *m.* Joan, dau. of Thomas de Dacre, first Baron, and had:

Sir William de Seymour, *d.* 1392, *m.* Margaret de Brockburn, and had:

Sir Henry de Bromflete, of Vesci, sheriff of Yorkshire, first Baron by writ, *d. s. p. m.* 1468, *m.* Eleanor, dau. of William, Baron Fitz-Hugh, and had:

John de Clifford, ninth Baron, *b.* 1461, who had:

Roger de Seymour, *m.* Maud d'Esturmé, and had:

Margaret de Bromflete.

John de Clifford, tenth Baron, *d.* 1485, *m.* Margaret, dau. of Sir Henry de Bromflete, and had:

Sir John de Seymour, *d.* 1465, *m.* Isabel MacWilliams, and had:

Mary de Clifford, *m.* Sir Philip Wentworth, of Nettlested, Suffolk, and had:

John de Seymour, *m.* Elizabeth Coker, and had:

Sir Henry Wentworth, of Nettlested, *m.* Anne, dau. of Sir John de Say, and had:

John de Seymour, *m.* Elizabeth Darrell, and had:

Elizabeth Wentworth.

Sir John de Seymour, of Wolf Hall, Wilts, *d.* 1536, *m.* Elizabeth, dau. of Sir Henry Wentworth, and had:

THE PEDIGREE OF LADY ANNA VON RYDINGSVÄRD—*Continued.*

William d'Albini, a Magna Charta Surety, *d.* 1236, *m.* Margaret, dau. of Odonel d'Umfraville, and had:

WILLIAM D'ALBINI, eldest son, *d.* 1285, *m.* secondly, Isabel ——, and had:

ISABEL D'ALBINI.

Eustace de Vesci, a Magna Charta Surety, *k.* 1216, *m.* Margaret, dau. of William the Lion, King of Scotland, and had:

WILLIAM DE VESCI, *d.* 1253, *m.* secondly, Agnes, dau. of William de Ferrers, Earl of Derby, and had:

WILLIAM DE VESCI, first Baron by writ, *d.* 1297, *m.* Isabel, dau. of Adam de Periton, and had:

Robert de Ros, a Magna Charta Surety, *d.* 1227, *m.* Isabel, dau. of William the Lion, King of Scotland, and had:

WILLIAM DE ROS, of Hamlake, *d.* 1258, *m.* Lucia, dau. of Reginald Fitz-Piers, and had:

ROBERT DE ROS, of Hamlake, first Baron by writ, *d.* 1285, *m.* Isabel, dau. of William d'Albini, and had:

WILLIAM DE ROS, of Hamlake, second Baron, *d.* 1317, *m.* Maud, dau. of John de Vaux, and had:

WILLIAM DE ROS, of Hamlake, third Baron, *d.* 1342, *m.* Margery, dau. of Bartholomew de Badlesmere, and had:

THOMAS DE ROS, of Hamlake, fifth Baron, *d.* 1384, *m.* Beatrice, dau. of Ralph de Stafford, K.G., first Earl of Stafford, and had:

DESCENDANTS OF MAGNA CHARTA BARONS 175

THOMAS DE ROS, of Hamlake, seventh Baron, d. 1414, m. Margaret, dau. of Sir John d'Arundel, and had:

ISABEL DE VESCI, m. William de Welles, lord of Alfourd, Lincolnshire, 1283, and had:

SIR ADAM DE WELLES, first Baron by writ, d. 1311, m. Joan, dau. of John d'Eugaine, of Gainsby, and had:

SIR ADAM DE WELLES, third Baron, second son, d. 1345, m. Margaret, dau. of John Bardolf, third Baron, and had:

MARGARET DE WELLES, m. William Deincourt, d. v. p. ante 1379, and had:

MARGARET DE ROS, m. James Touchet d'Audley, d. 1459, and had:

JOHN TOUCHET, first Baron d'Audley, d. 1491, m. Anne, dau. of Sir Thomas, Baron d'Eckingham, and had:

ANNE D'AUDLEY, m. Sir John Wingfield, and had:

ELIZABETH WINGFIELD, m. Sir William Fillol, of Woodlands, Dorset, and had:

CATHERINE FILLOL.

EDWARD SEYMOUR, K.G., Duke of Somerset, beheaded in 1552, m. Catherine, dau. of Sir William Fillol, and had:

THE PEDIGREE OF LADY ANNA VON RYDINGSVÅRD—*Continued.*

Robert Fitz-Walter, a Magna Charta Surety, the leader of the Barons, *d.* 1234, *m.* Gunora, dau. of Robert de Valonies, and had:

WALTER FITZ-WALTER, *d.* 1257, *m.* Maud ——, and had:

SIR ROBERT FITZ-WALTER, first Baron by writ, *d.* 1325, *m.* secondly, Alianore, dau. of William de Ferrers, Earl of Derby, and had:

ROBERT FITZ-WALTER, second Baron, *d.* 1328, *m.* Joan, dau. of John de Multon, of Egremont, second Baron, and had:

JOHN FITZ-WALTER, third Baron, *d.* 1361, *m.* Eleanor, dau. of Henry de Percy, of Alnwick, second Baron, and had:

ALICE FITZ-WALTER, *m.* Aubrey de Vere, Earl of Oxford, *d.* 1400, and had:

WILLIAM DEINCOURT, second Baron, *d.* 1381, *m.* Alice, dau. of John de Nevill, of Raby, third Baron, and had:

JOHN DEINCOURT, fourth Baron, *d.* 1406, *m.* Joan, dau. of Sir Robert de Grey, of Rotherfield, fifth Baron, and had:

ALICE DEINCOURT, *m.* secondly, Sir William Lovel, Baron Lovel and Holand, *d.* 1454, and had:

ROBERT WHITNEY, *m.* Elizabeth Morgan, and had:

DESCENDANTS OF MAGNA CHARTA BARONS 177

RICHARD DE VERE, K.G., Earl of Oxford, *d.* 1417, *m.* Alice, dau. of Sir John Sergeant, and had:

JOHN DE VERE, Earl of Oxford, beheaded in 1461, *m.* Elizabeth, dau. of Sir John Howard, and had:

JANE DE VERE, *m.* Sir William Norris, of Yattenden, Berks, second wife, and had:

SIR EDWARD NORRIS, of Yattenden, *m.* Frideswide, dau. of Sir John Lovel, Baron Lovel and Holand, and had:

SIR JOHN LOVEL, Baron Lovel and Holand, *d.* 1465, *m.* Joan, dau. of John, Viscount de Beaumont, and had:

FRIDESWIDE LOVEL.

◆◇◆

John Fitz-Robert, a Magna Charta Surety, *d.* 1249, *m.* Ada de Baliol, and had:

ROGER FITZ-JOHN, lord of Clavering and Warkworth, *d.* 1249, who had:

THE PEDIGREE OF LADY ANNA VON RYDINGSVÄRD—*Continued.*

ROBERT FITZ-ROGER DE CLAVERING, first Baron by writ, *d.* 1311, *m.* Margaret de la Zouche, and had:

JOHN FITZ-ROBERT DE CLAVERING, second Baron, *d.* 1332, *m.* Hawise, dau. of Robert de Tibetot, and had:

EVE DE CLAVERING, *m.* first, Ralph d'Ufford (second wife), *d.* 1346, and had by her:

SIR EDMUND D'UFFORD, second son, *m.* Sybil, dau. of Sir Robert Pierpont, and had:

SIR ROBERT D'UFFORD, *m.* Eleanor, dau. of Sir Thomas Felton, and had:

JOAN D'UFFORD, *m.* William Bowet, and had:

SIR EDWARD SEYMOUR, Baron Seymour, *d.* 1593, *m.* Catherine, dau. of Henry de Grey, Duke of Suffolk, beheaded in 1554, and had:

ELIZABETH BOWET, m. Sir Thomas Dacre, d. v. p., eldest son of Thomas, Baron de Dacre, and had:

JOAN DACRE, m. Sir Richard Fienes, Baron Dacre of the South, and had:

THOMAS FIENES, Baron Dacre of the South, m. Alice, dau. of Henry Fitz-Hugh, fifth Baron, and had:

THOMAS FIENES, Baron Dacre of the South, m. Anne Bouchier, and had:

THOMAS FIENES, Baron Dacre of the South, m. Jane Dudley de Sutton, and had:

THOMAS FIENES, Baron Dacre of the South, m. Mary, dau. of George Nevill, K.B.. Baron Bergavenny, and had:

MARY FIENES.

HENRY NORRIS, second son, beheaded in 1536, m. Mary, dau. of Thomas Fienes, Baron Dacre, and had:

THE PEDIGREE OF LADY ANNA VON RYDINGSVÅRD—*Continued.*

MARY NORRIS, *m.* secondly, Sir Arthur Champernon, of Darlington, Devon, and had:

ELIZABETH CHAMPERNON.

William de Huntingfield, a Magna Charta Surety, *d.* 1256, *m.* Alice de St. Liz, and had:

ROGER DE HUNTINGFIELD, *d.* 1257, who had:

SIR WILLIAM DE HUNTINGFIELD, *d.* 1282, who had:

ROGER DE HUNTINGFIELD, *d.* 1301, who had:

EDWARD SEYMOUR, Bart., of Berry-Pomeroy, *d. v. p.* 1613, *m.* Elizabeth, dau. of Sir Arthur Champernon, and had:

MARY SEYMOUR, *m.* Sir George Farwell, of Hill-Bishop, Somerset, *d.* 1647, and had:

THOMAS WHITNEY, of London, *m.* Mary Bray, and had:

DESCENDANTS OF MAGNA CHARTA BARONS 181

JOHN WHITNEY, *bapt.* July 20, 1592, removed from London to Massachusetts in 1635, with wife Eleanor, *d.* 1659, *d.* at Watertown, June 1, 1673, having:

William de Mowbray, a Magna Charta Surety, *d.* 1223, *m.* Agnes, dau. of William d'Albini, Earl of Arundel, and had:

ROGER DE MOWBRAY, *d.* 1266, *m.* Maud, dau. of William de Beauchamp, of Bedford, and had:

ROGER DE MOWBRAY, first Baron by writ, *d.* 1298, *m.* Rose de Clare, and had:

JOHN DE MOWBRAY, second Baron, beheaded in 1321, *m.* Alice, dau. of William de Braose, of Gower, and had:

JOHN DE MOWBRAY, third Baron, *d.* 1361, *m.* Joan, dau. of Henry Plantagenet, Earl of Lancaster, and had:

WILLIAM DE HUNTINGFIELD, *d.* 1314, who had:

ALICE DE HUNTINGFIELD, *m.* Sir John de Norwich, *d.* 1361, and had:

BLANCHE DE NORWICH, *m.* Sir Richard le Scrope, feudal lord of Bolton, chancellor to Richard II., first Baron by writ, *d.* 1403, and had:

SIR ROGER LE SCROPE, of Bolton, second Baron, *d.* 1403, *m.* Margaret, dau. of Robert, third Baron Tiptoft, or Tibetot, and had:

SIR RICHARD LE SCROPE, of Bolton, third Baron, *d.* 1420, *m.* Margaret, dau. of Ralph de Nevill, first Earl of Westmoreland, and his first wife, and had:

JOHN FARWELL, of Hill-Bishop, *m.* Dorothy, dau. of Sir John Routh, and had:

THE PEDIGREE OF LADY ANNA VON RYDINGSVÅRD—Continued.

JOHN DE MOWBRAY, fourth Baron, b. 1368, m. Elizabeth, dau. of John de Segrave, third Baron, and had:

    SIR HENRY LE SCROPE, of Bolton, fourth Baron, d. 1459, m. Elizabeth, dau. of John le Scrope, of Masham and Upsal, fourth Baron, d. 1455, and had:

        HENRY FARWELL, of Concord, 1639, d. at Chelmsford, Massachusetts, 1670, m. Olive ——, d. 1691-2, and had:

MARGARET DE MOWBRAY, m. John de Welles, second Baron by writ, d. 1421, and had:

    RICHARD SCROPE, second son, m. Eleanor Washburne, and had:

        JOSEPH FARWELL, of Dunstable, Massachusetts, 1642-1722, m. 1666, Hannah Learned, and had:

EUDO DE WELLES, eldest son, d. v. p., who m. Maud, dau. of Ralph de Greystock, fifth Baron, and had:

    ELEANOR SCROPE, m. Sir Thomas Wyndham, d. 1522, and had:

MARY DE WELLES, m. John Laurence, of Rixton, Lancastershire, 1418, M.P. 1419, and had:

    MARY WYNDHAM, m. Erasmus Paston, d. 1540, and had:

MARGARET LAURENCE, m. Robert Laurence, of Ashton, Lancastershire, and had:

    SIR WILLIAM PASTON, d. 1610, m. Frances Clere, and had:

JOHN WHITNEY, of Watertown, bapt. at Isleworth, September 14, 1621, d. 1692, m. 1642, Ruth Reynolds, and had:

    GERTRUDE PASTON, m. Sir William Reade, son of William Reade, of London, d. 1522, and had:

NATHANIEL WHITNEY, of Weston, Massachusetts, 1646-1732, m. 1673, Sarah Hagar, and had:

NATHANIEL WHITNEY, of Watertown, Massachusetts, 1675-1730, m. 1695, Mary Robinson, and had:

DESCENDANTS OF MAGNA CHARTA BARONS

SIR THOMAS READE, m. Mildred, dau. of Sir Thomas Cecil, first Earl of Exeter, and Dorothy, dau. of Sir John Nevill, Lord Latimer, and had:

THOMAS READE, of Barton, m. Ann, dau. of Thomas Hoo, and had:

THOMAS READE, m. Mary Stoneham, and had:

SIR THOMAS READE, Bart., m. Mary, dau. of Sir John Brockett, and had:

SIR THOMAS READE, m. Mary, dau. of Sir Thomas Cornwall, of Burford, Salop, and had:

WILLIAM READE, b. 1587, d. at New Castle-on-Tyne, 1656, came to New England and resided at Woburn, m. Mabel Kendall, d. June 5, 1690, and had:

WILLIAM LAWRENCE, of Sevenampton, Gloucestershire, d. 1559, m. Isabel Molineux, and had:

EDMUND LAWRENCE, of Withington, Gloucestershire, d. 1582, who had:

JOHN LAWRENCE, chief burgess and Mayor of St. Albans, Herts, 1553-1575, who had:

WILLIAM LAWRENCE, of St. Albans, Herts, m. Catherine Beamond, and had:

JOHN LAWRENCE, bapt. at St. Albans, 1561, m. secondly, 1586, Margaret Roberts, and had:

THOMAS LAWRENCE, 1588-9, d. 1624, m. 1609, Joan Antrobus, and had:

ISRAEL WHITNEY, of Killingby, Connecticut, 1710-1746, m. Hannah ——, and had:

SYBIL WHITNEY, 1733-1812, m. Captain Oliver Cummings, of Dunstable, d. 1810, and had:

CAPTAIN JOSIAH CUMMINGS, of Dunstable, Massachusetts, 1763-1834, m. 1785, Sally Taylor, and had:

SALLY CUMMINGS.

SARAH FARWELL, m. 1707, Jonathan Howard, of Chelmsford, Massachusetts, 1675-1758, and had:

JACOB HOWARD, of Chelmsford, 1719-1798, m. 1745, Rachel Fletcher, and had:

SARAH HOWARD, m. 1776, John Cummings, of Tyngsboro, Massachusetts, 1753-1837, and had:

JOHN CUMMINGS, of Tyngsboro, 1779-1866, m. 1806, Sally, dau. of Josiah Cummings, and had:

———◆◆◆———

THE PEDIGREE OF LADY ANNA VON RYDINGSVÄRD—*Continued.*

MARIE LAWRENCE, *b.* 1625, *m.* Thomas Burnham, of Ipswich, Massachusetts, *d.* 1694, and had:

RALPH REED, *b.* 1630, *d.* January 4, 1711–12, *m.* Mary Peirce, *b.* 1636, *d.* February 15, 1701, and had:

RUTH BURNHAM, *m.* 1678, John Carter, of Woburn, Massachusetts, 1653–1727, and had:

JOSEPH REED, of Woburn, Massachusetts, *m.* 1692, Phœbe, dau. of Ensign Israel Walker, *b.* March 11, 1676, and had:

JABEZ CARTER, of Woburn, Massachusetts, 1700–1771, *m.* 1773, Abigail Manning, 1699–1772, and had:

NATHANIEL REED, *b.* March 28, 1704, *m.* October 3, 1773, Hannah, *b.* October 1, 1716, dau. of Ebenezer Flagg, 1678–1700, and had:

MARY CARTER, 1731–1776, *m.* 1756, Eleazer Flagg Pooles, of Woburn, Massachusetts, 1734–1776, and had:

CAPTAIN JOSHUA REED, *b.* 1739, *d.* 1805, *m.* November 28, 1759, Rachel, *b.* 1737, *d.* 1818, dau. of Joshua Wyman, of Woburn, 1693–177–, and had:

ELEAZER FLAGG POOLE, of Woburn, 1761–1790, *m.* 1779, Mary Reed, 1760–1796, and had:

MARY REED.

MARY POOLE, 1780–1857, *m.* 1798, Joshua Davis, of Springfield, Vermont, and had:

DESCENDANTS OF MAGNA CHARTA BARONS 185

WILLARD CUMMINGS, of Tyngsboro, *b.* 1811, *m.* 1835, Mary Ann Pollard, and had:

ELLEN MARIA CUMMINGS.

JOSHUA DAVIS, of Boston, Massachusetts, 1805-1873, *m.* 1827, Catherine Parkhurst, and had:

JOSHUA FLAGG DAVIS, of Boston and Chalmsford, Massachusetts, *b.* 1822, *m.* 1853, Ellen Maria Cummings, and had:

ANNA MARIA DAVIS, *b.* March 20, 1856, *m.* June 30, 1886, Lord Karl von Rydingsvärd, of Sweden, son of Lord Axel George von Rydingsvärd and Emma Cecilia, dau. of Erik Hohnström, a lineal descendant of King Karl VIII. (Knutson) of Sweden, through his daughter, Princess Christina and Count Erik Gyllenstjerna.

PEDIGREE LVI

RICHARD DE CLARE, a Magna Charta Surety, had:
    GILBERT DE CLARE, a Magna Charta Surety, who had:
ISABEL DE CLARE, *m.* Robert Bruce, Earl of Annandale, and had:
ROBERT BRUCE, Earl of Annandale and Carrick, *d.* 1304, who had:
ROBERT BRUCE, KING OF SCOTLAND, who had:
MARGERY BRUCE, *m.* Walter, lord high steward of Scotland, and had:
ROBERT II., KING OF SCOTLAND, who had:
ROBERT III., KING OF SCOTLAND, who had:
JAMES I., KING OF SCOTLAND, who had:
JAMES II., KING OF SCOTLAND, who had:
MARY STUART, *m.* secondly, James, Lord Hamilton, and had:
JAMES HAMILTON, first Earl of Arran, who had:
JAMES HAMILTON, first Duke of Chatelherault, who had:
CLAUD, LORD HAMILTON, third son, *d.* 1621, who had:
JAMES HAMILTON, first Earl of Abercorn, who had:
SIR GEORGE HAMILTON, Bart., of Donalong, Tyrone, who had:
MARGARET HAMILTON, *m.* Matthew Ford, M.P., *d.* 1713, and had:
MATTHEW FORD, M.P., of Seaford, County Down, *d.* 1729, who had:
STANDISH FORD, fourth son, came to Philadelphia, Pa., in 1730, *d.* 1766. *Issue.*

PEDIGREE LVII

GILBERT DE CLARE, a Magna Charta Surety, had:
    ISABEL DE CLARE, *m.* Robert Bruce, Earl of Annandale, *d.* 1295, and had:
ROBERT BRUCE, Earl of Annandale and Carrick, *d.* 1304, who had:
ROBERT BRUCE, KING OF SCOTLAND, who had:
MARGERY BRUCE, *m.* Walter, lord high steward of Scotland, and had:
ROBERT I., KING OF SCOTLAND, who had:
CATHERINE STUART, *m.* Sir David Lindsay, Earl of Crawford, and had:
MARJORY LINDSAY, *m.* Sir William Douglas, laird of Lochlevan, and had:
SIR HENRY DOUGLAS, laird of Lochlevan and Lugton, 1421, who had:
ROBERT DOUGLAS, laird of Lochlevan and Kincross, *k.* 1513, who had:
SIR ROBERT DOUGLAS, laird of Lochlevan, who had:
THOMAS DOUGLAS, only son, *d. v. p.*, who had:
ELIZABETH DOUGLAS, *m.* Alexander Alexander, of Menstrie, *d.* 1515, and had:
ANDREW ALEXANDER, laird of Menstrie, 1545, eldest son, who had:
ALEXANDER ALEXANDER, laird of Menstrie, *d.* 1594, who had:
WILLIAM ALEXANDER, Bart., first Earl of Sterling, 1633, *d.* 1640, who had:
JOHN ALEXANDER, fourth son, of Stafford County, Va., 1659, *d.* 1677. *Issue.*

Genealogies of Founders and Members

of

The Order of Runnemede

descendants of

The Sureties for the Magna Charta

THE PEDIGREE OF CHAR

William
de Lanvallei — Geoffrey de Say — William Malet —
Hawise de Lanvallei — William de Say — Helewise Malet — John Fitz-Robert —   William de
John de Burgh — William de Say — John de Muscegros — Roger Fitz-John — Robert   William   Roger d
Margaret de Burgh — Lady de Say — Robert de Muscegros — Robert Fitz-Roger — de Ros — d'Albini — Roger d
John de Burgh — John de Sudley — Hawyse de Muscegros — Euphemia Fitz-Roger — William   William   John d
William de Burgh — Joan de Sudley — Robert de Ferrers — Ralph de Nevill — de Ros — d'Albini — John d
Elizabeth de Burgh — Elizabeth Boteler — Robert de Ferrers, John de Nevill — Robert de Ros — Isabel d'Albini. John d
Philippa Plantagenet — Robert de Ferrers — Ralph de Nevill — William de Ros — Jane d
Elizabeth de Mortimer — Mary de Ferrers — Ralph de Nevill, Alice de Ros — Thor
Henry Percy — John de Nevill — Elizabeth de Meinill — Philip d'Arcy — Elizabeth de Grey. Her
Henry Percy — William Gascoigne — Joan de Nevill, John d'Arcy — Margaret de Grey.
Margaret Percy — William Gascoigne.   Ph

Mar

Elea

Dorothy

Alice N

Dorothy

Ed
of W

L

Elizabeth

Gabriel Thre
of Ellington, H

Robert Thr
of

John Thr
of

Gabriel Thre
of Gloucester Co., Va.,

Mordecai Thre
of King and Queen Co., Va.,

Thomas Thre
of Frederick Co., Va., and Nicholas Co., Ky.,

Mordecai Thre
of Loudon Co., Va.,

Col. John Aris Thre
of Culpeper Co., Va.,

Major Charles B. Thre
U. S. Army, retired, of New York City; δ. Ma

Charles Wickliffe Th

WICKLIFFE THROCKMORTON.

Roger Bigod⸆						
Hugh Bigod⸆		Saher de Quincey⸆				Eustace de Vesci⸆
Ralph Bigod⸆		Robert de Quincey⸆	Robert de Vere⸆	Henry de Bohun⸆		William de Vesci⸆
Isabel Bigod⸆	Richard de Clare⸆	Margaret de Quincey	Hugh de Vere⸆	Humphrey de Bohun⸆		William de Vesci⸆
⸆bray⸆ John Fitz-John⸆	Gilbert de Clare⸆	m. John de Lacie⸆	Robert de Vere⸆	Humphrey de Bohun⸆		Isabel de Vesci⸆
⸆bray⸆ Maud Fitz-John⸆	Richard de Clare⸆	Maud de Lacie.	Joan de Vere⸆	Humphrey de Bohun⸆		Adam de Welles⸆
⸆bray⸆ Isabel de Beauchamp⸆	Gilbert de Clare⸆		Alice de Warren⸆	Humphrey de Bohun⸆		Adam de Welles⸆
⸆bray⸆ Maud de Chaworth⸆	Margaret de Clare⸆	Richard Fitz-Alan⸆		Alianore de Bohun⸆		John de Welles⸆
⸆bray⸆ Joan Plantagenet⸆	Margaret d'Audley⸆	Mary Fitz-Alan⸆		Petronella Butler⸆		John de Welles⸆
⸆bray⸆	Hugh de Stafford⸆	Ankaret Le Strange⸆	Richard de Talbot⸆			Margery de Welles⸆
⸆bray⸆	Margaret de Stafford⸆	John de Talbot⸆		Henry le Scrope⸆		
Grey⸆ Alice de Neville⸆		Thomas de Talbot⸆	Henry Fitz-Hugh⸆	Joan le Scrope⸆		
Grey⸆ Elizabeth de Talbot.			Henry Fitz-Hugh⸆			

'Arcy⸆ Eleanor Fitz-Hugh.
'Arcy⸆ John Conyers.
⸆nyers⸆ Thomas Markenfield.
⸆oigne⸆ Nyan Markenfield.
⸆afield⸆ Robert Mauleverer, of Wothersome, Yorkshire.
⸆verer⸆ John Kaye, of Woodersome.
⸆aye,⸆ Anna Tirwhitt.
⸆ome.
⸆Kaye⸆ John Pickering, of Techmersh, Northampton.
⸆ering⸆ Robert Throckmorton, of Ellington, Huntingdon.
⸆rton,⸆ Alice Bedles.
⸆don.
⸆rton,⸆ Judith Bromsall.
⸆gton.
⸆rton,⸆ (Name unknown.)
⸆gton.
⸆rton,⸆ Frances Cooke.
1737.
⸆rton,⸆ Mary Reade.
1767.
⸆rton,⸆ Mary Hooe (second wife).
1806.
⸆ton,⸆ Sarah McCarty Hooe (second wife).
1838.
⸆rton,⸆ Mary Barnes Tutt.
1891.
⸆rton,⸆ Fanny Hall Wickliffe.
1842.
⸆orton, of New York City.

Members of the Order of Runnemede

Charles Wickliffe Throckmorton

DESCENT from the Sureties for the observance of the Magna Charta:

William d'Albini,	William de Lanvallei,
Hugh Bigod,	William de Malet,
Roger Bigod,	William de Mowbray,
Henry de Bohun,	Saher de Quincey,
Gilbert de Clare,	Robert de Ros,
Richard de Clare,	Geoffrey de Say,
John Fitz-Robert,	Robert de Vere,
John de Lacie,	Eustace de Vesci.

1. **Robert de Ros,** lord of Furfan and of Hamelake and Werke Castles, one of the Sureties for the observance of the Magna Charta, *d.* a Knight Templar, in 1227. He *m.* Lady Isabel, a daughter of King William the Lion, of Scotland, and had:

2. WILLIAM DE ROS, lord of Hamelake, who was engaged with his father in the baronial wars, and was taken prisoner at the battle of Lincoln; *d.* 1258. He *m.* Lucia, daughter of Reginald Fitz-Piers, of Blewleveny, Wales, and had:

3. ROBERT DE ROS, lord of Hamelake and Belvoir Castles, *d.* 1285. He *m.* 1244, Lady Isabel, daughter and heiress of William d'Albini, lord of Belvoir, *d.* 1285, son of **William d'Albini,** one of the Sureties for the observance of the Magna Charta, and had:

4. WILLIAM DE ROS, lord of Hamelake, one of the competitors for the crown of Scotland, *d.* 1316. He *m.* Lady Maud, daughter of John de Vaux, of Feston and Boston, County Lincoln, and had:

5. LADY ALICE DE ROS, who *m.* Nicholas de Meinill, of Wherlton, Yorkshire, *d.* 1342, and had:

6. LADY ELIZABETH DE MEINILL, *d.* 1369, who *m.* first, Sir John d'Arcy, second Baron d'Arcy, *b.* 1317, one of the heroes of Cressy, constable of the Tower of London, *d.* 1356, and had:

7. SIR PHILIP D'ARCY, fourth Baron, second son, admiral of the Royal Navy, *d.* 1398. He *m.* Lady Elizabeth de Grey, whose descent was as follows:

William de Mowbray, one of the Sureties for the Magna Charta, a brother of Roger de Mowbray, also one of the Magna Charta Sureties, *m.* Lady Agnes, daughter of William d'Albini, second Earl of Arundel and Sussex, whose mother was Adeliza of Lorraine, Queen Dowager of England, the second wife and widow of King Henry I., and, dying in 1222, had issue:

ROGER DE MOWBRAY, second son, who took part in the Scotch wars of Henry III., and, dying in 1266, had issue by his wife, Lady Maud, daughter of William de Beauchamp, of Bedford:

ROGER DE MOWBRAY, eldest son, who served in the wars of Wales and Gascony, and was the first of this family summoned to Parliament as Baron Mowbray of Axholme, writ dated June 23, 1295. He *m.* Lady Rose, "a descendant of the Earl of Hertford," and, dying in 1298, had issue:

JOHN DE MOWBRAY, second Baron. In 6 Edward II. he was sheriff of Yorkshire and governor of the city of York, and was constituted one of the wardens of the marches adjoining the kingdom. But, subsequently taking a prominent part in the insurrection of the Earl of Lancaster, and being captured at the battle of Boroughbridge, he was hanged at York in 1321, and his family imprisoned for a time in the Tower of London. He *m*. Lady Alice, daughter of William de Braose, of Gower, and had:

JOHN DE MOWBRAY, third Baron, *d*. 1361. He was a favorite of Edward III., and attended the king through his memorable French campaigns. He *m*. Lady Joan Plantagenet, daughter of Henry, Earl of Lancaster (a grandson of HENRY III., KING OF ENGLAND), and his wife, Lady Maud, daughter of Patrick de Chaworth, by his wife, Lady Isabel, daughter of William de Beauchamp, a descendant of HENRY I., KING OF FRANCE, created Earl of Warwick, *d*. 1298, and his wife, Lady Maud, widow of Gerard de Furnival, of Sheffield, and daughter of John Fitz-John, justiciary of Ireland, 1258, the eldest son of John Fitz-Geoffrey, justiciary of Ireland, 1246 (son of Geoffrey Fitz-Piers, Earl of Essex, justiciary of England), and his wife, Lady Isabel, daughter of Sir Ralph, third son of 𝔥𝔲𝔤𝔥 𝔅𝔦𝔤𝔬𝔡, one of the Sureties for the observance of the Magna Charta, second Earl of Norfolk (and his wife, Lady Maud Marshall, sister of William Marshall, Jr., one of the Magna Charta Sureties, and daughter of William, Earl of Pembroke, the adviser of King John), son of 𝔯𝔬𝔤𝔢𝔯 𝔅𝔦𝔤𝔬𝔡, one of the Sureties for the observance of the Magna Charta, Earl of Norfolk and lord high steward of England. Baron de Mowbray and Lady Joan had:

JOHN DE MOWBRAY, fourth Baron, who was a crusader, and was killed in a conflict with the Turks in 1368. He *m*. Lady Elizabeth, only daughter and heiress of John, Baron de Segrave, *d. s. p. m.* 1353, and his wife Margaret, Duchess of Norfolk, *d*. 1399, daughter and eventually sole heiress of Thomas de Brotherton, Earl of Norfolk, earl marshal of England, son of EDWARD I., KING OF ENGLAND,

and his second wife, Princess Margaret, daughter of PHILIP III., KING OF FRANCE. Baron de Mowbray and Lady Elizabeth had:

LADY JANE DE MOWBRAY, who *m.* Sir Thomas de Grey, of Berwyke, constable of Norham Castle, 1390, and had:

SIR THOMAS DE GREY, of Heton, second son, who was beheaded for political reasons August 5, 1415. He *m.* Lady Alice, daughter of Ralph Nevill, K.G., of Raby, created, in 1399, Earl of Westmoreland and earl marshal of England for life, *d.* 1425, and his first wife, Lady Margaret, daughter of Hugh, K.G., second Earl of Stafford, *d.* 1386 (and his wife, Lady Philippa de Beauchamp), son of Ralph, K.G., Earl of Stafford, one of the original members of the order of Knights of the Garter, *d.* 1372, and his wife, Lady Margaret, daughter of Hugh, second Baron d'Audley, created, 1337; Earl of Gloucester, *d.* 1347-9, by his wife, Lady Margaret, widow of Piers de Gaveston, Earl of Cornwall, beheaded in 1210, and daughter of Gilbert de Clare, Earl of Hertford and Gloucester, *d.* 1295, and his second wife, Princess Joan d'Acre, *d.* 1305, daughter of EDWARD I., KING OF ENGLAND, and his first wife, Princess Eleanor, daughter of FERDINAND III., KING OF CASTILE AND LEON.

Gilbert de Clare was the son of Richard, Earl of Hertford and Gloucester, *d.* 1262 (by his second wife, Lady Maud, daughter of **John de Lacie,** one of the Sureties for the observance of the Magna Charta, Earl of Lincoln, and his second wife, Lady Margaret, daughter of Robert, *d. v. p.*, eldest son of **Saber de Quincey,** one of the Sureties for the observance of the Magna Charta), son of **Gilbert de Clare,** Earl of Hertford, one of the Sureties for the observance of the Magna Charta (and his wife, Lady Isabel Marshall, daughter of William, Earl of Pembroke, Protector of England, and sister of William Marshall, Jr., a Surety for the observance of the Magna Charta), son of **Richard de Clare**, one of the Sureties for the observance of the Magna Charta.

Sir Thomas de Grey and Lady Alice de Nevill aforesaid had Lady Elizabeth, who *m.* Sir Philip, Baron d'Arcy, and had:

8. JOHN D'ARCY, fifth Baron, *b.* 1377, *d.* 1411, *m.* Lady Margaret, *d.* 144-, daughter of Sir Henry, fifth Baron de Grey, of Wilton, *d.* 1394, and his wife, Lady Elizabeth, daughter of Thomas, Lord Talbot, *d. v. p.* in France, 145-, eldest son by his first wife, Lady Maud Nevill,* of the celebrated general, John de Talbot, K.G., Lord of Furnival, created, in 1448, Earl of Shrewsbury, lord lieutenant and lord chancellor of Ireland, Earl of Waterford and Wexford, in the peerage of Ireland, *k.* in France, 1453, aged eighty years. He was the second son of Sir Richard, fourth Baron Talbot, of Goodrich Castle, and his wife, Lady Ankaret, daughter of John, fourth Baron le Strange, of Blackmere, *d.* 1361, and his wife, Lady Mary, daughter of Richard Fitz-Alan, K.G., Earl of Arundel and Surrey, *d.* 1375, and his second wife, Lady Eleanor Plantagenet.† Sir Richard was the son of Edmund Fitz-Alan, K.B., eighth Earl of Arundel, beheaded 1326, and his wife, Lady Alice, daughter of William de Warren, *d.* December 15, 1285, and his wife, Lady Joan, daugh-

---

* Lady Maud was the daughter of Thomas Nevill, third Baron de Furnival, *d.* 1406, and his wife Joan, only child of William de Furnival, *d.* 1383, son of Thomas, *d.* 1339, son of Thomas, *d.* 1332, son of Gerard de Furnival, *d.* 1280, and his wife Maud, daughter of John Fitz-John, justiciary of Ireland, 1258, aforesaid, a descendant of **Roger Bigod** and **Hugh Bigod**, both Sureties for the Magna Charta.

† Lady Eleanor was the daughter of Henry Plantagenet, third Earl of Lancaster, *d.* 1345, and his wife Maud, *b.* 1280, daughter of Patrick de Chaworth, *b.* 1253, *d. s. p. m.* 1282, by his wife, Isabel de Beauchamp, aforesaid, a descendant of **Roger Bigod** and **Hugh Bigod**, both Sureties for the Magna Charta.

ter of Robert de Vere, fifth Earl of Oxford and sixth great chamberlain, son of Hugh, Earl of Oxford and great chamberlain, *d.* 1263,* the son of **Robert de Vere**, Earl of Oxford and great chamberlain, one of the Sureties for the observance of the Magna Charta.

Sir Richard, Baron Talbot, aforesaid, was the son of Gilbert, third Baron Talbot, of Goodrich Castle, 1332–1387, by his first wife, Lady Petronella, daughter of James Butler, second Earl of Carrick, created, in 1328, Earl of Ormond, seventh Lord Butler of Ireland,† and his wife, Lady Alianore, sister of three Earls of Hertford and of William, Earl of Northampton, daughter of Humphrey de Bohun, fourth Earl of Hertford and Essex, lord high constable of England, *k.* 1321 (and his wife, Princess Elizabeth, widow of John de Vere and daughter of EDWARD I., KING OF ENGLAND, and his first wife, Eleanor of Castile), son of Humphrey, Earl of Hertford and Essex, *d.* 1297, son of Humphrey, *d. v. p.*, eldest son of Humphrey, Earl of Hertford and Essex, *d.* 1274, the son of **Henry de Bohun**, one of the Sureties for the observance of the Magna Charta, by his wife, Lady Maud, a sister of Geoffrey de Mandeville, one of the Sureties for the Magna Charta.

John, fifth Baron d'Arcy, and Lady Margaret, had:

9. PHILIP D'ARCY, sixth Baron, *d.* 1418, *m.* Lady Eleanor, daughter of Henry, fourth Baron Fitz-Hugh (by his wife Elizabeth, daughter and heiress of Sir Robert Grey, Knt.), son of Henry, third Baron Fitz-Hugh, and his wife, Lady Joan, daughter of Henry, third Baron Scrope, of Masham,

---

* His wife was Lady Hawyse, daughter of **Saier de Quincey**, a Surety for the Magna Charta.

† He was the son of Theobald, fourth Lord Butler of Ireland, *d.* 1285, and his wife Joan, daughter of John Fitz-Geoffrey, justiciary of Ireland, 1246, and his wife, Isabel Bigod, a descendant of **Roger Bigod** and **Hugh Bigod**, both Sureties for the Magna Charta.

son of Sir Stephen le Scrope, second Baron, and his wife Margery, daughter of John, fifth Baron de Welles,* *d.* 1421, son of John, fourth Baron, *d.* 1361,† son of Sir Adam, third Baron, *d.* 1345, son of Adam, second Baron, *d.* 1311, son of William, Baron de Welles, of Alford, in Lincolnshire, and his wife, Lady Isabel, daughter of William, *d.* 1297, second son of William, *d.* 1253 (and his second wife, Agnes, daughter of William de Ferrers, Earl of Derby), the eldest son of **Eustace de Vesci,** one of the Sureties for the observance of the Magna Charta.

Philip, sixth Baron d'Arcy, and Lady Eleanor had:

10. LADY MARGERY D'ARCY, *m.* Sir John Conyers, K.G., and had:

11. LADY ELEANOR CONYERS, *m.* Sir Thomas Markenfield, of Markenfield, will dated April 8, 1497, and had:

12. SIR NYAN MARKENFIELD, *m.* Dorothy, daughter of Sir William Gascoigne, *d.* March 4, 1486, seized of the manors of Whalten, County Notts, and Bentley, County York, and his wife, Lady Margaret Percy. He was the son of Sir William Gascoigne, *d.* before 1463-4, and Lady Joan, daughter and heiress of John, Nevill, of Oversley, lord of Wymesley, who was the son of Ralph Nevill (and Margery,

---

* His wife was Lady Margaret (or Eleanor), daughter of John, fourth Baron de Mowbray, *k.* 1368, aforesaid, a descendant of **William de Mowbray, Roger Bigod,** and **Hugh Bigod,** Sureties for the Magna Charta.

† John, fourth Baron de Welles, *m.* Maud, daughter of William, Baron Ros, of Hamelake, and his wife, Margaret Badlesmere, son of William, second Baron, *d.* 1317, son of Robert de Ros, of Hamelake, and his wife, Isabel d'Albini, descendants of **Robert de Ros,** or **Roos,** and **William d'Albini,** Sureties for the Magna Charta. Lady Margaret Badlesmere was the daughter of Bartholomew, Baron Badlesmere, of Leeds Castle, and his wife Margaret, daughter of Thomas, son of Richard de Clare, Earl of Gloucester (and his wife Maud, daughter of **John de Lacie,** a Magna Charta Surety, by Margaret, granddaughter of **Saier de Quincey,** a Magna Charta Surety) the son of **Gilbert de Clare,** son of **Richard de Clare,** both Sureties for the Magna Charta.

daughter of Sir Robert, second Baron Ferrers, of Wemme), the son of Ralph, fourth Baron Nevill, of Raby, K.G., Earl of Westmoreland, member of the privy council of King Richard II., earl marshal of England (and his first wife, Lady Margaret Stafford,* daughter of Hugh, Earl of Stafford, K.G.), the son of Sir John, third Baron de Nevill, of Raby, K.G., constituted admiral of the king's fleet, *d.* October 17, 1385, the son of Ralph de Nevill, second Baron, *d.* 1367, son of Ralph, Baron de Nevill, of Raby, and his first wife, Lady Euphemia, sister of John de Clavering, and daughter of Robert Fitz-Roger, son of Roger Fitz-John, the son of John Fitz-Robert, one of the Sureties for the Magna Charta.

Sir Robert Ferrers, aforesaid, second Baron Ferrers, of Wemme, *m.* Lady Joan, daughter of John of Gaunt, Earl of Lancaster, son of EDWARD III., KING OF ENGLAND. He was the son of Sir Robert, first Baron Ferrers, of Wemme, *d.* 1410 (by his wife, Lady Elizabeth, only daughter and heiress of William, third Baron Boteler), the son of Robert, second Baron Ferrers, of Chartley, *d.* 1350,† son of John, first Baron Ferrers, of Chartley, seneschal of Aquitaine, *d.* 1324,‡ by his wife, Lady Hawyse, daughter and heiress of Sir Robert de Muscegros, of Charlton, County Somerset, son of John de Muscegros, of Charlton, *d.* 3 Edward I., son of Sir Robert de Muscegros, lord of Berwain and Norton, 38 Henry III., and his wife, Lady Helewise, daughter of

---

* Lady Margaret Stafford was descended from the Magna Charta Sureties Saier de Quincey, John de Lacie, Gilbert de Clare, Roger Bigod, Richard de Clare, and Hugh Bigod.

† His wife was Lady Agnes, *d. v. p.*, daughter of Humphrey de Bohun, Earl of Hereford and Essex, *k.* 1321, a descendant of Henry de Bohun, a Magna Charta Surety.

‡ He was the only son of Robert de Ferrers, eighth and last Earl of Derby, *d.* 1279, son of William, seventh Earl, *k.* 1254, and his wife Margaret, daughter of Roger, son of Saier de Quincey, a Magna Charta Surety.

William Malet, one of the Sureties for the observance of the Magna Charta.

William, third Baron Boteler, of Wemme, aforesaid, *d.* 1369, *m.* Lady Joan, daughter of John, Baron de Sudley, son of John, Baron de Sudley, lord chamberlain to King Edward I., *d.* 1336, and his wife, a daughter of William, Lord Say, *d.* 1295, who was the son of William de Say, governor of the Castle of Rochester, *d.* 1272, the son of **Geoffrey de Say,** one of the Sureties for the observance of the Magna Charta.

Lady Margaret, wife of Sir William Gascoigne aforesaid, was the daughter of Henry de Percy, third Earl of Northumberland, the son of Henry, second Earl,* the son of Sir Henry Percy, the celebrated "Hotspur," killed at the battle of Shrewsbury, 1403,† and his wife, Lady Elizabeth, daughter of Edmund de Mortimer, third Earl of March, *d.* 1381,‡ and his wife, Lady Philippa, only child of Lionel Plantagenet, Duke of Clarence (son of EDWARD III., KING OF ENGLAND), and his wife, Lady Elizabeth, daughter of William de Burgh, third Earl of Ulster, who

---

* His wife was Eleanor, daughter of Ralph de Nevill, first Earl of Westmoreland, and his second wife, Joan de Beaufort, daughter of John of Gaunt, son of Edward III., King of England.

† He was the son of Sir Henry Percy, of Alnwick, first Earl of Northumberland (and his wife Margaret, daughter of Ralph Nevill, of Raby, and Margaret, daughter of Hugh, Earl of Stafford, a descendant of **John de Lacie, Saier de Quincey,** and **John Fitz-Robert,** Sureties for the Magna Charta), son of Henry, third Baron Percy, and Mary Plantagenet, daughter of Henry, Earl of Lancaster (a grandson of Henry III.), and Maud de Chaworth, aforesaid, a descendant of **Hugh Bigod** and **Roger Bigod,** Sureties for the Magna Charta.

‡ Edmund, Earl of March, was the son of Earl Roger, son of Sir Edmund, Baron de Mortimer, *d.* 1331, and Elizabeth, daughter of Bartholomew de Badlesmere and his wife, Margaret de Clare, aforesaid, a descendant of **Richard de Clare, John de Lacie, Gilbert de Clare,** and **Saier de Quincey,** Sureties for the Magna Charta.

was murdered June 6, 1313, the son of John de Burgh,* son of Richard de Burgh, second Earl of Ulster, *d.* 1326, and his wife, Lady Margaret, daughter of John de Burgh, Baron of Lanvallei, the son of John de Burgh and his wife, Lady Hawise, daughter of William de Lanvallei, one of the sureties for the observance of the Magna Charta.

Sir Nyan Markenfield and Lady Dorothy had:

13. ALICE MARKENFIELD, who *m.* October 16, 1524, Robert Mauleverer, of Wothersome, Yorkshire, son of Sir William Mauleverer, Knight, of Wothersome and Arncliffe,† and his wife, *m.* 1492, Jane, daughter of Sir John Conyers, Knight, of Sockburn, and had:

14. DOROTHY MAULEVERER, *m.* 1542, John Kaye, of Woodersome, Yorkshire, and had:

15. EDWARD KAYE, of Woodersome, Yorkshire, who *m.* Anna, daughter of Robert Tirwhitt, of Ketelby, in County Lincoln, and had:

16. LUCIA KAYE, *m.* John Pickering, of Techmersh, in Northamptonshire, and had:

---

* His wife was Elizabeth, daughter of Gilbert de Clare, Earl of Hertford and Gloucester (and his wife Joan, daughter of King Edward I.), son of Earl Richard (and his wife Maud, daughter of John de Lacie, and a descendant of Saier de Quincey, Sureties for the Magna Charta), son of Gilbert de Clare, son of Richard de Clare, both Sureties for the Magna Charta.

† He was the son of Robert Mauleverer, *d.* 1495, son of Edmund, of Wothersome, and Eleanor, daughter of Sir James Strangeways, sheriff of Yorkshire, 1446 and 1469, by his wife Elizabeth, daughter of Philip, sixth Baron d'Arcy, and his wife, Eleanor Fitz-Hugh, aforesaid, descendants of William d'Albini, Robert de Roos, Gilbert de Clare, John de Lacie, Richard de Clare, Saier de Quincey, John Fitz-Robert, Eustace de Vesci, William de Mowbray, Robert de Vere, Henry de Bohun, Roger Bigod, and Hugh Bigod, all Sureties for the Magna Charta.

Edmund Mauleverer was the son of Sir William, of Wothersome, *temp.* 1418, and his wife Joan, daughter of Sir John Colville by his wife Alice, daughter of John, Baron d'Arcy, and Elizabeth Meinill, aforesaid, descended from William d'Albini and Robert de Roos, Sureties for the Magna Charta.

MEMBERS OF THE ORDER OF RUNNEMEDE   199

17. ELIZABETH PICKERING, *m.* Robert Throckmorton, of Ellington, Huntingdonshire, 1613, who was the son of Gabriel Throckmorton, of Ellington (and his wife Emma, daughter of John Lawrence, of Ramsays, Huntingdonshire), the son of Sir Richard Throckmorton, Knight, of Higham Ferrars, Northamptonshire, seneschal of the duchy of Lancashire, and his wife Jane, daughter of Humphrey Beaufo de Bereford, County Warwick, the son of Sir Robert Throckmorton, lord of Coughton, Warwickshire, and Weston Underwood, County Bucks, privy counsellor to Henry VII., commander in the king's army at the battle of Stoke, Knight of Bath, 10 Henry VII., will dated 1518, and his wife Catharine, daughter of Sir William Marrow, lord mayor of London. He was the son of Sir Thomas Throckmorton, lord of Throckmorton, County Worcester, and Coughton, County Warwick, sheriff of Warwick and Leicester, knight of the shire for County Worcester, 1447, *d.* 1472, aged sixty, buried at Fladbury (and his wife, *m.* 1446, Margaret, daughter and heiress of Sir Robert Olney, Knight, of Weston Underwood, County Bucks, by Goditha, his wife, daughter and coheiress of William Bosum), the son of Sir John Throckmorton, Knight, lord of Throckmorton and Coughton, under treasurer of England, knight of the shire for County Worcester, 2 and 8 Henry V. and 1 Henry VI., privy counsellor to Henry V., died April 13, 1446, will dated April 12, 23 Henry VI., buried at Fladbury, County Worcester, and his wife Eleanor, *m.* 1409, a daughter and coheiress of Sir Guy de la Spine, of Coughton, Warwick, by the heiress of Wyke. He was the son of Sir Thomas Throckmorton, Knight, lord of Throckmorton, 17 Richard II., constable of Elmley Castle, 6 Henry IV., knight of the shire, 3 Henry IV., escheator of Worcestershire, 3 Henry IV., *d.* about 1408, buried at Fladbury, and his wife, *m.* 1392, Agnes, daughter of Sir Alexander Besford, Knight, of County

Worcester. He was the son of John Throckmorton, lord of Throckmorton, 13 Edward III., *m.* Anne, daughter and heiress of Sir Richard Abberbury, of Doddington, County Oxon. He was descended from John de Throckmorton, lord of Throckmorton, *temp.* 1130.

Robert Throckmorton and Elizabeth Pickering had:

18. GABRIEL THROCKMORTON, of Ellington, *b.* 1586, *m.* Alice, daughter and heiress of William Bedles, of Bedfordshire, and had:

19. ROBERT THROCKMORTON, of Ellington, *b.* 1608, *d.* 1662, will dated September 14, 1657, proved at London, June 21, 1664, *m.* Judith Bromsall, and had:

20. JOHN THROCKMORTON, of Ellington, *b.* 1633, *d.* 1678, who had:

21. GABRIEL THROCKMORTON, of Ware Parish, Gloucester County, Virginia, second son, living in Virginia 1684, aged about nineteen; inherited by the will of his brother Robert Throckmorton, of Peyton Pawa, County Huntingdon, dated March 1, 1698, proved May 3, 1699, his plantation and effects in New Kent County, Virginia, presiding justice of Gloucester County, *d.* January, 1737, *m.* 1690, Frances, daughter of Mordecai Cooke, of Ware Parish, Gloucester County, and had:

22. MORDECAI THROCKMORTON, of Gloucester and King and Queen Counties, Virginia, captain of militia, sheriff of King and Queen County, 1740; *b.* about 1696, *d.* 1767; *m.* Mary, daughter of Thomas Reade, of Ware Parish (and his wife, Lucy Gwyn), son of Colonel George Reade (came to Virginia in 1637; was burgess for James City County, 1649, and for Gloucester County in December, 1656; secretary of state *pro tem.*, 1640; member of the council, March 13, 1657–8, and April 3, 1658, holding office until his death, 1671; will probated November 20, 1671), and his wife Elizabeth, daughter of Captain Nicholas Martian, of York,

CHARLES WICKLIFFE THROCKMORTON.

Virginia. His father was Robert Reade, of Linkenhot, Hampshire, will dated December 10, 1626, who *m*. Mildred (third wife), daughter of Sir Thomas Windebank, of Haines Hill, parish of Hurst, Berkshire, clerk of the signet to Elizabeth and James, *d*. October 24, 1607, and his wife Frances, a daughter of Sir Edward Dymoke, of Scrivelsby, Lincolnshire, hereditary champion of England, sheriff of Lincoln, officiated as champion at the coronations of Edward VI., Queen Mary, and Queen Elizabeth,* by his wife Anne, daughter of Sir George Talboys, heir of Gilbert, Lord Talboys, of Kyme, *d*. 1566.†

Captain Mordecai Throckmorton and Mary Reade had:

23. THOMAS THROCKMORTON, of Frederick County, Virginia, and Nicholas County, Kentucky, *b*. 1739, *d*. April 27, 1826; justice of Frederick County, Virginia, as late as 1790; member Kentucky House of Representatives from Nicholas County; State Senate, 1811–15, 1820–21 ; *m*. (second wife)

---

* He was the son of Sir Robert Dymoke, of Scrivelsby, king's treasurer, and sheriff of Lincolnshire, champion at the coronations of Richard III., Henry VII., and Henry VIII., *d*. 1544, son of Sir Thomas Dymoke, beheaded *temp*. Edward IV., and his wife Margaret, daughter of Sir Lionel, Baron de Welles, *k*. 1461, a descendant of Robert de Roos, William d'Albini, Eustace de Vesci, and William de Mowbray, Sureties for the Magna Charta.

† His wife was Elizabeth, daughter of Sir William Gascoigne and Margaret, daughter of Henry Percy, Earl of Northumberland. and descended from William de Lanvallei, John Fitz-Robert, Gilbert de Clare, Richard de Clare, John de Lacie, Saier de Quincey, Geoffrey de Say, William Malet, Roger Bigod, and Hugh Bigod, Sureties for the Magna Charta.

He was the son of Sir Robert Talboys and his wife Elizabeth, daughter of Sir John Heron, of Wetmore, *d*. 1425, and Elizabeth, daughter of William Heron, of Ford, by Anne, daughter of Sir Robert Ogle, Sheriff of Northumberland, *d*. 1437, and Maud, daughter of Sir Thomas Grey, of Heton, and his wife Alice, daughter of Ralph Nevill, first Earl of Westmoreland, a descendant of John Fitz-Robert, a Magna Charta Surety.

Sir Thomas Grey was the son of Sir Thomas Grey, of Berwick, and Jane, daughter of John, fourth Baron de Mowbray, a descendant of William de Mowbray, a Magna Charta Surety.

Mary, daughter of John Hooe, of Virginia, and Anne Fowke, and had by her:

24. MORDECAI THROCKMORTON, of "Meadow Farm," Loudon County, Virginia, *b.* March 10, 1777, *d.* April 7, 1838. He *m.* first, Mildred, daughter of Warner Washington and Hannah Fairfax, and *m.* secondly, February 6, 1812, Sarah McCarty, a daughter of Bernard Hooe, of Prince William County, Virginia; will probated, Prince William County, May 7, 1810, and his wife, Mary Symes, daughter of Colonel Richard Chichester, of Fairfax County, Virginia; county lieutenant of Fairfax County; will probated, Fairfax County, 1796; *m.* 1766, Sarah, daughter of Colonel Daniel McCarty, of Fairfax County; will probated, Fairfax County, 1792; *m.* 1748, Sinah, daughter of Major James Ball, of "Bewdley," Lancaster County, Virginia, *b.* 1678, *d.* October 13, 1754; will dated July 15, 1754, probated, Lancaster County, November 15, 1754; *m.* April 16, 1707, Mary, daughter of Edmund Conway (and relict of John Dangerfield), *d.* January, 1698; will probated, Richmond County, Virginia, September 7, 1698; *m.* Sarah, daughter of Lieutenant-Colonel Henry Fleet, of Maryland and Virginia.*

Mordecai Throckmorton and Sarah McCarty Hooe had:

25. COLONEL JOHN ARIS THROCKMORTON, of Loudon and Culpeper Counties, *b.* March 3, 1815, at "Meadow Farm;" colonel of militia; major Sixth Virginia Cavalry, C.S.A.; took part in thirty-four battles and many skirmishes; *d.* May 28, 1891; *m.* March 13, 1839, Mary Barnes, daughter of Colonel Charles Pendleton Tutt, of Loudon County, Virginia, colonel in the War of 1812, *b.* 1780, *d.* 1832, buried at Fort Pickens, Pensacola, and his wife, Anne Mason, *b.* October 16, 1789, *d.* July 12, 1882, daughter of Richard

---

* He was descended from Sureties for the Magna Charta, as shown in the pedigree of Professor Fleete.

McCarty Chichester, *b.* February 27, 1769, died August 29, 1817, *m.* Anne Thomson Mason. He was the son of Colonel Richard Chichester, of Fairfax County, Virginia, *b.* Lancaster County, 1736, *d.* August 22, 1796, and Sarah McCarty, *d.* June 25, 1826, aforesaid.

Colonel John Aris Throckmorton and Mary Barnes Tutt had:

26. MAJOR CHARLES B. THROCKMORTON, U.S.A., retired, *b.* May 27, 1842; page in United States Senate, 1852–3; clerk Committee of Elections, House of Representatives, 1858; private secretary to postmaster-general, 1860; commissioned second lieutenant, U.S.A., March 16, 1861; first lieutenant, May 14, 1861; captain, July 18, 1864; major, December 1, 1883; retired, at his own request, after thirty-three years' service, March 8, 1894; assistant general superintendent, Department Street-Cleaning, New York, January 1, 1894–February 2, 1895; served throughout the war; brevetted major, 1865, for gallant and meritorious conduct; engaged in the Modoc, Nez-Percé, Bannock, and Piute Indian wars. He *m.* at Bardstown, Kentucky, October 8, 1863, Fanny Hall, daughter of Robert Logan Wickliffe, of Bardstown, Kentucky, and had:

27. CHARLES WICKLIFFE THROCKMORTON, of New York City, member of the Society Sons of the Revolution, State of New York, Society of Colonial Wars, Virginia Historical Society, Colonial Order of the Acorn, and a founder of the Order of Runnemede.

Arms.—Quarterly of 8.
Throckmorton.—*Gu., a chevron, ar., three bars gemelles, sa., a crescent in dexter chief for difference.*
Abberbury.—*Or., a fesse crenellée, sa.*
Olney.—*Ar., on a fesse crenellée, between six cross-crosslets fitchée, gu., three crescents of the field.*

De la Spine.—*Sa., a chevron, ar., between three crescents, or.*
Olney.—*Ar., on a fesse crenellée, between six cross-crosslets patée fitchée, gu., three plates.*
Bosum.—*Gu., three bird-bolts feathered, ar.*
Wyke.—*Gu., a fesse, or, between six goutes d'or.*
Throckmorton.—As before.
Crests.—Throckmorton: *An elephant's head, couped, sa., armed and eared, or, charged with a crescent for difference.*
Throckmorton: *A falcon rising, ar., billed and belled, or, charged on the breast with a crescent for difference.*
Mottoes.—Throckmorton: *Virtus sola nobilitas* and *Moribus antiquis.*

Esek Steere Ballord

DESCENT from the Surety for the observance of the Magna Charta:

William de Lanvallei.

1. **William de Lanvallei,** one of the Sureties for the Magna Charta, governor of Colchester Castle, who *d. s. p. m.* in 1217, had issue by his wife, whom he *m.* in 1212, a daughter of Alan Basset, of Wycombe, a descendant of Ralph Basset, of Weldon, justiciary of England, who *d.* 1120:

2. LADY HAWYSE DE LANVALLEI, only child and heiress, *d.* 1330, who *m.* Sir John de Burgh, eldest son (but not heir to his earldom) of Hubert de Burgh, Earl of Kent; justiciary of England; guardian of King Henry III.; a prominent character during the reign of Kings John and Henry III.; *d.* March 4, 1243, and his second wife, Lady Beatrix, widow of Dodo Bardolf, of Shelford, and daughter of William de Warren, of Wirmgay, Norfolk, son of Reginald, second son of William, first Earl of Warren and Surrey, and his wife, Lady Gundred, daughter of Queen Maud.

Sir John de Burgh, who fought under the Barons' banner at the battles of Lewes and Evesham, and the Lady Hawyse had:

3. JOHN DE BURGH, only son and heir, Baron of Lanvallei, He *d. s. p. m.* 1279, having issue by his wife, whose name has not been preserved:

4. LADY HAWYSE DE BURGH, coheiress, with her sisters, of her father; aunt of Elizabeth, second wife of King Robert

Bruce, who *m.* before 1279, Robert de Greslei, or Greilly, lord of Ringston and Portesdale, *d.* 1283, son of Thomas de Greslei, warden of the king's forests south of Trent, *d.* 1261, and had:

5. LADY JOAN DE GRESLEI, only daughter, sister and heiress of Sir Thomas de Greslei, K.B., *d. s. p.* 1347, who *m.* Sir John, Baron de la Warre, K.C.B., *d.* 1342, son and heir of Roger, Baron de la Warre, governor of Burgh Castle, in Gascoigne, *d.* 1321, and his wife, Lady Clarice, *d.* 1301, daughter and coheiress of John, Baron Tregoz, of Ewyas-Harold, summoned to Parliament in 1299, who served in the Welsh and French campaigns of Edward I., son of Robert de Tregoz, who lost his life fighting under the baronial banner at Evesham. Sir John de la Warre and the Lady Joan had:

6. LADY CATHERINE DE LA WARRE, who *m.* Sir Warine le Latimer, second Baron Latimer, of Braybroke, Northamptonshire, *d.* 1350, and had:

7. LADY ELIZABETH LATIMER, eventually her father's heiress, sister of Sir Thomas Latimer, second son and heir, leader of the "Lollards," a religious sect, *temp.* Richard II., who *d. s. p.*, his brother Edward being his heir, *d. s. p.* 1411, when his large estate devolved upon Lady Elizabeth's eldest son, his nephew, John Griffin. Lady Elizabeth Latimer *m.* Sir Thomas Griffin, of Weston-Favell, Northamptonshire, and had:

8. RICHARD GRIFFIN, of Weston-Favell (his eldest brother, John Griffin, was heir to Edward, last Baron Latimer), who *m.* Anne, daughter of Richard Chamberlain and his wife, Catherine Cotes, of Northamptonshire, and had:

9. SIR NICHOLAS GRIFFIN, of Braybroke, high sheriff of Northamptonshire, 1457, who had by his first wife, Catherine, daughter of John (or Richard) Curzon (or Curson):

10. JOHN GRIFFIN, of Braybroke, eldest son, who *m.* Em-

mote, daughter of Richard Wheathill, or Whettles, of Callis, or Callyce, and had:

11. CATHERINE GRIFFIN, second daughter, sister of Sir Nicholas Griffin, K.B., of Braybroke, sheriff of Northamptonshire, 1504, who *m.* as her first husband and his first wife, Sir John de Digby, of Eye-Kettleby, in Leicestershire, who was knighted by King Henry VII. for gallant service on Bosworth Field, *d.* 1533, son of Everard de Digby, M.P., of Tilton, Leicestershire, high sheriff of Rutlandshire, 1459, and his wife Jacquette, daughter of Sir John d'Ellis, of Devonshire. Sir John and Catherine Digby had:

12. WILLIAM DIGBY, of Kettleby and Luffenham, Leicestershire, *d.* before August 1, 1529. He and his two wives are mentioned in his father's will. He *m.* first, Rose, daughter of William Perwich (or Prestwith), of Luffenham, and his wife, a daughter of Sir Thomas Poultney, and *m.* secondly, Helen, daughter of John Roper, of Eltham, who *m.* secondly, Sir Edward Montague, lord chief justice of the King's Bench, an executor of the will of King Henry VIII. Her stepson, William Digby, was the executor of Lady Montague's will, and he had by his first wife:

13. SIMON DIGBY, of Bedale (or Beadell) manor, in Rutlandshire, who was condemned and executed for high treason in 1570, and lost his estates by attainder. He *m.* Anne, daughter of Reginald Grey, "of a Yorkshire family," and had:

14. EVERARD DIGBY, second son, who *m.* Katrina, daughter of Magister Stockbridge de Van der Shaff Theober de Newkirk, and had:

15. ELIZABETH DIGBY, *b.* 1584, *d.* 165-, who *m.* in 1614, Enoch Lynde, merchant, of London, *d.* 1636, aged fifty-six, a grandson of Nathan and Elizabeth Lynde, and had:

16. JUDGE SIMON LYNDE, of Boston, Massachusetts, *b.* London, 1624, *d.* 1687. He came to New England in 1650;

m. 1653, Hannah, *b.* 1635, daughter of John Newdigate, of London, *d.* Massachusetts, 1665, and had by her, who *d.* 1684:

17. JUDGE SAMUEL LYNDE, eldest child, *b.* December 1, 1653, *d.* October, 1721, *m.* October 20, 1674, Mary, daughter of Jervis Ballard. She was *b.* in Boston, May 27, 1657, *d.* February 1, 1697–8, and had:

18. MARY LYNDE, *b.* Boston, November 16, 1680, *d.* March 26, 1732, *m.* April 6, 1702, John Valentine, of Boston, *d.* 1742. He was the son of Rev. John Valentine, vicar of Frankfort, Sligo, Ireland, and was a lawyer and "notary and tabellion publick for Massachusetts Bay" in 1706, or crown advocate-general of the province of Massachusetts Bay and New Hampshire and colony of Rhode Island, and was warden of King's Chapel, Boston, and buried there. They had:

19. THOMAS VALENTINE, fifth child, *b.* August 3, 1713, *d.* April 17, 1783, *m.* in July, 1735, Elizabeth, daughter of James and Elizabeth (Hobby) Gooche. Elizabeth Hobby was the daughter of Sir Charles Hobby. He commanded the Boston regiment at the taking of Porte Royal (Annapolis), and was appointed vice-governor of that place. They had:

20. ELIZABETH VALENTINE, *b.* May 18, 1739, *d.* March 26, 1807, *m.* Zaccheus Ballord, *b.* March 21, 1731, *d.* Thompson, Connecticut, in 1800, who was fourth in descent from William Ballord, of Lynn, a soldier in the French and Indian War, also in the Revolution, in Colonel Shepard's (the Fourth Massachusetts) regiment. *Issue:*

21. LYNDE BALLORD, *b.* May 15, 1774, *d.* June 7, 1825, at Thompson, Connecticut; *m.* December 4, 1794, Polly, *b.* 1777, *d.* June 22, 1816, daughter of John Bates and Chloe Fuller, his wife. Polly Bates was fifth in descent from Clement Bates, 1595–1671, of Hingham, England, and Massachusetts, and her mother was fourth from Robert Fuller, of Salem, and fifth from Isaac Allerton, the Pilgrim. *Issue:*

22. REV. JOHN BATES BALLORD, eldest son, *b.* October 25, 1795, *d.* January 29, 1856. He was educated for the ministry at Madison University (now Colgate), and died in New York City. He *m.* May 28, 1824, Augusta Maria Gilman, *b.* in Gilmanton, New Hampshire, June 26, 1804, *d.* May 17, 1890, in Colchester, Connecticut. She was sixth in descent from Edward Gilman, who came from Hingham, England, to Hingham, Massachusetts, in 1638. Her family were descendants of Cilmin Troed-dhu, founder of the IV Noble Tribe of Wales, who was a descendant of Coel Godeboc, King of Briton and Duke of Colchester, *circa* A.D. 300. Rev. John Bates Ballord and Augusta Gilman, his wife, had:

23. ESEK STEERE BALLORD, of Davenport, Iowa, a founder of the Order of Runnemede and member of the Society Sons of the Revolution and Society of Colonial Wars, *b.* July 26, 1830, Bloomfield, Connecticut; *m.* September 4, 1862, Frances A. Webb, *b.* January 20, 1836, seventh in descent from Christopher Webb and seventh from Henry Adams, both of Braintree, Massachusetts, and had issue, all born in Davenport:

I. Katharine Augusta (Wellesley College), *b.* August 5, 1864, *m.* June 26, 1888, Leon M. Allen, and had:
   1. Leon Ballord, *b.* January 9, 1891, Davenport, Iowa.
   2. Frances Priscilla, *b.* April 17, 1894.
   3. Allerton, b. February 6, 1898.

II. Bessie Webb Ballord (Wellesley College), *b.* November 19, 1866.

III. Belle Ballord, *b.* September 16, 1868; *m.* June 7, 1893, Jennis Brock Richardson.

IV. John Gilman Ballord, *b.* June 14, 1870, of St. Hilaire, Minnesota.

V. Webb Rysse Ballord, *b.* March 12, 1876, naval architect.

THE PEDIGREE OF ANTHONY J. BLEECKER.

```
                                    Roger Bigod.
                                    Hugh Bigod.
William de Lanvallei.  Richard de Clare.  Ralph Bigod.                              Saber
Hawise de Lanvallei.   Gilbert de Clare.  Isabel Bigod.      Robert de Vere.          de
John de Burgh.         Isabel de Clare.   John Fitz-John.    Hugh de Vere—Hawise de
Margaret de Burgh.     Robert de Bruce.   Maud Fitz-John.    Robert de Vere.         Quincey.
   Elizabeth de Burgh—Robert Bruce, King  Isabel de Beauchamp.  Joan de Vere.
   Margaret de Bruce.        of Scotland. Maud de Chaworth.     Alice de Warren.
   William de Sutherland.           Eleanor Plantagenet—Richard Fitz-Alan.
   Robert de Sutherland.            Alice Fitz-Alan.
   John de Sutherland.              Margaret de Holland.
      John de Sutherland—           Joan de Beaufort—James I., King of Scotland.
                        Annabel Stewart—George Gordon.
                    Elizabeth de Sutherland—Adam Gordon, of Aboyne.
           Alexander Gordon, Earl of Sutherland,—Lady Janet Stewart.
           Sir John Gordon, Earl of Sutherland,—Lady Helen Stewart.
           Alexander Gordon, Earl of Sutherland—Lady Jean Gordon.
                     Sir Robert Gordon, Bart.,—Louise Gordon.
                     Catherine Gordon—Col. David Barclay, of Ury.
     John Barclay, Deputy-Governor of East Jersey,—Cornelia Van Schaick.
               Rev. Thomas Barclay, of Albany, N. Y.,—Anna Dorothea Draiyer.
               Andrew Barclay, of New York City,—Helena Roosevelt.
               Anna Dorothy Barclay—Theophylact Bache, of N. Y.
                           Sarah Bache—James Bleecker, of N. Y.
               Anthony J. Bleecker, of N. Y.,—Cornelia Van Benthuysen.
                     James Bleecker, of N. Y.,—Jane Clarkson Hill.
                        Anthony J. Bleecker, of New York City.
```

Anthony James Bleecker

DESCENT from the Sureties for the observance of the Magna Charta:

Hugh Bigod,
Roger Bigod,
Gilbert de Clare,
Richard de Clare,

William de Lanvallei,
Saher de Quincey,
Robert de Vere.

1. **William de Lanvallei,** one of the Sureties for the Magna Charta, *d. s. p. m.* 1217, who *m.* 1212, a daughter of Alan Basset, of Wycombe, and had:

2. LADY HAWYSE DE LANVALLEI, *d.* 3 Edward I., who *m.* Sir John, second Baron de Burgh, knighted by Henry III. in 1229, eldest son of Hubert de Burgh, Earl of Kent, chief justice of England, guardian of King Henry III., *d.* May 4, 1243, and had:

3. JOHN DE BURGH, Baron of Lanvallei, *d. s. p. m.* 1279, eldest son and heir, who had by his wife, whose name has not been preserved:

4. LADY MARGARET DE BURGH, who *m.* Richard de Burgh, Baron of Connaught and Trim, second Earl of Ulster, called the Red Earl, lord justice of Ireland, in 1296, *d.* 1326, a descendant of Andelm de Burgh, steward to King Henry III. of England, and his wife, Princess Agnes, daughter of Louis VII., KING OF FRANCE, and had:

5. LADY ELIZABETH DE BURGH, *d.* October 26, 1327, who *m.* in 1302, as his second wife, ROBERT BRUCE, KING OF SCOTLAND, when he was the Earl of Carrick. Robert de Bruce, Earl of Carrick, the restorer of the Scottish mon-

archy, crowned as Robert I., King of Scotland, was the eldest son of Robert de Bruce, *d.* 1304, Earl of Annandale, eldest son of Robert, Earl of Annandale, *d.* 1295, and his first wife, *m.* 1244, Lady Isabel, daughter of Gilbert de Clare, son of Richard de Clare, both Sureties for the Magna Charta.

Lady Elizabeth de Burgh and Robert I., King of Scotland, had:

6. PRINCESS MARGARET BRUCE, *d.* 1358, sister of David II., King of Scotland, and widow of Robert Glen, of Pittedy, Fife. She *m.* secondly, 1344, as his first wife, William, Earl of Sutherland, *d.* 1370, and had:

7. WILLIAM, EARL OF SUTHERLAND, second and only surviving son, who died "towards the close of the sixteenth century," having issue by his wife, whose name has not been preserved:

8. ROBERT, EARL OF SUTHERLAND, *d.* 1442. He was at the battle of Homildon, 1402, and in 1427 was sent to England as a hostage for James I. He *m.* Lady Mabilla, daughter of John, Earl of Moray, second son of Patrick Dunbar, Earl of Dunbar and March, *d.* 1369,* and his first wife, Lady Agnes Randolph,† known as "Black Agnes," who,

---

* He was the eldest son of Patrick, Earl of Dunbar, one of the competitors for the crown of Scotland, in 1291, as the great-grandson of Lady Ada, a daughter of KING WILLIAM THE LION, OF SCOTLAND, the eldest son of Patrick, Earl of Dunbar, a regent of the kingdom and a guardian of the king and queen, 1255, *d.* 1289, by his wife, Lady Christiana, only daughter of Robert de Bruce, Earl of Annandale and Carrick, *d.* 1304, aforesaid, a descendant of Gilbert de Clare and Richard de Clare, both Sureties for the Magna Charta.

† Her father, Thomas Randolph, first Earl of Moray, regent of Scotland, was the only son of Sir Thomas Randolph, of Strathwith, high chamberlain of Scotland, 1296, and his wife, Lady Isabel, sister of King Robert Bruce and daughter of Robert, Earl of Annandale and Carrick, *d.* 1304, eldest son of Robert, Earl of Annandale, *d.* 1295, one of the competitors for the crown of Scotland, 1290 (son of Robert de Bruce, Earl of Annandale, and his wife, Lady Isabel, second daughter of David, Earl of Huntingdon, a brother of

during the absence of her husband, successfully defended the Castle of Dunbar for nineteen weeks against the English in 1337.

Robert, Earl of Sutherland, and Lady Mabilla Dunbar had:

9. JOHN, EARL OF SUTHERLAND, who died in 1460, leaving issue by his wife, Lady Margaret, daughter of Sir William Baillie, of Lamington, Lanark:

10. JOHN, EARL OF SUTHERLAND, who, dying in 1508, had issue by his wife, Lady Margaret Macdonald, eldest daughter of Alexander, Earl of Ross, lord of the Isles, *d.* 1448–9, and his wife, Lady Elizabeth, only daughter of Alexander Seton, lord of Gordon and Huntly:

11. ELIZABETH, COUNTESS OF SUTHERLAND, only daughter, sister and heiress of John, Earl of Sutherland, who *d. s. p.* 1514. She was enfeoffed in the earldom June 30, 1515, *d.* in September, 1535. She *m. ante* October 3, 1514, Adam Gordon, of Aboyne, *d.* March 17, 1527, who in right of his wife was Earl of Sutherland. He was the second son of George Gordon, second Earl of Huntly,* and his wife,

---

King William the Lion, and son of Prince Henry, Earl of Huntingdon, the son of DAVID I., KING OF SCOTLAND, whose mother was the daughter of Prince Edward, the exile, of England, son and heir of EDMUND IRONSIDES, KING OF ENGLAND), and his first wife, *m.* 1344, Lady Isabel, daughter of Gilbert de Clare, son of Richard de Clare, both Sureties for the Magna Charta.

* He was the eldest son of Alexander de Seton, lord of Gordon, created Earl of Huntley in 1445, *d.* 1470, eldest son of Sir William de Seton by his wife, Lady Elizabeth, only child of Sir Adam Gordon, of Huntly, slain at Homildon, September 14, 1402, by his wife, Lady Elizabeth, daughter of Sir William de Keith, great marshal of Scotland, *d.* 1406–8, and his wife, Lady Margaret, only child of Sir John Fraser, eldest son of Sir Alexander Fraser, high chamberlain of Scotland, and his wife, Lady Mary, sister of King Robert I. and daughter of Robert de Bruce, Earl of Annandale, aforesaid, *d.* 1304, and his wife Marjory, Countess of Carrick, descendants of DAVID I., KING OF SCOTLAND, and of Gilbert de Clare and Richard de Clare, both Sureties for the observance of the Magna Charta.

214 THE MAGNA CHARTA BARONS

Princess Annabella, daughter of JAMES I., KING OF SCOTLAND,* by his wife, Lady Joan de Beaufort.

Lady Joan de Beaufort, aforesaid, who *m*. 1424, as her first husband, King James I., was a daughter of John de Beaufort, K.G., Earl of Somerset, Marquis of Dorset, lord high admiral and high chamberlain of England, *d*. 1410 (a son of John, Duke of Lancaster, King of Castile and Leon, son of EDWARD III., KING OF ENGLAND, and his wife, Lady Philippa, of Hainault), and his wife, Lady Margaret de Holland, daughter of Thomas, second Earl of Kent, earl marshal of England, *d*. 1397 (son of Sir Thomas de Holland, K.G., Earl of Kent, captain-general of France and Normandy, *d*. 1360, by his wife, Lady Joan Plantagenet, the Fair Maid of Kent, daughter of Edmund, Earl of Kent, a son of EDWARD I., KING OF ENGLAND, and his second wife, Princess Margaret, daughter of PHILIP III., KING OF FRANCE), and his wife, Lady Alice, daughter of Richard Fitz-Alan, K.G., Earl of Arundel and Surrey, *d*. 1375–6, by his second wife, Lady Eleanor Plantagenet, *d*. 1372, daughter of Henry, third Earl of Lancaster, *d*. 1345 (son of Edmund, Earl of Lancaster, *d*. 1295, a son of HENRY III., KING OF ENGLAND), and his wife, Lady Maud, daughter of Patrick de Chaworth by his wife, Lady Isabel, daughter of William de Beauchamp, created Earl of Warwick, *d*. 1298, and his wife, Lady Maud, widow of Gerard de Furnival, of Sheffield, and daughter of John Fitz-John, chief justice of Ireland, 1258, son of John Fitz-Geoffrey, lord of Berkhampsted and Kirkling, sheriff of Yorkshire, 1234, lord justice of Ireland, 30 Henry III., by his wife, Lady Isabel, widow of Gilbert de Lacie and

---

* KING JAMES I., murdered at Perth, February 21, 1437–8, was the third son of KING ROBERT III., the son of KING ROBERT II., the only son of Walter, lord high steward of Scotland, by his second wife, Princess Marjory Bruce, daughter of KING ROBERT I., a descendant of Gilbert de Clare and Richard de Clare, both Sureties for the Magna Charta.

MEMBERS OF THE ORDER OF RUNNEMEDE   215

daughter of Sir Ralph Bigod, son of **Hugh Bigod**, son of **Roger Bigod**, both Sureties for the Magna Charta and Earls of Norfolk.

Richard Fitz-Alan was son of Edmund Fitz-Alan, K.B., Earl of Arundel, beheaded in 1326, and his wife, *m.* 1305, Lady Alice, daughter of William de Warren, *d.* 1286, by his wife, Lady Joan, daughter of Robert de Vere, Earl of Oxford, *d.* 1296, son of Hugh, Earl of Oxford, great high chamberlain, *d.* 1263 (by his wife, Lady Hawyse, daughter of **Saber de Quincey**, one of the Sureties for the Magna Charta, Earl of Winchester), son of **Robert de Vere**, Earl of Oxford, one of the Sureties for the Magna Charta.

Elizabeth, Countess of Sutherland, and Adam Gordon had:

12. ALEXANDER GORDON, who was enfeoffed in the earldom of Sutherland in 1527, *d.* January 15, 1529. He *m.* Lady Janet, eldest daughter of Sir John Stewart, of Balvany,* created, in 1457, Earl of Athol, uterine brother to King James II., *d.* September 19, 1512, and his first wife, Lady Margaret of Galloway,† and had:

---

* He was the eldest son of Lady Joan de Beaufort, queen dowager of Scotland, a lineal descendant, as before stated, of kings of England and France, and of **Hugh Bigod**, **Roger Bigod**, **Saber de Quincey**, and **Robert de Vere**, Sureties for the Magna Charta, and her second husband, *m.* 1439, Sir James Stewart, the Black Knight of Lorn, who was the third son of Sir John Stewart, lord of Innermeth, and his wife, Lady Isabel, daughter of John d'Ergadia, lord of Lorn, by his wife, Lady Joanna, daughter of Thomas Isaac, Esq., and his wife, Princess Matilda, daughter of ROBERT BRUCE, KING OF SCOTLAND, by his second wife, Lady Elizabeth de Burgh, lineal descendants of **Gilbert de Clare**, **Richard de Clare**, and **William de Lanvallei**, Sureties for the observance of the Magna Charta.

¶ Margaret of Galloway, dowager of William, Earl of Douglas, was the only daughter of Archibald, Earl of Douglas and second Duke of Touraine, and his second wife, Lady Euphemia, eldest daughter of Sir Patrick Graham and his wife Euphemia, Countess of Strathern, daughter of David, Earl of Strathern, only son of ROBERT II., KING OF SCOTLAND, and his second wife,

13. SIR JOHN GORDON, eldest son, *b.* 1525, who succeeded as Earl of Sutherland, and, dying in July, 1567, had issue by his second wife, Lady Helen, *d.* 1563-5, widow of William, Earl of Erroll, and daughter of John Stewart, third Earl of Lennox, *k.* 1526,* and his wife, Lady Anne Stewart, daughter of John, first Earl of Athol, aforesaid:

14. ALEXANDER GORDON, Earl of Sutherland, *b.* 1552, *d.* December 6, 1594. He *m.* secondly, December 13, 1573, Lady Jean Gordon,† daughter of George, fourth Earl of

---

m. 1355, Euphemia, Countess of Moray, widow of John Randolph, Earl of Moray, *k.* 1346, and daughter of Hugh, Earl of Ross, and his second wife, Princess Matilda, sister of King Robert Bruce and daughter of Robert de Bruce, Earl of Annandale, *d.* 1304, a descendant of 𝔊ilbert de Clare and Ricbard de Clare, both Sureties for the Magna Charta.

* He was the second son of Matthew, second Earl of Lennox, *k.* at Flodden, 1513, and his wife, Lady Elizabeth Hamilton, niece of King James III. and daughter of James, first Lord Hamilton, *d.* 1479, and his wife, Princess Mary Stewart, daughter of JAMES II., KING OF SCOTLAND (and his wife, Lady Mary, daughter of Arnold, Duke of Gueldres), eldest son of Sir James Hamilton, of Cadyow, son of Sir John Hamilton, of Cadyow, *d.* 1397, by his wife, Lady Janet, daughter of James Douglas, lord of Dalkeith and Liddesdale, *d.* 1420, by his first wife, *m.* 1372, Lady Agnes Dunbar, daughter of Patrick, Earl of Dunbar, March, and Moray, *d.* 1369, and his first wife, Lady Agnes Randolph, descendants of 𝔊ilbert de Clare and Ricbard de Clare, both Sureties for the observance of the Magna Charta.

Earl Matthew was the son of Sir John Stewart, of Darnley, created Earl of Lennox, *d.* before September 11, 1495, son of Sir Alan Stewart, of Darnley, murdered in 1439, and his wife, Lady Catherine, daughter of Sir William de Seton, *k. v. p.* August 17, 1424, only son of Sir John de Seton, *d.* 1441, and his first wife, Lady Janet Dunbar, daughter of George, Earl of Dunbar and March, son of Patrick, ninth Earl, and his wife, Lady Agnes Randolph, descendants of Ricbard de Clare and 𝔊ilbert de Clare, both Sureties for the observance of the Magna Charta.

† Her mother was Lady Elizabeth, daughter of Robert, Lord Keith, *k.* at Flodden, 1513, and his wife, Lady Elizabeth Douglas, daughter of John, second Earl of Morton, eldest son of William Keith, third earl marshal, *d.* 1530 (and his wife, *m.* 1482, Lady Elizabeth Gordon, daughter of George, second Earl of Huntly, by Lady Annabella, daughter of JAMES I., KING OF SCOTLAND), son of William, second earl marshal, and his wife, Lady Mariota, or Muriella,

Huntly,* and formerly the wife of James, Earl of Bothwell, by whom she was divorced May 7, 1567, on account of a

daughter of Thomas, Lord Erskine, son of Sir Robert Erskine, Earl of Marr, 1435, d. 1453, and his wife, a daughter of Robert Stewart, lord of Lorn and Innermeth, by his wife, Lady Margaret Stewart, daughter of Robert, Duke of Albany, governor of Scotland, son of ROBERT II., KING OF SCOTLAND, a descendant of Richard de Clare and Gilbert de Clare, Sureties for the Magna Charta.

William, second earl marshal, aforesaid, was the son of Sir William de Keith, great marshal of Scotland, created earl marshal July 4, 1458, d. 1476, by his wife, Lady Mary, daughter of Sir James, eldest son of Sir John Hamilton, of Cadyow, d. 1397–8, by his wife, Lady Janet Douglas, aforesaid, a descendant of Gilbert de Clare and Richard de Clare, Sureties for the Magna Charta.

John, second Earl of Morton, aforesaid, was the son of James Douglas, of Dalkeith, created Earl of Morton 1457 (and his wife, Princess Joanna, widow of James, third Earl of Angus, and daughter of JAMES I., KING OF SCOTLAND, by his wife, Lady Joan de Beaufort, aforesaid, descendants of Gilbert de Clare, Richard de Clare, Hugh Bigod, Roger Bigod, Saber de Quincey, and Robert de Vere, Sureties for the Magna Charta), son of James Douglas, of Dalkeith, d. 1456, son of Sir James de Douglas, d. 1450–1 (by his wife, Princess Elizabeth Stewart, daughter of ROBERT III., KING OF SCOTLAND, a descendant of Richard de Clare and Gilbert de Clare, Sureties for the Magna Charta), son of Sir James de Douglas, d. 1420, and his first wife, Lady Agnes Dunbar, second daughter of Patrick, Earl of Dunbar and March, by his first wife, Agnes, Countess of Moray, aforesaid, descendants of Gilbert de Clare and Richard de Clare, Sureties for the Magna Charta.

* He was one of the regents of Scotland, 1536, and was constituted high chancellor, 1546, and was one of the chief commanders at the battle of Pinkie. He was granted the earldom of Moray, February 13, 1548–9, but subsequently he had the ill-will of the queen, and attacked her forces, under Moray, at Corrichil, October 28, 1562, when Huntly's men were defeated and himself trampled to death in the retreat. He was the son of John, Lord Gordon, d. v. p. December 5, 1517, eldest son of Alexander, third Earl of Huntly, a privy councillor to James IV., with whom he was at the battle of Flodden, September 9, 1513, and, with Lord Home, commanded the left wing of the Scottish army, and was one of the few who escaped the carnage of that disastrous day, and d. January 16, 1523–4. He m. first, October 14, 1474, Lady Joanna, or Janet, Stewart (mother of John, Lord Gordon), daughter of John, first Earl of Athol, d. 1512, uterine brother of King James II. and his wife, Margaret of Galloway, descendants of ROBERT II., KING OF SCOTLAND, and Richard de Clare and Gilbert de Clare, both Sureties for the Magna Charta.

Alexander, Earl of Huntly, was the eldest son of George, second Earl of

dispensation to marry not having been obtained, in order to make way for his nuptials with Queen Mary, and had:

15. SIR ROBERT GORDON, of Gordonstown, fourth son, *b.* May 14, 1580. In 1606 he was a gentleman of the privy chamber to King James VI., and was created a Baronet of Nova Scotia, being the first creation of that order, May 28, 1625, when he had a charter of the barony of Gordon, in Nova Scotia, and *d.* in 1656. He *m.* at London, February 16, 1613, Louise, *b.* December 20, 1597, only daughter and heiress of John Gordon, of Longormes, and dean of Salisbury, eldest son of Rev. Alexander Gordon, titular Archbishop of Athens, Bishop of Galloway, 1558, *d.* 1576, a brother of George Gordon, fourth Earl of Huntly, aforesaid, and a descendant of JAMES I., KING OF SCOTLAND, and Gilbert de Clare and Richard de Clare, Sureties for the Magna Charta. Sir Robert Gordon had by Louise Gordon:

16. LADY CATHERINE GORDON, second daughter, *b.* January 11, 1621–2, *d.* 1663, *m.* December 26, 1647–8, Colonel David Barclay, of Ury, in Kincardine, *b.* 1610, *d.* 1681, governor of Strathbogie, member of Parliament, 1654–58. He was imprisoned in Edinburgh Castle, 1663–4; joined the religious Society of Friends in 1666, and was again imprisoned, 1666–7, because of his religious belief. He received the title of colonel from Charles I., having served some time as major in the Swedish army. Lady Catherine Gordon had by Colonel David Barclay:

17. JOHN BARCLAY, *b.* 165–, second son, brother of Robert Barclay, author of the celebrated "Apology for the Quakers," and governor of East (New Jersey) Jersey for life, 1682. He resided at Perth Amboy, as deputy governor under his

---

Huntly, and his first wife, Princess Annabella Stewart, daughter of JAMES I., KING OF SCOTLAND, as aforesaid, descendants of Gilbert de Clare and Richard de Clare, Sureties for the Magna Charta.

elder brother, and, dying in 1731, left issue by his wife, *m.* in Perth Amboy, Cornelia van Schaick:

18. REV. THOMAS BARCLAY, minister at Albany, New York, younger son, who *m.* Anna Dorothea Draüyer, member of the Dutch Church, Albany, 1700, daughter of Andries Draüyer, admiral (Schout by Nacht) of the Danish naval force on the American coast, and his wife Gerritje, daughter of Levinius van Schaick, chosen alderman of Albany, New York, in July, 1686, and had:

19. ANDREW BARCLAY, of New York, who *m.* 1737, Helena, daughter of Jacobus Roosevelt, of New York, *b.* 1692, *d.* 1776, and his wife, Catherine Hardenbrook, and had:

20. ANNA DOROTHY BARCLAY, *b.* 1741, *d.* 1795, who *m.* 1760, Theophylact Bache, of New York, *b.* 1734, *d.* 1807, and had:

21. SARAH BACHE, *b.* 1774, *d.* 1852, who *m.* James Bleecker, of New York, and had:

22. ANTHONY J. BLEECKER, of New York, *b.* 1799, *d.* 1884, who *m.* Cornelia van Benthuysen, of Poughkeepsie, New York, and had:

23. JAMES BLEECKER, of New York, *b.* 1836, who *m.* Jane Clarkson Hill, *b.* 1839, and had:

24. ANTHONY JAMES BLEECKER, of New York City, one of the founders of the Order of Runnemede, a member of the Society of Colonial Wars, *b.* 1864, who *m.* September 8, 1892, Bertha de la Vergne Gilman, and had: Anthony Lispenard Bleecker, *b.* November 5, 1893, and Winthrop Gilman Bleecker, *b.* October 18, 1897.

    Arms.—*Per pale, az. and ar., on the first two chevronels embattled counter-embattled, or; on the second an oak branch fructed in pale, ppr.*

    Crest.—*A bleecker's brush, ar., in pale, above an inverted chevronel embattled, or.*

THE PEDIGREE OF DAVID S. BISPHAM.

Richard de Clare.
Gilbert de Clare. — Saber de Quincey.
Richard de Clare — John de Lacie — Margaret de Quincey. — Roger Bigod.
Gilbert de Clare. — Maud de Lacie. — Hugh Bigod.
Alianore de Clare — Hugh le Despencer. — Hugh le Despencer — Isabel de Beauchamp. — Ralph Bigod. — John Fitz-John. — Isabel Bigod. — Maud Fitz-John. — Robert de Vere. — Hugh de Vere. — Henry de Bohun. — Humphrey de Bohun. — William de Mowbray. — Roger de Mowbray.
Isabel le Despencer — Richard Fitz-Alan. — Edmund Fitz-Alan — Alice de Warren. — Robert de Vere. — Humphrey de Bohun. — Roger de Mowbray.
Richard Sergeaux — Philippa Fitz-Alan. — Richard Fitz-Alan — Eleanor Plantagenet. — Joan de Vere. — Humphrey de Bohun. — John de Mowbray.
Philippa Sergeaux — Robert Pashley. — Elizabeth Fitz-Alan — Thomas de Mowbray. — William de Bohun. — John de Mowbray.
John Pashley — Lowyn Gower. — Margaret de Mowbray — Robert Howard. — Elizabeth de Bohun.
Elizabeth Pashley — Reginald de Pympe. — Catherine Howard — Edward Nevill.
Anne de Pympe — John Scott. — Margaret Nevill — John Brooke.
Reginald Scott — Emeline Kempe. — Thomas Brooke — Dorothy Hayden.
Elizabeth Brooke — Thomas Wyatt.
Charles Scott — Jane Wyatt. — Thomas Wyatt — Jane Hawte.
Thomas Scott, of Edgerton, — Jane Knatchbull.
Dorothy Scott — Major Daniel Gotherson.
Dorothy Gotherson — John Davis, of Salem Co., N. J.
Judge David Davis, of Salem Co., N. J. — Dorothy Cousins.
Jacob Davis, of Salem Co., N. J. — Esther Wilkins.
Esther Davis — Joshua Lippincott, of Salem Co., N. J.
Lydia Lippincott — David Scull, of Philadelphia.
Jane Lippincott Scull — William D. Bispham, of Philadelphia.

David Scull Bispham

DESCENT from the Sureties for the observance of the Magna Charta:

Hugh Bigod,	John de Lacie,
Roger Bigod,	William de Mowbray,
Henry de Bohun,	Saher de Quincey,
Gilbert de Clare,	Robert de Vere.
Richard de Clare,	

1. **Richard de Clare,** one of the Sureties for the observance of the Magna Charta, sixth Earl of Clare and fourth Earl of Hertford, *d.* 1218, had by his wife, Lady Amicia, sister of King John's divorced wife, and second daughter of William, second Earl of Gloucester:

2. **Gilbert de Clare,** one of the Sureties for the Magna Charta, Earl of Clare and Hertford, and Earl of Gloucester, in right of his mother, *d.* 1229. He had by his wife, Lady Isabel Marshall, a sister of William Marshall, one of the Sureties for the Magna Charta, and daughter of William, Earl of Pembroke, the adviser of King John:

3. RICHARD DE CLARE, Earl of Clare, Hertford, and Gloucester, who was poisoned by a political enemy, in 1262. He *m.*, as his second wife, Lady Maud, daughter of **John de Lacie,** Earl of Lincoln, one of the Sureties for the observance of the Magna Charta, and his second wife, Lady Margaret, daughter of Robert de Quincey, second son of **Saher de Quincey,** one of the Sureties for the observance of the Magna Charta, and had by her:

4. GILBERT DE CLARE, surnamed the Red, Earl of Clare,

Hertford, and Gloucester, *d.* 1295. He *m.* May 2, 1290, as his second wife, the Princess Joan d'Acre, *d.* 1305, daughter of EDWARD I., KING OF ENGLAND, and his first wife, Eleanor of Castile, and had by her:

5. LADY ALIANORE DE CLARE, who *m.* May 1, 1306, as her first husband, Hugh le Despencer, Jr., one of the hapless favorites of King Edward I. He was the son of Hugh le Despencer and his wife, Lady Isabel de Beauchamp, and widow of Patrick de Chaworth, whom he *m.* without license and was heavily fined by King Edward I.

Hugh Spencer, the elder, to the very close of the reign of Edward I., enjoyed the favor of the king. When the Spencers, father and son, attained extraordinary eminence and influence with Edward II., the indignant Barons assembled and marched to St. Albans, whence they sent to Edward II. a demand that the Spencers should be banished. This the king declined to do, and thereupon the Barons, under Lancaster, proceeded towards London to seize it. The king then, at the instance of the queen, acquiesced, whereupon the Barons called a parliament and the Spencers were banished by them. However, the king soon raised an army, recalled the Spencers, and gave them important commands, and encountered and defeated the Barons at Boroughbridge. The Spencers now became more powerful than before, and the elder Hugh was created Earl of Winchester, and loaded with grants of forfeited estates. Hugh, Jr., also obtained many valuable grants, and the two used their influence to have the queen and the young prince banished as traitors. When the excitement had somewhat subsided the queen returned, rallied the defeated Barons about her, and marched to Bristol, where the king and his favorites were. They seized Hugh, the elder, and hanged him, in October, 1326. Hugh, Jr., and the king escaped, but were shortly captured, and by the queen's order his Majesty was consigned to Berkeley Castle, and was murdered the next year, and Hugh, Jr., was sentenced "to be drawn upon a hurdle, with trumps and trumpets, throughout all the city of Hereford," and was then hanged and quartered November 29, 1326. Thus terminated two of the most celebrated royal favorites in the history of England.

Lady Isabel de Beauchamp, aforesaid, was the daughter of William, Earl of Warwick (in right of his mother, Lady Isabel, daughter of William Mauduit, and sister and heiress to William Mauduit, Earl of Warwick), and his wife, Lady Maud, widow of Gerard de Furnival and a daughter of John Fitz-John, chief justice of Ireland, 1258, the son of John Fitz-Geoffrey, also chief justice of Ireland, by his wife, Lady Isabel, daughter of Sir Ralph, third son of **Hugh Bigod**, second Earl of Norfolk, eldest son of **Roger Bigod**, Earl of Norfolk, both Sureties for the observance of the Magna Charta, and descendants of HENRY I., KING OF FRANCE.

Lady Alianore de Clare and her first husband, Hugh le Despencer, the younger, had:

6. LADY ISABEL LE DESPENCER, who *m.*, as his first wife, Richard Fitz-Alan, K.G., ninth Earl of Arundel and seventh Earl of Surrey, from whom she was divorced, with the sanction of the Pope, having had by him an only child. He was the son of Edmund Fitz-Alan, K.B., Earl of Arundel, who was involved in the rebellion of the Earl of Lancaster, but was pardoned by Edward II. and given an important command in his army. He was captured by Barons and beheaded at Hereford, in 1326. His wife was Lady Alice, *m.* 1305, daughter of William de Warren, who *d. v. p.* 1286 (eldest son of John, seventh Earl of Warren and Surrey), and his wife, Lady Joan de Vere, daughter of Robert, fifth Earl of Oxford and sixth lord great chamberlain, *d.* 1296, son of Hugh, fourth Earl of Oxford, lord great chamber-

lain (and his wife, Lady Hawyse, daughter of **Saber de Quincey,** one of the Sureties for the Magna Charta), the son of **Robert de Vere,** one of the Sureties for the Magna Charta, Earl of Oxford, and lord great chamberlain, *d.* 1221.

Lady Isabel le Despencer and Richard Fitz-Alan, K.G., had:

7. LADY PHILIPPA FITZ-ALAN, only child, *m.* Sir Richard Sergeaux, lord of Sergeaux, in Cornwall, and had:

8. PHILIPPA SERGEAUX, *m.* Sir Robert Pashley, and had:

9. SIR JOHN PASHLEY, *m.* Lowys Gower, and had:

10. ELIZABETH PASHLEY, who *m.* Reginald de Pympe, of Nettlestead, in Kent, and their only daughter:

11. ANNE PYMPE, *m.* Sir John Scott, of Scott's Hall, high sheriff of Kent, 1528, and had:

12. SIR REGINALD SCOTT, of Scott's Hall, high sheriff of Kent, 1541–2, captain of the castle of Calais, *d.* December 16, 1554, who *m.* first, Emeline, daughter of Sir William Kempe, and had by her:

13. CHARLES SCOTT, of Edgerton, in Kent, *d.* 1617, who *m.* Jane, daughter of Sir Thomas Wyatt, of Allington Castle, Kent, executed as a rebel on Tower Hill, April 11, 1554, son of Sir Thomas Wyatt, of Allington Castle, poet laureate to King Henry VIII., *b.* 1503, *d.* 1542, by his wife, *m.* 1520, Lady Elizabeth, daughter of Thomas Brooke, third Baron Cobham, who served gallantly in Henry VIII.'s French campaigns, *d.* July 19, 1529.

Thomas, Baron Cobham, was the son of John, second Baron Cobham, in Kent, who distinguished himself in arms in the reigns of Edward IV. and Henry VII., and *d.* March 9, 1511–12, and his first wife, Lady Margaret, daughter of Edward Nevill, K.G., and his second wife, *m.* 1448, Lady Catherine, daughter of Sir Robert Howard, Duke of Norfolk, and earl marshal, *jure uxoris.* His wife, Lady Margaret, was the daughter, and eventually coheiress, of Thomas de Mowbray, K.G., created Earl of Nottingham, 1383, and constituted, in 1386, earl marshal of England, being the first who had the title of earl attached to the office, and in 1396 was created Duke of Norfolk. For political reasons, the duke was subsequently banished for life, and *d.* in 1400, of pestilence in Venice.

William de Mowbray, a Magna Charta Surety, had by his wife, Lady Agnes d'Albini, a daughter or a sister of William, second Earl of Arundel and Sussex: Roger de Mowbray, *d.* 1266, father of Roger, first Baron by writ, *d.* 1298, whose son John, second Baron, was executed in 1321, having issue by his wife, Lady Aliva de Braose: John, third Baron, *d.* 1361, *m.* Lady Joan, daughter of Henry Plantagenet, Earl of Lancaster, and his wife, Lady Maud de Chaworth,* and had: John, fourth Baron, *d.* 1368, *m.* Lady Elizabeth, daughter of John de Segrave, and his wife, Margaret Plantagenet, Duchess of Norfolk, only child of Thomas de Brotherton, Earl of Norfolk, earl marshal of England, a son of EDWARD I., KING OF ENGLAND, and his second wife, Princess Margaret, daughter of PHILIP III., THE HARDY, KING OF FRANCE, and had: Thomas de Mowbray, K.G., Earl of Nottingham, aforesaid.

Sir Thomas's second wife, the mother of Lady Margaret Howard, was Lady Elizabeth Fitz-Alan, daughter of Richard, tenth Earl of Arundel and Surrey, and his first wife, Lady Elizabeth de Bohun, daughter of William, K.G., Earl of Northampton, a hero of Cressy (and his wife, Lady Elizabeth, daughter of Bartholomew de Badlesmere, who was captured at the battle of Boroughbridge and hanged, drawn,

---

* She was a daughter of Patrick de Chaworth, 1253–1282, and his wife, Lady Isabel, daughter of William de Beauchamp, first Earl of Warwick, and his wife, Lady Maud Fitz-John, aforesaid, a descendant of **Hugh Bigod,** and **Roger Bigod,** both Magna Charta Sureties.

and quartered, 1322), fourth son of Humphrey de Bohun, Earl of Hereford and Essex, lord high constable, who was slain at Boroughbridge, fighting under the banner of the Barons, March 16, 1321-2 (and his wife, Princess Elizabeth Plantagenet, widow of John, Earl of Holland, and daughter of EDWARD I., KING OF ENGLAND, and his first wife, Eleanor of Castile), the eldest son of Humphrey, third Earl of Hereford and Essex, lord high constable of England, *d.* 1397, the son of Humphrey, *d. v. p.*, taken prisoner with his father, eldest son of Humphrey de Bohun, taken prisoner at the battle of Evesham, *d.* 1274, the son of **Henry de Bohun,** one of the Sureties for the observance of the Magna Charta, created Earl of Hereford and Essex.

Charles Scott, of Edgerton, and his wife, Jane Wyatt, had:

14. THOMAS SCOTT, of Edgerton, *b.* 1567, will dated in 1635. His estates in Kent County were sold in 167-. He *m.* 1604, Jane (Mary), second daughter of Joan Knatchbull, of Mershom Hatch, and had by her, who *d.* in 1616:

15. DOROTHY SCOTT, *bapt.* September 22, 1611. She *m.* secondly, about 1670, Joseph Hogben, who *d.* before 1680, and in 1680 she came to Oyster Bay, Long Island, New York, with her children by her first husband. She had by her first husband, Major Daniel Gotherson, of Cromwell's army, who visited Long Island and purchased land at Oyster Bay, August 28, 1633, returned home, and *d.* in 1666:

16. DOROTHY GOTHERSON, who *m.* 1680, John Davis, of Oyster Bay, Long Island. In 1705 they removed to Pilesgrove Township, Salem County, New Jersey. Their son:

17. JUDGE DAVID DAVIS, of Salem County, New Jersey, *m.* Dorothy Cousins, *b.* 1693, *d.* 1789, and had:

18. JACOB DAVIS, of Woodstown, Salem County, New

Jersey, *b.* 1734, *d.* 1820, who *m.* first, 1761, Esther Wilkins, *b.* 1736, *d.* 1785, and had by her:

19. ESTHER DAVIS, *b.* 1778, *d.* 1809, who *m.* 1800, Joshua Lippincott, of Salem County, New Jersey, *b.* 1774, *d.* 18—, and had:

20. LYDIA LIPPINCOTT, *b.* 1801, *d.* 1854, who *m.* 1823, David Scull, of Philadelphia, Pennsylvania, *b.* 1799, son of Gideon and Sarah Scull, of Sculltown, New Jersey, and had:

21. JANE LIPPINCOTT SCULL, who *m.* William D. Bispham, of Philadelphia, and had:

22. DAVID SCULL BISPHAM, of London, England, one of the founders of the Order of Runnemede. He *m.* Caroline, daughter of General Charles Seymour Russell, United States army, and had Vida and Francesca Leonie Bispham.

Arms.—*Gu., a chevron, ar., between three lions' heads, erased, ar., on a canton, or, a rose of the first, barbed and seeded of the second.*

Crest.—*On a ducal cap of maintenance, gu., turned up erm., a lion passant, ar., his dexter paw resting on an escutcheon of the first.*

THE PEDIGREE OF FREDERIC H. BETTS.

- Saher de Quincey.
  - Robert de Quincey.
    - Margaret de Quincey = John de Lacie.
- Richard de Clare.
  - Gilbert de Clare.
    - Richard de Clare = Maud de Lacie.
      - Gilbert de Clare.
        - Margaret de Clare.
          - Margaret d'Audley.
            - Hugh de Stafford = Phillippa Beauchamp.
              - Margaret de Stafford.
                - Phillippa de Nevill.
                  - Thomas de Dacre = Elizabeth Bowet.

- Roger Bigod.
  - Hugh Bigod.
    - Ralph Bigod.
      - Isabel Bigod.

- John Fitz-Robert.
  - Roger Fitz-John.
    - Robert Fitz-Roger.
      - Maud Fitz-John.
        - Guy de Beauchamp.
          - Thomas de Beauchamp.
      - John de Clavering.
        - Eve de Clavering.
          - Edmund d'Ufford.
            - Robert d'Ufford.
              - William Bowet = Amy d'Ufford.

- Geoffrey de Say.
  - William de Say.
    - William de Say.
      - Geoffrey de Say.
        - Geoffrey de Say.
          - Joan de Say.
            - William Fienes.
              - Roger Fienes.

- Robert de Vere.
  - Hugh de Vere.
    - Robert de Vere.
      - Joan de Vere.
        - Alice de Warren.
          - Richard Fitz-Alan.
            - Alice Fitz-Alan.
              - Eleanor de Holland.
                - Alice de Montacute.
                  - Alice de Nevill.

- Henry de Bohun.
  - Humphrey de Bohun.
    - Humphrey de Bohun.
      - Humphrey de Bohun.
        - William de Bohun.
          - Humphrey de Bohun.
            - Alianore de Bohun.
              - Anne Plantagenet.
                - John Bouchier.
                  - Humphrey Bouchier.

- Joan de Dacre = Richard Fienes.
- John Fienes = Alice Fitz-Hugh.
- Thomas Fienes = Anne Bouchier.
- Catherine Fienes = Richard Loudenoys, of Briede, Sussex.
- Mary Loudenoy = Thomas Harletenden, of Worthern, Kent.
- Roger Harletenden, of Kenardiston, Kent, = Elizabeth Hardres.
- Richard Harletenden, of Kenardiston, Kent, = Mary Hubbart.
- Mabel Harletenden = John Haynes, Governor of Massachusetts and Connecticut.
- Ruth Haynes = Samuel Wyllys.
- Mary Wyllys = Rev. Joseph Eliot.
- Abiel Eliot = Mary Leete.
- Wyllys Eliot = Abigail Ward.
- Sarah Eliot = John Scoville.
- Mary Ward Scoville = Frederic J. Betts.
- Frederic Henry Betts, of New York City.

Frederic Henry Betts

DESCENT from the Sureties for the observance of the Magna Charta:

Hugh Bigod,
Roger Bigod,
Henry de Bohun,
Gilbert de Clare,
Richard de Clare,

John Fitz-Robert,
John de Lacie,
Saher de Quincey,
Geoffrey de Say,
Robert de Vere.

1. **Richard de Clare,** one of the Sureties for the Magna Charta, Earl of Hertford, had by his wife, Lady Amicia, daughter of William, Earl of Gloucester:

2. **Gilbert de Clare,** one of the Sureties for the Magna Charta, Earl of Hertford, who had by his wife, Lady Isabel, daughter of William Marshall, Earl of Pembroke, Protector of England:

3. RICHARD DE CLARE, Earl of Hertford and Gloucester, who *m.* secondly, Lady Maud, daughter of **John de Lacie,** one of the Sureties for the Magna Charta, Earl of Lincoln, by his second wife, Lady Margaret, daughter of Robert de Quincey, *d. v. p.*, second son of **Saher de Quincey,** one of the Sureties for the Magna Charta, Earl of Winchester, and had:

4. SIR GILBERT DE CLARE, called the Red, Earl of Hertford and Gloucester, *d.* 1295, who had, by his second wife, *m.* May 2, 1290, Princess Joan Plantagenet, *d.* 1305, a daughter of EDWARD I., KING OF ENGLAND, by his wife, the Princess Eleanor, of Castile:

5. LADY MARGARET DE CLARE, widow of Piers de Gaves-

ton, Earl of Cornwall, who *m.* secondly, Hugh d'Audley, who was created, in 1377, Earl of Gloucester, and had by him, who *d.* 1347-9:

6. LADY MARGARET D'AUDLEY, only child, who *m.* Ralph de Stafford, K.G., one of the original members of the Order of Knights of the Garter, seneschal and captain-general of Aquitaine, a commander at Cressy, created, in 1351, Earl of Stafford, *d.* 1372, and had:

7. HUGH DE STAFFORD, K.G., second Earl of Stafford, a crusader, who *d.* in 1386. He *m.* Lady Philippa, daughter of Thomas de Beauchamp, K.G., third Earl of Warwick, one of the original Knights of the Garter, a commander at Cressy and Poictiers, and a crusader; *d.* 1369. His father was Guy, second Earl of Warwick, who died from poisoning August 12, 1315, the son of William de Beauchamp, of Elmley, Earl of Warwick (in right of his mother, Lady Isabel, sister and heiress of William de Mauduit, Earl of Warwick), by his wife, Lady Maud, widow of Gerard de Furnival, and the eldest daughter and coheiress of John Fitz-John, chief justice of Ireland, 1258, son of John Fitz-Geoffrey, sheriff of Yorkshire, 1234, chief justice of Ireland, 1246, and his wife, Lady Isabel, widow of Gilbert de Lacie, and daughter of Sir Ralph Bigod, third son of **Hugh Bigod**, son of **Roger Bigod**, both Sureties for the Magna Charta, and Earls of Norfolk.

Hugh, Earl of Stafford, and Lady Philippa had:

8. LADY MARGARET DE STAFFORD, *d.* 1370, who *m.*, as his first wife, Ralph de Nevill, K.G., created Earl of Westmoreland and great marshal of England, who took a leading part in the political drama of his day, and was active in raising Henry of Lancaster to the throne, *d.* 1425, and had:

9. LADY PHILIPPA DE NEVILL, who *m.* Thomas, Baron de Dacre, of Gillesland, 1387-1457, who was constituted chief forester of Inglewood, Cumberland, in 8 Henry V., and a

commissioner to treat for peace with James I. of Scotland, and had:

10. THOMAS DE DACRE, eldest son, who *d. v. p.* His brother, Humphrey de Dacre, third son, was summoned to Parliament in 1482 as Baron Dacre of Gillesland, or of the North, his chief seat being in Cumberland, to distinguish him from Sir Richard Fienes, who was summoned as Baron Dacre, and was known as Baron Dacre of the South, his chief possessions being in County Sussex.

Thomas de Dacre *m*. Lady Elizabeth, daughter and heiress of Sir William Bowet, of Cumberland, *d*. 1423, and his wife, Lady Amy, daughter and coheiress of Sir Robert d'Ufford, *d*. 1400 (by his wife Helen, daughter of Sir Thomas Felton), eldest son of Sir Edmund d'Ufford (heir to his elder brother, John, Baron Ufford), of Horsford, *d*. 1374 (and his wife, Lady Sibilla, daughter of Sir Simon Pierpont, of Henstead, Suffolk), youngest son of Sir Ralph d'Ufford (brother of Robert d'Ufford, K.G., created, 1337, Earl of Suffolk), justice of Ireland, *d*. 1346, and his second wife, Lady Eve, only daughter and heiress of John de Clavering, Lord of Horsford, Norfolk, second Baron by summons, 1299–1331, *d*. 1332, eldest son of Robert Fitz-Roger, lord of Warkworth and Clavering, a gallant soldier in the Scottish wars of Edward I., summoned to Parliament 1295, *d*. 1311, eldest son of Roger Fitz-John, feudal Baron of Warkworth and Clavering, *d*. 1249, eldest son of **John Fitz-Robert,** one of the Sureties for the Magna Charta.

Thomas de Dacre had by the Lady Elizabeth Bowet:

11. LADY JOAN DE DACRE, *b*. 1432, heir-general to her grandfather. Her will was proved June 14, 1486. She *m. ante* 1457, Sir Richard Fynes, or Fiennes, who was declared Baron Dacre, in right of his wife, by Edward IV., and was so summoned to Parliament, 1459–82. He was constable of the Tower of London and lord chamberlain to the

household of King Edward IV., and *d.* 1484-5. He and his wife were buried in All Saints' Church, Hertsmonceaux, Sussex.

Sir Richard Fienes was the son of Sir Roger, treasurer of the household to Henry VI., the son of Sir William, high sheriff of Surrey and Sussex, 1297, the son of Sir William Fynes, and his wife, Lady Joan, daughter of Sir Geoffrey, second Baron de Say, admiral of the king's fleet, *d.* 1359, by his wife, Lady Maud, a daughter of the above Guy, Earl of Warwick, a descendant of **Roger Bigod** and **Hugh Bigod,** both Sureties for the Magna Charta. He was the eldest son of Geoffrey, *d.* 1322, son of William, *d.* 1295, son of William, *d.* 1272, the son of **Geoffrey de Say,** one of the Sureties for the Magna Charta.

Sir Richard Fienes, Baron Dacre, and Lady Joan had:

12. SIR JOHN FIENES, eldest son, who *d. v. p.* He *m.* Lady Alice, daughter of Henry, Baron Fitz-Hugh, of Ravensworth, who was, during the reign of Henry VI., firmly attached to the Lancastrian interest, but on the accession of Edward IV., the champion of the Yorkists, he was employed by him in a military capacity and as a diplomatist. In 1468 he made a pilgrimage to the Holy Sepulchre, and *d.* at Ravensworth in 1472. His wife, and mother of Lady Alice Fitz-Hugh, was Lady Alice, daughter of Richard Nevill, K.G., Earl of Salisbury,* by his wife, Lady Alice Mont-

---

* He was the eldest son of Ralph de Nevill, K.G., first Earl of Westmoreland, by his second wife, Lady Joan de Beaufort, daughter of John, Duke of Lancaster, son of EDWARD III., KING OF ENGLAND. Sir Richard obtained from Henry VI. numerous substantial grants and some of the highest and most important trusts; yet he was one of the earliest to espouse the cause of the House of York, and one of the most determined in maintaining it. His lordship fought and won, in conjunction with the Duke of York, the first pitched battle—that of St. Albans—between the contending "Roses," and himself defeated Audley at Bloreheath in 1458-9, and again in 1460 at Northampton, when he was constituted, by the Yorkists, lord great chamberlain. At the

MEMBERS OF THE ORDER OF RUNNEMEDE   233

acute, daughter and heiress of Thomas, Earl of Salisbury, who was concerned in so many military exploits that to give an account of them all would be to write the history of the reign of Henry V. His first wife, mother of Lady Alice Montacute, was Lady Eleanor, daughter of Thomas de Holland, second Earl of Kent, who, upon the accession of his half-brother, King Richard II., was constituted marshal of England. His wife, mother of Lady Eleanor de Holland, was Lady Alice, daughter of Richard Fitz-Alan, K.G., Earl of Arundel and Surrey, *d.* 1375-6, by his second wife, Lady Eleanor Plantagenet.* He was the son of Edmund, K.B., eighth Earl of Arundel, who fell a victim to the ill-will of Mortimer and the queen, and was executed at Hereford in 1326. His wife was Lady Alice, daughter of William de Warren, *d.* 1286, by his wife, Lady Joan de Vere, daughter of Robert, Earl of Oxford, lord great chamberlain, *d.* 1296, the son of Hugh, Earl of Oxford, lord great chamberlain, *d.* 1203 (by his wife, Lady Hawyse, daughter of **Saber de Quincey,** one of the Sureties for the Magna Charta, Earl of Winchester), the son of **Robert de Vere,** Earl of Oxford and lord great chamberlain, one of the Sureties for the Magna Charta.

Sir John Fienes and Lady Alice Fitz-Hugh had:

13. THOMAS FIENES, K.B., *b.* 1470, who, as heir to his grandfather, succeeded as Baron Dacre of the South, and was made a Knight of the Bath by Henry VII. in 1495-6. His will was probated in 1534. His wife was Lady Anne,

---

battle of Wakefield he was captured, when his head was immediately cut off and fixed upon a pole over one of the gates of York, in December, 1460.

* She was the daughter of Henry, third Earl of Lancaster, *d.* 1345 (son of Edmund, Earl of Lancaster, *d.* 1295, the son of HENRY III., KING OF ENGLAND, and his wife, Lady Eleanor, of Provence), by his wife, Lady Maud, daughter of Patrick de Chaworth, 1253-1282, and his wife, Lady Isabel, daughter of William de Beauchamp, first Earl of Warwick, by his wife, Lady Maud Fitz-John, aforesaid, descended from **Hugh Bigod** and **Roger Bigod,** both Sureties for the Magna Charta.

16

daughter of Sir Humphrey Bouchier, who was *k. v. p.* at Barnetfield, fighting under the banner of Edward IV., eldest son of John Bouchier, K.G.

"John Bouchier de Berners, Chevalier" appears to have played a safe game between the Houses of York and Lancaster, as in the reign of Henry VI. he fought at St. Albans under the Red Rose, and in that of Edward IV. was a stanch adherent of the White Rose, and was made constable of Windsor Castle, and *d.* in 1474. Sir John, who *m.* Lady Margery, daughter and heiress of Richard Berners, of West Horsley, Surrey, was the fourth son of William de Bouchier, Earl of Ewe, and his wife, Lady Anne Plantagenet, widow of both Thomas and Edmund, Earls of Stafford, a daughter of Thomas, Duke of Gloucester, *d.* 1397 (youngest son of EDWARD III., KING OF ENGLAND), by his wife, Alianore de Bohun, a daughter and coheiress of Humphrey, the last Earl of Hereford and Essex and second Earl of Northampton, *d.* 1372, and his wife, Lady Joan Fitz-Alan.*

Humphrey, the last Earl of Hereford and Essex, was the only son of Sir William de Bohun, K.G., a person of great eminence in the turbulent times in which he lived, and one of the gallant heroes of Cressy, and was created, March 17, 1337, Earl of Northampton, and from this date was a constant companion in arms of the martial Edward and his illustrious son, and *d.* in 1360. Earl William was the brother of three Earls of Hereford and Essex, and the fourth son of Humphrey de Bohun, Earl of Hereford and

---

* She was a daughter of Richard Fitz-Alan, K.G., ninth Earl of Arundel (by his second wife, Lady Eleanor Plantagenet, daughter of Henry, third Earl of Lancaster, a grandson of HENRY III., KING OF ENGLAND, and his wife, Lady Maud de Chaworth, aforesaid, a descendant of Hugh Bigod and Roger Bigod, both Sureties for the Magna Charta), who was, as before stated, a descendant of Sabet de Quincey and Robert de Vere, both Sureties for the Magna Charta.

Essex, lord high constable of England, who was slain in the battle of Boroughbridge, March 16, 1321-2, and his wife, *m.* November 14, 1302, Lady Elizabeth Plantagenet, widow of John de Vere and daughter of EDWARD I., KING OF ENGLAND, and his wife Eleanor, of Castile.

This latter Earl Humphrey was the son of Humphrey de Bohun, also Earl of Hereford and Essex and lord high constable, *d.* in 1297, the eldest son of Humphrey de Bohun, *d. v. p.*, who was taken prisoner at Evesham with his father, also named Humphrey, who was the eldest son of **Henry de Bohun**, one of the Sureties for the Magna Charta, Earl of Hereford and lord high constable of England.

Sir Thomas Fienes, K.B., and Lady Anne had:

14. LADY CATHERINE FIENES (sister of Sir Thomas Fienes, eldest son, who *d. v. p.*, father of Thomas, Baron Dacre of the South, executed in 1541, aged twenty-four years), second daughter, who *m.* Richard Loudenoys, son of Richard Loudenoys, or Londoniis, of Briade, or Breame, in Sussex, and had:

15. MARY LOUDENOYS, only child, who *m.* Thomas Harlakenden, of Worthorn, or Warhorn, Kent, his will proved in 1564 (see the "Visitations of Kent," 1574, Nichol's "Topographer and Genealogist," I. 228, Savage's "Geneal. Dic. of New England," Waters's "Genealogical Gleanings in England," the N. E. Hist. Geneal. Reg., xiv. and xv. etc.), and had:

16. ROGER HARLAKENDEN, of Kenardiston and Woodchurch, Kent, third son; *b.* 1535, *d.* 1603. He was steward to Edward de Vere, Earl of Oxford, and in 1583 purchased from him the manor of Earl's Colne, Essex. He *m.* first, Elizabeth, daughter of Thomas Hardres, of Kentshire, and widow of George Harlakenden, of Woodchurch, and had by her:

17. RICHARD HARLAKENDEN, of Kenardiston, Earl's Colne,

and Staple's Inn, *b.* 1565, *d.* August 24, 1631, who *m.* Mary (or Margaret), daughter of Edward Hubbart, or Hobart, of Stanstead-Montfichet, and had:

18. MABEL HARLAKENDEN, seventh daughter, *b.* at Earl's Colne, September 27, 1614. In 1635 she came with her brother, Roger Harlakenden, to New England, and *m.* first, in 1636, as his second wife, John Haynes, of Cambridge, Massachusetts, 1594–1653, and *m.* secondly, November 17, 1654, Samuel Eaton, son of Theophilus Eaton, first governor of the New Haven Colony.

John Haynes, of Copford Hall, Essex, *b.* May 1, 1594, arrived at Boston September 4, 1633. He was made freeman "at a General Court holden at Boston," May 14, 1634; elected an assistant in 1634 and 1636, and governor of the Bay Colony in 1635. He was colonel of the Second Regiment Massachusetts Militia in 1636. In 1637 he removed to Connecticut and settled at Hartford, and was elected the first governor of that colony in April, 1639, and every second year afterwards until his death, March 1, 1654. His will was of October 27, 1646, and was exhibited to the court of magistrates July 11, 1654. He had by his wife, Mabel Harlakenden:

19. RUTH HAYNES, *b.* Hartford, Connecticut, 1639, who *m.*, in 1655, Samuel Wyllys, *b.* February 19, 1631–2, *d.* 1709, assistant governor of the Connecticut Colony, son of George Wyllys (son of Richard Wyllys, of Fenny Compton manor, Warwickshire), who came to New England and settled at Hartford in 1638, and became governor of the Connecticut Colony in 1642, and had:

20. MARY WYLLYS, *b.* 1656, *d.* October 11, 1689, who *m.*, 1684, Rev. Joseph Eliot, of Guilford, Connecticut, *b.* December 20, 1638, *d.* May 26, 1694, son of Rev. John Eliot, the apostle to the Indians, and had:

21. ABIAL ELIOT, *b.* 1686–7, *d.* October 28, 1776, who *m.*

1726, Mary Leete, *b.* February 18, 1701, *d.* January 12, 1778, a great-granddaughter of William Leete, governor of the Connecticut Colony, and had:

    22. WYLLYS ELIOT, *b.* February 9, 1731, *d.* September 23, 1777, who *m.* Abigail, *b.* April 22, 1731, daughter of Colonel Andrew Ward, who served at Louisburgh in 1745, and was a member of the House of Deputies of Connecticut, and sister of General Andrew Ward, and had:

    23. SARAH ELIOT, *b.* February 28, 1772, *d.* February 12, 1852, who *m.* John Scoville, *b.* August 12, 1770, *d.* August 19, 1816, and had:

    24. MARY WARD SCOVILLE, *b.* August 13, 1812, *d.* July 2, 1868, who *m.* Frederic J. Betts, *b.* July 2, 1803, *d.* October 19, 1879, acting district attorney of Orange County, New York, 1823, master in chancery, New York, quartermaster on staff of Governor Clinton, New York, 1826, clerk of the United States Circuit Court in New York and judge of Hustings Court of Campbell County, Virginia, who was descended from Thomas Betts, one of the founders of Guilford, Connecticut, and Edward Rosseter, one of the early assistants of the colony of Massachusetts Bay, and had:

    25. FREDERIC H. BETTS, of New York City, a member of the Society Sons of the Revolution and of the Society of Colonial Wars, a founder of the Order of Runnemede, *b.* March 8, 1843, *m.* October 16, 1867, Mary Louise Holbrook, and had:

    I. Louis Frederic Holbrook Betts, *b.* May 21, 1870.

    II. Mary Eliot, *b.* October 19, 1871, who *m.* January 28, 1892, Russell H. Hoadley, and has two children:

        1. Sheldon Eliot, *b.* November 20, 1894.

        2. Louise Russell, *b.* March 20, 1896.

    III. Wyllys Rosseter Betts, *b.* May 12, 1875.

THE PEDIGREE OF ROBERT C. LAWRENCE.

- Saher de Quincey.
- Robert de Quincey.
- Margaret de Quincey=John de Lacie.
  - Maud de Lacie=Richard de Clare.
    - Roger Bigod.
    - Hugh Bigod.
    - Ralph Bigod.
    - Isabel Bigod=Gilbert de Clare.
      - John Fitz-John=Richard de Clare.
      - Maud Fitz-John=Thomas de Clare.
      - Guy de Beauchamp=Thomas de Clare.
      - Thomas de Beauchamp=Maud de Clare.
        - Roger de Clifford=Maud de Beauchamp.
          - Catherine de Clifford.
            - Maud de Greystock=Eudo de Welles.
              - William de Mowbray.
              - Roger de Mowbray.
              - Roger de Mowbray.
              - John de Mowbray.
              - John de Mowbray.
              - John de Mowbray.
              - Margery de Mowbray=John de Welles.
                - Mary de Welles=John Lawrence, of Rixton Manor.
                  - Margaret Lawrence=Robert Lawrence, of Ashton.
                    - William Lawrence, of Withington,=Isabel Molineaux.
                      - Edmund Lawrence, of Withington,=Eleanor ——
                        - John Lawrence, of St. Albans,
                          - William Lawrence, of St. Albans,=Catherine Beamond.
                            - John Lawrence, of St. Albans,=Margaret Roberts.
                              - Thomas Lawrence, of St. Albans,=Joan Antrobus.
                                - William Lawrence, of Flushing, L. I.,=Elizabeth Smith.
                                  - William Lawrence, of Flushing, L. I.,=Deborah Smith.
                                    - Samuel Lawrence, of Blackstone, L. I.,=Mary Hicks.
                                      - Augustine Lawrence, of New York City,=Johanna Van Zant.
                                        - Augustine Hicks Lawrence, of New York City,=Catherine Laqueer.
                                          - Augustine Nicholas Lawrence, of New York City,=Frances J. Powell.
                                            - Joseph Dangerfield Lawrence, of New York City,=Margaretta La Forge.
- Eustace de Vesci.
- William de Vesci.
- William de Vesci.
- Isabel de Vesci.
- Adam de Welles.
- Adam de Welles.
- John de Welles.
- John de Welles.

Robert Cutting Lawrence

DESCENT from the Sureties for the observance of the Magna Charta:

Hugh Bigod,
Roger Bigod,
Gilbert de Clare,
Richard de Clare,

John de Lacie,
William de Mowbray,
Saher de Quincey,
Eustace de Vesci.

1. **Saber de Quincey,** one of the Sureties for the Magna Charta, first Earl of Winchester, had by his wife, Lady Margaret de Bellomont, daughter of Robert, Earl of Leicester, lord high steward of England, and his wife, Lady Petronella, daughter of Hugh Grantemaisnill, lord high steward:

2. ROBERT DE QUINCEY, eldest son, *d. v. p.* in the Holy Land, leaving issue by Lady Hawyse (Margaret) de Meschines, daughter of Hugh de Keveliock, fifth earl palatine of Chester, *d.* 1181:

3. LADY MARGARET DE QUINCEY, only child, who *m.*, as his second wife, **John de Lacie,** one of the Sureties for the Magna Charta, first Earl of Lincoln, *d.* 1240, and had:

4. LADY MAUD DE LACIE, who *m.*, as his second wife, Richard de Clare, eighth Earl of Clare, sixth Earl of Hertford, and second Earl of Gloucester, a distinguished personage in the reign of Henry III., *d.* 1262, son of **Gilbert de Clare** and grandson of **Richard de Clare,** both Sureties for the Magna Charta and Earls of Clare and Hertford, and had:

5. THOMAS DE CLARE, second son, governor of St. Briarch's Castle in Gloucestershire and constable of Gloucester Castle, 50 Henry III. In the following year he made a pilgrimage to the Holy Land; returned in 1271; was constituted governor of the City of London by Edward I. upon his accession, and *d.* September 4, 1287, in Ireland, and was buried in Grey Friars, Limerick, having issue by his wife, Lady Amy, daughter of Sir Maurice Fitz-Maurice, of Mollahuffe Castle, Desmond (by his first wife, Joanna, daughter of Miles Fitz-Henry, chief justice of Ireland), eldest son of Raymond le Gros Fitz-William, viceroy of Ireland, 1177:

6. THOMAS DE CLARE, third son, father, by his wife, whose name has not been preserved, of:

7. LADY MAUD DE CLARE, who *m.* Robert, Baron de Clifford, of Appleby, who participated in the Scottish wars of Edward I., and was slain at the battle of Bannockburn, 1313. His grandfather, Roger de Clifford, for his stanch adherence to Henry III., was appointed, after the victory at Evesham, justice of all the king's forests south of Trent, whose grandfather, Walter de Clifford, was a brother of "the Fair Rosamond." Lady Maud and Robert, Baron de Clifford, had:

8. ROGER, SECOND BARON DE CLIFFORD, of Appleby, lord of Westmoreland, *d.* July 13, 1390, who *m.* Lady Maud de Beauchamp, daughter of Thomas, K.G., third Earl of Warwick, hereditary sheriff of Worcestershire and chamberlain of the exchequer, one of the original members of the Order of the Knights of the Garter, *d.* 1369. Sir Thomas was very distinguished in arms in the reign of Edward III., and had a principal command at the battle of Cressy. His wife, whom he *m.* when he was fifteen years old, in 1328, by special dispensation, as she was his cousin, was Lady Catherine, daughter of Sir Roger, second Baron de Mortimer,

of Wigmore, best known as the lover of Queen Isabel, consort of Edward II., who participated in the Scottish wars, and was appointed lord lieutenant of Ireland. He attached himself to the interests of Queen Isabel, and fled to France with her and Prince Edward. When the latter became king he was created Earl of March, and held a "round table" to celebrate his advancement, and soon, by his mode of living, became known as the King of Folly. Subsequently he was arrested by order of Edward III. and convicted under various charges of treason, was executed, and all his honors became forfeited.

His father, Sir Edmund Mortimer, of Wigmore Castle, was mortally wounded at the battle of Buelt, against the Welsh, 1303, and his grandfather, Roger de Mortimer, was captain-general of all the king's forces in Wales and governor of Hereford Castle, and was on the side of Henry III. in his contest with his Barons, and rescued Prince Edward, and was greatly instrumental in winning the battle of Evesham, August 4, 1265, by which the king was restored to his freedom and his crown. After the accession of Edward I. he continued to enjoy royal favor, and became very wealthy. In honor of the knighting by the king of his three sons he caused a tournament to be held, at his cost, at Kenilworth Castle, where he entertained a very large party of guests, for several days, more sumptuously than was ever before known in England, and began there the "round table" and other celebrated follies which made him known the world over, and *d.* 1282.

The wife of Roger de Mortimer (son of Ralph, fifth Baron Mortimer, *d.* 1246, and his wife Gladuse-duy, daughter of Llewellyn the Great, Prince of Wales) was Lady Maud, a daughter and coheiress of William, sixth Baron de Braose, of Brecknock, by his wife, Lady Eva Marshall, sister of William le Mareschall, one of the Sureties for the Magna

Charta, and daughter of William, Earl of Pembroke, Protector of England, and his first wife, Lady Isabel de Clare, daughter of Richard the Strongbow, Earl of Pembroke, lord justice of Ireland, son of Gilbert, Earl of Pembroke, *d.* 1149, and his wife, Lady Elizabeth de Beaumont, daughter of Robert, Earl of Mellent, and first Earl of Leicester, *d.* 1118, by Lady Isabel (grandmother of the aforesaid Robert, third Earl of Leicester), daughter of Hugh Magnus, Count de Vermandois, a son of HENRY I., KING OF FRANCE.

Thomas de Beauchamp, K.G., aforesaid, was the eldest son of Guy, second Earl of Warwick, *d.* 1315, son of William, sixth Baron de Beauchamp, of Elmly, created Earl of Warwick, *d.* 1298, by his wife, Lady Maud, daughter of John Fitz-John, chief justice of Ireland, 1258, son of John Fitz-Geoffrey, chief justice of Ireland, 1246, by his wife, Lady Isabel, daughter of Sir Ralph Bigod, third son of **Hugh Bigod**, and grandson of **Roger Bigod**, both Sureties for the Magna Charta.

Roger, second Baron Clifford, and Lady Maud had:

9. LADY CATHERINE DE CLIFFORD, who *m.* Ralph, fifth Baron de Greystock, who was very active in the wars with the Scots, and was captured by George, Earl of Dunbar, and ransomed, *d.* 1417, and had:

10. LADY MAUD DE GREYSTOCK, who *m.* Eudo de Welles, *d. v. p.*, eldest son of Sir John, fifth Baron de Welles, of Gainsby, knighted 47 Edward III., ambassador to Scotland, 19 Richard II., *d.* 1421, and his wife, Lady Margery, sister of Sir Thomas de Mowbray, Duke of Norfolk, earl marshal of England, and daughter of John, fourth Baron de Mowbray, who served in the French wars, and was killed by Turks, near Constantinople, 1368, and his wife, Lady Elizabeth, daughter and heiress of John, third Baron de Segrave, who took an active part in the wars of Edward III., *d.* 1353, and

his wife Margaret, Duchess of Norfolk, daughter and eventually sole heiress of Thomas de Brotherton, Earl of Norfolk, earl marshal, etc., *d.* 1338, son of EDWARD I., KING OF ENGLAND, by his second wife, Princess Margaret, daughter of PHILIP III., KING OF FRANCE, and his first wife, Princess Isabel, daughter of JAMES I., KING OF ARRAGON.

William de Mowbray, a Surety for the Magna Charta, had by his wife, Lady Agnes, daughter of William d'Albini, Earl of Arundel and Sussex: Roger de Mowbray, second son, *d.* 1266, *m.* Lady Maud, daughter of William de Beauchamp, of Bedford, and had: Roger de Mowbray, *d.* 1298, *m.* Lady Rose de Clare, and had: John de Mowbray, who took part in the insurrection of Thomas of Lancaster, was taken prisoner and executed at York in 1321, *m.* Lady Aliva, daughter of William de Braose, of Gower, and had: John de Mowbray, third Baron, *d.* 1361, who was the father of the aforesaid John de Mowbray, *d.* 1368, by his wife, Lady Joan Plantagenet, daughter of Henry, third Earl of Lancaster, *d.* 1345, and his wife, Lady Maud,* eldest son of Edmund the Crouchback, Earl of Leicester, Lancaster, and Chester, high steward of England, *d.* 1295 (son of HENRY III., KING OF ENGLAND), and his second wife, Lady Blanche, widow of Henry I., King of Navarre, and daughter of Robert of Artois, a son of LOUIS VIII., KING OF FRANCE, by his wife, the Princess Blanche, daughter of ALPHONSO VIII., KING OF CASTILE, and Princess Eleanor Plantagenet, daughter of HENRY II., KING OF ENGLAND.

Eustace de Vesci, a Magna Charta Surety, had by his wife, Lady Margaret, a daughter of William the Lion, King of Scotland: William de Vesci, *m.* secondly, Lady Agnes,

---

* She was daughter of Patrick, Baron de Chaworth, and his wife, Lady Isabel de Beauchamp, daughter of William, first Earl of Warwick, *d.* 1298, and his wife, Lady Maud Fitz-John, aforesaid, a lineal descendant of **Hugh Bigod** and **Roger Bigod,** Sureties for the Magna Charta.

daughter of William de Ferrers, Earl of Derby, and had: William de Vesci, second son, appointed by Edward I. justice of the royal forests beyond Trent, governor of Scarborough Castle, first Baron by writ, *m.* Lady Isabel, daughter of Adam de Periton, and widow of Robert de Welles, and had: Lady Isabel, *m.* William de Welles, of Alford, and had: Adam, first Baron by writ, 1299, whose second son, Sir Adam, third Baron, had: John, fourth Baron, *d.* 1361, who had: John, fifth Baron, *d.* 1421, *m.* Lady Margery de Mowbray, and had: Eudo de Welles, eldest son *d. v. p.*, who *m.* as aforesaid, Lady Maud de Greystock, and had:

11. LADY MARY DE WELLES, sister to Sir Lionel, or Leo, sixth Lord Welles, lord lieutenant of Ireland, *k.* 1461, and Sir William de Welles, lord chief justice of Ireland, 1442, who *m.* John Laurence, of Rixton Manor, Lancastershire, returned to Parliament for Lancaster County, October 16, 1419. He was a commissioner for musters in Londale Wapentake, commission dated April 28, 6 Henry V., and had:

12. MARGARET LAURENCE, who *m.* her cousin, Robert Laurence (his nephew Sir Thomas, son of his brother, Sir James Laurence, of Standish, *m.* Lady Eleanor, a daughter of Sir Lionel, Lord Welles), eldest son of Sir Robert Laurence, of Ashton Hall, Lancastershire, member of Parliament, 1459 (whose pedigree, beginning in 1190, is preserved in the Herald's Visitation to Gloucestershire, 1682–3), and his wife, Amphibis, a daughter of Edward de Longford, Lancastershire, and had:

13. WILLIAM LAWRENCE, of Withington, 1509, and Sevenhampton, which he bought, in Gloucestershire, Sea House, in Somersetshire, and Blackley Park and Norton, in Worcestershire. He also owned the manors of Staple Farm, New House, Upcot Farm, etc. His will was proved

in 1559.* He *m.* before 1518, Isabel, daughter of John Molineaux, of Sefton Manor and Chorly (Sorely), in Lancashire, and had :

14. EDMUND LAWRENCE, of Withington parish, Gloucestershire, fourth son. His will dated August 30, 1558, proved January 10, 1559. He had issue by his wife Eleanor, whose surname has not been preserved :

15. JOHN LAWRENCE, of St. Albans, in Hertfordshire. He was chief burgess in 1553, and mayor of St. Albans in 1567 and 1575, and had by his wife, whose name has not been preserved :

16. WILLIAM LAWRENCE, of St. Albans, who *m.* there, November 25, 1559, Catherine Beamond, or Beaumont, and had :

17. JOHN LAWRENCE, *bapt.* at Abbey Church, St. Albans, January 12, 1561–2, who had by his second wife, *m.* January 25, 1586–7, Margaret Roberts :

18. THOMAS LAWRENCE, of St. Albans, second son, *bapt.* at St. Albans, February 2, 1588–9, *d.* March 20, 1624–5. He was an assistant of the borough of St. Albans, 1622, and *m.* October 23, 1609, Joan, daughter of Walter and Joan Antrobus (Anterbus), of St. Albans. Joan *m.* secondly, John Tuthill (or Tuttell), of Ipswich, and came with him to New England in April, 1635, bringing John, *b.* 1618, and William, children of her first husband, Thomas Lawrence, of whom :

19. WILLIAM LAWRENCE, *bapt.* at St. Albans, July 27, 1622, *d.* 1680 (no will). In 1645 he and his brother John, who was one of the patentees of Hampstead, Long Island, New York, obtained the patent of Flushing, Long Island,

---

* In the Herald's pedigree (Gloucestershire Visitations, 1682) he is given as son of John, the son of the aforesaid William and Margaret, but by Sir Thomas Phillips, in the pedigree of Lawrence, of Sevenhampton, as brother to John, son of Robert.

New York, from the Dutch Governor Keift, and were of the number to whom the confirmatory patent was issued by Governor Nicoll, in 1666. He was a magistrate of Flushing, 1655, and one of its largest land-owners; was a member of the governor's council, 1700; captain of a foot company, 1665; high sheriff, 1673; justice of the North Riding, 1675. He *m.* secondly, March 4, 1664-5, Elizabeth, daughter of Richard Smith (she *m.* secondly, Philip Carteret, governor of New Jersey, and *m.* thirdly, Colonel Richard Townley, of Elizabeth, New Jersey, which city was so named in her honor by her second husband), and had by her:

20. WILLIAM LAWRENCE, of Flushing, Long Island, *d.* 1719 (N. Y. Wills, ix. 152), having issue by his wife Deborah, *d.* 1743 (N. Y. Wills, xv. 47), daughter of Richard Smith:

21. SAMUEL LAWRENCE, of Blackstone, Long Island, *d.* 1760 (N. Y. Wills, xxii. 148), having issue by his wife Mary, *d.* 1782 (N. Y. Wills, xxxvii. 230), daughter of Thomas Hicks:

22. AUGUSTINE LAWRENCE, of New York, *b.* 1727, *d.* April, 1794 (N. Y. Wills, xli. 285), having issue by his wife Johanna, *b.* August 20, 1729, *d.* May, 1809, daughter of Wynant Van Zant:

23. AUGUSTINE HICKS LAWRENCE, of New York, *b.* 1769, *d.* September 10, 1828 (N. Y. Wills, lxii. 262, and New York *Evening Post*, September 11, 1828), having issue by his wife Catherine, *b.* April 23, 1771 (King's County, N. Y. Wills, iii. 1), daughter of Abraham Luqueer:

24. AUGUSTINE NICHOLAS LAWRENCE, of New York, *b.* December 1, 1794, *d.* March 28, 1872, who *m.* secondly, May 4, 1846, Frances J., *b.* February 6, 1810, *d.* October 5, 1895, daughter of Joseph Powell, and had:

25. JOSEPH DANGERFIELD LAWRENCE, of New York, *b.* February 2, 1850, who *m.* June 17, 1874, Margaretta La

Forge, *b.* May 9, 1856, daughter of Peter Clarkson La Forge, and had:

26. ROBERT CUTTING LAWRENCE, of New York, *b.* April 20, 1875, a member of the Society of Colonial Wars, and one of the founders of the Order of Runnemede. He *m.* January 30, 1896, Jessie, *b.* July 27, 1875, daughter of Edward and Laura (Perry) Monteath.

> Arms.—*Ar., a cross raguly, gu., on a chief of the second, a lion passant guardant, or.*
> Crest.—*A demi-turbot, couped, tail upward, in pale, gu.*
> Motto.—*In cruce solus.*

THE PEDIGREE OF STEPHEN WHITNEY.

Roger Bigod.
Hugh Bigod.
Ralph Bigod.
Isabel Bigod.
Maud de Lacy.
Peter de Genevill.
Joan de Genevill.
Joan de Mortimer.
Joan d'Audley.
John Touchet—Margery de Mortimer.

Richard de Clare.
Gilbert de Clare.
Richard de Clare—Maud de Lacy.
Thomas de Clare.
Thomas de Clare.
Margaret de Clare.
Elizabeth Badlesmere.
Roger de Mortimer.

Saher de Quincey.
Robert de Quincey.
John de Leche—Margaret de Quincey.

Eustace de Vesci.
William de Vesci.
William de Vesci.
Isabel de Vesci.
Adam de Welles.
Adam de Welles.
John de Welles.
John de Welles—Margery de Mowbray.

William de Mowbray.
Roger de Mowbray.
Roger de Mowbray.
John de Mowbray.
John de Mowbray.
John de Mowbray.

John Touchet
à qua
Henry Whitney—Hannah Eugenia Lawrence
à qua
Stephen Whitney, of New Haven, Conn.

Eudo de Welles
à quo

Stephen Whitney

DESCENT from the Sureties for the observance of the Magna Charta:

Hugh Bigod,
Roger Bigod,
Gilbert de Clare,
Richard de Clare,

John de Lacie,
William de Mowbray,
Saher de Quincey,
Eustace de Vesci.

1. **Roger Bigod**, one of the Sureties for the observance of the Magna Charta, second Earl of Norfolk, had by his wife, Lady Isabel Plantagenet, daughter of Hameline, Earl of Surrey:

2. **Hugh Bigod**, one of the Sureties for the Magna Charta, and third Earl of Norfolk, who had by his wife, Lady Maud Marshall, daughter of William, Earl of Pembroke:

3. SIR RALPH BIGOD, third son, who had by his wife, Lady Berta de Furnival:

4. LADY ISABEL BIGOD, who *m.* first, Gilbert de Lacie, *d. v. p.* (son of Walter de Lacie, the celebrated lord of Meath, in Ireland, who *d.* 1241), and had by him:

5. LADY MAUD DE LACIE, widow of Peter de Geneva, who *m.* 1254, Geoffrey de Genevill, lord of Trim Castle, Ireland, and had:

6. PETER DE GENEVILL, who *m.* Lady Joan, daughter of Hugh le Brune, Earl of Angoulême, and had:

7. LADY JOAN DE GENEVILL, who *m.* Roger de Mortimer, of Wigmore, second Baron by writ, 1299–1326, the favorite of Isabel, consort of King Edward II., created Earl

of March; impeached before Parliament and convicted under various charges, he was executed, and had:

8. LADY JOAN DE MORTIMER, who *m.* James d'Audley, K.G., Baron Audley, one of Edward III.'s noted generals, *d.* 1386, and had:

9. LADY JOAN D'AUDLEY, *m.* Sir John Touchet, and had:

10. JOHN TOUCHET D'AUDLEY, who *m.* Lady Margery Mortimer, daughter of Roger, K.G., Baron de Mortimer, of Wigmore, restored to the earldom of March, 26 Edward III., *d.* 1360 (and his wife, Lady Philippa, daughter of William de Montacute, first Earl of Salisbury), son and heir of Sir Edmund, Baron de Mortimer, *d.* 1331 (and his wife, Lady Elizabeth, daughter and coheiress of Bartholomew the Rich, Baron Badlesmere, of Leeds Castle, in Kent), and Lady Margaret de Clare, eldest son of the unfortunate Roger, Earl of March, aforesaid.

Lady Margaret de Clare, aforesaid, was the daughter of Thomas, son of Thomas de Clare, governor of London, 1274, son of Richard, Earl of Clare, Hertford, and Gloucester, *d.* 1262 (and his second wife, Lady Maud, daughter of **John de Lacie**, one of the Sureties for the Magna Charta, by his second wife, *m.* 1232, Lady Margaret, daughter of Robert, *d. v. p.*, second son of **Saber de Quincey**, one of the Sureties for the Magna Charta), son of **Gilbert de Clare**, and grandson of **Richard de Clare**, both Sureties for the Magna Charta, and Earls of Hertford.

Sir John Touchet and the Lady Margery had:

11. SIR JOHN TOUCHET, first Baron d'Audley by writ, 1405, who *m.* Lady Eleanor de Holland, and had:

12. LADY CONSTANCE TOUCHET, who *m.* Robert de Whitney, of Predwarden, and had:

13. HUGH DE WHITNEY, of The Hay, Hereford, and Bramhall, Chester, 1551, who *m.* Constance, daughter of

Richard Vaun, of Leckryd, and his wife Constance, daughter of Griffith Preis, and had:

14. RICHARD WHITNEY, of Bramhall, Chester, *d.* 1549, who *m.* Mary, daughter of Owen Parry, of Bredwardyn, or Predwarden, by Margery, daughter and heiress of Thomas Vaughn, and had:

15. JOHN WHITNEY, of Audlem, in Chester, and Grimdon, in Stafford, who had by his wife, whose surname has not been preserved:

16. NICHOLAS WHITNEY, of Leeke, Staffordshire, and Brooke-Walden, Essex, *d.* before 1590, who *m.* Mary ———, of Brooke-Walden, *d.* 1590, and had:

17. GEORGE WHITNEY, *d.* before 1604, who *m.* Penelope, daughter of William and Penelope Pardoe, of Walden, in Essex, and had:

18. THOMAS WHITNEY, the younger, of Northchurch, St. Mary, and Berkhampstead, in Herts, *d.* March 5, 1624, who *m.* Jane, daughter of Thomas Warne, of Walden, *d.* 1627, and had:

19. THOMAS WHITNEY, of Berkhampstead, St. Mary, or Northchurch, Herts, *d.* 1659; will proved May 4, 1659; who *m.* Mary, daughter of John Roach, and had:

20. HENRY WHITNEY, who came to New England in 1635. He resided and died at Norwalk, Connecticut; will dated June 5, 1672; inventory of his estate taken November 8, 1673. In his aunt's (Mrs. Anne Roberts, of Borrington, Herts, father's sister) will, dated October 4, 1655, proved at Hitchin, December 25, 1655, and also in his father's will, he is mentioned as "living in New England." His son:

21. JOHN WHITNEY, of Norwalk, Connecticut, *b.* before 1644, *d.* before October 11, 1720, *m.* March 17, 1674-5, Elizabeth, *d.* after April 30, 1741, daughter of Richard Smith, of Norwalk, and had:

22. JOSIAH WHITNEY, of Norwalk, *d.* 1750, *m.* October 30, 1729, Eunice, daughter of Eleazer and Hannah Hanford, of Norwalk, and had:

23. HENRY WHITNEY, of Derby, Connecticut, *b.* February 19, 1735–6, *d.* May 1, 1811, *m.* 1761, Eunice, *b.* April 15, 1746, *d.* August 21, 1794, daughter of William and Hannah Clark, of Derby, and had:

24. STEPHEN WHITNEY, of New York City, *b.* Derby, September 14, 1776, *d.* February 16, 1860, who *m.* August 4, 1803, at Newtown, Long Island, New York, Harriet, *b.* September 1, 1782, *d.* May 12, 1860, daughter of Hendrick and Phœbe (Skidmore) Suydam, of Hallett's Cove, Long Island, and had:

25. HENRY WHITNEY, of New Haven, Connecticut, *b.* New York, August 23, 1812, *d.* March 21, 1856, who *m.* first, January 27, 1835, Hannah Eugenia, *b.* New York, January 27, 1815, *d.* March 16, 1844, daughter of Isaac Lawrence and his wife Anna, daughter of Rev. Abraham Beach, D.D., of New York.

Isaac Lawrence was a descendant of Captain John Lawrence, of Newtown, Long Island, high sheriff of Queens County, New York, 1698, *d.* 1729, a son of Captain Thomas Lawrence, a patentee of Newtown, 1645, *d.* 1703, son of Thomas Lawrence, of St. Albans, Hertfordshire, *d.* 1624, second son of John Lawrence, of St. Albans, *bapt.* 1561, son of William Lawrence, of St. Albans, Herts, and St. Ives, Huntingdonshire, high sheriff of Huntingdon and Cambridge shires, son of John Lawrence, mayor of St. Albans, 1567 and 1575, son of Edmund Lawrence, of Whittington, Gloucestershire, *d.* 1582, fourth son of William Lawrence, of Sevenhampton, Gloucestershire, *d.* 1559, son of Robert Lawrence, and his wife, Margaret, daughter of John Lawrence, of Rixton Manor, Lancashire, by his wife, Lady Mary, daughter of Eudo de Welles, *d. v. p.* (and

MEMBERS OF THE ORDER OF RUNNEMEDE 253

his wife, Lady Maud de Greystock),* eldest son of Sir
John, fifth Baron Welles, of Gainsby, *d.* 1422, and his wife,
Lady Eleanor, daughter of John, fourth Baron de Mowbray,
of Axholme, the son of John, third Baron, *d.* 1361 (and his
wife, Lady Joan Plantagenet†), the son of John, second
Baron, *d.* 1321, son of Roger, first Baron by writ, *d.* 1298,
the son of Roger, *d.* 1266, second son of 𝔚𝔦𝔩𝔩𝔦𝔞𝔪 𝔡𝔢
𝔐𝔬𝔴𝔟𝔯𝔞𝔶, one of the Sureties for the Magna Charta.

Sir John, fifth Baron de Welles, aforesaid, *d.* 1422, was
the son of John, fourth Baron, *d.* 1361, son of Sir Adam, *d.*
1345, son of Adam de Welles, first Baron by writ in 1299,
son of William de Welles, lord of Alford, in Lincolnshire,
and his wife, Lady Isabel, daughter of William de Vesci, *d.*
1297, son of William de Vesci, *d.* 1253 (and his second wife,
Lady Agnes, daughter of William de Ferrers, Earl of Derby,
and his first wife, Lady Sibil, a daughter of William, Earl
of Pembroke, and sister of William Marshall, a Magna

---

* She was a daughter of Ralph de Greystock, *d.* 1417, and his wife, Lady
Catherine, daughter of Roger de Clifford, *d.* 1390, and his wife Lady Maud,
daughter of Sir Thomas de Beauchamp, third Earl of Warwick, son of Guy,
second Earl, son of William, first Earl, and his wife, Lady Maud, daughter of
John Fitz-John, chief justice of Ireland, 1258, son of John Fitz-Geoffrey, chief
justice of Ireland, 1246, by his wife, Lady Isabel, daughter of Sir Ralph, third son
of 𝔥𝔲𝔤𝔥 𝔅𝔦𝔤𝔬𝔡, the son of 𝔕𝔬𝔤𝔢𝔯 𝔅𝔦𝔤𝔬𝔡, both Sureties for the Magna Charta.

Roger de Clifford, aforesaid, was the son of Robert de Clifford, of Appleby,
and his wife, Lady Maud, daughter of Thomas, third son of Thomas, second
son of Richard de Clare, Earl of Hertford and Gloucester, *d.* 1262 (son of
𝔊𝔦𝔩𝔟𝔢𝔯𝔱 𝔡𝔢 𝔄𝔩𝔞𝔯𝔢, the son of 𝔕𝔦𝔠𝔥𝔞𝔯𝔡 𝔡𝔢 𝔄𝔩𝔞𝔯𝔢, both Sureties for the Magna
Charta), by his wife, Lady Maud, daughter of 𝔍𝔬𝔥𝔫 𝔡𝔢 𝔏𝔞𝔠𝔦𝔢, a Surety for the
Magna Charta, and his wife, Lady Margaret, daughter of Robert, eldest son of
𝔖𝔞𝔥𝔢𝔯 𝔡𝔢 𝔔𝔲𝔦𝔫𝔠𝔢𝔶, one of the Sureties for the Magna Charta.

† She was the daughter of Henry, Earl of Lancaster, *d.* 1345, a descendant
of LOUIS VIII., KING OF FRANCE, and HENRY III., KING OF ENGLAND, and
his wife, Lady Maud, daughter of Patrick de Chaworth and his wife, Lady
Isabel, daughter of William de Beauchamp, first Earl of Warwick, and his
wife, Lady Maud Fitz-John, a descendant of 𝔥𝔲𝔤𝔥 𝔅𝔦𝔤𝔬𝔡, and 𝔕𝔬𝔤𝔢𝔯 𝔅𝔦𝔤𝔬𝔡,
both Sureties for the Magna Charta.

Charta Surety), son of **Eustace de Vesci,** a Magna Charta Surety.

Henry Whitney had by his wife, Hannah Lawrence:

26. STEPHEN WHITNEY, of New Haven, Connecticut, a member of the Society of Colonial Wars, and a founder of the Order of Runnemede, *b.* New Haven, October 20, 1841. He served in the army during the Civil War as first lieutenant in the Fourth United States Artillery, August 5, 1861–November 12, 1863. He *m.* in New York, April 27, 1864, Margaret Lawrence, daughter of Bradish and Louisa Anna (Lawrence) Johnson, of New York.

Arms.—*Az., a cross chequy, or and sa.*

Crest.—*A bull's head, couped, sa. armed ar., the points gu.*

Motto.—*Magnanimiter crucem sustine.*

Morgan G. Bulkeley

DESCENT from the Sureties for the observance of the Magna Charta:

Roger Bigod,   Hugh Bigod.

1. **Roger Bigod,** one of the Sureties for the observance of the Magna Charta, Earl of Norfolk, *d.* 5 Henry III., had by his first wife, Lady Isabel de Warren, daughter of Hameline Plantagenet, Earl of Warren and Surrey:

2. **Hugh Bigod,** eldest son and heir, also one of the Sureties for the Magna Charta, second Earl of Norfolk, *d.* 1225, who had by his wife, Lady Maud (or Matilda), daughter of William Marshall, Earl of Pembroke, one of the advisers of King John, and Protector of England during the nonage of Henry III., and sister of William Marshall, one of the Sureties for the Magna Charta:

3. SIR HUGH BIGOD, second son, chief ranger of Farnedale, 1255, governor of Castle Pickering. He was appointed, June 22, 41 Henry III., 1257, justiciary of England and governor of the Tower of London and of Dover Castle, and chamberlain of Sandwich. He resigned the office of chief justice in 1260, and, dying before November 7, 1266, he had issue by his first wife, Joan, daughter of Robert Burnet:

4. SIR JOHN BIGOD, second son, and heir at law of his elder brother, Roger Bigod, the last Earl of Norfolk, who *d. s. p.* 1307. Sir John was unjustly deprived of his inheritance by Earl Roger making a complete surrender of his

honors and estates to the crown. He had by his wife, whose name has not been preserved:

5. ROGER BIGOD, lord of Settrington, youngest son, whose daughter:

6. JOAN BIGOD, *m.* Sir William de Chauncy, the last feudal Baron of Skirpenbeck, in Yorkshire. He was the eldest son of Thomas de Chauncy, lord of the manors of Skirpenbeck, Willington, Thoralby, etc., who, in 1358, paid twenty marks for "leave to enfeoff William, *primo genitum*, and Johannam, daughter of Roger Bygot," with rectine, lands, etc., in Thoralby and Skirpenbeck, and the next year he did enfeoff William and Joan with a part of the manor of Skirpenbeck. Sir William obtained license, 1399, to alienate Skirpenbeck and to purchase estates in Stepney, Middlesex, and received from Richard II. confirmation of his charter and liberties. Sir William de Chauncy and Joan had:

7. JOHN CHAUNCY, of Stepney, near London, eldest son, who, dying in February, 1444–5, had issue by his wife Margery, or Margaret, daughter and coheiress of William Gifford, of Gedleston:

8. JOHN CHAUNCY, eldest son, *d.* May 7, 1479, and buried in the church of Sawbridgeworth, Herts. He *m.* Anne, daughter of John Leventhorp, of Shingey Hall, and had:

9. JOHN CHAUNCY, eldest son, *d.* June 8, 1510. He had by his wife, a daughter of Thomas Boyce:

10. JOHN CHAUNCY, of Pishobury manor, son and heir, *d.* June 4, 1546. He *m.* Elizabeth (Proffit), widow of Richard Mansfield, and had:

11. HENRY CHAUNCY, second son and heir, who inherited ten manors, located in the counties of Kent, Sussex, Hertford, and Essex. He resided on his manor of Gifford, or Gelston, Herts, where he erected a mansion, called "New Place," and *d.* April 14, 1587. He had by his wife Lucy, whose surname has not been preserved:

12. GEORGE CHAUNCY, of New Place, Herts, second son and eventual heir, who succeeded his father in the manors of Gifford, Nether Hall, etc. He *m.* first, Jane, daughter and heiress of John Cornwall, of Stebbing, Essex, and became possessed of Yardley and other manors. He *m.* secondly, Anne (or Agnes), daughter of Edward Welsh, of Great Wymondly, and widow of Edward Humberston, and, dying in 1625 (buried at Barking, Essex), had by her:

13. REV. CHARLES CHAUNCY, fifth son, and third son of the second wife, *bapt.* and registered in Yardley Bury Church, Herts, November 5, 1592. He was a Fellow of Trinity College, Cambridge, and came to New England in May, 1638, and was the pastor at Scituate, Massachusetts, 1641, and November 29, 1654, was installed as the second president of Harvard College, with a salary of one hundred pounds per annum. He *d.* February 19, 1671–2, having issue by his wife, whom he *m.* in England, March 17, 1630, Catherine, *d.* March 23, 1667, aged sixty-six, daughter of Robert Eyre, of Sarum, Wilts, by his wife Agnes, or Anne, daughter of Rev. John Still, Bishop of Bath and Wells, 1592–1607:

14. SARAH CHAUNCY, eldest daughter, *b.* at Ware, England, June 13, 1631, *bapt.* June 22, *d.* June 9, 1699. She *m.* October 26, 1659, Rev. Gershom Bulkeley, *b.* December, 1636, son of Rev. Peter Bulkeley, of Concord, Massachusetts, a Fellow of St. John's College, Cambridge, England, and his wife Grace, daughter of Sir Richard Chetwood. He was graduated at Harvard College, 1655, was minister at New London, Connecticut, and Wethersfield, Connecticut, and then became a physician, practising in Glastonbury, Connecticut, and served as surgeon in an Indian war, and, dying December 2, 1713, had issue by Sarah Chauncy:

15. REV. JOHN BULKELEY, who was graduated at Harvard College in 1699, and was minister at Colchester, Connecti-

cut, 1703, *d.* June, 1731. He *m.* 1701, Patience, daughter of John and Sarah Prentice, of New London, Connecticut, and had:

16. JOHN BULKELEY, *b.* April 19, 1705, second child, *m.* October 29, 1738, Mrs. Mary (Adams) Gardiner, and had:

17. ELIPHALET BULKELEY, *b.* 1746, fifth child, who *m.* Anna Bulkeley, and had:

18. JOHN CHARLES BULKELEY, *b.* 1772, third child, who *m.* 1798, Sally Taintor, and had:

19. ELIPHALET ADAMS BULKELEY, *b.* 1803, third child, who *m.* 1830, Lydia S. Morgan, and had:

20. MORGAN GARDNER BULKELEY, of Hartford, Connecticut, *b.* December 26, 1837, at East Haddam, third child. He was eight years mayor of Hartford, and was elected governor of Connecticut in November, 1888. He is a member of the Society of Colonial Wars, the Society *Mayflower* Descendants, the Military Order of Foreign Wars of the United States, the Society of the War of 1812, the Military Order of the Loyal Legion, the Society Sons of the Revolution, the Society Sons of the American Revolution, and the Grand Army of the Republic, and a founder of the Order of Runnemede. He *m.* 1885, Fannie Briggs Houghton, of San Francisco, California, and had Morgan Gardner, *b.* December 25, 1885; Elinor Houghton, *b.* April 7, 1893; and Houghton, *b.* August 9, 1896.

Arms.—Sa., *a chevron between three bulls' heads, cabossed, or.*

Crest.—*Out of a ducal coronet, or, a bull's head, ar., armed of the first.*

Motto.—*Nec temere, nec timide.*

GEORGE ALEXANDER LYMAN.

George Alexander Lyman

❦

DESCENT from the Surety for the observance of the Magna Charta:

Saher de Quincey.

1. **Saber de Quincey,** one of the Sureties for the Magna Charta, Earl of Winchester, *m.* Lady Margaret de Beaumont, daughter of Robert-blanchemaines, third Earl of Leicester, lord high steward of England, *d.* 1190. He was the son of Robert-bossu, second Earl of Leicester, a stanch supporter of the interests of Henry I. and II., lord justice of England, *d.* 1167, son of Robert de Bellemont, or Beaumont, Earl of Mellent, who came to England with the Conqueror, and greatly contributed to the victory at Hastings, and was rewarded with ninety-one lordships, and was created by Henry I. Earl of Leicester, and in his latter days became a monk, and *d.* in the Abbey of Preaux in 1118. His wife was Lady Isabel, or Elizabeth, daughter of Hugh Magnus, Count of Vermandois and Valois, son of HENRY I., KING OF FRANCE, by his wife Anne, daughter of Jaroslaus, Czar of Russia, 1015–1051.

Saher de Quincey and Lady Margaret had:

2. ROGER DE QUINCEY, second son, who succeeded as Earl of Winchester, constable of Scotland, *jure uxoris*, *d.* in 1264, when the earldom became extinct. He *m.* Lady Helen, eldest daughter and coheiress of Alan McDonal, lord of Galloway, constable of Scotland, *d.* 1233, by his

wife, Lady Margaret, sister of Derverguile, mother of John Baliol, and sister of Isabel, mother of King Robert Bruce, and daughter of David, Earl of Huntingdon, brother of William the Lion, King of Scots, son of Henry, Earl of Northumberland, *d. v. p.* 1152, eldest son of DAVID I., KING OF SCOTLAND, (by his wife, Lady Matilda, daughter of Waltheof, Earl of Northampton and Northumberland, beheaded in 1075, son of Syward the Saxon), son of MALCOLM-CANMORE, KING OF SCOTLAND, and his wife, Princess Margaret, daughter of Prince Edward, the exile, eldest son of EDMUND IRONSIDES, KING OF ENGLAND.

Roger de Quincey and Lady Helen had:

3. LADY ELIZABETH DE QUINCEY, third daughter and coheiress, who *m.* Alexander, Baron Cumyn, second Earl of Buchan, who acted a conspicuous part in the busy reigns of Kings Alexander II. and III. He was one of the guarantees of the peace with England in 1244; was appointed justiciary of Scotland, 1251; constable of Scotland, *jure uxoris*, 1270; was one of the guardians of Scotland, 1286, and *d.* in 1289. Their third daughter:

4. LADY AGNES CUMYN, *m.* Gilbert d'Umfraville, of Riddesdale and Harbottle, in Northumberland, and had:

5. GILBERT D'UMFRAVILLE, Earl of Angus, *jure uxoris*, so summoned to Parliament by writ, January 26, 1297. He was governor of the castles of Dundee and Forfar, and of the whole territory of Angus, in 1291, when the competitors for the crown of Scotland agreed that seisin of that kingdom and its fortifications should be delivered to King Edward of England. On this occasion, Gilbert d'Umfraville declared that he had received his castles in charge from the Scottish nation, and that he would not surrender them to the English unless King Edward and all the competitors entered into an obligation to indemnify him. They submitted finally to these conditions, and "Angus was the only nobleman in all Scot-

land who acted with integrity and spirit on this trial of national integrity and spirit." He *m.* Matilda, Countess of Angus, widow of John Cumyn, and daughter of Malcolm, Earl of Angus, and, dying in 1307, was succeeded by his eldest son:

6. ROBERT D'UMFRAVILLE, second Earl of Angus, of new creation, *b.* 1274–5, *d.* 1326, second and surviving son. He was appointed by Edward II., of England, joint guardian of Scotland, with William, Lord Ros, 1308, and sole guardian of the kingdom, August 26, 1309. He was forfeited by King Robert Bruce, but was one of the commissioners to treat with Bruce for a truce, 11 Edward II. He had by his second wife, Lady Alianore, whose surname has not been preserved (she *m.* secondly, Robert Mauduit):

7. SIR THOMAS D'UMFRAVILLE, second son by second wife (half-brother of Gilbert, third Earl of Angus), who succeeded by special entail to the castle of Harbottle, and the manor of Otterburn, estates of his half-brother, to whom he was next heir male. He *m.* Joan, daughter of Adam de Rodam, in Northumberland, and had:

8. SIR THOMAS D'UMFRAVILLE, of Riddesdale and Kyme, second son, brother of Sir Robert d'Umfraville, K.G., *d. s. p.* 1436. He had by his wife, Lady Agnes, whose surname has not been preserved:

9. LADY JOAN D'UMFRAVILLE, second daughter, sister of Gilbert d'Umfraville, styled Earl of Kyme, *k. s. p.* in the French wars, in 1422, who *m.* Sir William Lambert, of Owlton, in Durham, and Harbottle, in Northumberland, who was of royal descent in the following line:

ROBERT THE PIOUS, KING OF FRANCE, was the father of Almaric de Montfort, whose son, Simon de Montfort, had: Lady Isabel, who *m.* Ralph de Toni, lord of Flamsted, *d.* 1142 (eldest son of Ralph de Toni, standard bearer to

William of Normandy, and his wife, Lady Alice, daughter of William Fitz-Osborne, Count of Bretville, the king's lieutenant and steward, in Normandy, first Earl of Hereford), and had: Lady Alianore de Toni, who *m.* Sir Randulphus Lambert, who was with the Conqueror at the battle of Hastings, and for his services received grants of manors in Yorkshire, his chief seat being at Skipton, and had: Sir Hugh Lambert, second feudal lord of Skipton, *temp.* Henry I., who *m.* Lady Maud, daughter of Peter de Ros, of Holderness, *d.* 1157, and his wife, Lady Adeline, sister of the celebrated Walter d'Espec, lord of Hamelake, and had: Sir Henry Lambert, of Skipton, *temp.* Stephen, from whom was descended Sir Thomas Lambert, who *m.* Lady Joan d'Umfraville, and had:

10. ROBERT LAMBERT, of Owlton, or Owton, Durham, who had:

11. HENRY LAMBERT, of High Ongar, Essex, *temp.* 1447, whose heiress:

12. ELIZABETH LAMBERT, *m.* about 1488, Thomas Lyman, of Navistoke and Westersfield, or Wethersfield, Essex, 1486, *d.* 1509, son of John Lyman, a citizen and merchant of London, *temp.* Henry V., who purchased lands at Navistoke and Wethersfield, by Joanna, daughter and heiress of Roger Trethewy, of Southampton, and had:

13. HENRY LYMAN, eldest son, of Navistoke, Westersfield, and High Ongar, in Essex, living in 1517, who *m.* Alicia, daughter of Simon Hyde, of Wethersfield, Essex, and had:

14. JOHN LYMAN, eldest son, of High Ongar and Navistoke, at which latter place he died in 1587, having issue by his wife Margaret, daughter of William Gérard, of Beauchamp, St. Paul, Essex:

15. HENRY LYMAN, eldest son, of High Ongar and Navistoke, living in 1598, *d.* about 1609, who *m.* secondly, Phillis,

daughter of John Scott, of Navistoke (she *m.* secondly, Ralph Greene, of High Ongar, and was living as his widow in 1629), and had:

16. RICHARD LYMAN, *b.* at High Ongar, 1580; came to Charlestown, New England, in 1631 (his brother Henry, *bapt.* June 7, 1591, came with him and *d. s. p.*); settled at Roxbury, Massachusetts, 1635; was one of the founders of Hartford, Connecticut, 1635-6, where he *d.* in 1640. He *m.* before 1617, Sarah Osborne, of Halsted, Kent, and had by her, who *d.* at Hartford, in 1640:

17. RICHARD LYMAN, of Northampton, Massachusetts, *b.* 1617, *d.* 1662, *m.* Hepzibah Ford, of Windsor, Connecticut, and had:

18. JOHN LYMAN, of Northampton, Massachusetts, *b.* 1655, *d.* 1727, *m.* Abigail ——, and had:

19. JOSHUA LYMAN, of Northfield, Massachusetts, *b.* 1704, *d.* 1777, *m.* Sarah Norman, of Sheffield, Connecticut. He was in Captain Dwight's company from Fort Dummer in the spring of 1725,—Father Ralle's War. After the establishment of the trading-post at Fort Dummer he became fourth officer, and afterwards had the title of lieutenant, and had issue:

20. SETH LYMAN, of Northfield, Massachusetts, *b.* February 1, 1736, *d.* October 14, 1817, *m.* Eunice Graves, of Sunderland, Massachusetts. He served as corporal in Captain John Burk's company, Colonel Timothy Ruggles's regiment, in the expedition to Ticonderoga and Crown Point, March 31–December 25, 1759. He was also a private in Captain Allen's company, Colonel Fellow's regiment, Continental Army, dating from October 7, 1775, and went with the army to Quebec in September, 1776. His name appears on the Continental army rolls as late as February 7, 1779. He served with the rank of sergeant in Captain Samuel Merriman's company, Phineas Wright's regiment

(Sixth Hampshire Regiment) in the expedition to Northern Department in 1777. His company took part in the battle of Saratoga, and he was present at Burgoyne's surrender, October 27, 1777. Seth and Eunice Lyman had:

21. TERTIUS LYMAN, of Winchester, New Hampshire, *b.* 1761, *d.* 18—, *m.* Hannah (Alexander) Foster, of Winchester, New Hampshire, and had:

22. TERTIUS ALEXANDER LYMAN, of Winchester, New Hampshire, *b.* March 13, 1812. He moved to Lee Centre, Illinois, in 1856, where he still resides. He *m.* March 13, 1834, Sarah P. Codding, who died February 15, 1898, aged eighty-eight years, and had:

23. GEORGE ALEXANDER LYMAN, of Amboy, Illinois, one of the founders of the Order of Runnemede, *b.* June 26, 1839, at Winchester, New Hampshire. He moved to Lee County, Illinois, in March, 1856; is now editor and proprietor of the *Amboy Journal;* was among the first to offer his services to his country in the war of the Rebellion; in February, 1865, raised a company of twenty-nine volunteers to fill the quota of the town of Bradford, Lee County, Illinois; is a member of several patriotic societies, and Lecturer for the American Institute of Civics; *m.* 1866, Mary E. Jones, and has two children:

James Alexander Lyman, A.B. and A.M., Beloit College, Beloit, Wisconsin, and Ph.D., Johns Hopkins University, Baltimore, Maryland, *b.* October 17, 1866; professor of chemistry in Portland Academy, Portland, Oregon; *m.* June 7, 1897, Miss Ethel Anna Skinner, of Portland, Oregon.

George Richard Lyman, *b.* December 1, 1871; graduated from Beloit College, Beloit, Wisconsin, June, 1894; B.A., Harvard University, 1897. Graduate student in biology at Harvard University, Cambridge, Massachusetts,

and assistant in the botanical department under Professor Farlow.
  Arms.—*Per chevron, gu. and ar., in base an annulet of the first.*
  Or,
  Arms.—*Quarterly, 1 and 4, per chevron, gu. and az., in base an annulet of the first,* for Lyman; 2, *gu., a chevron between three lambs, ar.,* for Lambert; 3, *quarterly erm. and gu., over all a cross, or,* for Osborne.
  Crest.—Lyman: *A demi-bull, ar., attired and hoofed, or, langued, gu.*
  Motto.—*Quod verum tutum.*

THE PEDIGREE OF FREDERICK H. WINSTON.

```
                            Roger Bigod.
                            Hugh Bigod.
                 Saher de   Ralph Bigod.
Robert de Vere.  Quincey.   Isabel Bigod.        Richard de Clare.    William de Lanvallei.
  Hugh de Vere—Hawise de      John Fitz-John.      Gilbert de Clare.    Hawise de Lanvallei
  Robert de Vere.  Quincey.     Maud Fitz-John.      Isabel de Clare.     John de Burgh.
  Joan de Vere.                   Isabel de Beauchamp.  Robert Bruce.       Margaret de Burgh.
  Alice de Warren.                  Maud de Chaworth.     King Robert I.,—Elizabeth de Burgh.
  Richard Fitz-Alan—Eleanor Plantagenet.           Matilda Bruce.
  Alice Fitz-Alan.                                   Joanna Isaac.
  Margaret Holland—John de Beaufort.                   Isabel d'Ergadia—John Stewart.
      Joan de Beaufort, widow of King James I.,—James Stewart, the Black Knight, of Lorn.
              John Stewart, Earl of Athol,—Lady Eleanor Sinclair.
              John Stewart, Earl of Athol,—Lady Mary Campbell.
                    Lady Isabel Stewart—Kenneth Mackenzie, lord of Kintail.
                        Agnes Mackenzie—Lachlan-mohr Macintosh, chief of Clan Chattan.
                    William Macintosh, of Borlum,—Elizabeth Innes.
                        Lachlan-mohr Macintosh—Anne ——, second wife.
      John-mohr Macintosh, of Georgia, 1733; d. 1761,—Marjory Fraser.
          Maj.-Gen. Lachlan McIntosh, 1727—1806,—Sarah Treadcroft.
                  John Hampden McIntosh—Charlotte Nephew.
                         Mary McIntosh—Rev. Dennis M. Winston.
                  Frederick Hampton Winston, of Chicago, Ill.
```

Frederick Hampden Winston

DESCENT from the Sureties for the observance of the Magna Charta:

Hugh Bigod,
Roger Bigod,
Gilbert de Clare,
Richard de Clare,
William de Lanvallei,
Saher de Quincey,
Robert de Vere.

1. **Robert de Vere,** third Earl of Oxford, one of the Sureties for the observance of the Magna Charta, d. 1221, had by his wife, Lady Isabel, daughter of Hugh de Bolebec, d. 1261:

2. HUGH DE VERE, fourth Earl of Oxford, great high chamberlain of England, d. 1263. He m. Lady Hawyse, daughter of **Saher de Quincey,** one of the Sureties for the observance of the Magna Charta, Earl of Winchester, d. 1219, and had:

3. ROBERT DE VERE, fifth Earl of Oxford, d. 1296, who had by his wife, Lady Alice, daughter of Gilbert, Baron de Saundford, chamberlain-in-fee to Eleanor, queen consort of Henry III.:

4. LADY JOAN DE VERE, who m. William de Warren, d. v. p. December 15, 1286, son of John, seventh Earl of Warren and Surrey, d. 1304, son of William, sixth Earl, and his second wife, Lady Maud Marshall, widow of Hugh Bigod, a Surety for the Magna Charta, and a sister of William le Mareschal, also one of the Sureties for the Magna Charta, and had:

268 THE MAGNA CHARTA BARONS

5. LADY ALICE DE WARREN, who *m.* 1305, Edmund Fitz-Alan, K.B., eighth Earl of Arundel, beheaded in 1326, and had:

6. RICHARD FITZ-ALAN, K.G., ninth Earl of Arundel, and seventh Earl of Surrey, *d.* January 24, 1375-6, who *m.*, as his second wife, and her second husband, Lady Eleanor Plantagenet, *d.* January 11, 1372, daughter of Henry, Earl of Lancaster, *d.* 1345, son of Edmund, Earl of Leicester, Lancaster, and Chester, high steward of England, *d.* 1295, the son of HENRY III., KING OF ENGLAND, and his wife, Lady Eleanor de Provence.

The Earl of Lancaster's wife, Lady Maud, was a daughter of Patrick de Chaworth, *d. s. p. m.* 1282, and his wife, Lady Isabel, daughter of William, sixth Baron de Beauchamp, of Elmley, created Earl of Warwick, *d.* 1298, by his wife, Lady Maud, widow of Gerard de Furnival, and daughter of John Fitz-John, justiciary of Ireland, 1258, son of John Fitz-Geoffrey, of Berkhampstead, sheriff of Yorkshire, 1234, justiciary of Ireland, 30 Henry III., and his wife, Lady Isabel, widow of Gilbert de Lacie, lord of Meath, in Ireland, and daughter of Sir Ralph Bigod, third son of **Hugh Bigod**, one of the Sureties for the Magna Charta, second Earl of Norfolk, *d.* 1225 (by his wife, Lady Maud Marshall, sister of William le Mareschal, a Surety for the Magna Charta), son of **Roger Bigod**, one of the Sureties for the Magna Charta, Earl of Norfolk, lord high steward of England, *d.* 1220.

Sir Richard, Earl of Arundel, and his second wife, Lady Eleanor Plantagenet, had:

7. LADY ALICE FITZ-ALAN, who *m.* Thomas de Holland, second Earl of Kent, earl marshal of England, *d.* 1397, son of Thomas, K.G., Earl of Kent, captain-general of France and Normandy, *d.* 1360, by his wife, Lady Joan, the Fair Maid of Kent, daughter of Edmund of Woodstock, Earl

of Kent, beheaded in 1330, the son of EDWARD I., KING OF
ENGLAND, by his second wife, Princess Margaret, daughter
of PHILIP THE HARDY, KING OF FRANCE, and had :

8. LADY MARGARET DE HOLLAND (she *m.* secondly, Thomas,
Duke of Clarence, son of King Henry IV.), who *m.* first,
John de Beaufort, K.G,, Earl of Somerset, marquis of
Dorset, lord high admiral and chamberlain of England, *d.*
1410, son of John of Gaunt, Duke of Lancaster, son of
EDWARD III., KING OF ENGLAND, by his wife Philippa, of
Hainault, and had :

9. LADY JOAN DE BEAUFORT, who *d.* in 1445, at Dunbar,
and was buried at the side of her first husband, in the Car-
thusian church at Perth. She *m.* first, in 1423-4, James I.,
King of Scotland, who was murdered at Perth by con-
spirators, February 21, 1437-8, and was the mother by him
of King James II. Her Majesty *m.* secondly, 1439, Sir
James Stewart, the Black Knight, of Lorn, who was taken
prisoner at sea in 1448 by a Flemish ship, and *d.* in Flanders.

Sir James was the third son of Sir John Stewart, of Lorn
and Innermeth, who obtained the great barony of Lorn, in
Argyleshire, by his marriage with Lady Isabel, daughter and
heiress of John d'Ergadia, lord of Lorn, by his wife, Lady
Joanna, daughter of Thomas Isaac, Esq., and his wife, the
Princess Matilda Bruce, who *d.* at Aberdeen, July 20, 1353,
and was buried at Dunfermline, sister of King David II.,
and second daughter of ROBERT I., KING OF SCOTLAND, and
his second wife, *m.* in 1302, Lady Elizabeth de Burgh.

Robert Bruce, or Robert I., King of Scotland, the restorer of the Scottish monarchy, was the eldest son of
Robert de Brus, sixth Earl of Annandale, and Earl of Carrick, in right of his wife, *d.* 1304 (and his wife, *m.* 1271,
Marjorie, Countess of Carrick, *d.* 1292, widow of Adam de
Kilconeath, and daughter and heiress of Niel, second Earl
of Carrick, a regent of Scotland, 1255, and his wife Mar-

garet, daughter of Walter, lord high steward of Scotland), eldest son of Robert de Brus, fifth Earl of Annandale, 1210–1295, one of the competitors for the crown of Scotland, 1290 (son of Robert de Brus, Earl of Annandale, and his wife, Lady Isabel, second daughter of David, Earl of Huntingdon, son of Henry, Earl of Huntingdon, Northumberland, etc., the son of DAVID I., KING OF SCOTLAND, whose mother, the wife of Malcolm-canmore, King of Scots, was the daughter of Prince Edward the Exile, the son and heir of EDMUND IRONSIDES, KING OF ENGLAND), and his first wife, *m.* 1244, Lady Isabel, daughter of **Gilbert de Clare**, Earl of Hertford and Earl of Gloucester, a Surety for the Magna Charta, *d.* 1229, the son of **Richard de Clare**, Earl of Hertford, one of the Sureties for the observance of the Magna Charta.

The second wife of King Robert Bruce, Lady Elizabeth de Burgh, was the eldest daughter of Richard de Burgh, Baron of Connaught and Trim, second Earl of Ulster, known as the "Red Earl," lord justice of Ireland in 1296, *d.* 1326. He was the son of Walter de Burgh, Baron of Connaught and Trim, Earl of Ulster, in right of his wife, *d.* 1271, son of Richard de Burgh the Great, lord lieutenant of Ireland, 1227, son of Willliam de Burgh, governor of Ireland, 1177, the son of Andelm de Burgh, steward to Henry II., by his wife, Princess Agnes, daughter of LOUIS VII., KING OF FRANCE. His wife was Lady Margaret, a daughter of John de Burgh, Baron de Lanvallei, *d.* 1279, eldest son and heir of Sir John de Burgh (son of Hubert, Baron de Burgh, third Earl of Kent, chief justice of England, and of Ireland, 1215 ; guardian of Henry III.), and his wife, Lady Hawyse, daughter of **William de Lanvallei,** one of the Sureties for the Magna Charta.

Lady Joan de Beaufort had by her second husband, Sir James Stewart, of Lorn:

10. SIR JOHN STEWART, of Balveny, eldest son, uterine brother of King James II. In 1457 he was created Earl of Athol, and had a new investure of the earldom in 1480. He was very instrumental in suppressing the rebellion of the Earl of Ross, and was one of the conservators of the the peace with England in 1484. He had a principal command in the army of James III. against his son and the rebel lords, 1488, for which he was imprisoned in the castle of Dunbar, on the death of that monarch. He *d.* September 19, 1512, and was buried in Dunkeld Cathedral.

Sir John Stewart, Earl of Athol, *m.* secondly, Lady Eleanor, daughter of William Sinclair, third Earl of Orkney, and Earl of Caithness,* and his second wife, Marjory, Countess of Caithness, daughter of Alexander Sutherland, of Dunbeath, third son of Robert, Earl of Sutherland, *d.* 1442, and his wife, Lady Mabilla, daughter of John Dunbar, Earl of Moray, second son of Patrick Dunbar,† ninth Earl of

---

* He was one of the hostages for James I., 1421, admiral and high chancellor of Scotland, and was the only son of Henry, second Earl of Orkney, admiral of Scotland, *d. ante* 1418, and his wife, Lady Egidia, only daughter and heiress of William Douglas, lord of Niddisdale and Galloway, by his wife, Princess Egidia Stewart, daughter of ROBERT II., KING OF SCOTLAND (and his first wife Elizabeth, daughter of Sir Adam Mure, of Rowallan), only child of Walter, lord high steward of Scotland, *d.* 1326, and his wife, Princess Marjory Bruce, daughter of ROBERT I., KING OF SCOTLAND (and his first wife, Lady Isabel, daughter of Donald, tenth Earl of Marr), son of Robert de Bruce, Earl of Annandale and Carrick, *d.* 1304, aforesaid, a descendant of Richard de Clare and Gilbert de Clare, both Sureties for the observance of the Magna Charta.

† He was the son of Patrick, eighth Earl of Dunbar, one of the competitors for the Scottish crown in 1291, as the great-grandson of Lady Ada, a daughter of KING WILLIAM THE LION, which claim was withdrawn, and he appeared as one of the nominees of his grandfather, Bruce, in the competition; he swore fealty to Edward I., of England, 1291, and when hostilities commenced between the Scots and English, in 1296, the earl adhered to the latter, but his wife, Lady Marjory, daughter of Alexander Comyn, Earl of Buchan, favoring the former, held the castle of Dunbar for Baliol and the Scots. He was eldest

Dunbar and March, *d.* 1369, and his first wife, Lady Agnes Randolph.*

Sir John Stewart, Earl of Athol, who *d.* 1512, had by his second wife, Lady Eleanor Sinclair:

11. SIR JOHN STEWART, second Earl of Athol, who was slain at the battle of Flodden, September 9, 1513. He *m.* Lady Mary Campbell, daughter of Archibald, second Earl of Argyle,† who was also killed at Flodden, and his wife,

---

son of Patrick, seventh Earl of Dunbar, a regent of the kingdom and a guardian of the king and queen, 1255; he led his warlike vassals to the battle of Largs, 1263, and aided in the defeat of the Norwegians, and was a party to the treaty of Perth, 1266, whereby the Scots got the Isle of Man and the Hebrides from them, *d.* 1289, and his wife, Lady Christian, only daughter of Robert de Bruce, Earl of Annandale and Carrick, *d.* 1304, aforesaid, a descendant of Gilbert de Clare and Richard de Clare, both Sureties for the observance of the Magna Charta.

* She was the daughter of Thomas, first Earl of Moray, regent of Scotland. Lady Agnes, known as "Black Agnes," during the absence of her husband, successfully defended the castle of Dunbar for nineteen weeks against the English forces in 1337–8. Her father was the only son of Sir Thomas Randolph, of Strathwith, high chamberlain of Scotland, 1296, and his wife, Lady Isabel Bruce, sister of King Robert Bruce, and daughter of Robert Bruce, Earl of Annandale and Carrick, *d.* 1304, aforesaid, a descendant of Richard de Clare and Gilbert de Clare, both Sureties for the observance of the Magna Charta.

† He was the son of Sir Colin Campbell, who succeeded his grandfather as second Lord Campbell, of Lochow, and was created, in 1457, Earl of Argyle, and appointed, 1483, lord high chancellor of Scotland, *d.* May 10, 1493, and his wife, Lady Isabel, daughter of John Stewart, second lord of Lorn, son of Robert Stewart, created, in 1439, Lord Lorn and Innermeth, and his wife, Lady Margaret, daughter of Robert Stewart, Duke of Albany, regent of Scotland, brother of King Robert III., and son of ROBERT II., KING OF SCOTLAND, aforesaid, a descendant of Richard de Clare and Gilbert de Clare, both Sureties for the observance of the Magna Charta.

Lord Lorn was the son of Sir John Stewart, of Innermeth, and his wife, Lady Isabel, daughter and heiress of John d'Ergadia, lord of Lorn, and his wife, Lady Joan, daughter of Thomas Isaac, Esq., and his wife, Princess Matilda Bruce, daughter of ROBERT I., KING OF SCOTLAND, and his second wife, Lady Elizabeth de Burgh, aforesaid, descendants of Gilbert de Clare, Richard de Clare, and William de Lanvallei, Sureties for the Magna Charta.

Lady Elizabeth Stewart, daughter of John, first Earl of Lennox.

Sir John Stewart, Lord Derneley, first Earl of Lennox, was warden of the west borders in 1481; was one of the confederated lords who seized James III. at Lander, in 1482, but subsequently attended his majesty during his confinement in the castle of Edinburgh, by his request, as a protector, and later enlisted in the party of James IV. against his father, and was rewarded with the earldom of Lennox, and had the custody of Dunbarton Castle committed to him in 1488. In 1489 he entered into a conspiracy against the government and joined the discontented nobles with a considerable force, but soon deserted them for the king and was pardoned, and *d. ante* September 11, 1495. He *m.* before May 15, 1438, Lady Margaret, daughter of Alexander, first Lord Montgomery. He was the eldest son of Sir Alan Stewart, of Derneley (and his wife, Lady Catherine, daughter of Sir William Seton, of Seton, *k.* 1424*), son of Sir John Stewart, of Derneley, *k.* 1429 (and his wife, *m.* 1392,

---

Earl Colin was the son of Archibald, *d. v. p.*, second, but eldest surviving son of Sir Duncan Campbell, created, in 1445, Lord Campbell, of Lochow, *d.* 1453, and his first wife, Lady Marjory Stewart, daughter of Robert, Duke of Albany, son of ROBERT II., KING OF SCOTLAND, aforesaid, a descendant of 𝕽icharð ðe Clare and 𝕲ilbert ðe Clare, Sureties for the Magna Charta.

Lord Campbell was the son of Sir Colin Campbell, of Lochow, son of Sir Archibald, son of Sir Colin, son of Sir Neil Campbell, of Lochow, *d.* 1316, and his wife, Lady Mary Bruce, sister of King Robert Bruce, and daughter of Robert de Bruce, Earl of Carrick and Annandale, *d.* 1304, aforesaid, a descendant of 𝕲ilbert ðe Clare and 𝕽icharð ðe Clare, Sureties for the Magna Charta.

* Sir William de Seton was killed at the battle of Verneuil, in Normandy, August 17, 1424. He was the only son of Sir John de Seton, *d.* 1441, and his wife, Lady Janet, daughter of George Dunbar, tenth Earl of Dunbar and March, *d.* 1420, son of Patrick, ninth Earl of Dunbar and March, and Earl of Moray, *d.* 1369, and his wife, Lady Agnes Randolph, aforesaid, descendants in several lines from 𝕲ilbert ðe Clare and 𝕽icharð ðe Clare, Sureties for the Magna Charta.

Lady Elizabeth, daughter of Duncan, Earl of Lennox), son of Sir Alexander Stewart, of Derneley (and his wife, Lady Janet, daughter of William Keith, of Galstoun), son of Sir Alexander, the third son of Sir Alan, of Dreghorn, the second son of Sir John Stewart, of Bonkyl, who was the second son of Alexander, the sixth high steward of Scotland.

Sir John Stewart, second Earl of Athol, and his wife, Lady Mary Campbell, had:

12. LADY ISABEL STEWART, who *m.* Kenneth Mackenzie, tenth lord of Kintail, *d.* June 6, 1568. He was the only son of John Mackenzie, of Kintail, *d.* 1556 (and his wife, Elizabeth Grant), the eldest son of Sir Kenneth Mackenzie,* of Kintail, who was knighted by James IV., and contributed greatly to the civilization of the northern parts of Scotland, *d.* 1506-7, and his second wife, Lady Agnes Fraser, only daughter of Hugh, second Lord Lovat, whose wife's name is unknown; his father entered into a contract with Thomas Dunbar, Earl of Moray, August 9, 1422, that his unborn son and heir should marry a daughter of the Earl, but failing of sons, that his daughter and heiress should marry the Earl's son, and to bind the bargain the Earl granted him the barony of Abertarf; if Hugh Fraser had married a daughter of the Earl, then the Frasers, of Lovat, would have eventually inherited the earldom of Moray, and as they did not, Lord Lovat probably married some other lady.

Kenneth Mackenzie, of Kintail, and his wife, Lady Isabel Stewart, had:

---

* He was the only child of Alexander Mackenzie, of Kintail, who aided in crushing the rebellion of the Earl of Ross, and received grants of estates belonging to the Earl in 1477, *d.* 1488, and his first wife, Lady Agnes, sixth daughter of Colin, second Lord Campbell, of Lochow, first Earl of Argyle, *d.* 1493, and his wife, Lady Isabel Stewart, aforesaid, descendants of Richard de Clare, Gilbert de Clare, and William de Lanvallei, Sureties for the Magna Charta, and of ROBERT I., KING OF SCOTLAND.

13. LADY AGNES MACKENZIE, second daughter, sister of Colin Mackenzie, eldest son and heir, who *d.* June 14, 1594. She *m.* 1567, Lachlan-mohr Macintosh, of Dunachtane and Knocknagail, sixteenth chief of Clan Chattan, and had:

14. WILLIAM MACINTOSH, of Essick and Borlum, second son, *d.* 1630 (brother of Lachlan, eldest son and chief of Clan Chattan, father of the celebrated Sir Lachlan MacIntosh), who *m.* 1594, Elizabeth (Beatrix), daughter of Robert Innes, of Invermarkie,* and had:

15. LACHLAN-MOHR MACINTOSH, the second of Borlum and of Bolkeskine. He *m.* first, Helen Gordon, according to a minute of agreement, dated at Ruthyn, August 28, 1637, whereby George Gordon, second Marquis of Huntly, undertakes to give him sasine, and *m.* secondly, Annie, the widow of Sir Lachlan MacIntosh, of that ilk, by whom he had:

16. CAPTAIN JOHN-MOHR MACINTOSH, *b.* at Bolkeskine (or Badenoch), March 24, 1700, came to America with his family in January, 1733, with Oglethorpe, and settled in that part of Georgia called after him, McIntosh County. He entered actively upon the defence of the colony against the Spaniards, and commanded the first company of Highlanders organized in America. He was severely wounded and taken prisoner at Fort Moosa, and sent to Madrid, Spain, and exchanged after the treaty of Aix la Chapelle. He *d.* at his seat, "Borlum," near Darien, Georgia, in 1761. He *m.* in Scotland, March 4, 1725, Marjory, *b.* 1701, daughter of John Fraser, of Garthmore, and his wife, Elizabeth Fraser, of Errogy, and had:

---

* He was the son of John, the son of Robert Innes, of Innerbrakie, and his wife, Lady Elspeth Stewart, daughter of Sir John, first Earl of Athol, *d.* 1512, and his second wife, Lady Eleanor Sinclair, aforesaid, descendants in several lines from Richard de Clare and Gilbert de Clare, both Sureties for the observance of the Magna Charta, and of ROBERT I., KING OF SCOTLAND.

17. MAJOR-GENERAL LACHLAN MCINTOSH, second son, *b.* at Badenoch, 1727, *d.* 1806. He served faithfully in the American army and became a major-general. He *m.* Sarah Treadcroft, and had:

18. JOHN HAMPDEN MCINTOSH, who *m.* Charlotte, daughter of James Nephew, and had:

19. MARY MCINTOSH, who *m.* Rev. Dennis M. Winston, and had:

20. FREDERICK HAMPDEN WINSTON, of Chicago, Illinois, one of the founders of the Order of Runnemede. Mr. Winston is also a member of the Society of Colonial Wars, the Society of the Cincinnati, and the Society of the Sons of the American Revolution. He has been twice married, —first to Maria Garrard Dudley, by whom he has now living six children: Frederick Seymour Winston, Eliza Talbot Winston (now Grover), Dudley Winston, Bertram McIntosh Winston, Marie Winston (now Walker), and Ralph Talbot Winston. His present wife was Sallie Reeves Hews, by whom he has no children.

Arms.—*Sa., a plate between three towers, ar.*

Crest.—*A dexter hand holding four arrows, all ppr.*

Marmaduke Richardson and Charles Henry Browning

DESCENT from the Sureties for the observance of the Magna Charta:

William d'Albini,
Hugh Bigod,
Roger Bigod,
Henry de Bohun,
Gilbert de Clare,
Richard de Clare,
John Fitz-Robert,
John de Lacie,
William de Lanvallei,
William de Malet,
William de Mowbray,
Saher de Quincey,
Robert de Roos,
Geoffrey de Say,
Robert de Vere,
Eustace de Vesci.

Richard de Clare, a Magna Charta Surety, had: **Gilbert de Clare**, a Magna Charta Surety, who had: RICHARD, *m.* Maud, dau. of **John de Lacie**, a Magna Charta Surety (and MARGARET, dau. of ROBERT, son of **Saher de Quincey**, a Magna Charta Surety), and had: GILBERT, who had: ELIZABETH, *m.* Theobald de Verdon, and had: ISABEL, *m.* Henry de Ferrers, and had: WILLIAM, who had: MARGARET, *m.* THOMAS DE BEAUCHAMP, and had:

RICHARD, who had: ELEANOR, *m.* EDMUND DE BEAUFORT, and had:

Roger Bigod, a Magna Charta Surety, had: **Hugh Bigod**, a Magna Charta Surety, who had: RALPH, who had: ISABEL, *m.* John Fitz-Geoffrey, and had: JOHN, who had: MAUD, *m.* William de Beauchamp, and had: GUY, who had: THOMAS, father of this THOMAS DE BEAUCHAMP.

Robert de Vere, a Magna Charta Surety, had: HUGH, who had: ROBERT, who had: JOAN, *m.* William de Warren, and had: ALICE, *m.* Edmund Fitz-Alan, and had: RICHARD, who had: ALICE, *m.* Thomas de Holland, and had: MAGRARET, *m.* John de Beaufort, and had this EDMUND DE BEAUFORT.

Eustace de Vesci, a Magna Charta Surety, had: WILLIAM, who had: WILLIAM, who had: ISABEL, *m.* William de Welles, and had: ADAM, who had: ADAM, who had: JOHN, who had: JOHN, *m.* MARGARET DE MOWBRAY (dau. of JOHN, son of JOHN, son of JOHN, son of ROGER, son of ROGER, son of **William de Mowbray**, a Magna Charta Surety), and had: EUDO, who had: WILLIAM, who had: ELIZABETH, *m.* Christopher Plunket, and had this JEANETTE PLUNKET.

JOAN, *m.* Robert St. Lawrence, and had: NICHOLAS, *m.* JEANETTE PLUNKET, and had:

William de Lanvallei, a Magna Charta Surety, had: HAWISE, *m.* John de Burgh, and had: JOHN, who had: MARGARET, *m.* Richard de Burgh, and had: JOAN, *m.* John d'Arcy, and had: ELIZABETH, *m.* James Butler (son of ELEANOR, dau. of HUMPHREY, son of HUMPHREY, son of HUMPHREY, son of HUMPHREY, son of **Henry de Bohun**, a Magna Charta Surety), and had: THOMAS, who had: ELEANOR, *m.* Robert de la Field, and had: ROBERT, who had: THOMAS, who had: JOHN, who had: THOMAS, who had: ISABEL, *m.* Gerald Fitz-Gerald, and had this ALISON FITZ-GERALD.

ELEANOR, *m.* Walter Cheever, and had: CHRISTOPHER, who had: MARGARET, *m.* Bartholomew Aylmer, and had: GERALD, *m.* ALISON FITZ-GERALD, and had:

Robert de Roos, a Magna Charta Surety, had: WILLIAM, who had: ROBERT, *m.* ISABEL (dau. of WILLIAM, son of **William d'Albini**, a Magna Charta Surety), and had: WILLIAM, who had: ALICE, *m.* Nicholas de Meinill, and had: ELIZABETH, *m.* John d'Arcy, and had: PHILIP, *m.* ELIZABETH (dau. of Thomas de Grey and ALICE, dau. of RALPH, son of JOHN, son of RALPH, son of RALPH DE NEVILL and EUPHEMIA, dau. of ROBERT, son of ROGER, son of **John Fitz-Robert**, a Magna Charta Surety), and had: JOHN, who had: JOHN, *m.* JOAN [dau. of John de Grey-

BARTHOLOMEW AYLMER, who had:

CHRISTOPHER AYLMER, who had: stock and ELIZABETH, dau. of ROBERT, son of ROBERT (son of ROBERT, son of John de Ferrers and HAWISE, dau. of ROBERT, son of JOHN, son of Robert de Muscegros and HELEWISE, dau. of 𝔚illiam 𝔐alet, a Magna Charta Surety) and ELIZABETH, dau. of William Boteler and JOAN, dau. of JOHN, son of John de Sudley and a dau. of WILLIAM, son of WILLIAM, son of Geoffrey de Say, a Magna Charta Surety], and had: JOHN, who had: ELIZABETH, *m.* Thomas de Rochefort, and had: ROGER, who had: JOHN, who had: JOHN, who had: CATHERINE, *m.* Oliver Plunket, and had: THOMAS, who had: OLIVER, who had: MATTHEW, who had:

SIR CHRISTOPHER AYLMER, Baronet, *m.* MARGARET PLUNKET, *d.* 1673, and had:

LADY CATHERINE AYLMER, will proved December 20, 1726, sister of Matthew Aylmer, who was created Lord Aylmer in the peerage of Ireland. She *m.* first, Sir Nicholas Plunket, of Dublin, and *m.* secondly, Captain Michael Warren, of Warrenstown, County Meath, an officer in King James's Irish army, *d.* 1712, and had:

OLIVER WARREN, a second lieutenant, Royal Navy, 1719, brother of Vice Admiral Sir Peter Warren, K.B., R.N., *d.* Dublin, 1752, who with General Pepperell and his New England troops captured Louisburgh from the French in 1745, and uncle of General Sir William Johnson, Bart., of New York, superintendent of Indian affairs. Lieutenant Warren was the father of:

RT. HON. NATHANIEL WARREN, M.P., of "Warren Mount," Dublin, and "Neilstown House" and "Balgatty," in County Dublin, *d.* at his official residence, in William Street, Dublin, January 15, 1796.—Obituary in the *Gentleman's Magazine.* He was sheriff for the city of Dublin, 1773; sheriff's peer, 1775; alderman of Dublin, 1775; first master of the Guild of Merchants, 1777; captain of the Dublin Volunteer Corps, 1777; a delegate with Henry Grattan to the non-importation and non-consumption convention, May, 1779, and in July following he was on the national committee to put the country in a state of defence; elected lord mayor of Dublin 1782; a delegate from the county of Dublin to the convention of the volunteers, at Dungannon, February, 1783, and in November following a delegate to the Irish National Convention; was member of Parliament for Dublin City, 1783–90; high sheriff of Dublin County, 1786; His Majesty's first police commissioner and the organizer of the national police system, 1786; member of Parliament for the borough of Callan, County Kilkenny, 1790–96; justice of the peace for County Dublin, 1794–5. In May, 1793, with the Dublin troops, he quelled the "Liberty mob," and was appointed superintendent magistrate for protecting the peace of the city of Dublin.

In 1763, Alderman Warren *m.* first, Katherine Higgins, *d.* 1773, and had by her five children, named in his will, proved February, 1796, and *m.* secondly, 1774, Agnes Bermingham, *d.* 1826, and had by her six children, of whom:

1. ELEANOR LA TOUCHE WARREN, *b.* 1776, *d.* New York City, 1860, a sister of Lieutenant-Colonels Nathaniel and Samuel R. Warren, and aunt of Major-General Lionel S.

Warren, of the English army. She *m.* in Dublin, Robert Crean, *d.* at Madrid, Spain, 1831, a descendant of Andrew O'Crean, of the barony of Carbury, County Sligo, 1641, and had:

HELENA MARGARETTA CREAN, *b.* Dublin, March 9, 1819, *d.* New York City, March 3, 1887. She *m.* first, in Dublin, September 13, 1834, Lindsay Downes Richardson, *d.* New York City, May 1, 1845, a son of Marmaduke John Richardson, captain of the Rothsay and Caithness Fencibles, son of Captain John Richardson, of Farlough, high sheriff of County Tyrone, 1778, and his wife Hannah, dau. of Rev. Alexander Lindsay, rector of Kilmac, County Monaghan, and had:

MARMADUKE RICHARDSON, of New York City and Paris, a founder of the Order of Runnemede. He was appointed August 12, 1890, by King Humbert, an officer of the Order of the Crown of Italy.

Arms.—*Aurcate; a bull's head, ppr., ship, sa., quarterly; as. band, with saltire cross, ar., fessè point.*

Crest.—*An esquire's helmet, ppr., surmounted by a lion rampant, gu., holding a wreath of oak-leaves.*

Motto.—*Virtuti paret robur.*

2. ELIZA SIDNEY WARREN, *b.* Dublin, October, 1787, *d.* Philadelphia, Pennsylvania, March, 1856, *m.* in Dublin, 1803, Cain Hanlon, of Roscommon, a descendant of Sir Eocha O'Hanlon, Knight, of Tonregee, lord of Upper and Lower Orior, in County Armagh, hereditary Irish royal standard bearer for Ulster, attainted but pardoned, February 12, 1605, and had:

ELEANOR AGNES HANLON, *b.* Dublin, March 17, 1809, *d.* Cincinnati, Ohio, October 27, 1857, *m.* at Christ Church, New York City, December 13, 1829, Robert Lewright Browning, lieutenant United States navy, *b.* Mason County, Kentucky, May 22, 1803, drowned in Trinidad Bay, California, March 27, 1850, son of Thomas and Elizabeth (Lewright) Browning, of Mason County, Kentucky, *m.* at Culpeper Court-House, Virginia, October 29, 1793, *b.* December 17, 1767, *d.* June 4, 1834, son of Joshua Browning, of Culpeper County, Virginia, and had:

CHARLES HENRY BROWNING, of Philadelphia and Ardmore, Pennsylvania, *b.* Cincinnati, a founder of the Order of Runnemede, *m.* at St. Paul's Roman Catholic Church, Philadelphia, January 1, 1884, by the acting archbishop, Vicar-General Walsh, to Katherine Aloysius Campbell, of Philadelphia, and had:

ROBERTA LEWRIGHT BROWNING, *b.* Ardmore, September 1, 1891.

Edward Clinton Lee

DESCENT from the Sureties for the observance of the Magna Charta:

Hugh Bigod,   Roger Bigod.

1. **Roger Bigod**, one of the Sureties for the Magna Charta, Earl of Norfolk, lord high steward of England, *d.* 1220, *m.* first, before 1195, Lady Isabel de Warren, daughter of Hameline Plantagenet, fifth Earl of Warren and Surrey, *jure uxoris*, who bore one of the three swords at the second coronation of Richard I., and was with that king in the army in Normandy, and *d.* 1202, and his wife, Isabella, Countess of Surrey, widow of William de Blois, and only daughter and heiress of William, third Earl of Warren and Surrey, who zealously espoused the cause of King Stephen and had a chief command in his army, son of William, second Earl of Warren and Surrey, and his wife, Lady Isabel (or Elizabeth), daughter of Hugh the Great, Count of Valois and Vermandois, son of HENRY I., KING OF FRANCE, and his wife, Anne of Russia.

Roger Bigod had by his first wife, Lady Isabel:

2. **Hugh Bigod**, eldest son, also one of the Sureties for the Magna Charta, second Earl of Norfolk, *d.* 1225. He *m.*, as her first husband, Lady Maud (or Matilda) Marshall, a sister of William Marshall, one of the Sureties for the Magna Charta, and daughter of William Marshall, created Earl of Pembroke, Protector of England during the minority of Henry III., and his first wife, Lady Isabel de Clare,

daughter of Richard the Strongbow, second Earl of Pembroke, lord justice of Ireland, by his wife, Princess Eva, daughter of DERMOT, LAST KING OF LEINSTER.

Hugh Bigod and Lady Maud had:

3. SIR RALPH BIGOD, third son (brother of Roger, the last Earl of Norfolk), who *m.* Lady Berta, daughter of the Baron Furnival, and had:

4. LADY ISABEL BIGOD, widow of Gilbert de Lacy, lord of Meath, Ireland, who *m.* secondly, John Fitz-Piers Fitz-Geoffrey, lord of Berkhampstead and Kirkling, sheriff of Yorkshire, 1234, chief justice of Ireland, 30 Henry III., son of Geoffrey Fitz-Piers, Baron de Mandeville, created, in 1199, Earl of Essex, justiciary of England, and his second wife, Lady Aveline, and had:

5. JOHN FITZ-JOHN, chief justice of Ireland, 1258, *d.* 42 Henry III., leaving issue by his wife, whose name has not been preserved:

6. LADY MAUD FITZ-JOHN, widow of Gerard de Furnival, *d. ante* 1280, who *m.* secondly, William, sixth Baron de Beauchamp, of Elmley Castle, Earl of Warwick, in right of his mother, Lady Isabel, daughter of William, fourth Baron Mauduit, of Hanslape, County Bucks, heritable chamberlain of the exchequer, *d.* 1256, and sister and heiress of William Mauduit, seventh Earl of Warwick. William de Beauchamp was a distinguished captain in Welsh and Scottish wars of Edward I., and *d.* 1298. The mother of Lady Isabel Mauduit was Lady Alice, daughter of Waleran de Newburgh, fourth Earl of Warwick, *d.* 1205 (by his second wife, Lady Alice de Harcourt), son of Roger, second Earl of Warwick, *d.* 1153, by his wife, Lady Gundred de Warren, daughter of the aforesaid William, second Earl of Warren and Surrey, and his wife, Lady Isabel de Vermandois, widow of Robert, Earl of Mellent, and a descendant of HUGH CAPET, KING OF FRANCE.

William de Beauchamp and Lady Maud had:

7. LADY SARAH DE BEAUCHAMP, sister of Guy, Earl of Warwick, who *m.* Richard, sixth Baron Talbot, of Goodrich Castle, who served in the wars in Wales and in Gascony, and was constituted governor of Cardiff Castle, 25 Edward I. He was a member of the great council held at Lincoln, 29 Edward I., which asserted the right of Edward to the realm of Scotland. His mother was Princess Gwenllian, daughter and heiress of RHESE AP GRIFFITH, PRINCE OF SOUTH WALES, *d.* 1136. He had by his wife, Lady Sarah:

8. LADY GWENLLIAN TALBOT, sister of Sir Gilbert, seventh Baron Talbot, lord justice of South Wales, who *m.* Sir Payne de Turberville, custos of Glamorganshire, 134-, and had:

9. SARAH DE TURBERVILLE, fourth daughter, and coheiress of her brother, who *m.* William de Gamage, high sheriff of Gloucestershire, 1325, and had:

10. GILBERT DE GAMAGE, lord of Rogiad, who *m.* Lettice, daughter of Sir William Seymour, of Penhow, and had:

11. SIR WILLIAM GAMAGE, lord of Rogiad and Coyty, who *m.* Mary, daughter of Thomas de Rodburg, Knight, and had:

12. SIR THOMAS GAMAGE, lord of Rogiad and Coyty, who *m.* Matilda, daughter of John Dennis, Knight, and had:

13. JANE GAMAGE, who *m.* Roger Arnold, of Llanthony, Monmouthshire, Wales, son of Arnholt ap Arnholt Vychan, and his wife, Sybil, daughter of Madoc ap Einon ap Thomas (*N. E. His. Gen. Reg.*, October, 1879), and had:

14. THOMAS ARNOLD, of Llanthony, who *m.* Agnes, daughter of Richard Waimstead, Knight, and had:

15. RICHARD ARNOLD, of Street parish, Somersetshire, who *m.* Emmote, daughter of Pearce Young, of Damerham, Wilts, and had:

16. RICHARD ARNOLD, of Bagbere, Dorsetshire, *d.* 1595, who had by his wife, name unknown:

17. THOMAS ARNOLD, of Melcomb-Horsey, Cheselbourne, Dorsetshire, who had by his second wife, whose name has not been preserved:

18. THOMAS ARNOLD, *b.* 1599, who came to New England in 1635, and finally settled in Providence, Rhode Island, in 1654, and was a deputy, 1666–67, 1670–72, member of the town council, 1672, and *d.* in 1674. He *m.* first in England,—wife's name has not been preserved,—and *m.* secondly, Phebe, daughter of George Parkhurst, of Watertown, Massachusetts, *d.* 1700, and had by the latter:

19. ELEAZER ARNOLD, of Providence, Rhode Island, *b.* at Watertown, Massachusetts, June 17, 1651, *d.* August 29, 1722. He was member of the town council, 1684–6; deputy, 1686, 1700, 1703, 1706–7, 1711, and 1715; justice of the peace, 1705. He *m.* Eleanor, daughter of John Smith, of Providence, and had:

20. JOSEPH ARNOLD, *d.* November 4, 1746, at Smithfield, Rhode Island. He *m.* June 20, 1716, Mercy, daughter of Amos and Mary (Burlingame) Stafford, and had:

21. CALEB ARNOLD, of Gloucester, Rhode Island, *b.* at Smithfield, May 26, 1725, *d.* February 5, 1784. He was deputy from Gloucester, 1773 and 1778; a corporal in 1776; purchasing agent in 1778; bounty agent in 1778; member of the committee on recruits and of the war committee in 1780. He *m.* January 26, 1746, Patience Brown, and had:

22. NEHEMIAH ARNOLD, of Providence, Rhode Island, *b.* Gloucester, March 15, 1748, *d.* March 12, 1833. He *m.* Alice, daughter of James and Mary (Anthony) Brown, of Taunton, Massachusetts, and Barrington and Providence, Rhode Island, and a descendant of John Brown, of Plymouth, Rehoboth, and Swanzey, Massachusetts, who was commissioner of the United Colonies in 1643, and of John Coggeshall, first governor of Rhode Island, 1647, and had:

23. AMY ARNOLD, *b.* April 7, 1778, *d.* March 28, 1862,

who *m.* at Providence, Rhode Island, September 19, 1796, Caleb Earle, *b.* at Swanzey, Massachusetts, February 25, 1771, *d.* at Providence, July 13, 1851, lieutenant-governor of Rhode Island, 1821–24, a descendant of Captain Ralph Earle, one of the founders of Portsmouth, Rhode Island, its treasurer, 1649 and 1651, deputy in 1650, and had:

24. ELIZABETH TERRY EARLE, *b.* Providence, September 8, 1799, *d.* Philadelphia, Pennsylvania, September 30, 1853, who *m.* at Providence, Rhode Island, February 1, 1825, Zebediah Lothrop, *b.* at Stratton, Vermont, September 27, 1798, and removed to Philadelphia, Pennsylvania, where he *d.* April 17, 1863. He was a descendant of Mark Lothrop, of Bridgewater, Massachusetts, 1656; of John Alden, a passenger in the *Mayflower*, 1620, deputy governor of Plymouth Colony, 1664–1677; of John Washburne, the first "Secretary of the governor and Company of Massachusetts Bay in New England" in 1628. *Issue:*

25. SARAH ELIZA LOTHROP, *b.* Providence, Rhode Island, January 8, 1826, *d.* Brooklyn, New York, March 21, 1889, who *m.* in Philadelphia, January 31, 1854, Richard Henry Lee, M.D., *b.* Pineville, Bucks County, Pennsylvania, May 13, 1826, graduate University of Pennsylvania, Medical Department, 1848, member of the Philadelphia County Medical Society, *d.* Philadelphia, March 21, 1881, and had:

26. EDWARD CLINTON LEE, of Philadelphia, *b.* December 5, 1857, a member of the Society of Colonial Wars, Society Sons of the Revolution, Society of *Mayflower* Descendants, etc., and a founder of the Order of Runnemede. He *m.* April 8, 1885, Mai, daughter of George Philler, of Philadelphia, president of the First National Bank, and his wife, Rebecca Horner Ruckman, and had: Lothrop, *b.* January 8, 1886; Ruckman, *b.* October 13, 1887; Helen Philler, *b.* June 6, 1890; Alden, *b.* October 31, 1893; and Philler, *b.* May 23, 1896.

THE PEDIGREE OF WILLIAM HERRICK GRIFFITH.

Roger Bigod.
Hugh Bigod.
Ralph Bigod.
Isabel Bigod.
Maud de Lacie.
Peter de Geneville.
Joan de Geneville.
Joan de Mortimer.
Joan d'Audley.
  John Touchet—Margery de Mortimer.
  John Touchet—Eleanor de Holland.

Richard de Clare.
Gilbert de Clare.
Richard de Clare—Maud de Lacie.
Thomas de Clare.
Thomas de Clare.
Margaret de Clare.
Elizabeth Badlesmere.
Roger de Mortimer.

John de Lacie—Margaret de Quincey.

William d'Albini.
William d'Albini.
Isabel d'Albini—Robert de Ros.

Saher de Quincey.
Robert de Quincey.

Robert de Ros.
William de Ros.
William de Ros.
William de Ros.
Thomas de Ros.
Thomas de Ros.

    James Touchet—Margaret de Ros.
    Anne Touchet—Sir Thomas de Dutton.
    Isabel de Dutton—Sir Christopher Southworth.
    Sir John Southworth—Ellen Langton.
    Christopher Southworth—(Name unknown.)
    Edward Southworth—Jane Lloyd.
    Thomas Southworth—Jane Mynne.
    Edward Southworth—Alice Carpenter.
    Constant Southworth—Elizabeth Collier.
    Mercy Southworth—Samuel Freeman.
    Constant Freeman—Jane Treat.
    Robert Freeman—Mary Paine.
    Robert Freeman—Anna ———.
    John Freeman—Sybil Lewis.
    Susan Freeman—Leonard Rowe.
    Sybil Ann Rowe—George W. Knowlton.
  Mary Louisa Knowlton—Edwin Henry Griffith.
  William Herrick Griffith, of Albany, N. Y.

William Herrick Griffith

꧁

DESCENT from the Sureties for the observance of the Magna Charta:

William d'Albini, Richard de Clare,
Hugh Bigod, John de Lacie,
Roger Bigod, Saher de Quincey,
Gilbert de Clare, Robert de Ros.

1. **Saher de Quincey,** one of the Sureties for the Magna Charta, first Earl of Winchester, had by his wife, Lady Margaret, daughter of Robert de Bellomont, third Earl of Leicester:

2. ROGER DE QUINCEY, second Earl of Winchester and constable of Scotland, in right of his wife, who accompanied his father to the Holy Land, 1264. He *m.* Lady Helen, daughter and coheiress of Alan Macdonald, *d.* 1234, lord of Galloway and constable of Scotland, one of the Barons on whose advice King John granted the Magna Charta, and his wife, Lady Margaret, daughter of David, Earl of Huntingdon, the son of Earl Henry, son of DAVID I., KING OF SCOTLAND, and had:

3. LADY HELEN DE QUINCEY, who *m.* Alan de la Zouche, Baron Zouche, one of the king's justices, constable of the Tower of London and governor of the castle of Northampton, *d.* 1285, and had:

4. ROGER, BARON DE LA ZOUCHE, of Ashby, *d.* 1285, who *m.* Lady Eleanor, daughter and heiress of Stephen, youngest son of William Longespee, Earl of Salisbury, a natural son of Henry II. and the "Fair Rosamond," and had:

5. ALAN, BARON DE LA ZOUCHE, of Ashby, who served in

the Scottish and French wars, governor of Buckingham Castle and Forest, and was summoned to Parliament, 25 Edward I. to 7 Edward II., *d.* 1314. He *m.* Lady Eleanor, daughter of Nicholas, Baron de Segrave, and had:

6. LADY MAUD DE LA ZOUCHE, who *m.* Sir Robert de Holland, K.G., summoned to Parliament 1314, *d.* 1328, and had:

7. LADY JOAN HOLLAND, who *m.* Sir Hugh de Dutton, 1276–1326, steward of Halton Castle, son of Hugh, son of Sir Thomas de Dutton, sheriff of Lancaster, son of Hugh, third son of Hugh, second son of Hugh Fitz-Odard, whose father, Odard, came in with William the Conqueror, son of William, Earl d'Eu, and Jeanne, sister to Hugh Lupus, Earl of Chester, and daughter of Richard d'Abrincis, by Emma, half-sister to William the Conqueror. Sir Hugh de Dutton and Lady Joan had:

8. SIR THOMAS DE DUTTON, 1314–1381, seneschal and governor of Halton Castle and sheriff of Cheshire, 30 and 33 Edward III., who *m.* Ellen, daughter of Sir Peter Thornton, of Thornton, and had:

9. EDMUND DE DUTTON, who *m.* Joan, daughter of Henry Minshall de Church Minshall, and had:

10. SIR PETER DE DUTTON, *d.* 1433, who had:

11. JOHN DE DUTTON, who *m.* Margaret, daughter of Sir John Savage, K.G., and had:

12. SIR THOMAS DE DUTTON, *k.* at Blore Heath, September 23, 1459, *m.* Lady Anne, daughter of James Touchett, sixth Baron Audley, of Heleigh, *k.* at Blore Heath, and his wife, Lady Margaret de Ros. He was the son of John Touchett, first Baron by writ, 1405, *d.* 1409, son of Sir John (and his wife, Lady Margery de Mortimer), son of Sir John Touchett, *temp.* Edward III., and his wife, Lady Joan, daughter of James d'Audley, K.G., fourth Baron Audley, of Heleigh, 1316–1387, and his first wife, Lady Joan, daughter of Roger de Mortimer, Earl of March, and his wife, Lady

WILLIAM HERRICK GRIFFITH.

Joan, only child of Sir Peter de Genevil, son of Geoffrey de Genevil, lord of Trim, and his wife, Lady Maud, daughter of Gilbert de Lacy and Lady Isabella, daughter of Ralph, son of **Hugh Bigod**, son of **Roger Bigod**, both Sureties for the Magna Charta and Earls of Norfolk.

Robert de Ros, a Magna Charta Surety, *d.* 1227, *m.* Lady Isabel, a daughter of William the Lion, King of Scotland, and had: William de Ros, lord of Hamlake, *d.* 1258, *m.* Lady Lucia, daughter of Reginald Fitz-Piers, of Blewleveny, Wales, and had: Robert de Ros, lord of Hamlake, *d.* 1285, *m.* Lady Isabel, daughter of William d'Albini, *d.* 1285, and his second wife, Lady Isabel, the son of **William d'Albini,** a Magna Charta Surety, *d.* 1236, and his wife, Lady Margery, daughter of Odonel d'Umfraville.

Robert de Ros and Lady Isabel d'Albini had: William de Ros, lord of Hamlake, *d.* 1317, *m.* Lady Maud, daughter of John de Vaux, of Feston, and had: William de Ros, lord of Hamlake, *d.* 1342, *m.* Lady Margery, daughter of Bartholomew de Badlesmere,* and had: Thomas de Ros, lord of Hamlake, *d.* 1384, *m.* Lady Beatrice, daughter of Ralph de Stafford, K.G., first Earl of Stafford, *d.* 1372, and had: Thomas de Ros, lord of Hamlake, *d.* 1414, *m.* Lady Margaret, daughter of Sir John d'Arundel, and had: Lady Margaret de Ros, aforesaid, who *m.* James Touchett, Baron d'Audley, *k.* 1459.

Richard de Clare, a Magna Charta Surety, was the father of **Gilbert de Clare,** also a Magna Charta Surety, whose son, Richard de Clare, *m.* Lady Maud, daughter of **John de Lacie,** a Magna Charta Surety, and his wife, Lady Mar-

---

* His wife, Lady Margaret, was a daughter of Thomas, third son of Thomas, governor of London, 1274, son of Richard de Clare, Earl of Hertford and Gloucester (and his wife, Lady Maud, daughter of **John de Lacie,** a Magna Charta Surety), son of **Gilbert de Clare,** the son of **Richard de Clare,** both Magna Charta Sureties.

garet, daughter of Robert, a son of **Saber de Quincey**, a Magna Charta Surety, and had: Thomas de Clare, whose son Thomas was the father of Lady Margaret de Clare, who *m.* Bartholomew de Badlesmere, who was captured by the Earls of Kent and Surrey at the battle of Boroughbridge, and hanged, drawn, and quartered at Canterbury, and his head set upon a pole at Burgate in 1332. Their daughter, Lady Elizabeth de Badlesmere, *m.* first, Sir Edmund de Mortimer, *d.* 1331, and had: Roger, Baron Mortimer, of Wigmore, Earl of March, *d.* 1360, *m.* Lady Philippa, a daughter of William de Montacute, Earl of Salisbury, and had: Lady Margery de Mortimer, who *m.* Sir John Touchett, second Baron d'Audley, aforesaid.

Sir Thomas de Dutton and Lady Anne had:

13. LADY ISABEL DE DUTTON, second daughter and coheiress, who *m.* Sir Christopher Southworth, of Salmesbury, 1443–1487, and had:

14. SIR JOHN SOUTHWORTH, of Salmesbury, 1478–1519, *m.* Lady Ellen, daughter of Sir Richard Langton, Baron of Newton and lord of Walton, by his wife Isabel, daughter of Peter Gerard, of Kingsley and Bryn, *d. v. p.* 1492, and his wife, Lady Margaret Stanley, whose descent from royalty was as follows:

HENRY I., KING OF FRANCE, 1031, had by his third wife, Anne of Russia, Hugh the Great, Count de Vermandois, whose daughter, Isabel, or Elizabeth,* *m.* first, Robert de

---

* Her mother was of the following royal descent: CHARLEMAGNE, the Emperor, had by his third wife, Hildegarde of Suabia: Pepin, King of Lombardy, *m.* Bertha, daughter of William, Count of Toulouse, and had: Bernard, King of Lombardy, *m.* Cunegonde, and had: Pepin, first Count of Vermandois, who had: Herbert, second Count, who had: Herbert, third Count, who had: Albert the Pious, fourth Count, who had by his wife Gerberga, a daughter of Louis IV., King of France (*see* Anderson's "Royal Genealogies"), Hubert, fifth Count, who had: Otto, seventh Count, who had: Herbert, eighth Count de Vermandois, whose daughter Adelheid *m.* Hugh Magnus.

Bellomont, Earl of Mellent and Leicester, a commander in the battle of Hastings, *d.* 1118, and had: Robert, second Earl of Leicester, lord justice of England, *d.* 1163, who had by his wife Amicia, daughter of Ralph de Waer, Earl of Norfolk, Suffolk, and Cambridge: Isabel de Bellomont, widow of Simon de St. Liz, Earl of Northampton, who *m.* secondly, Sir Gervaise Paganel, Baron de Dudley, and their only child: Hawyse, Baroness de Dudley, *m.* John de Someri, in Cambridgeshire, Baron Dudley, in right of his wife, and had: Roger de Someri, second son, Baron Dudley, *d.* 1230, having issue by his second wife, Amabel, widow of Gilbert de Segrave, and daughter of Sir Robert de Chaucombe: Margaret, widow of Uriean St. Pierre, who *m.* secondly, Ralph, first Baron Basset, of Drayton, in Staffordshire, *k.* at Evesham, and had: Ralph, second Baron Basset, *d.* 1299, whose daughter, Margaret, *m.* Edmund, first Baron de Stafford, *d.* 1308, and had: Ralph, second Baron Stafford, *d.* 1372, who had a principal command at Cressy, and in 1351 was created Earl of Stafford. He had by his second wife, Catherine, daughter of Sir John Hastings: Jane, who *m.* Sir Nicholas Beke, or Beck, and had: Elizabeth, *m.* Sir Robert de Swynnerton, and had: Maud, *m.* thirdly, Sir John Savage, of Clifton, *d.* 1450, and had: Sir John Savage, of Clifton, *d.* 1468, who had by his wife Elena, daughter of Sir William de Brereton: Mary, *m.* William de Stanley, lord of Stanley, Stourton, and Hoghton, sheriff of Cheshire, 2 Edward IV., and had: Sir William de Stanley, of Hoghton, who *m.* Alice, daughter of Sir Richard de Hoghton, of Molynton-Banastre,* and had: Sir William

---

* He was of the following royal descent: Lady Isabel de Vermandois, widow of Robert, Earl of Mellent, and granddaughter of HENRY I., KING OF FRANCE, *m.* secondly, William de Warren, second Earl of Surrey, and had: Gundred, widow of Roger de Newburg, Earl of Warwick, *m.* secondly, William de Lancaster, lord of Kendal, and had: William de Lancaster, steward to Henry II.,

de Stanley, sheriff of Cheshire, 10 Edward IV., *m.* Margaret, daughter of Sir John Bromley, and had the aforesaid Margaret, wife of Peter Gerard.

Sir John Southworth, of Salmesbury, and Lady Ellen had:

15. CHRISTOPHER SOUTHWORTH, of Salmesbury, who had:

16. EDWARD SOUTHWORTH, of London, merchant, who had by his wife Jane, daughter of Edward Lloyd, of Llwynymaen:

17. THOMAS SOUTHWORTH, recorder at Wells, in Somersetshire, *m.* Jane, daughter of Nicholas Mynne, of Norfolk, and had:

18. EDWARD SOUTHWORTH, of Duke Place, London, 1595, *d.* at Leyden, Holland, in August, 1620, leaving sons, Constant and Thomas (who came to America), by his wife, *m.* May 28, 1613, Alice, *b.* 1599, daughter of Alexander Carpenter, of Wrington, Somerset. Mrs. Southworth, after the decease of her husband, came to New England in the ship *Anne*, in July, 1623, and, on August 14, 1623, *m.* Governor William Bradford, of the Plymouth Colony, and *d.* April 5, 1670. The son of Edward Southworth:

19. CONSTANT SOUTHWORTH, *b.* 1615, came to Massachusetts in 1628, and resided and *d.* at Duxbury, March 10, 1679. He served in the Pequot War, 1637; ensign of the Duxbury company, 1646; lieutenant, 1653; deputy from 1647 for twenty-two years; treasurer of Plymouth Colony sixteen years; a member of the council of war, 1658; commissioner for the United Colonies, 1663; commissary-general during King Philip's War, and governor of Kennebec. He *m.* November 2, 1637, Elizabeth, daughter of William Collier, of Duxbury, and had:

---

father of Henry de Lea, who had: John, who had: Henry, who had: Sir William de Lea, *m.* Clemence Banastre, and had: Sybil, *m.* Sir Richard de Hoghton, and had: Sir Adam, who had: Sir Richard, who had: Sir William, father of this Sir Richard de Hoghton.

20. MERCY SOUTHWORTH, *b.* 1638, *m.* May 12, 1658, Deacon Samuel Freeman, *b.* May 11, 1638, at Watertown, Massachusetts, *d.* at Eastham November 25, 1712, and had:

21. CONSTANT FREEMAN, *b.* at Eastham, Massachusetts, March 31, 1669, *d.* at Truro June 8, 1745, where he settled in 1705, and was treasurer of the town, August 1, 1709, and in 1715 chosen its representative at the general court, and was commander of the military company. He *m.* October 11, 1694, Jane, *b.* December 6, 1675, *d.* September 1, 1729, daughter of Rev. Samuel Treat, of Eastham, 1648-1716, son of Robert Treat, governor of Connecticut, 1686, *d.* at Milford, Connecticut, 1710, and his wife, Jane Tapp, and had:

22. ROBERT FREEMAN, *b.* August 12, 1696, *d.* at Pomfret, Connecticut, September 27, 1755. He *m.* April 5, 1722, at Eastham, Mary, *b.* February 1, 1695-6, *d.* September 25, 1755, daughter of Elisha Paine, *d.* at Canterbury, Connecticut, February 7, 1735, son of Thomas Paine, 1611-1706, and Mary, daughter of Nicholas Snow and Constance, daughter of Stephen Hopkins, who was a passenger in the *Mayflower*, and had:

23. ROBERT FREEMAN, *b.* December 31, 1727, at Truro, *d.* at Amenia, Dutchess County, New York, September 29, 1798. He served in the Revolution as captain and major in Colonel Sutherland's regiment, New York Line. He had by his wife Anna, *d.* September 4, 1809, whose surname is unknown:

24. JOHN FREEMAN, *b.* 1754, in the Amenia precinct, New York, *d.* at Amenia, November 8, 1815. He was a soldier in the Revolution and the War of 1812, and *m.* about 1780, Sybil, born July 29, 1753, *d.* July 18, 1812, daughter and coheiress of Edward Lewis, of Ashford, Connecticut, and had:

25. SUSAN FREEMAN, *b.* about 1783, *d.* May 21, 1827, at Schodack, New York, who *m.* Leonard Rowe, *b.* July 27,

1785, at Hillsdale, New York, *d.* August 1, 1844, at Newburgh, New York, and had:

26. SYBIL ANN ROWE, *b.* November 15, 1812, at Schodack, *d.* August 20, 1897. She *m.* at Troy, New York, May 23, 1832, George Washington Knowlton, *b.* at East Greenbush, New York, January 18, 1804, *d.* at Albany, New York, October 11, 1884, grandson of Lieutenant Daniel Knowlton, of Connecticut, a hero of the French and Indian, Revolutionary, and 1812 wars, whose brother, Colonel Thomas Knowlton, slain at Harlem Heights, was commended highly by Washington, and buried with military honors, and had daughter and co-heiress:

27. MARY LOUISA KNOWLTON, *b.* at Greenbush, March 26, 1833, member of the Society Daughters of the American Revolution, Society of *Mayflower* Descendants, and the Order of Descendants of Colonial Governors. She *m.* at Nassau, New York, September 29, 1852, Edwin Henry Griffith, banker, of Castleton-on-Hudson, New York, *b.* December 1, 1830, at Nassau, *d.* May 16, 1875, at Albany, New York, grandson of Major Joshua Griffith (1812), and great-grandson of William Griffith, a Revolutionary soldier, who was a lineal descendant of Llewellyn, last King of Wales, beheaded by the English in 1282, through Griffith, his son. Mr. Griffith was the son of Smith Griffith, 1793–1878, of Nassau, New York, and his wife Lemira, daughter and heiress of John and Nancy (Platt) Herrick, of Greenbush, New York, and granddaughter of Colonel Rufus Herrick, of New York, Continental Line, Revolutionary War. She was seventh in lineal descent from Sir William Herrick, of London, Leicester, and Beau Manor Park, England, and was eighteenth in lineal descent from Eric, King of Danes. Edwin Henry and Mary Louisa (Knowlton) Griffith had:

28. WILLIAM HERRICK GRIFFITH, of Albany, New York,

third son, named for Sir William Herrick, of London and Beau Manor, from whom he is ninth in descent, and twenty-sixth from Eric, King of Danes, *b.* at Castleton-on-Hudson, January 27, 1866, a founder and member of the Order of Runnemede, and member of the Society Sons of the Revolution, Society Sons of the American Revolution, Society of Colonial Wars, Society of *Mayflower* Descendants, Order of Founders and Patriots, Society of the War of 1812, Order of Descendants of Colonial Governors, Order of the Old Guard, of Illinois, New England Historic Genealogical Society, New York Historical Society, Albany Institute, secretary of the Knowlton Association of America, and a 32° Scottish Rite Mason. He *m.* February 3, 1892, at Albany, Grace Elizabeth Clute, daughter of Hon. Matthew Henry Robertson, of Albany, and had issue: Margaret Frances, *b.* December 27, 1892.

Arms.—Quarterly, 1 and 4, Griffith and Herrick impaled; 2 and 3, Knowlton; over all, Freeman and Southworth impaled.

Crests.—Herrick and Knowlton.

Motto.—(Herrick) *Virtus omnia nobilitat.*

Griffith.—*Gu., three lions passant, ar. in pale, armed, az.*

Herrick.—*Ar., a fesse vairé, or and gu.*

    Crest: *A bull's head, couped, ar., horned and eared, sa., gorged with a chaplet of roses, ppr.*

Knowlton.—*Ar., a chevron, gu., between three ducal coronets, sa.*

    Crest: *A demi-lion rampant, sa., armed, gu.*

Freeman.—*Az., three lozenges, or.*

Southworth.—*Ar., a chevron, sa., between three cross-crosslets, sa.*

THE PEDIGREE OF CHARLES SAMUEL WARD, M.D.

Saher de Quincey.	Roger Bigod.		Henry de Bohun.
Robert de Quincey.	Hugh Bigod.	Robert de Vere.	Humphrey de Bohun.
Margaret de Quincey	Ralph Bigod.	Hugh de Vere.	Humphrey de Bohun.
=	Isabel Bigod.	Robert de Vere.	Humphrey de Bohun.
John de Lacie.	John Fitz-Robert.	Joan de Vere.	Humphrey de Bohun.
	Roger Fitz-John.	Alice de Warren.	William de Bohun.
	Robert Fitz-Roger.	Richard Fitz-Alan.	Humphrey de Bohun.
	John de Clavering.	Alice Fitz-Alan.	Allianore de Bohun.
	Eve de Clavering.	Eleanor de Holland.	Anne Plantagenet.
	Edmund d'Ufford.	Alice de Montacute.	John Bouchier.
	Robert d'Ufford.	Alice de Nevill.	Humphrey Bouchier.

Richard de Clare.
Gilbert de Clare.
Richard de Clare ═ Maud de Lacie.
Gilbert de Clare.
Margaret de Clare.
Margaret d'Audley.
Hugh de Stafford ═ Philippa Beauchamp.
Margaret de Stafford.
Philippa de Nevill.
Thomas de Dacre ═ Elizabeth Bowet.

Geoffrey de Say.
William de Say.
William de Say.
Geoffrey de Say.
Joan de Say.
William Fienes.
Roger Fienes.

Thomas de Beauchamp.

William Bowet ═ Amy d'Ufford.

Joan de Dacre ═ Richard Fienes.
John Fienes ═ Alice Fitz-Hugh.
Thomas Fienes ═ Anne Bourchier.

Catherine Fienes ═ Richard Loudenoye, of Briade, Sussex.
Roger Harlakenden, of Kenardiston, Kent, ═ Mary Loudenoye ═ Thomas Harlakenden, of Worthorn, Kent.
Richard Harlakenden, of Kenardiston, Kent, ═ Mary Hubbart.
Mabel Harlakenden ═ John Hayes, Governor of Massachusetts and Connecticut.
Ruth Haynes ═ Samuel Wyllys.
Mehitable Wyllys ═ Rev. Daniel Russell, of Charlestown, Mass.
Mabel Russell ═ Rev. John Hubbard, of Jamaica, L. I., N. Y.
Lt.-Col. John Hubbard, M.D., of New Haven, Conn., ═ Elizabeth Stevens.
Col. Leverett Hubbard, of New Haven, Conn., ═ Sarah Whitehead.
Mary Hubbard ═ Rev. John Lewis, of New Haven, Conn.
Mary Whiteleey Lewis ═ Samuel Ward, of New York and New Haven.
Charles Samuel Ward, M.D., of New York, ═ Lucinda Jane Taggart.
Charles Samuel Ward, M.D., of Bridgeport, Conn.

Charles Samuel Ward, M.D.

DESCENT from the Sureties for the observance of the Magna Charta:

Hugh Bigod,	John Fitz-Robert,
Roger Bigod,	John de Lacie,
Henry de Bohun,	Saher de Quincey,
Gilbert de Clare,	Geoffrey de Say,
Richard de Clare,	Robert de Vere.

1. **Richard de Clare,** one of the Sureties for the Magna Charta, Earl of Hertford, had by his wife, Lady Amicia, daughter of William, Earl of Gloucester:

2. **Gilbert de Clare,** one of the Sureties for the Magna Charta, Earl of Hertford, who had by his wife, Lady Isabel, daughter of William Marshall, Earl of Pembroke:

3. RICHARD DE CLARE, Earl of Hertford and Gloucester, who *m.* secondly, Lady Maud, daughter of **John de Lacie,** a Surety for the Magna Charta, Earl of Lincoln, and had:

4. SIR GILBERT DE CLARE, Earl of Hertford and Gloucester, *d.* 1295, who had, by his second wife, *m.* May 2, 1290, Princess Joan Plantagenet, *d.* 1305, a daughter of EDWARD I., KING OF ENGLAND, by his wife, Eleanor of Castile:

5. LADY MARGARET DE CLARE, widow of Piers de Gaveston, Earl of Cornwall, who *m.* secondly, Hugh d'Audley, first Earl of Gloucester, and had by him, who *d.* 1347-9:

6. LADY MARGARET D'AUDLEY, only child, who *m.* Ralph de Stafford, one of the original members of the Order of Knights of the Garter, seneschal and captain-general of Aquitaine, first Earl of Stafford, *d.* 1372, and had:

7. HUGH DE STAFFORD, K.G., second Earl of Stafford, *d.* 1386. He *m.* Lady Philippa, daughter of Thomas de Beauchamp, third Earl of Warwick, one of the original members of the Order of Knights of the Garter, a commander at Cressy and Poictiers, and a crusader; *d.* 1369. His father was Guy, second Earl of Warwick, *d.* 1315, the son of William de Beauchamp, first Earl of Warwick, by his wife, Lady Maud, widow of Gerard de Furnival, and daughter of John Fitz-John, chief justice of Ireland, 1258, son of John Fitz-Piers Fitz-Geoffrey, chief justice of Ireland, 1246, and his wife, Lady Isabel, widow of Gilbert de Lacie, and daughter of Sir Ralph, third son of **Hugh Bigod**, son of **Roger Bigod**, both Sureties for the Magna Charta and Earls of Norfolk.

Sir Hugh, Earl of Stafford, and Lady Philippa had:

8. LADY MARGARET DE STAFFORD, *d.* 1370, who *m.*, as his first wife, Ralph de Nevill, K.G., created Earl of Westmoreland and marshal of England, who took a leading part in the political drama of his day, *d.* 1425, and had:

9. LADY PHILIPPA DE NEVILL, who *m.* Thomas, Baron de Dacre, of Gillesland, *d.* 1457, and had:

10. THOMAS DE DACRE, eldest son, who *d. v. p.* He *m.* Lady Elizabeth, daughter of Sir William Bowet, *d.* 1423, and his wife, Lady Amy, daughter of Sir Robert d'Ufford, *d.* 1400, eldest son of Sir Edmund d'Ufford, of Horsford, *d.* 1374, youngest son of Sir Ralph d'Ufford (brother of Robert d'Ufford, K.G., Earl of Suffolk), justice of Ireland, *d.* 1346, and his second wife, Lady Eve, daughter of John de Clavering, Lord of Horsford, Norfolk, second Baron by writ, *d.* 1332, eldest son of Robert Fitz-Roger, *d.* 1311, eldest son of Roger Fitz-John, feudal Baron of Warkworth and Clavering, *d.* 1249, eldest son of **John Fitz-Robert**, one of the Sureties for the Magna Charta.

Thomas de Dacre had by the Lady Elizabeth Bowet:

MEMBERS OF THE ORDER OF RUNNEMEDE 299

11. LADY JOAN DE DACRE, will proved June 14, 1486. She *m. ante* 1457, Sir Richard Fienes, Baron Dacre in right of his wife. He was constable of the Tower of London and lord chamberlain to the household of King Edward IV., and *d.* 1484-5.

Sir Richard Fienes was the son of Sir Roger, treasurer of the household to Henry VI., the son of Sir William, high sheriff of Surrey and Sussex, 1297, the son of Sir William Fynes, and his wife, Lady Joan, daughter of Sir Geoffrey, second Baron de Say, admiral of the king's fleet, *d.* 1359 (by his wife, Lady Maud, a daughter of the above Guy, Earl of Warwick, a descendant of **Roger Bigod** and **Hugh Bigod**, both Sureties for the Magna Charta), the eldest son of Geoffrey, *d.* 1322, son of William, *d.* 1295, son of William, *d.* 1272, the son of **Geoffrey de Say**, one of the Sureties for the Magna Charta.

Sir Richard Fienes, Baron Dacre, and Lady Joan had:

12. SIR JOHN FIENES, eldest son, who *d. v. p.* He *m.* Lady Alice, daughter of Henry, Baron Fitz-Hugh, of Ravensworth, *d.* 1472, and his wife, Lady Alice, daughter of Richard Nevill, K.G., Earl of Salisbury, by his wife, Lady Alice Montacute, daughter of Thomas, Earl of Salisbury, and his first wife, Lady Eleanor, daughter of Thomas de Holland, second Earl of Kent, marshal of England, and his wife, Lady Alice, daughter of Richard Fitz-Alan, K.G., Earl of Arundel and Surrey, *d.* 1375, the son of Edmund, K.B., eighth Earl of Arundel, executed in 1326, and his wife, Lady Alice, daughter of William de Warren, *d.* 1286, by his wife, Lady Joan de Vere, daughter of Robert, Earl of Oxford, lord great chamberlain, *d.* 1296, the son of Hugh, Earl of Oxford, lord great chamberlain, *d.* 1203 (by his wife, Lady Hawyse, daughter of **Saber de Quincey**, one of the Sureties for the Magna Charta, Earl of Winchester), the son of

Robert de Vere, Earl of Oxford and lord great chamberlain, one of the Sureties for the Magna Charta.

Sir John Fienes and Lady Alice Fitz-Hugh had:

13. THOMAS FIENES, Baron Dacre of the South, made a Knight of the Bath by Henry VII., *d.* 1534. He *m.* Lady Anne, daughter of Sir Humphrey Bourchier, who was *k. v. p.* at Barnetfield, fighting under the royal banner, eldest son of John Bourchier, K.G., the fourth son of William, Earl of Eue, and his wife, Lady Anne Plantagenet, widow of both Thomas and Edmund, Earls of Stafford, and a daughter of Thomas, Duke of Gloucester, *d.* 1397, youngest son of EDWARD III., KING OF ENGLAND.

The wife of the Earl of Eue was Lady Alianore de Bohun, a daughter of Humphrey, the last Earl of Hereford and Essex and second Earl of Northampton, *d.* 1372. He was the only son of Sir William de Bohun, K.G., Earl of Northampton, *d.* 1360, the fourth son of Humphrey de Bohun, Earl of Hereford and Essex, lord high constable of England, who was slain in the battle of Boroughbridge, March 16, 1321–2, and his wife, *m.* November 14, 1302, Lady Elizabeth Plantagenet, widow of John de Vere and daughter of EDWARD I., KING OF ENGLAND.

This latter Earl Humphrey was the son of Humphrey de Bohun, also Earl of Hereford and Essex and lord high constable, *d.* in 1297, the eldest son of Humphrey de Bohun, *d. v. p.*, who was taken prisoner at Evesham with his father, also named Humphrey, who was the eldest son of **Henry de Bohun,** one of the Sureties for the Magna Charta, Earl of Hereford.

Thomas Fienes, K.B., Baron Dacre, and Lady Anne had:

14. LADY CATHERINE FIENES, second daughter, who *m.* Richard, son of Richard Loudenoys, of Breame, in Sussex, and had:

15. MARY LOUDENOYS, only child, *m.* Thomas Harlaken-

MEMBERS OF THE ORDER OF RUNNEMEDE 301

den, of Warhorn, Kent, his will proved in 1564, and had:

16. ROGER HARLAKENDEN, of Earl's Colne, Essex, Kenardiston and Woodchurch, Kent, third son, *b.* 1535, *d.* 1603. He *m.* first, Elizabeth, daughter of Thomas Hardres, of Kentshire, and widow of George Harlakenden, of Woodchurch, and had by her:

17. RICHARD HARLAKENDEN, of Earl's Colne, *b.* 1565, *d.* August 24, 1631, who *m.* Mary (or Margaret), daughter of Edward Hubbart, of Stanstead-Montfichet, and had:

18. MABEL HARLAKENDEN, seventh daughter, *b.* at Earl's Colne, September 27, 1614. In 1635 she came with her brother, Roger Harlakenden, to New England, and *m.* first, in 1636, as his second wife, John Haynes, of Cambridge, Massachusetts, *b.* 1594,* *d.* 1653, who was elected an assistant in 1634 and 1636, and governor of Massachusetts Colony in 1635; colonel of the Second Regiment Massachusetts Militia in 1636. In 1637 he removed to Hartford, Connecticut, and was elected the first governor of that colony in April, 1639, and every second year afterwards until his death, March 1, 1653-4. His will is printed in the N. E. Hist. and Geneal. Register, xvi. 167. He had by his wife, Mabel Harlakenden:

19. RUTH HAYNES, *b.* 1639, *m.* in 1655, Samuel Wyllys, *b.* February 19, 1631-2, *d.* 1709, assistant governor of the Connecticut Colony, son of George Wyllys, who came to Hartford in 1638, and became governor of the Connecticut Colony in 1642, and had:

20. MEHITABLE WYLLYS, *b.* about 1658, who *m.* Rev. Daniel Russell, *b.* at Charlestown, Massachusetts, graduated, in 1669, at Harvard College, of which he was a Fellow, and was invited, in 1678, to settle as the minister of

---

* See N. E. Hist. and Geneal. Register, xxxii. 311.

Charlestown,* but he died January 4, 1678-9,† having issue :

21. MABEL RUSSELL, *b*. March, 1678-9, *d.* May 10, 1730; *m*. June 12, 1701, Rev. John Hubbard, *b*. in Ipswich, Massachusetts, January 9, 1677, graduated at Harvard College, 1695, and *d*. October 5, 1705, while pastor of the Presbyterian church at Jamaica, Long Island. He was the grandson of Rev. William Hubbard, minister at Ipswich, and the historian of New England, *b*. in England, 1621, and graduated at Harvard College, 1642; and on the maternal side he was a grandson of John Leverett, governor of Massachusetts, 1673.‡ He had by his wife, Mabel Russell :

22. LIEUTENANT-COLONEL JOHN HUBBARD, M.D., *b*. November 30, 1703. He was judge of the New Haven Probate District from 1748 till his death, October 30, 1773, and served during the French and Indian Wars (1754-1763), holding commission as major and commissary for the Crown Point Expedition, under date March 13, 1755, and was promoted lieutenant-colonel Second Connecticut Militia, October, 1757, and resigned May, 1771.§ He *m*. August 30, 1724, Elizabeth, *b*. 1703, *d*. August 25, 1744, daughter of Ensign Samuel Stevens, of Killingworth, Connecticut, and his wife Melatiah, daughter of Major William Bradford, the son of William Bradford, governor of Plymouth Colony, and had :

23. COLONEL LEVERETT HUBBARD, *b*. Killingworth, July 21, 1725, graduated at Yale College, 1744, *d*. October 10, 1794. In 1745 he went on the expedition to Louisburg, to

---

* See 3d Series Col. Mass. Hist. Soc., i. 261.

† Farmer's "First Settlers of New England," p. 250.

‡ Farmer's "First Settlers of New England ;" Macdonald's "Two Centuries in the History of the Presbyterian Church, Jamaica, Long Island ;" New Haven Colony Historical Society Papers, ii. 257.

§ "Colonial Records of Connecticut," vol. x. p. 349, and vol. xiii. p. 428.

familiarize himself with surgical as well as medical cases. In September, 1755, he left New Haven for Crown Point at the head of a company of volunteers, and the next year he was regularly commissioned as one of the surgeons in the intended expedition against the same fortifications. He was promoted in 1771 to the rank of lieutenant-colonel in the militia, and two years later to that of colonel, but resigned his position in October, 1775.* Colonel Hubbard was a loyalist, and resigned his commission, but he did not refuse his services to the State as examiner of such as presented themselves desiring to secure positions on the medical staff in the Continental army, for which service he was appointed.† He was fourth in descent from Major-General Robert Sedgwick, of the Massachusetts forces, 1652, in the expedition against Acadia, and also, in 1656, in the expedition against Jamaica, West Indies, where he died, having been made governor and major-general by the Protector. He *m.* May 22, 1746, Sarah Whitehead, of New Haven, Connecticut, *b.* October 27, 1729, *d.* December 5, 1769, and had:

24. MARY HUBBARD, *b.* April 13, 1752, *d.* August 11, 1786, who *m.* March 9, 1777, Rev. John Lewis, of New Haven, *b.* March, 1746, *d.* April 28, 1792, the son of Captain Eldad Lewis, Second Regiment, Connecticut forces, French and Indian Wars, 1755-58, and had:

25. MARY WHITTLESEY LEWIS, *b.* November 3, 1780, *d.* January 18, 1863, who *m.* November 3, 1802, Samuel Ward, *b.* February 22, 1764, *d.* March 13, 1828, a merchant in New York and New Haven, fifth in descent from Andrew Ward, 1600-1659, the first of the name to settle in America. He was a son of Richard Warde, Knight, whose arms, as below, were granted July 12, 1593. He came to Boston in Win-

---

* Dexter's "Yale Biographies and Annals," p. 760.
† "Public Records of Connecticut," vol. i. p. 24.

throp's fleet; was made freeman at Boston, May 14, 1634, and for a short time resided at Watertown, Massachusetts; was appointed by the General Court of the Bay Colony one of the commissioners "to govern the people at Connecticut."* He was one of the five persons who held the first court in the colony, in April, 1636,—tried the first cause and made the first law. He was one of the six magistrates who, with committees of the lower house, first asserted the sovereignty of the colony by the formal declaration of war against the nation of the Pequots, May 1, 1637 (O.S.).

Mary Whittlesey Lewis had by Samuel Ward:

26. CHARLES SAMUEL WARD, M.D. (Woodstock, Vermont), 1834, of New York, *b*. March 16, 1813, *d*. May 24, 1849. He never practised or engaged in any pursuit. He *m*. June 1, 1840, Lucinda Jane Taggart, of Peterborough, New Hampshire, *b*. March 6, 1821, and had:

27. CHARLES SAMUEL WARD, JR., M.D., *b*. October 28, 1842; graduated, Yale, 1863; medical cadet, United States army, 1862 to 1864, both inclusive; practised in New York City, 1868-1891; resident physician, New York Lying-in Asylum, 1869-1873; visiting and consulting obstetric surgeon to the same institution, 1873-1891; assistant surgeon, Woman's Hospital, 1873-1885; consulting physician, Manhattan Hospital, 1885-1891; retired from practice, 1891; one of the founders of the Order of Runnemede and a member of the Society of Colonial Wars. He *m*. January 30, 1873, Julia Marion Tuttle, *b*. June 30, 1845, *d*. August 21, 1874, and had only one child, Edith, *b*. March 3, 1874, *d*. October 21, 1880.

Arms.—*Az., a cross between four eagles, displayed, ar.*
Crests.—*On a mount vert, a hind couchant, ar.*

THE PEDIGREE OF AND

			Roger Bigod.		Eustace de Vesci.	
			Hugh Bigod.		William de Vesci.	
			Ralph Bigod.	William de Lanvallei.	William de Vesci.	
Geoffrey de Say.	William Malet.		Isabel Bigod.	Hawise de Lanvallei.	Isabel de Vesci.	
William de Say.	Helewise Malet.	John Fitz-Robert.	John Fitz-John.	John de Burgh.	Adam de Welles.	
William de Say.	John de Muscegros.	Roger Fitz-John.	Maud Fitz-John.	Margaret de Burgh.	Adam de Welles.	
Lady de Say.	Robert de Muscegros.	Robert Fitz-Roger.	Guy de Beauchamp.	John de Burgh.	John de Welles.	Robert
John de Sudley.	Hawise de Muscegros.	Euphemia de Clavering.	Thomas de Beauchamp.	John de Burgh.	John de Welles.	William
Joan de Sudley.	Robert de Ferrers.	Ralph de Nevill.	Philippa Beauchamp.	William de Burgh.	Margery de Welles.	Rob
Elizabeth Boteler—Robert de Ferrers.	John de Nevill.		Elizabeth de Burgh.	Henry le Scrope.	Will
	Robert de Ferrers.	Ralph de Nevill—Margaret de Stafford.	Philippa Plantagenet.	Joan le Scrope.	Willia
	Margery de Ferrers—Ralph de Nevill.		Elizabeth Mortimer.	Henry Fitz-Hugh.	Thom
			John de Nevill.	Henry de Percy.	Eleanor Fitz-Hugh.	
			Joan de Nevill.	Henry de Percy.	Margery d'Arcy.	
			William Gascoigne—Margaret Percy.	Eleanor Conyers.	
			Dorothy Gascoigne—Ninian Markenfield.		
			Alice Markenfield—Robert Mauleverer.		

Dorothy Mauleverer—John Kaye.
Robert Kaye—Ann Flower.
Grace Kaye—Sir Richard S
Richard Saltons
Col. Nathaniel Saltons
Gov. Gurdon Saltons
Brig.-Gen. Gurdon Saltons
Rosewell Saltons
William Saltons
Mary Susan Saltons
Isabel Be
* Andrew H. M. Saltons
Sophie Forrest M. Saltonstall.

* In conformity with legal requirements, asce

REW H. M. SALTONSTALL.

```
                                                        Saher de Quincey.   Robert de Vere.                              Henry de Bohun.
                                                          Hawise de Quincey—Hugh de Vere.                                Humphrey de Bohun.
                                       Richard de Clare.                    Robert de Vere.     William de Mowbray.      Humphrey de Bohun.
 de Ros.   William d'Albini.    Gilbert de Clare.   John de Lacie.   Joan de Vere.    Roger de Mowbray.                  Humphrey de Bohun.
 de Ros.     William d'Albini.     Richard de Clare—Maud de Lacie.   Alice de Warren.  John de Mowbray.                  William de Bohun.
rt de Ros—Isabel d'Albini.           Thomas de Clare.                Richard Fitz-Alan.  John de Mowbray.                Humphrey de Bohun.
 de Ros.                              Maud de Clare.                 Richard Fitz-Alan.  John de Mowbray.                Eleanor de Bohun.
 de Ros.                              Robert de Clifford.            Elizabeth Fitz-Alan—Thomas de Mowbray.              Anne Plantagenet.
 de Ros.                              Roger de Clifford.                                  Margaret de Mowbray.           John Bourchier.
        Elizabeth de Ros—Thomas de Clifford.                                                John Howard.                 Humphrey Bourchier.
         Maud de Clifford—Richard Wentworth.                            Katherine Howard—John Bourchier.
         Richard Wentworth—Isabel Fitz-William.                          Jane Bourchier—Edmund Knyvett.
         Matthew Wentworth—Elizabeth Woodruffe.                           John Knyvett—Agnes Harcourt.
         Beatrice Wentworth—Arthur Kaye.                                 Thomas Knyvett—Muriel Parry.
                                                                          Abigail Knyvett—Martin Sedley.
                                                                             Muriel Sedley—Brampton Gurdon.
```

ltonstall.
ll—Muriel Gurdon.
ll—Elizabeth Ward.
ll—Elizabeth Rosewell.
ll—Rebecca Winthrop.
ll—Elizabeth Stewart.
ll—Maria Hudson.
all—Thomas Marston Beare.
re—George B. Mickle.
ll—Susan S. Hunter.
    Muriel Winthrop Saltonstall.

med by judicial decree the name of Saltonstall.

Andrew H. M. Saltonstall

DESCENT from the Sureties for the observance of the Magna Charta:

William d'Albini,	William de Lanvallei,
Hugh Bigod,	William de Malet,
Roger Bigod,	William de Mowbray,
Henry de Bohun,	Saher de Quincey,
Gilbert de Clare,	Robert de Ros,
Richard de Clare,	Geoffrey de Say,
John Fitz-Robert,	Robert de Vere,
John de Lacie,	Eustace de Vesci.

1. **Saber de Quincey,** a Surety for the Magna Charta, Earl of Winchester, had by his wife, Lady Margaret de Bellomont, or Beaumont:

2. LADY HAWISE DE QUINCEY, who *m.* Hugh de Vere, Earl of Oxford, eldest son of **Robert de Vere,** a Magna Charta Surety, Earl of Oxford, and had:

3. ROBERT DE VERE, Earl of Oxford, lord great chamberlain, *m.* Lady Alice, daughter of Gilbert, Baron Saundford, chamberlain-in-fee to Queen Eleanor, and had:

4. LADY JOAN DE VERE, *m.* William de Warren, *k. v. p.* 1285, eldest son of John Plantagenet, Earl of Warren and Surrey, and had:

5. LADY ALICE DE WARREN, *m.* Edmund Fitz-Alan, K.B., Earl of Arundel, beheaded 1326, and had:

6. RICHARD FITZ-ALAN, K.G., Earl of Arundel, *m.* secondly, Lady Eleanor, daughter of Henry Plantagenet, Earl of Lancaster, a grandson of King Henry III., and had:

7. RICHARD FITZ-ALAN, K.G., Earl of Arundel, beheaded

1397, *m.* first, Lady Elizabeth, daughter of William de Bohun, Earl of Northampton, and had:

8. Lady Elizabeth Fitz-Alan, *m.* secondly, as second wife, Thomas de Mowbray, Earl of Nottingham, Duke of Norfolk, first earl marshal of England, *d.* in banishment, 1400, whose descent was:

William de Mowbray, a Magna Charta Surety, had by his wife, Lady Agnes, daughter of William d'Albini, Earl of Arundel and Sussex:

Roger de Mowbray, *d.* 1266, *m.* Lady Maud, daughter of William de Beauchamp, of Bedford, and had:

Roger de Mowbray, *d.* 1298, *m.* Lady Rose de Clare, a granddaughter of Richard de Clare, and had:

John de Mowbray, executed 1321, *m.* Lady Aliva, daughter of William de Braose, of Gower, and had:

John de Mowbray, *d.* 1361, *m.* Lady Joan, daughter of Henry Plantagenet, Earl of Lancaster, a grandson of King Henry III., and had:

John de Mowbray, *d.* 1368, *m.* Lady Elizabeth, daughter of John de Segrave and Margaret, Duchess of Norfolk, a granddaughter of King Edward I., and had:

Thomas de Mowbray, Duke of Norfolk, *d.* 1400, who had by Lady Elizabeth Fitz-Alan, aforesaid:

9. Lady Margaret de Mowbray, *m.* Sir Robert Howard, and had:

10. Sir John Howard, Duke of Norfolk, earl marshal, *m.* Lady Margaret Chedworth, and had:

11. Lady Catherine Howard, *m.* Sir John Bourchier, Baron Berners, *d.* 1532, who was descended as follows:

Henry de Bohun, a Magna Charta Surety, Earl of Hereford and Essex, had by his wife, Lady Maud, daughter of Geoffrey Fitz-Piers de Mandeville, Earl of Essex, and sister of Geoffrey de Mandeville, a Magna Charta Surety:

Humphrey de Bohun, Earl of Hereford and Essex, lord

high constable, *d.* 1274, *m.* first, Lady Maud, daughter of Henry d'Eue, and had:

Humphrey de Bohun, eldest son, *d. v. p.*, who *m.* Lady Eleanor, daughter of William de Braose, of Brecknock, and had:

Humphrey de Bohun, Earl of Hereford and Essex, lord high constable, *d.* 1297, *m.* Lady Maud, daughter of Ingelram de Fienes, and had:

Humphrey de Bohun, Earl of Hereford and Essex, lord high constable, *k.* 1321, *m.* Lady Elizabeth, daughter of King Edward I., and had:

William de Bohun, K.G., Earl of Northampton, *d.* 1360, *m.* Lady Elizabeth, daughter of Bartholomew de Badlesmere, and had:

Humphrey de Bohun, second Earl of Northampton, *d.* 1372, *m.* Lady Joan, daughter of Richard Fitz-Alan, K.G., Earl of Arundel, *d.* 1375, and had:

Lady Eleanor de Bohun, *m.* Thomas, of Woodstock, Duke of Gloucester, son of King Edward III., and had:

Lady Anne Plantagenet, *m.* Sir William Bourchier, Earl of Ewe, *d.* 1412, and had:

John Bourchier, K.G., Baron Berners, *d.* 1474, *m.* Lady Margery, daughter of Richard Berners, of West Horsley, Surrey, and had:

Sir Humphrey Bourchier, eldest son, *k. v. p.*, who *m.* Elizabeth, daughter of Sir Frederick Tilney, and had:

Sir John Bourchier, Baron Berners, aforesaid, *d.* 1532, who had by Lady Catherine Howard:

12. LADY JANE BOURCHIER, *d.* 1561, *m.* Edmund Knyvett, of Ashwelthorpe, sergeant-porter to King Henry VIII., *d.* 1539, and had:

13. JOHN KNYVETT, of Plumstead, Norfolk, *m.* Agnes, daughter of Sir John Harcourt, of Stanton-Harcourt, Oxford, and had:

14. Sir Thomas Knyvett, *d.* 1616–17, *m.* Muriel Parry, and had:

15. Abigail Knyvett, *m.* Sir Martin Sedley, and had:

16. Muriel Sedley, *m.* Brampton Gurdon, of Assington, Suffolk, high sheriff, 1629, member of Parliament for Sudbury, 1620, and had:

17. Muriel Gurdon, *m.* Richard Saltonstall, of Ipswich, Massachusetts, whose descent was as follows:

Robert de Ros, a Magna Charta Surety, had by his wife, Lady Isabel, a natural daughter of William the Lion, King of Scotland:

William de Ros, of Hamelake, *d.* 1258, *m.* Lady Lucia, daughter of Reginald Fitz-Piers, of Blewleveny, Wales, and had:

Robert de Ros, of Hamelake, *d.* 1285, *m.* Lady Isabel, daughter of William, eldest son of **William d'Albini,** a Magna Charta Surety, and had:

William de Ros, of Hamelake, *d.* 1316, *m.* Lady Maud, daughter of John de Vaux, of Feston, and had:

William de Ros, of Hamelake, *d.* 1342, *m.* Margery, sister and coheiress of Giles de Badlesmere, of Leeds Castle, and had:

Thomas de Ros, of Hamelake, *d.* 1384, *m.* Beatrix, daughter of Ralph, K.G., first Earl of Stafford, and had:

Lady Elizabeth de Ros, *m.* Thomas de Clifford, of Appleby, *d.* 1392, whose descent was as follows:

Richard de Clare, a Magna Charta Surety, Earl of Hertford, had by his wife, Lady Amicia, daughter of William, Earl of Gloucester:

Gilbert de Clare, a Magna Charta Surety, Earl of Hertford and Gloucester, *m.* Lady Isabel, daughter of William Marshall, Earl of Pembroke, and sister of William Marshall, a Magna Charta Surety, and had:

Richard de Clare, Earl of Hertford and Gloucester, *m.*

secondly, Lady Maud, daughter of **John de Lacie**, a Magna Charta Surety, Earl of Lincoln, and had:

Thomas de Clare, governor of London, 1274, *d.* 1287, *m.* Amy, daughter of Sir Maurice Fitz-Maurice, and had:

Lady Maud de Clare, *m.* Robert de Clifford, of Appleby, *k.* 1313, and had:

Robert de Clifford, *d.* 1340, *m.* Lady Isabel de Berkeley, and had:

Roger de Clifford, of Appleby, *m.* Lady Maud, daughter of Thomas de Beauchamp, Earl of Warwick, and had:

Thomas de Clifford, of Appleby, *d.* 1392, aforesaid, who had by Lady Elizabeth de Ros, or Roos:

Lady Maud de Clifford, *m.* Richard Wentworth, of Bretton, and had:

Richard Wentworth, *d.* 1448, *m.* Isabel, daughter of Sir William Fitz-William, of Sprotsborough, and had:

Matthew Wentworth, of Bretton, *d.* 1504, *m.* Elizabeth Woodruffe, and had:

Beatrice Wentworth, *m.* Arthur Kaye, of Woodsome, Yorkshire, and had:

John Kaye, of Woodsome, 1585, *m.* Dorothy Mauleverer, whose descent was as follows:

Roger Bigod, a Magna Charta Surety, Earl of Norfolk, *m.* first, Lady Isabel, daughter of Hameline Plantagenet, Earl of Surrey, and had:

Hugh Bigod, a Magna Charta Surety, Earl of Norfolk, *m.* Lady Maud, daughter of William Marshall, Earl of Pembroke, and sister of William Marshall, a Magna Charta Surety, and had:

Sir Ralph Bigod, third son, *m.* Berta, daughter of Baron de Furnival, and had:

Lady Isabel Bigod, *m.* secondly, John Fitz-Piers Fitz-Geoffrey, justiciary of Ireland, 1246, and had:

John Fitz-John, justiciary of Ireland, 1258, who had:

Lady Maud Fitz-John, *m.* secondly, William de Beauchamp, first Earl of Warwick, *d.* 1298, and had:

Guy de Beauchamp, Earl of Warwick, *d.* 1315, *m.* Lady Alice, daughter of Ralph de Toni, and had:

Thomas de Beauchamp, K.G., Earl of Warwick, *d.* 1369, *m.* Lady Catherine, daughter of Roger de Mortimer, Earl of March, and had:

Lady Philippa de Beauchamp, *m.* Hugh de Stafford, K.G., second Earl of Stafford, *d.* 1386, and had:

Lady Margaret de Stafford, *m.* Ralph de Nevill, K.G., first Earl of Westmoreland, *d.* 1425, whose descent was:

John Fitz-Robert, a Magna Charta Surety, had by his wife, Lady Ada de Baliol:

Roger Fitz-John, lord of Clavering, *d.* 1249, who had:

Robert Fitz-Roger de Clavering, first Baron by writ, *d.* 1311, *m.* Lady Margaret de la Zouche, and had:

Lady Euphemia de Clavering, who *m.*, as his first wife, Ralph, Baron de Nevill, of Raby, *d.* 1331, and had:

Ralph de Nevill, of Raby, second Baron, *d.* 1367, *m.* Lady Alice, daughter of Hugh d'Audley, and had:

John de Nevill, K.G., third Baron, admiral of the fleet, *d.* 1388, *m.* Lady Maud, daughter of Henry, Baron Percy, of Alnwick, and had:

Ralph de Nevill, K.G., fourth Baron, created Earl of Westmoreland, earl marshal, aforesaid, who had by Lady Margaret de Stafford:

Ralph de Nevill, second son, *m.* Lady Margery, daughter of Sir Robert, second Baron de Ferrers, of Wemme, by his wife, Lady Joan de Beaufort, a granddaughter of King Edward III. Lord Ferrers was descended as follows:

William de Malet, a Magna Charta Surety, *m.* a daughter of Thomas Basset, and had:

Lady Helewise de Malet, who *m.* Sir Robert de Muscegros, lord of Norton and Berwain, and had:

MEMBERS OF THE ORDER OF RUNNEMEDE 311

John de Muscegros, of Charlton, Somerset, *d.* 1275, who had:

Sir Robert de Muscegros, of Charlton, who had:

Hawyse de Muscegros, who *m.* John, first Baron Ferrers, of Chartley, *d.* 1324, and had:

Robert de Ferrers, second Baron, *d.* 1350, *m.* Lady Agnes, daughter of Humphrey de Bohun, Earl of Hereford and Essex, *k.* 1321, a descendant of **Henry de Bohun**, a Magna Charta Surety, and had:

Sir Robert, first Baron de Ferrers, of Wemme, *d.* 1410, *m.* Lady Elizabeth, daughter and heiress of William, third Baron Boteler, of Wemme, *d.* 1369, and his wife, Lady Joan, daughter of John, Baron de Sudley, son of John de Sudley, lord chamberlain to Edward I., *d.* 1336, and his wife, a daughter of William, Baron de Say, *d.* 1295, the son of William, Baron de Say, governor of Rochester Castle, *d.* 1272, the son of **Geoffrey de Say**, a Magna Charta Surety, and had:

Sir Robert, second Baron de Ferrers, of Wemme and Oversley, aforesaid, whose daughter, Lady Margery, *m.* Ralph de Nevill, and had:

John Nevill, of Wymesley, York, *d.* 1482, *m.* first, Elizabeth, daughter of Robert, Baron de Newmarch, and had, only child:

Joan Nevill, *m.* first, Sir William Gascoigne, of Gawthorpe, York, *d.* 1464, and had:

Sir William Gascoigne, of Gawthorpe, *m.* Lady Margaret Percy, whose descent was as follows:

William de Lanvallei,, a Magna Charta Surety, had by his wife, a daughter of Alan Basset, of Wycombe:

Lady Hawise de Lanvallei, *d.* 1330, *m.* Sir John de Burgh, son of Hubert, Earl of Kent, and had:

John de Burgh, Baron of Lanvallei, *d. s. p. m.*, 1279, who had:

Lady Margaret de Burgh, *m*. Richard de Burgh, second Earl of Ulster, justiciary of Ireland, *d*. 1326, and had:

John de Burgh, *m*. Lady Elizabeth, daughter of Gilbert de Clare, Earl of Hertford and Gloucester, *d*. 1295, and Lady Joan, daughter of King Edward I., and had:

William de Burgh, Earl of Ulster, *m*. Lady Maud, daughter of Henry Plantagenet, Earl of Lancaster and Leicester, a grandson of King Henry III., and had, only child:

Lady Elizabeth de Burgh, *m*. Lionel Plantagenet, Duke of Clarence, a son of King Edward III., and had:

Lady Philippa Plantagenet, only child, *m*. Edmund de Mortimer, Earl of March, *d*. 1381, and had:

Lady Elizabeth de Mortimer, *m*. Sir Henry Percy ("Hotspur"), *k*. 1403, at Shrewsbury, and had:

Henry Percy, second Earl of Northumberland, *k*. at St. Albans, 1455, *m*. Lady Eleanor, daughter of Ralph de Nevill, first Earl of Westmoreland, and his second wife, Lady Joan de Beaufort, a granddaughter of King Edward III., and had:

Henry Percy, third Earl of Northumberland, *m*. Lady Eleanor, daughter of Richard, Baron Poynings, and had:

Lady Margaret Percy, who *m*. Sir William Gascoigne, whose descent is given above, and had:

Dorothy Gascoigne, *m*. Sir Ninian, or Nyan, de Markenfield (see his descent on p. 195), whose descent was:

Eustace de Vesci, a Magna Charta Surety, *m*. Lady Margaret, daughter of William the Lion, King of Scots, and had: William, *d*. 1253, who had by his second wife, Lady Agnes, daughter of William de Ferrers, Earl of Derby: William, second son, second Baron by writ, *d*. 1297, *m*. Isabel, daughter of Adam Periton, and had: Isabel, *m*. William de Welles, and had: Adam, first Baron by writ, 1299, who had: Adam, second son and third Baron, *d*. 1345, who had: John, fourth Baron, *d*. 1361, who had: John, fifth Baron, who had: Margery, widow of John de Huntingfield, *m*. secondly,

ANDREW H. M. SALTONSTALL.

Sir Stephen le Scrope, second Baron, of Masham, and had: Sir Henry, third Baron, *m.* first, Philippa, daughter of Sir Guy de Brien, and had: Lady Joan, *m.* Henry Fitz-Hugh, second Baron, and had: Henry, third Baron, who had: Lady Eleanor, *m.* Philip, sixth Baron d'Arcy, *d.* 1418, and had: Margery, *m.* Sir John Conyers, K.G., and had: Eleanor, *m.* Sir Thomas de Markenfield, *d.* 1497, and had: Ninian Markenfield, who *m.* Dorothy Gascoigne, aforesaid, and had:

Alice Markenfield, *m.* Robert Mauleverer, son of Sir William Mauleverer, of Wothersome, Yorkshire (see p. 198), and had:

Dorothy Mauleverer, *m.* John Kaye, aforesaid, and had:

Robert Kaye, of Woodsome, 1612, *m.* Ann, daughter of John Flower, of Whitewell, and had:

Grace Kaye, *m.* Sir Richard Saltonstall, of Huntwick, *b.* 1586. He was one of the first-named associates of the original patentees of the Massachusetts Bay Colony in the charter granted May 4, 1628, also first named among the assistants appointed thereby, and was one of the original patentees of Connecticut. He came to America in April, 1630, and was the founder of Watertown, Massachusetts. He returned to England and was ambassador to Holland, and was a member of the high court of justice held to try the Duke of Hamilton and others for high treason. His eldest son by Grace Kaye was:

Richard Saltonstall, of Ipswich, Massachusetts, *b.* at Woodsome, York, 1610, *d.* at Hulme, England, 1694. He came to New England with his father, and was deputy to the general court, 1635–7; assistant, 1637–1683; sergeant-major in Colonel Endicott's regiment, 1641. He *m.*, as above, Muriel Gurdon, and had:

18. NATHANIEL SALTONSTALL, of Haverhill, Massachusetts, *b.* Ipswich, 1639, *d.* May 21, 1707. He was assist-

ant, 1679-92; member of the governor's council, and judge and colonel, and *m.* December 28, 1663, Elizabeth, daughter of Rev. John Ward, and had:

19. GURDON SALTONSTALL, of New London, Connecticut, eldest son, *b.* March 27, 1666, *d.* September 20, 1724. He was governor of Connecticut Colony, 1708-24, and had by his second wife, Elizabeth, daughter of William Rosewell:

20. GURDON SALTONSTALL, of New London, *b.* 1708. He served as delegate to several colonial conventions; was a member of the several committees of New London conducting continental affairs, and was made a brigadier-general in 1776. He *m.* March 15, 1732, Rebecca, daughter of John Winthrop, F.R.S., *d.* London, 1747 (a son of Chief Justice Wait Still Winthrop, son of John Winthrop, governor of Connecticut and New Haven Colonies, 1657-1676, son of John Winthrop, the "Father of the Massachusetts Colony," governor of Massachusetts Bay Colony, 1629-1649), and his wife Anne, daughter of Joseph Dudley, president of the colony of Massachusetts, New Hampshire, and Maine, 1686; chief justice of New York, 1692; governor of Massachusetts, 1702-15, son of Thomas Dudley, governor of Massachusetts Colony, 1634-1650; major-general, 1646, and had:

21. ROSEWELL SALTONSTALL, seventh child, 1741-1804, *m.* Elizabeth, daughter of Matthew Stewart, of New London, and had:

22. WILLIAM SALTONSTALL, of New York, seventh child, *d.* 1842, *m.*, in England, Maria Hudson, and had:

23. MARY SUSAN SALTONSTALL, who *m.* Thomas Marston Beare, of New York, and had:

24. ISABEL BEARE, *m.* George B. Mickle, of Bayside, Long Island, New York, and had:

25. ANDREW H. M. SALTONSTALL (who, in conformity with legal requirements, assumed, by judicial decree, the name

of Saltonstall), of Berkeley Springs, West Virginia, a founder and member of the Order of Runnemede, Society of Colonial Wars, and Society Sons of the Revolution. He *m.* June 9, 1892, Susan Summers, daughter of Dr. John Harrison and Sophie (Forrest) Hunter, of Berkeley Springs, and had: Sophie Forrest and Muriel Winthrop Saltonstall.

Arms.—Quarterly, 1 and 4, Saltonstall; 2, Mickle; 3, Beare.

Crests.—Saltonstall and Mickle.

Motto.—*Teneo tenuere majores.*

Saltonstall.—*Or, a bend between two eaglets, displayed, sa.*

Crest.—*An eaglet's head and neck, couped, az., issuing out of ducal coronet, or.*

Mickle.—*Gu., a chevron between three crosses pattée fitchée, each cantoned with four cross-crosslets, ar.*

Crest.—*A stag's head, couped at the neck, or.*

Beare.—*Ar., a bear rampant, sa., a canton, gu.*

Ferdinand P. Earle

DESCENT from the Sureties for the observance of the Magna Charta:

Hugh Bigod,   Geoffrey de Say.   Roger Bigod,

1. **Geoffrey de Say,** one of the Sureties for the Magna Charta, *d.* 1230, had by his wife, Lady Alice, daughter and coheiress of John de Cheney:

2. WILLIAM DE SAY, governor of the castle of Rochester, 44 Henry III., and was at the battle of Lewes, on the side of the king. He *d.* in 1272, and was succeeded by his son:

3. WILLIAM DE SAY, who had, with others, in 22 Edward II., summons to advise with the king upon affairs of the realm, and subsequently did military duty in Gascony. He *d.* 1295, and was succeeded by his son:

4. GEOFFREY DE SAY, then only fourteen years old, whose wardship was given to William, first Baron de Leyburne, in order that he might marry Idonæ, daughter of the said William. In 7 Edward II. he had summons to Parliament as a Baron, and *d.* in 1322, having issue by the Lady Idonæ:

5. GEOFFREY DE SAY, second Baron. Being of age, 19 Edward II., he had livery of his lands and was summoned to Parliament, and 10 Edward III. he was constituted an admiral of the king's fleet, and was constantly afterwards employed in the wars of France and Flanders, and *d.* 1359. He *m.* Lady Maud (Matilda), daughter of Guy de Beauchamp, second Earl of Warwick, *d.* 1315, and his wife, Lady

Alice, daughter of Ralph de Toni, of Flamstead, Herts, and widow of Thomas de Leyburne.

Guy, Earl of Warwick, aforesaid, was the son of William de Beauchamp, of Elmley Castle, created Earl of Warwick, *d.* 1298, and his wife, Lady Maud, widow of Gerard de Furnival, of Sheffield, and daughter of John Fitz-John, chief justice of Ireland, 1258, son of John Fitz-Geoffrey, chief justice of Ireland, 1246, and his wife, Lady Isabel, widow of Gilbert de Lacie, lord of Meath, and daughter of Sir Ralph Bigod, third son of **Hugh Bigod**, son of **Roger Bigod**, both Sureties for the Magna Charta and Earls of Norfolk.

Geoffrey de Say and the Lady Maud had:

6. LADY IDONÆ DE SAY, who *m.* Sir John, third Baron de Clinton, of Mantoch, governor of Warwick Castle, *b.* 1326, *d.* 1397, and had:

7. LADY MARGARET CLINTON, who *m.* Sir Baldwin de Montfort, Knight, and had:

8. SIR WILLIAM DE MONTFORT, Knight, *d.* 1453, who *m.* Margaret, granddaughter of Sir John Peche, *d.* 1376, and daughter of Sir John Peche, *d.* 1386, and had:

9. SIR BALDWIN DE MONTFORT, Knight, *b.* 1445, *d.* 1475, who *m.* Joanna Vernon, and had:

10. ROBERT DE MONTFORT, of Bescote, Staffordshire, and Monkspath, Warwickshire, who had:

11. CATHERINE MONTFORT, heiress, who *m.* George Bothe, *d.* 1483, eldest son of Sir William Bothe, of Dunham-Massie, County Chester, high sheriff of Chester for life, *d.* 1476, and his wife Maud, daughter of John Dutton, of Dutton, Cheshire, *d.* 1445, and sister of Sir Thomas de Dutton, *k.* at Bloreheath in 1459, and had:

12. SIR WILLIAM BOTHE, eldest son, *d* November 9, 1520, who had by his second wife, Ellen, daughter of Sir John Montgomery, of Trewly, Staffordshire:

13. JANE BOTHE, widow of Hugh, son of Sir Piers de Dutton, County Chester, who *m.* secondly, Thomas Holford, of Holford, County Chester, and had:

14. DOROTHY HOLFORD, who *m.* (as his second wife) John Bruen, of Bruen-Stapleford, County Chester, *b.* 1510, *d.* May 14, 1580, and had:

15. JOHN BRUEN, eldest son; *bapt.* 1560; *d.* January 18, 1625–6; buried at Tarrin. He was known as "the celebrated John Bruen" (see Omerod's "History of Cheshire," ii. 320), and had by his second wife, Ann, daughter of John Fox:

16. OBADIAH BRUEN, second son and fourth child by second wife, *bapt.* December 25, 1606, who came to the Plymouth Colony, New England, before 1640, and was one of the founders of New London, Connecticut, 1650, and of Newark, New Jersey, 1667, where he *d.* after 1680, having issue by his wife Sarah, whose surname has not been preserved:

17. JOHN BRUEN, of Newark, New Jersey, *d. ante* 1696, who had by his wife, Esther Lawrence, *m. ante* 1680:

18. REBECCA BRUEN, who *m.* Thomas Montagne, of New York, *b.* 1691, son of Vincent Montagne, *b.* 1657, and had:

19. HANNAH MONTAGNE, *b.* 1737, who *m.* February 8, 1755, Morris Earle, of New York, *b.* 1734, son of Marmaduke Earle, *b.* Bergen, New Jersey, October 6, 1696, and had:

20. WILLIAM EARLE, *b.* Watertown, Massachusetts, April 22, 1775, who *m.* Martha Pinto, *b.* New Haven, Connecticut, May 19, 1780, and had:

21. WILLIAM PITT EARLE, *b.* Worcester, Massachusetts, June 14, 1812, who *m.* April 13, 1836, Elizabeth, *b.* December 25, 1817, daughter of Judge Benjamin Pinney, of Ellington, Connecticut, *b.* July 4, 1780, and Susannah McKinney, *b.* July 6, 1780, and had:

22. FERDINAND PINNEY EARLE, of New York City, *b.* Hartford, Connecticut, September 11, 1839. He was appointed, January 1, 1889, on his staff by Governor Hill, of New York, with the rank of brigadier-general, and served also on the staff of Governor Flower. He is one of the founders of the Order of Runnemede, a member of the Society of Colonial Wars, and a member of other American patriotic and historical societies. He *m.* first, December 4, 1861, Mary Lay Hutchings, who *d. s. p.* in Paris, September 11, 1870, and *m.* secondly, November 6, 1871, Lydia Jones, *b.* May 29, 1844, widow of Dorephus Tuttle, of Boston, *d. s. p.*, and daughter of David George Smith, of Halifax, Nova Scotia, and his wife Catherine, daughter of Captain Jacob Locke, of Shelborn, Nova Scotia, a descendant of the Emperor Charlemagne (see "Americans of Royal Descent," pp. 825, 826), and had issue: Ferdinand Pinney, *b.* June 8, 1878; Victor de la Montagne, *b.* May 24, 1880; William Pitt Striker, *b.* December 28, 1882; and Guyon Locke Crocheron, *b.* May 25, 1884.

Arms.—*Quarterly,* 1 *and* 4, *gu., a St. George cross, ar., 2 and 3, az., three escollopes, gu.; over all a St. George cross, ar.*

Crest.—*A nag's head, erased, sa., maned, or, on an esquire's helmet.*

Motto.—*Vulneritus non victus.*

THE PEDIGREE OF SCHUYLER L. PARSONS.

```
                                    Roger Bigod.
                                    Hugh Bigod.
William de Lanvallei.   Richard de Clare.   Ralph Bigod.                                    Saher
                                                                                              de
Hawise de Lanvallei.    Gilbert de Clare.   Isabel Bigod.      Robert de Vere.            Quincey.
John de Burgh.          Isabel de Clare.    John Fitz-John.    Hugh de Vere—Hawise de
Margaret de Burgh.      Robert de Bruce.    Maud Fitz-John.    Robert de Vere.           Quincey.
       Elizabeth de Burgh—Robert Bruce, King   Isabel de Beauchamp.  Joan de Vere.
Margaret de Bruce.              of Scotland.   Maud de Chaworth.     Alice de Warren.
William de Sutherland.                         Eleanor Plantagenet—Richard Fitz-Alan.
Robert de Sutherland.                          Alice Fitz-Alan.
John de Sutherland.                            Margaret de Holland.
       John de Sutherland—                     Joan de Beaufort—James I., King of Scotland.
                                               Annabel Stewart—George Gordon.
              Elizabeth de Sutherland—Adam Gordon, of Aboyne.
              Alexander Gordon, Earl of Sutherland,—Lady Janet Stewart.
                Sir John Gordon, Earl of Sutherland,—Lady Helen Stewart.
              Alexander Gordon, Earl of Sutherland,—Lady Jean Gordon.
                        Sir Robert Gordon, Bart.,—Louise Gordon.
                             Catherine Gordon—Col. David Barclay, of Ury.
       John Barclay, Deputy-Governor of East Jersey,—Cornelia Van Schaick.
              Rev. Thomas Barclay, of Albany, N. Y.,—Anna Dorothea Drailyer.
              Rev. Henry Barclay, D.D., of New York City,—Mary Rutgers.
              Col. Thomas Barclay, of New York City,—Susan de Lancey.
                             Anne Barclay—William Burrington Parsons, R.N.
              William Barclay Parsons, of New York City,—Eliza Livingston.
                      Schuyler Livingston Parsons, of New York City.
```

Schuyler Livingston Parsons

DESCENT from the Sureties for the observance of the Magna Charta:

Hugh Bigod,
Roger Bigod,
Gilbert de Clare,
Richard de Clare,

William de Lanvallei,
Saher de Quincey,
Robert de Vere.

1. **William de Lanvallei,** a Surety for the Magna Charta, *m.* a daughter of Alan Basset, of Wycombe, and had:

2. LADY HAWYSE DE LANVALLEI, who *m.* Sir John, eldest son of Hubert de Burgh, Earl of Kent, chief justice of England, and had:

3. JOHN DE BURGH, Baron of Lanvallei, *d.* 1279, who had:

4. LADY MARGARET DE BURGH, who *m.* Richard de Burgh, second Earl of Ulster, lord justice of Ireland, *d.* 1326, and had:

5. LADY ELIZABETH DE BURGH, *d.* 1327, who *m.* in 1302, as his second wife, ROBERT BRUCE, KING OF SCOTLAND, the eldest son of Robert, Earl of Annandale, *d.* 1304, the eldest son of Robert, Earl of Annandale, *d.* 1295, and his first wife, Lady Isabel, daughter of **Gilbert de Clare,** son of **Richard de Clare,** both Sureties for the Magna Charta and Earls of Hertford.

Lady Elizabeth and Robert I., King of Scotland, had:

6. PRINCESS MARGARET BRUCE, *d.* 1358, widow of Robert Glen, of Pittedy. She *m.* secondly, 1344, as his first wife, William, Earl of Sutherland, *d.* 1370, and had:

7. WILLIAM, EARL OF SUTHERLAND, second son, who had by his wife, whose name has not been preserved:

8. ROBERT, EARL OF SUTHERLAND, *d.* 1442. He *m.* Lady Mabilla, daughter of John, Earl of Moray, second son of Patrick Dunbar, Earl of Dunbar and March, *d.* 1369 (a descendant of **Gilbert de Clare** and **Richard de Clare**, both Sureties for the Magna Charta), and his first wife, Lady Agnes Randolph, known as "Black Agnes" (daughter of Thomas, first Earl of Moray, regent of Scotland, only son of Sir Thomas Randolph, of Strathwith, high chamberlain of Scotland, 1296, and his wife, Lady Isabel, sister of King Robert Bruce and daughter of Robert, Earl of Annandale and Carrick, a descendant of **Gilbert de Clare**, son of **Richard de Clare**, both Sureties for the Magna Charta), who, during the absence of her husband, successfully defended the Castle of Dunbar for nineteen weeks against the English in 1337.

Robert, Earl of Sutherland, and Lady Mabilla had:

9. JOHN, EARL OF SUTHERLAND, *d.* 1460, *m.* Margaret, daughter of Sir William Baillie, of Lamington, and had:

10. JOHN, EARL OF SUTHERLAND, *d.* 1508, *m.* Lady Margaret Macdonald, daughter of Alexander, Earl of Ross, *d.* 1448, and had:

11. ELIZABETH, COUNTESS OF SUTHERLAND, *d.* 1535, sister and heiress of John, Earl of Sutherland, who *d. s. p.* 1514. She *m.* Adam Gordon, of Aboyne, *d.* March 17, 1527, who in right of his wife was Earl of Sutherland. He was the second son of George Gordon, second Earl of Huntly (a descendant of DAVID I., KING OF SCOTLAND, and of **Gilbert de Clare** and **Richard de Clare**, both Sureties for the Magna Charta), and his wife, Princess Annabella, daughter of JAMES I., KING OF SCOTLAND, (a descendant of **Gilbert de Clare** and **Richard de Clare**, both Sureties for the Magna Charta), by his wife, Lady Joan de Beaufort.

MEMBERS OF THE ORDER OF RUNNEMEDE 323

Lady Joan de Beaufort, who *m.* 1424, as her first husband, King James I., was a daughter of John, Earl of Somerset, Marquis of Dorset, lord high admiral and high chamberlain of England, *d.* 1410 (a son of John, Duke of Lancaster, a son of EDWARD III., KING OF ENGLAND, and his wife, Lady Philippa, of Hainault), and his wife, Lady Margaret de Holland, daughter of Thomas, second Earl of Kent, earl marshal of England, *d.* 1397, son of Sir Thomas de Holland, K.G., Earl of Kent, captain-general of France and Normandy, *d.* 1360, by his wife, Lady Joan Plantagenet, the Fair Maid of Kent, daughter of Edmund, Earl of Kent, a son of EDWARD I., KING OF ENGLAND, and his second wife, Princess Margaret, daughter of PHILIP III., KING OF FRANCE.

The wife of the second Earl of Kent was Lady Alice, daughter of Richard Fitz-Alan, K.G., Earl of Arundel and Surrey, *d.* 1375, by his second wife, Lady Eleanor Plantagenet, daughter of Henry, third Earl of Lancaster, *d.* 1345 (son of Edmund, Earl of Lancaster, *d.* 1295, a son of HENRY III., KING OF ENGLAND), and his wife, Lady Maud, daughter of Patrick de Chaworth by his wife, Lady Isabel, daughter of William de Beauchamp, created Earl of Warwick, *d.* 1298, and his wife, Lady Maud, daughter of John Fitz-John, chief justice of Ireland, 1258, son of John Fitz-Geoffrey, chief justice of Ireland, 1246, by his wife, Lady Isabel, widow of Gilbert de Lacie and daughter of Sir Ralph Bigod, son of **Hugh Bigod**, son of **Roger Bigod**, both Sureties for the Magna Charta and Earls of Norfolk.

Richard Fitz-Alan, aforesaid, was the son of Edmund, K.B., Earl of Arundel, beheaded in 1326, and his wife, Lady Alice, daughter of William de Warren, *d.* 1286, by his wife, Lady Joan, daughter of Robert de Vere, Earl of Oxford, *d.* 1296, son of Hugh, Earl of Oxford, great high chamberlain, *d.* 1263 (by his wife, Lady Hawyse, daughter of **Saber de Quincey**, one of the Sureties for the Magna Charta,

Earl of Winchester), son of **Robert de Vere,** Earl of Oxford, one of the Sureties for the Magna Charta.

Countess Elizabeth and Adam Gordon had:

12. ALEXANDER GORDON, Earl of Sutherland, *d.* 1529, *m.* Lady Janet, daughter of Sir John Stewart, of Balveny, the eldest son of Lady Joan de Beaufort, queen dowager of Scotland, a lineal descendant, as before stated, of kings of England and France, and of **Hugh Bigod, Roger Bigod, Saber de Quincey,** and **Robert de Vere,** Sureties for the Magna Charta, and her second husband, Sir James Stewart, of Lorn, a descendant of **Gilbert de Clare, Richard de Clare,** and **William de Lanvallei,** Sureties for the Magna Charta, created, in 1457, Earl of Athol, *d.* 1512, and his first wife, Lady Margaret, dowager of William, Earl of Douglas, and daughter of Archibald, Earl of Douglas and second Duke of Touraine, and his second wife, Lady Euphemia, daughter of Sir Patrick Graham and his wife Euphemia, daughter of David, Earl of Strathern, only son of ROBERT II., KING OF SCOTLAND, and his second wife, Euphemia, Countess of Moray, a descendant of **Gilbert de Clare** and **Richard de Clare,** both Sureties for the Magna Charta.

Alexander, Earl of Sutherland, and Lady Janet had:

13. SIR JOHN GORDON, Earl of Sutherland, *d.* 1567, *m.* secondly, Lady Helen, *d.* 1563-5, widow of William, Earl of Erroll, and daughter of John Stewart, third Earl of Lennox, *k.* 1526, a descendant of **Gilbert de Clare** and **Richard de Clare,** both Sureties for the Magna Charta, and his wife, Lady Anne Stewart, daughter of John, first Earl of Athol, and had:

14. ALEXANDER GORDON, Earl of Sutherland, *d.* 1594, *m.* secondly, December 13, 1573, Lady Jean Gordon, a descendant, through her parents, of **Gilbert de Clare, Richard de Clare, Hugh Bigod, Roger Bigod, Saber de Quincey,** and **Robert de Vere,** Sureties for the Magna Charta, daugh-

ter of George, fourth Earl of Huntly, and his wife, Lady Elizabeth, daughter of Robert, Lord Keith, *k.* at Flodden, 1513, and had by her:

15. SIR ROBERT GORDON, of Gordonstown, fourth son, *b.* May 14, 1580. He was created a Baronet of Nova Scotia, being the first creation of that order, May 28, 1625, when he had a charter of the barony of Gordon, in Nova Scotia, and *d.* in 1656. He *m.* at London, February 16, 1613, Louise, daughter of John Gordon, of Longormes, and dean of Salisbury, eldest son of Alexander Gordon, titular Archbishop of Athens, Bishop of Galloway, *d.* 1576, a brother of George Gordon, fourth Earl of Huntly, and a descendant of JAMES I., KING OF SCOTLAND, and of **Gilbert de Clare** and **Richard de Clare,** Sureties for the Magna Charta.

Sir Robert Gordon, Bart., had by his wife, Louise Gordon:

16. LADY CATHERINE GORDON, second daughter, *b.* January 11, 1621, *d.* 1663. She *m.* December 26, 1647, Colonel David Barclay, of Ury, in Kincardine, *b.* 1610, *d.* 1681, governor of Strathbogie, and member of Parliament, 1654–58. He was imprisoned in Edinburgh Castle, 1663–4; joined the religious Society of Friends in 1666, and was again imprisoned, 1666–7, because of his religious belief. He received the title of colonel from Charles I., having served some time as major in the Swedish army. Lady Catherine Gordon had by Colonel David Barclay:

17. JOHN BARCLAY, *b.* 165–, second son, brother of Robert Barclay, governor of East Jersey (New Jersey), 1682. He came to New Jersey, and resided at Perth Amboy, as deputy governor, and, dying in 1731, left issue by his wife, Cornelia van Schaick:

18. REV. THOMAS BARCLAY, minister at Albany, New York, younger son, who *m.* Anna Dorothea, daughter of Andries Draüyer, admiral (Schout by Nacht) of the Danish naval force on the American coast, and had:

19. Rev. HENRY BARCLAY, D.D., who succeeded, in 1746, as rector of Trinity Church, New York City, and so continued until his decease, August 20, 1764, aged fifty-three years. He *m.* Mary, daughter of Anthony Rutgers, of New York, and had:

20. COLONEL THOMAS BARCLAY, of New York, eldest son, *b.* 1753, *d.* 1830, British consul-general in the United States. He *m.* Susan, *d.* 1837, daughter of Peter de Lancey, of New York (and his wife Elizabeth, daughter of Cadwalader Colden, governor of the province of New York), son of Etienne de Lanci, Viscount de Laval, and his wife, Alice van Cortlandt, of New York, and had:

21. ANNE BARCLAY, *b.* 1788, *d.* 1869, who *m.* 1815, William Burrington Parsons, Royal navy, and had:

22. WILLIAM BARCLAY PARSONS, of New York, *b.* 1828, *d.* December 31, 1887, who *m.* in 1851, ELIZA, daughter of SCHUYLER LIVINGSTON, of New York (and his first wife, Ann Eliza Hosie), son of SCHUYLER LIVINGSTON and his wife Elizabeth, 1776–1817, a daughter of the above Colonel Thomas Barclay, 1753–1830.

SCHUYLER LIVINGSTON, aforesaid, was a son of WALTER LIVINGSTON, of New York (and his wife Cornelia, daughter of Peter Schuyler, of New York), a son of ROBERT LIVINGSTON, the third lord of the manor of Livingston, New York, whose father, PHILIP LIVINGSTON, the second lord of the manor, was the son of ROBERT LIVINGSTON, to whom the manor of Livingston, in New York, was granted, who was *b.* at Ancram, 1651; came to New York in 1676, and was a member and speaker of the Provincial Assembly, 1718–1725, *d.* 1728. He was a son of REV. JOHN LIVINGSTON, of Ancram, in Tivotdale, who was *b.* at Monyabrook, June 21, 1603, and *d.* in Holland in 1672, being one of the persecuted Scotch ministers. His father, REV. WILLIAM LIVINGSTON, minister at Lanark, was the son of the Rev. Alexander Livingston, minister at Monyabrook, Sterlingshire, Scotland (whose father was slain at the battle of Pinkie), and his wife BARBARA, a daughter of WILLIAM LIVINGSTON, of Kilsyth (heir to his grandfather), son and heir of WILLIAM LIVINGSTON, *k. v. p.* at the battle of Flodden, 1513, eldest son of WILLIAM LIVINGSTON, of Kilsyth, *d.* 1540, the son and heir of William Livingston, the third laird of Kilsyth, in Sterlingshire, and his wife, LADY MARY ERSKINE.

LADY MARY ERSKINE was a daughter of THOMAS, LORD ERSKINE, second Earl of Marr, *d.* 1494, the son of Sir Robert Erskine, Earl of Marr, *d.* 1453, and his wife, LADY MARGARET, daughter of Robert Stuart, lord of Lorn and Innermeth, by his wife, LADY MARGARET, daughter of ROBERT STUART, Duke of Albany, *d.* 1419, the son of ROBERT II., KING OF SCOTLAND, whose mother, LADY MARGERY, was the daughter of ROBERT BRUCE, KING OF SCOTLAND, the son of ROBERT BRUCE, Earl of Annandale, *d.* 1304, whose mother, LADY ISABEL, was the daughter of Gilbert de Clare, son of Richard de Clare, both Sureties for the Magna Charta.

William B. Parsons and Eliza Livingston had:

23. SCHUYLER LIVINGSTON PARSONS, of New York City and Islip, Long Island, one of the founders of the Order of Runnemede, who *m.* 1877, Helena, daughter of Bradish Johnson, of New York, and had issue: Helena Johnson, Evelyn Knapp, and Schuyler Livingston, Jr.

 Arms.—*Per chevron, az. and or., in chief two crosses pattée; in base a sea-lion segant guardant, counterchanged.*
 Crest.—*On a wreath a sword erect, ppr., pommel and hilt, or, between two crosses pattée, or.*
 Motto.—*Vitam impendere vero.*

THE PEDIGREE OF ALEXANDER FREDERICK FLEETE, LL.D.

```
Richard de Clare.
Gilbert de Clare.
    John de Lacie—Margaret de Quincey.        Saber de Quincey.
Richard de Clare—Maud de Lacie.                  Robert de Quincey.
Gilbert de Clare.                                                    Roger Bigod.
    Alianore de Clare—Hugh le Despencer.                             Hugh Bigod.
                                                Ralph Bigod.
        Hugh le Despencer—Isabel de Beauchamp.  Isabel Bigod.   John Fitz-John.
                                                                Maud Fitz-John.
            Isabel le Despencer—Richard Fitz-Alan—Eleanor Plantagenet.
                                   Edmund Fitz-Alan—Alice de Warren.   Robert de Vere.   Henry de Bohun.
                Richard Sergeaux—Philippa Fitz-Alan.                   Hugh de Vere.     Humphrey de Bohun.    William de Mowbray.
                Philippa Sergeaux—Robert Pashley.                      Robert de Vere.   Humphrey de Bohun.    Roger de Mowbray.
                    John Pashley—Lowys Gower.                          Joan de Vere.     Humphrey de Bohun.    Roger de Mowbray.
                    Elizabeth Pashley—Reginald de Pympe.                                 Humphrey de Bohun.    John de Mowbray.
                        Anne de Pympe—John Scott.                          Richard Fitz-Alan—Elizabeth de Bohun.   John de Mowbray.
                        Reginald Scott—Emeline Kempe.                      Elizabeth Fitz-Alan—Thomas de Mowbray.  John de Mowbray.
                                                                               Margaret de Mowbray—Robert Howard.
                                                                                   Catherine Howard—Edward Nevill.
                                                                                       Margaret Nevill—John Brooke.
                                                                                           Thomas Brooke—Dorothy Hayden.
                                                                                               Elizabeth Brooke—Thomas Wyatt.
                                                                                                   Thomas Wyatt—Jane Hawte.
                            Charles Scott—Jane Wyatt.
                                Dorothea Scott—William Fleete, Gent., of Chatham, Kent.
                                    Capt. Henry Fleete, of Md. and Va.; d. 1660,—Sarah
                                        Henry Fleete, of Lancaster Co., Va.; d 1729,—Elizabeth Wildey.
                                            Capt. William Fleete, of Lancaster Co., Va.,—Sarah Jones.
                                                William Fleete, of King and Queen Co., Va.,—Susannah Walker.
                                                    Capt. William Fleete, of King and Queen Co., Va.,—Sarah Browne Tomlin.
                                                        Benjamin Fleete, M.D., of King and Queen Co., Va.,—Maria Louise Wacker.
```

Alexander F. Fleete

DESCENT from the Sureties for the observance of the Magna Charta:

Hugh Bigod,
Roger Bigod,
Henry de Bohun,
Gilbert de Clare,
Richard de Clare,

John de Lacie,
William de Mowbray,
Saher de Quincey,
Robert de Vere.

1. **Richard de Clare,** a Surety for the Magna Charta, Earl of Hertford, *d.* 1218, *m.* Lady Amicia, daughter of William, second Earl of Gloucester, and had:

2. **Gilbert de Clare,** a Surety for the Magna Charta, Earl of Hertford and Gloucester, *d.* 1229, *m.* Lady Isabel Marshall, a sister of William Marshall, a Surety for the Magna Charta, and daughter of William, Earl of Pembroke, and had:

3. RICHARD DE CLARE, Earl of Hertford and Gloucester, *d.* 1262, *m.*, as his second wife, Lady Maud, daughter of **John de Lacie,** Earl of Lincoln, a Surety for the Magna Charta, and had by her:

4. GILBERT DE CLARE, Earl of Hertford and Gloucester, *d.* 1295, *m.* May 2, 1290, as his second wife, the Princess Joan, daughter of EDWARD I., KING OF ENGLAND, and his first wife, Eleanor of Castile, and had by her:

5. LADY ALIANORE DE CLARE, who *m.* May 1, 1306, Hugh le Despencer, one of the hapless favorites of King Edward I. He was the son of Hugh le Despencer, Earl of Winchester, and his wife, Lady Isabel de Beauchamp, widow of

Patrick de Chaworth, and the daughter of William, Earl of Warwick, and his wife, Lady Maud, widow of Gerard de Furnival and a daughter of John Fitz-John, chief justice of Ireland, 1258, the son of John Fitz-Piers Fitz-Geoffrey, also chief justice of Ireland, by his wife, Lady Isabel, daughter of Sir Ralph, third son of **Hugh Bigod**, second Earl of Norfolk, eldest son of **Roger Bigod**, Earl of Norfolk, both Sureties for the Magna Charta.

Hugh le Despencer and Lady Alianore de Clare had:

6. LADY ISABEL LE DESPENCER, who *m.*, as his first wife, Richard Fitz-Alan, K.G., Earl of Arundel and Surrey, from whom she was divorced, with the sanction of the Pope, having had by him an only child. He was the son of Edmund Fitz-Alan, K.B., Earl of Arundel, who was captured by the Barons and beheaded at Hereford, in 1326, and his wife, Lady Alice, daughter of William de Warren, *d. v. p.* (eldest son of John, seventh Earl of Warren and Surrey), and his wife, Lady Joan de Vere, daughter of Robert, fifth Earl of Oxford, lord great chamberlain, *d.* 1296, son of Hugh, fourth Earl, lord great chamberlain (and his wife, Lady Hawyse, daughter of **Saber de Quincey**, a Surety for the Magna Charta, Earl of Winchester) the son of **Robert de Vere**, a Surety for the Magna Charta, Earl of Oxford, and lord great chamberlain, *d.* 1221.

Richard Fitz-Alan, K.G., and Isabel le Despencer had:

7. LADY PHILIPPA FITZ-ALAN, only child, *m.* Sir Richard Sergeaux, lord of Sergeaux, in Cornwall, and had:

8. PHILIPPA SERGEAUX, *m.* Sir Robert Pashley, and had:

9. SIR JOHN PASHLEY, *m.* Lowys Gower, and had:

10. ELIZABETH PASHLEY, who *m.* Reginald de Pympe, of Nettlestead, in Kent, and their only daughter:

11. ANNE DE PYMPE, *m.* Sir John Scott, of Scott's Hall, high sheriff of Kent, 1528, and had:

12. SIR REGINALD SCOTT, of Scott's Hall, high sheriff of

Kent, 1541-2, captain of the castle of Calais, *d.* December 16, 1554, who *m.* first, Emeline, daughter of Sir William Kempe; *m.* secondly, Mary, daughter of Sir Bryan Tuke, secretary to Cardinal Wolsey, and had:

13. CHARLES SCOTT, of Edgerton, in Kent, *d.* 1617, who *m.* Jane, daughter of Sir Thomas Wyatt, of Allington Castle, Kent, executed as a rebel on Tower Hill, April 11, 1554,* son of Sir Thomas Wyatt, of Allington Castle, poet laureate to King Henry VIII., *b.* 1503, *d.* 1542, by his wife, *m.* 1520, Lady Elizabeth, daughter of Thomas Brooke, third Baron Cobham, *d.* July 19, 1529, the son of John, second Baron *d.* 1511, and his first wife, Lady Margaret, daughter of Edward Nevill, K.G., and his second wife, Lady Catherine, daughter of Sir Robert Howard, by his wife, Lady Margaret, daughter of Thomas de Mowbray, K.G., Earl of Nottingham, and first earl marshal, created Duke of Norfolk.

William de Mowbray, a Magna Charta Surety, had by his wife, Lady Agnes d'Albini, a daughter or a sister of William, second Earl of Arundel and Sussex: Roger de Mowbray, *d.* 1266, father of Roger, first Baron by writ, *d.* 1298, whose son John, second Baron, was executed in 1321, having issue: John, third Baron, *d.* 1361, who had: John, fourth Baron, *d.* 1368, *m.* Lady Elizabeth, daughter of John de Segrave, and his wife, Margaret Plantagenet, Duchess of Norfolk, only child of Thomas, Earl of Norfolk, a son of EDWARD I., KING OF ENGLAND, and his second wife, Princess Margaret, daughter of PHILIP III., KING OF FRANCE, and had: Thomas de Mowbray, K.G., Earl of Nottingham, aforesaid.

The Earl of Nottingham's second wife, the mother of

---

* See Encyc. Brit.; Am. Encyc.; Green's "English People;" Brown's "Genesis of the United States;" Berry's "Kent Pedigrees;" Virginia Magazine, ii. 70-76.

Lady Margaret Howard, was Lady Elizabeth Fitz-Alan, daughter of Richard, Earl of Arundel and Surrey, and his first wife, Lady Elizabeth de Bohun, daughter of William, K.G., Earl of Northampton, fourth son of Humphrey de Bohun, Earl of Hereford and Essex, lord high constable, who was slain at Boroughbridge, fighting under the banner of the Barons, March 16, 1321-2 (and his wife, Princess Elizabeth Plantagenet, widow of John, Earl of Holland, and daughter of EDWARD I., KING OF ENGLAND, and his first wife, Eleanor of Castile), the eldest son of Humphrey, third Earl of Hereford and Essex, lord high constable of England, *d.* 1397, the son of Humphrey, *d. v. p.*, taken prisoner with his father, eldest son of Humphrey de Bohun, taken prisoner at the battle of Evesham, *d.* 1274, the son of **Henry de Bohun**, one of the Sureties for the observance of the Magna Charta, created Earl of Hereford and Essex.

Charles Scott, of Edgerton, and Jane Wyatt had:

14. DOROTHEA SCOTT, who *m.* William Fleete, gent., of Chatham, in Kent, an incorporator of the third Virginia charter, and had issue: Edward, Reginald, John, members of the Maryland Assembly, and

15. CAPTAIN HENRY FLEETE, of St. George's, Maryland, and Fleete Bay, Lancaster County, Virginia; *d.* 1660.* He was associated with Calvert in establishing the province of Maryland, and was a member of the assembly, 1637-8. In 1652 he was burgess for Lancaster County, Virginia; a justice, 1653 and 1656, and lieutenant-colonel of the county militia. He received grants for over thirteen thousand acres of land in Virginia. Captain Fleete had by his wife Sarah, whose surname has not been preserved (she *m.* secondly, Colonel John Walker, of Virginia, and had issue, see *Virginia Magazine*, July, 1894):

---

* See Neill's "Founders of Maryland;" Streeter's "Papers Relating to the Early History of Maryland."

16. HENRY FLEETE, who was a justice, 1695, and high sheriff of Lancaster County, Virginia, 1718-19. His will is dated January 31, 1728-9. He *m.* Elizabeth Wildey (her mother Jane Wildey's will was proved December 19, 1701), and had:

17. CAPTAIN WILLIAM FLEETE, who was high sheriff of Lancaster County, 1719-20, and was the executor of his father's will. He *m.* Sarah, daughter of Robert Jones, of King and Queen County, Virginia, and had:

18. WILLIAM FLEETE, *b.* October 19, 1726. He resided in King and Queen County, and had issue by his second wife, Susannah, daughter of John Walker, of King and Queen County:

19. CAPTAIN WILLIAM FLEETE, *b.* December 18, 1757; *d.* at "Goshen," King and Queen County, Virginia, April 11, 1833. He was a member of the constitutional convention of 1788, and high sheriff of King and Queen County. He *m.* Mrs. Sarah Browne Tomlin, widow, daughter of Bennet Browne, of Essex County, Virginia, and his wife, Mary Hill.

Bennet Browne, aforesaid, was a son of Charles Browne and PRISCILLA, daughter of ROGER BROOKE, a son of ROGER BROOKE, *b.* 1637, a son of ROBERT BROOKE, *b.* in London, June 3, 1602; A.M. Wadham College, Oxford; came to Maryland, June 29, 1650, was acting governor of the province, 1652, *d.* July 20, 1655 (and his wife Mary, daughter of Rev. Roger Mainwaring, D.D., Bishop of St. David's, 1636, and Dean of Worcester), who was a son of Thomas Brooke, member of Parliament, 1604-11, *d.* September 13, 1612, aged fifty-two, and his wife SUSAN, daughter of SIR THOMAS FOSTER, counsel to Queen Anne of Denmark, *d.* May 18, 1612, aged sixty-four (and his wife Susan, daughter of Thomas Foster, Jr., of Iden, Sussex), son of THOMAS FOSTER (by his wife, Margaret Browning, of Clemesford, Sussex), son of ROGER, second son of THOMAS FOSTER, of Etherstone (by his wife, Elizabeth Featherstonehaugh, of Stanhope Hall, Durham), son of THOMAS FOSTER (by his wife, Elizabeth d'Etherstone, heiress to her brother Roger), son of Thomas Foster, of Buckton, and his wife, LADY JOAN D'ELMEDON.

LADY JOAN D'ELMEDON, aforesaid, was a daughter of Sir William Elmedon, county palatine knight, 1393-1447, and his wife, LADY ELIZABETH, daughter of THOMAS, *d.* February 14, 1390-1, aged twenty-three, son and heir of SIR THOMAS D'UMFRAVILLE, lord of Holmaid and Whitley, governor of Harbotel Castle, county palatine knight (and his wife Joan, daughter of Adam Rodam), second son of ROBERT D'UMFRAVILLE, second Earl of Angus, 1274-1325-6 (and his second wife, Lady Alianore), second and surviving son of Gilbert d'Umfraville, 1238-1307-8, Earl of Angus, in right of his wife, LADY AGNES COMYN, daughter of Alexander, Baron Comyn, second Earl of Buchan, justiciary of Scotland, 1251, *d.* 1289, and his wife, LADY ELIZABETH DE QUINCEY, third daughter and coheiress of ROGER DE QUINCEY, second Earl of Winchester, *d.* 1264, (by his wife, Lady Helen, daughter of Alan, lord of Galloway, constable of Scotland, *d.* 1233, and his wife, Lady Margaret, daughter of David, Earl of Huntingdon, a grandson of DAVID I., KING OF SCOTS, who was a descendant of ALFRED THE GREAT, KING OF ENGLAND), second son of **Saber de Quincey**, one of the Sureties for the Magna Charta.

Captain William Fleete, 1757-1833, and his wife, Sarah Browne Tomlin, had:

20. BENJAMIN FLEETE, M.D., of King and Queen County, Virginia, *b.* January 25, 1818; *d.* March 8, 1865. He *m.* Maria Louisa, daughter of Jacob D. Wacker, M.D., of King and Queen County, and had:

21. PROFESSOR ALEXANDER FREDERICK FLEETE, A.M., LL.D., *b.* June 6, 1843; educated University of Virginia;

assistant adjutant-general, Henry A. Wise's brigade, C. S. army; professor of Greek at the Missouri State University; founder of the Missouri Military Academy and superintendent of the Culver Military Academy, Culver, Indiana; one of the founders of the Order of Runnemede; one of the founders and governor of the Missouri Society of Colonial Wars; one of the founders and historian of the Missouri Society of Sons of the Revolution. Professor Fleete *m.* Belle, daughter of Major John Seddon, of "Snowden," Stafford County, Virginia, and had issue: Mary, Belle, John Seddon, Henry Wyatt, William Alexander, Charles Preston, and Reginald Scott.

THE PEDIGREE OF GEORGE RICHARD SCHIEFFELIN.

```
Saher de Quincey.
 |
Robert de Quincey.                          Roger Bigod.
 |                                           |
Margaret de Quincey═John de Lacie.          Hugh Bigod.
                |                            |
   Maud de Lacie═Richard de Clare.          Ralph Bigod.                         Eustace de Vesci.
                     |                       |                                    |
                Richard de Clare.           Isabel Bigod.                         William de Vesci.
                     |                       |                                    |
                Gilbert de Clare.           John Fitz-John.                       William de Vesci.
                     |                       |                                    |
                Thomas de Clare.            Maud Fitz-John.        William de Mowbray.   Isabel de Vesci.
                     |                       |                     |                     |
                Thomas de Clare.            Guy de Beauchamp.      Roger de Mowbray.     Adam de Welles.
                     |                       |                     |                     |
                Maud de Clare.              Thomas de Beauchamp.   Roger de Mowbray.     Adam de Welles.
                     |                       |                     |                     |
              Roger de Clifford═Maud de Beauchamp.                 John de Mowbray.      John de Welles.
                         |                                         |                     |
                 Catherine de Clifford.                            John de Mowbray.      John de Welles.
                         |                                         |                     |
              Maud de Greystock═Eudo de Welles.                    John de Mowbray.      John de Welles.
                                      |                            |                     |
                                      |                          Margery de Mowbray═John de Welles.
                                      |                                   |
                              Mary de Welles═John Lawrence, of Rixton Manor.
                                                  |
                          Margaret Lawrence═Robert Laurence, of Ashton.
                                                  |
              William Lawrence, of Withington,═Isabel Molineaux.
                                                  |
              Edmund Lawrence, of Withington,═Eleanor ———.
                                                  |
                          John Lawrence, of St. Albans,═———.
                                                  |
                         William Lawrence, of St. Albans,═Catherine Beaumond.
                                                  |
                          John Lawrence, of St. Albans,═Margaret Roberts.
                                                  |
                       Thomas Lawrence, of St. Albans,═Joan Antrobus.
                                                  |
                   William Lawrence, of Flushing, L. I.,═Elizabeth Smith.
                                                  |
                         Joseph Lawrence, of New York,═Mary Townley.
                                                  |
                        Richard Lawrence, of New York,═Hannah Bowne.
                                                  |
                           John Lawrence, of New York,═Ann Burling.
                                                  |
                       Hannah Lawrence, of New York,═Jacob Schieffelin, of New York.
                                                  |
                  Richard Lawrence Schieffelin, of New York,═Margaret H. McKay.
                                                  |
                           George Richard Schieffelin, of New York City.
```

George Richard Schieffelin

DESCENT from the Sureties for the observance of the Magna Charta:

Hugh Bigod,	John de Lacie,
Roger Bigod,	William de Mowbray,
Gilbert de Clare,	Saher de Quincey,
Richard de Clare,	Eustace de Vesci.

1. **Saher de Quincey,** a Surety for the Magna Charta, Earl of Winchester, *m.* Lady Margaret, daughter of Robert, Earl of Leicester, lord high steward of England, and had:

2. ROBERT DE QUINCEY, eldest son, *d. v. p.* in the Holy Land, leaving issue by Lady Hawyse de Meschines, daughter of Hugh, fifth earl palatine of Chester, *d.* 1181:

3. LADY MARGARET DE QUINCEY, only child, who *m.*, as his second wife, **John de Lacie,** one of the Sureties for the Magna Charta, first Earl of Lincoln, *d.* 1240, and had:

4. LADY MAUD DE LACIE, who *m.*, as his second wife, Richard de Clare, Earl of Hertford and Gloucester, *d.* 1262, son of **Gilbert de Clare** and grandson of **Richard de Clare,** both Sureties for the Magna Charta and Earls of Hertford, and had:

5. THOMAS DE CLARE, second son, constable of Gloucester Castle, 1266, was constituted governor of the city of London by Edward I. upon his accession, and *d.* 1287, in Ireland, having issue by his wife, Lady Amy, daughter of Sir Maurice Fitz-Maurice, of Mallahuffe Castle, Desmond:

6. THOMAS DE CLARE, third son, father of:

7. LADY MAUD DE CLARE, who *m.* Robert de Clifford, of

Appleby, first Baron by writ, 1299, who was slain at the battle of Bannockburn, 1313, and had:

8. ROGER DE CLIFFORD, second Baron of Appleby, lord of Westmoreland, *d.* 1390, who *m.* Lady Maud, daughter of Thomas de Beauchamp, K.G., third Earl of Warwick, one of the original members of the Order of Knights of the Garter, *d.* 1369, and his wife, Lady Catherine, daughter of Sir Roger, second Baron de Mortimer, of Wigmore Castle, the favorite of Queen Isabel, consort of Edward II. In 1328 he was created Earl of March, and subsequently was arrested by order of King Edward III., convicted under various charges of treason, and executed, when all his honors became forfeited. He was the son of Sir Edmund Mortimer, of Wigmore Castle, mortally wounded in 1303, who was the son of Roger de Mortimer, captain-general of the king's forces in Wales and governor of Hereford Castle, *d.* 1282, and his wife, Lady Maud, a daughter of William, sixth Baron de Braose, of Brecknock, by his wife, Lady Eva Marshall, sister of William Marshall, one of the Sureties for the Magna Charta, and daughter of William, Earl of Pembroke, Protector of England, and his first wife, Lady Isabel de Clare, daughter of Richard the Strongbow, Earl of Pembroke, lord justice of Ireland, son of Gilbert, Earl of Pembroke, *d.* 1149, and his wife, Lady Elizabeth de Beaumont, daughter of Robert, Earl of Mellent and Leicester, *d.* 1118, by Lady Isabel, daughter of Hugh Magnus, Count de Vermandois, a son of HENRY I., KING OF FRANCE.

Thomas de Beauchamp, K.G., aforesaid, was the eldest son of Guy, second Earl of Warwick, *d.* 1315, son of William, sixth Baron de Beauchamp, of Elmly, created Earl of Warwick, *d.* 1298, and his wife, Lady Maud, daughter of John Fitz-John, chief justice of Ireland, 1258, son of John Fitz-Piers Fitz-Geoffrey, chief justice of Ireland, 1246, by his wife, Lady Isabel, daughter of Sir Ralph Bigod, third son of

Hugh Bigod, and grandson of **Roger Bigod**, both Sureties for the Magna Charta.

Roger, second Baron Clifford, and Lady Maud had:

9. LADY CATHERINE DE CLIFFORD, who *m.* Ralph, fifth Baron de Greystock, *d.* 1417, and had:

10. LADY MAUD DE GREYSTOCK, who *m.* Eudo de Welles, *d. v. p.*, eldest son of Sir John, fifth Baron de Welles, of Gainsby, *d.* 1421, and his wife, Lady Margery, daughter of John, fourth Baron de Mowbray, *k.* 1368, and his wife, Lady Elizabeth, daughter of John, third Baron de Segrave, *d.* 1353, and his wife Margaret, Duchess of Norfolk, daughter of Thomas Plantagenet, Earl of Norfolk, *d.* 1338, son of EDWARD I., KING OF ENGLAND, by his second wife, Princess Margaret, daughter of PHILIP III., KING OF FRANCE.

William de Mowbray, a Surety for the Magna Charta, had by his wife, Lady Agnes, daughter of William d'Albini, Earl of Arundel and Sussex: Roger de Mowbray, second son, *d.* 1266, *m.* Lady Maud, daughter of William de Beauchamp, of Bedford, and had: Roger de Mowbray, *d.* 1298, *m.* Lady Rose de Clare, and had: John de Mowbray, who took part in the insurrection of Thomas of Lancaster, was taken prisoner and executed at York in 1321; he *m.* Lady Aliva, daughter of William de Braose, of Gower, and had: John de Mowbray, third Baron, *d.* 1361, *m.* Lady Joan Plantagenet, daughter of Henry, third Earl of Lancaster, *d.* 1345 (and his wife, Lady Maud, daughter of Patrick de Chaworth, and his wife, Lady Isabel de Beauchamp, daughter of William, first Earl of Warwick, and his wife, Lady Maud FitzJohn, aforesaid, a descendant of **Hugh Bigod** and **Roger Bigod**, Sureties for the Magna Charta), eldest son of Edmund, Earl of Leicester, Lancaster, and Chester, high steward of England, *d.* 1295 (a son of HENRY III., KING OF ENGLAND), and his second wife, Lady Blanche, widow of Henry I., King of Navarre, and daughter of Robert of Artois, a son of Louis VIII., King of France, and had: John de Mowbray, *d.* 1368, aforesaid.

Eustace de Vesci, a Magna Charta Surety, had by his wife, Lady Margaret, a daughter of William the Lion, King of Scotland: William de Vesci, who had by his second wife, Lady Agnes, daughter of William de Ferrers, Earl of Derby: William de Vesci, second son, first Baron by writ, *m.* Lady Isabel, daughter of Adam de Periton, and widow of Robert de Welles, and had: Lady Isabel, *m.* William de Welles, of Alford, and had: Adam, first Baron by writ, 1299, whose second son, Sir Adam, third Baron, had: John, fourth Baron, *d.* 1361, who had: John, fifth Baron, *d.* 1421, *m.* Lady Margery de Mowbray, and had: Eudo de Welles, eldest son *d. v. p.*, who *m.* as aforesaid, Lady Maud de Greystock, and had:

11. Lady Mary de Welles, who *m.* John Laurence, of Rixton Manor, Lancastershire, returned to Parliament for Lancaster County, October 16, 1419, and had:

12. Margaret Laurence, who *m.* Robert Laurence, son of Sir Robert Laurence, of Ashton Hall, Lancastershire, and had:

13. William Lawrence, of Withington, 1509, and Sevenhampton, in Gloucestershire, which he bought; will proved in 1559. He *m.* before 1518, Isabel, daughter of John Molineaux, of Sefton Manor and Chorly, in Lancashire, and had:

14. Edmund Lawrence, of Withington parish, Gloucestershire, fourth son; will proved January 10, 1559. He had by his wife Eleanor:

15. John Lawrence, of St. Albans, in Hertfordshire. He was chief burgess in 1553, and mayor of St. Albans in 1567 and 1575, and had:

16. William Lawrence, of St. Albans, who *m.* November 25, 1559, Catherine Beamond, or Beaumont, and had:

17. JOHN LAWRENCE, *bapt.* at Abbey Church, St. Albans, January 12, 1561-2, who had by his second wife, *m.* January 25, 1586-7, Margaret Roberts:

18. THOMAS LAWRENCE, of St. Albans, second son, *bapt.* at St. Albans, February 2, 1588-9, *d.* March 20, 1624-5. He was an assistant of the borough of St. Albans, 1622, and *m.* October 23, 1609, Joan, daughter of Walter and Joan Antrobus, of St. Albans. Joan *m.* secondly, John Tuthill (or Tuttell), of Ipswich, and came with him to New England in April, 1635, bringing John and William, children of her first husband, Thomas Lawrence, whose son:

19. WILLIAM LAWRENCE, *bapt.* at St. Albans, July 27, 1622, *d.* 1680. In 1645 he was one of the patentees of Hampstead and Flushing, Long Island. He was a magistrate of Flushing, 1655, and one of its largest land-owners; was a member of the governor's council, 1700; captain of a foot company, 1665; high sheriff, 1673; justice of the North Riding, 1675. He *m.* secondly, March 4, 1664-5, Elizabeth, daughter of Richard Smith, and had by her:

20. JOSEPH LAWRENCE, of Flushing, *b.* 1665-8, commissioned ensign in 1684, *d.* April, 1759, *m.* 1690, Mary Townley (see the *American Historical Register*, February, 1896), and had:

21. RICHARD LAWRENCE, of Flushing, *b.* 1691, *d.* 1781, *m.* April 6, 1717, Hannah, daughter of Samuel Bowne, and had:

22. JOHN LAWRENCE, of Flushing, *b.* January 22, 1731, *d.* July, 1794, *m.* August 13, 1755, Ann Burling, and had:

23. HANNAH LAWRENCE, *b.* July 8, 1758, *d.* October 3, 1838, *m.* August 16, 1780, Jacob Schieffelin, of New York, and had:

24. RICHARD LAWRENCE SCHIEFFELIN, of New York, *b.* November 9, 1801, *d.* November 21, 1889, *m.* August 3, 1833, Margaret H. McKay, and had:

25. GEORGE RICHARD SCHIEFFELIN, of New York City, *b.* July 27, 1836, a founder of the Order of Runnemede, and member of the Society of Colonial Wars. Mr. Schieffelin *m.* Julia M., daughter of Hon. Isaac C. and Matilda Delaplaine, and had issue :

I. Julia Florence Schieffelin, *m.* J. Bruce Ismay, of Liverpool, England, and had :
  1. Margaret Bruce.
  2. Thomas Bruce.
  3. Evelyn Constance.

II. Margaret Helen Schieffelin, *m.* Henry Graff Trevor, of New York, and had :
  1. George Schieffelin.
  2. Margaret Estelle.
  3. Louisa Stephanie Stewart.

III. Constance Schieffelin.

IV. Dorothy Schieffelin.

V. George Richard Delaplaine Schieffelin.

Arms.—*Tierce per fesse, sa. and or, on three piles, two conjoined with one between transposed, invected, counterchanged, as many cross-crosslets of the first.*

Crest.—*A holy lamb, passant, crowned with glory, and bearing cross, staff, and pennon, ppr.*

Motto.—*Per fidem et constantiam.*

Melville M. Bigelow

DESCENT from the Sureties for the observance of the Magna Charta:

Henry de Bohun,   Saher de Quincey,
Robert de Vere.

1. **Henry de Bohun,** one of the Sureties for the Magna Charta, Earl of Hereford, lord high constable of England, *d.* 1220, *m.* Lady Maud, daughter of Geoffrey Fitz-Piers, Baron de Mandeville, first Earl of Essex, lord high justice of England, and sister of Geoffrey de Mandeville, one of the Sureties for the Magna Charta, and had:

2. HUMPHREY DE BOHUN, Earl of Hereford and Essex, *d.* 1274-5. He was a very distinguished person among the rebellious Barons, *temp.* Henry III. In 47 Henry III. he and other Barons were excommunicated for plundering churches in time of war, and was one of the commanders at the battle of Lewes, and was constituted governor of Goodrich and Winchester Castles. He *m.* first, Lady Maud, daughter of Raoul, Baron d'Eue, *d. s. p. m.*, and had by her;

3. HUMPHREY DE BOHUN, eldest son, taken prisoner at Evesham, and *d. v. p.** He commanded the infantry at the battle of Evesham, and died in Beeston Castle soon after being imprisoned. He *m.* Lady Eleanor, daughter and coheiress of William, sixth Baron de Braose, of Brecknock,

---

* See American Historical Review, April and July, 1896, "Bohun Wills" and authorities there cited, and Doyle's "Official Baronage."

and coheiress of her mother, Lady Eva, one of the daughters and coheiresses of William Marshall, Earl of Pembroke, and sister of William Marshall, one of the Sureties for the Magna Charta, and had:

4. HUMPHREY DE BOHUN, who succeeded as Earl of Hereford and Essex and lord high constable, *d.* 1298. He *m.* Lady Maud, daughter of Ingelram de Fienes, or of William, Baron de Fienes, and had:

5. HUMPHREY DE BOHUN, Earl of Hereford and Essex, lord high constable. He was taken prisoner in the Scotch wars and was exchanged for the wife of Robert Bruce, then a captive in England. Subsequently he joined the banner of the insurrectionary Barons, under Lancaster, and was killed at Boroughbridge, March 16, 1321-2. He *m.* November 14, 1302, Princess Elizabeth, *b.* 1282, *d.* 1316, widow of Sir John, Earl of Holland, and daughter of EDWARD I., KING OF ENGLAND, by his first wife, Eleanor of Castile, and had:

6. LADY MARGARET DE BOHUN, sister of Sir William de Bohun, K.G., created Earl of Northampton, and of John and Humphrey, Earls of Hereford and Essex. She *d.* 15 Richard II.,* having *m.*† 1325, Sir Hugh Courtenay, K.G., second Earl of Devon, *d.* 1377, who distinguished himself in arms in the warlike reign of Edward III., and was one of the original members of the Order of Knights of the Garter.

He was the second son of Sir Hugh Courtenay, feudal Baron of Oakhampton, summoned to Parliament, as Baron Courtenay, 1299, and created Earl of Devon February 22, 1335 (and his wife, whom he *m.* when he was only seventeen years old, Lady Agnes, daughter of Sir John St. John, of Basing, and sister of the first Baron St. John, of Basing), son of Sir Hugh de Courtenay, Baron of Oakhampton

---

* Her will dated January 28, 1390, given among the "Bohun Wills," American Historical Review, vol. i. 639.

† See her father's will, dated August 11, 1319.

(and his wife, Lady Alianore, sister of Hugh le Despencer, first Earl of Winchester, and daughter of Hugh, Baron le Despencer, justiciary of England, *k*. at Evesham, and his wife, Lady Aliva Basset, widow of Roger Bigod, Earl of Norfolk), son of John de Courtenay, Baron of Oakhampton (son of Robert de Courtenay, feudal Baron of Oakhampton, Devonshire, and his wife, Lady Mary, daughter of William de Redvers, sixth Earl of Devon, *d.* 1216, a supporter of King John, and his wife, Lady Mabel, daughter of Robert, Earl of Mellent), and his wife, Lady Isabel, daughter of Sir Hugh de Vere, fourth Earl of Oxford, lord great chamberlain, *d.* 1263 (and his wife, Lady Hawise, daughter of **Saber de Quincey**, one of the Sureties for the Magna Charta), eldest son of **Robert de Vere**, one of the Sureties for the Magna Charta.

Lady Margaret de Bohun, who *d*. December 16, 1391, had by Sir Hugh, Earl of Devon:

7. EDWARD COURTENAY, of Godrington, Devon, second son, who *d. v. p.*, having issue by his wife, Lady Emeline, daughter and heiress of Sir John d'Auney, of Modeford Terry, Somerset, and Cheviock, Cornwall:

8. SIR HUGH COURTENAY, of Haccomb, Devonshire, and Boconnock, Cornwall, second son, brother of Edward, third Earl of Devon, who *m*., as his third wife, Lady Maud, daughter of Sir John Beaumont, of Sherwill, Dorset, and had by her:

9. MARGARET COURTENAY (sister of Sir Hugh Courtenay, of Boconnock, Cornwall, *k*. at Tewkesbury, father of Edward, created Earl of Devon, 1485), who *m*. Sir Theobald Grenville, Knight, of Stowe, Cornwall, and had:

10. SIR WILLIAM GRENVILLE, Knight, of Bideford, who *m*. Lady Philippa, daughter of Sir William Bonville, K.G., Lord Bonville, of Chuton, and had:

11. THOMAS GRENVILLE, of Stowe, Cornwall, high sheriff

of Gloucestershire, who *m*. Elizabeth, daughter of Sir Theobald Gorges, Knight, of Devonshire, and had:

12. SIR THOMAS GRENVILLE, Knight, of Stowe, Cornwall, who *m*. Elizabeth, daughter of Sir Otis Gilbert, of Compton, Devon, high sheriff of Devonshire, 1474, *d*. 1494, and his wife Elizabeth, daughter of John Hill, of Shilston, and had:

13. SIR ROGER GRENVILLE, of Stowe and Bideford, who *m*. Margaret, daughter of Richard Whitleigh, of Efford, Devon, and had:

14. AMY GRENVILLE (sister of Sir Richard Grenville, grandfather of Vice-Admiral Sir Richard Grenville, R.N.), who *m*. John Drake, of Ashe and Exmouth, Devon, high sheriff of Devonshire, 1561-2, eldest son of John Drake, of Ashe, and his wife Margaret, daughter of John Cole, of Rill, in Devonshire, and had:

15. ROBERT DRAKE, of Wiscombe Park, Devon (his brother, Bernard Drake, was knighted in 1585), who *m*. Elizabeth, daughter of Humphrey Prideaux, of Thewborough, Devon, *d*. 1550, and his wife Edith, daughter of William Hatch, of Aller, South Molton, Devon, and had:

16. WILLIAM DRAKE, of Wiscombe Park, who *m*. Philippa, daughter of Sir Robert Dennys, of Holcombe, Devon, *d*. 1592, and his second wife, Margaret, daughter of Sir William Godolphin, of Cornwall, and had:

17. JOHN DRAKE, *b*. 1585, who came to New England in 1630 and settled, in 1635, at Windsor, Connecticut, and, dying August 17, 1659, had issue by his wife, Elizabeth Rogers, who *d*. October 7, 1681:

18. ELIZABETH DRAKE, *b*. 1621, *d*. 1716, who had by her second husband, John Elderkin, of Norwich, Connecticut:

19. JOHN ELDERKIN, of Norwich, *b*. 1664, who had by his first wife, Abigail Fowler, *b*. 1660, *d*. 1713-14, of New Haven, Connecticut:

20. JOHN ELDERKIN, of Norwich, *b.* 1694, *d.* 1736, who *m.* Susanna Baker, of Norwich, and had:

21. SUSANNA ELDERKIN, *b.* 1722, *d.* 1797, who had by her third husband, Jabez Bigelow, of Norwich and Hebron, Connecticut, and New Lebanon, New York:

22. JABEZ BIGELOW, of New Lebanon, New York, *b.* 1760, *d.* 1829, who had by his first wife, Almy Gardner, of Stephentown, New York:

23. JOB GARDNER BIGELOW, of New Lebanon, New York, and Milford, Michigan, *b.* 1792, *d.* 1838, who *m.* Thankful Enos, of Nassau, New York, and had:

24. WILLIAM ENOS BIGELOW, of Flint, Michigan, *b.* 1820, *d.* 1890, who had by his first wife, Daphne Florence Mattison, of Perry, New York, *b.* 1824, *d.* 1878:

25. MELVILLE MADISON BIGELOW, PHD. (Harvard), of Cambridge, Massachusetts, *b.* 1846, one of the founders of the Order of Runnemede and a member of the Society of Colonial Wars, who had by his first wife, Elizabeth Chamberlin Bragg, of Cambridge, *d.* 1881 : Ada Hawthorn, *d.* 1876; Charlotte Gray, *d.* 1876; and Leslie Melville, A.B. (Harvard, 1895), *b.* 1873, *d.* 1898, in his third year in Harvard Law School.

THE PEDIGREE OF GEORGE DAVIS TERRY.

- Saber de Quincey.
- Robert de Quincey.
- Margaret de Quincey *m.* John de Lacie.
- Richard de Clare.
- Gilbert de Clare.
- Richard de Clare—Maud de Lacie.
- Gilbert de Clare.
- Margaret de Clare.
- Margaret d'Audley.
- Hugh de Stafford—Philippa Beauchamp.
- Margaret de Stafford.
- Philippa de Nevill.
- Thomas de Dacre—Elizabeth Bowet.

- Roger Bigod.
- Hugh Bigod.
- Ralph Bigod.
- Isabel Bigod.
- John Fitz-John.
- Maud Fitz-John.
- Guy de Beauchamp.
- Thomas de Beauchamp.

- William Bowet—Amy d'Ufford.

- John Fitz-Robert.
- Roger Fitz-John.
- Robert Fitz-Roger.
- John de Clavering.
- Eve de Clavering.
- Edmund d'Ufford.
- Robert d'Ufford.

- Robert de Vere.
- Hugh de Vere.
- Robert de Vere.
- Joan de Vere.
- Alice de Warren.
- Richard Fitz-Alan.
- Alice Fitz-Alan.
- Eleanor de Holland.
- Alice de Montacute.

- Geoffrey de Say.
- William de Say.
- William de Say.
- Geoffrey de Say.
- Geoffrey de Say.
- Joan de Say.
- William Fiennes.
- Roger Fiennes.

- Henry de Bohun.
- Humphrey de Bohun.
- Humphrey de Bohun.
- Humphrey de Bohun.
- William de Bohun.
- Humphrey de Bohun.
- Alianore de Bohun.
- Anne Plantagenet.
- John Bourchier.
- Humphrey Bourchier.

- Joan de Dacre—Richard Fiennes.
- John Fiennes—Alice Fitz-Hugh.
- Thomas Fiennes—Anne Bourchier.
- Catherine Fiennes—Richard Loudenoys, of Briade, Sussex.
- Mary Loudenoys—Thomas Harlakenden, of Worthorn, Kent.
- Roger Harlakenden, of Kenardiston, Kent,—Elizabeth Hardres.
- Richard Harlakenden, of Kenardiston, Kent,—Mary Hubbart.
- Mabel Harlakenden—John Haynes, Governor of Massachusetts and Connecticut.
- Ruth Haynes—Samuel Wyllys.
- Ruth Wyllys—Rev. Edward Taylor.
- Eldad Taylor—Thankful Day.
- Rev. John Taylor—Elizabeth Terry.
- Harriet Taylor—Roderick Terry.
- Edmund Terry—Anna Prentice.
- George Davis Terry, of Brooklyn, N. Y.

George Davis Terry

Descent from the Sureties for the observance of the Magna Charta:

Hugh Bigod,
Roger Bigod,
Henry de Bohun,
Gilbert de Clare,
Richard de Clare,

John Fitz-Robert,
John de Lacie,
Saher de Quincey,
Geoffrey de Say,
Robert de Vere.

1. **Robert de Vere**, Earl of Oxford, a Surety for the observance of the Magna Charta, *d.* 1221, had by his wife, Lady Isabel, daughter of Hugh de Bolebec, *d.* 1261:

2. Hugh de Vere, fourth Earl of Oxford, chamberlain of England, *d.* 1263. He *m.* Lady Hawyse, daughter of **Saher de Quincey**, one of the Sureties for the Magna Charta, Earl of Winchester, and had:

3. Robert de Vere, fifth Earl of Oxford, *d.* 1296, who had by his wife, Lady Alice, daughter of Gilbert, Baron de Saundford:

4. Lady Joan de Vere, who *m.* William de Warren, *d.* 1286, son of John, seventh Earl of Warren and Surrey, *d.* 1304, and had:

5. Lady Alice de Warren, who *m.* 1305, Edmund Fitz-Alan, K.B., Earl of Arundel, beheaded in 1326, and had:

6. Richard Fitz-Alan, K.G., Earl of Arundel and Surrey, *d.* 1375, who *m.*, as his second wife, and her second husband, Lady Eleanor Plantagenet, daughter of Henry, Earl of Lancaster, *d.* 1345, son of Edmund, Earl of Leices-

ter, Lancaster, and Chester, high steward of England, *d.* 1295, the son of HENRY III., KING OF ENGLAND, and his wife, Lady Eleanor de Provence, and had:

7. LADY ALICE FITZ-ALAN, who *m.* Thomas de Holland, second Earl of Kent, earl marshal, *d.* 1397, son of Thomas, K.G., Earl of Kent, *d.* 1360, by his wife, Lady Joan, the Fair Maid of Kent, daughter of Edmund, Earl of Kent, beheaded in 1330, the son of EDWARD I., KING OF ENGLAND, by his second wife, Princess Margaret, daughter of PHILIP III., KING OF FRANCE, and had:

8. LADY ELEANOR DE HOLLAND, *m.* Thomas de Montacute, Earl of Salisbury, a prominent character in the reign of Henry V., and had:

9. LADY ALICE DE MONTACUTE, *m.* Richard de Nevill, K.G., Earl of Salisbury, eldest son of Ralph, first Earl of Westmoreland, and his second wife, Lady Joan, daughter of John, Duke of Lancaster, a son of EDWARD III., KING OF ENGLAND, and had:

10. LADY ALICE DE NEVILL, *m.* Henry, Baron Fitz-Hugh, of Ravensworth, *d.* 1472, and had:

11. LADY ALICE FITZ-HUGH, *m.* Sir John Fienes, *d. v. p.*, eldest son of Sir Richard Fienes, Baron Dacre, *jure uxoris*, and his wife, Lady Joan de Dacre, who was descended as follows from Magna Charta Sureties:

Richard de Clare, one of the Sureties for the Magna Charta, Earl of Hertford, had by his wife, Lady Amicia, daughter of William, Earl of Gloucester:

Gilbert de Clare, one of the Sureties for the Magna Charta, Earl of Hertford, who had by his wife, Lady Isabel, daughter of William Marshall, Earl of Pembroke:

Richard de Clare, Earl of Hertford and Gloucester, who *m.* secondly, Lady Maud, daughter of **John de Lacie,** a Surety for the Magna Charta, Earl of Lincoln, by his second wife, Lady Margaret, daughter of Robert de Quincey, *d. v. p.*, second son of **Saber de Quincey**, a Surety for the Magna Charta, Earl of Winchester, and had:

Sir Gilbert de Clare, Earl of Hertford and Gloucester, *d.* 1295, who had by his second wife, Princess Joan Plantagenet, *d.* 1305, a daughter of EDWARD I., KING OF ENGLAND, by his wife, the Princess Eleanor of Castile:

Lady Margaret de Clare, widow of Piers, Earl of Cornwall, who *m.* secondly, Hugh d'Audley, created, in 1377, Earl of Gloucester, and had by him, who *d.* 1347–9:

Lady Margaret d'Audley, only child, who *m.* Ralph de Stafford, K.G., one of the original members of the Order of Knights of the Garter, a commander at Cressy, created, in 1351, Earl of Stafford, *d.* 1372, and had:

Hugh de Stafford, K.G., second Earl of Stafford, a crusader, *d.* 1386. He *m.* Lady Philippa, daughter of Thomas, third Earl of Warwick, one of the original Knights of the Garter, a commander at Cressy and Poictiers, and a crusader, *d.* 1369, son of Guy, second Earl of Warwick, *d.* 1315, the son of William de Beauchamp, of Elmley, Earl of Warwick (in right of his mother, Lady Isabel, sister and heiress of William de Mauduit, Earl of Warwick), by his wife, Lady Maud, widow of Gerard de Furnival, and the eldest daughter and coheiress of John Fitz-John, chief justice of Ireland, 1258, son of John Fitz-Geoffrey, chief justice of Ireland, 1246, and his wife, Lady Isabel, widow of Gilbert de Lacie, and daughter of Sir Ralph, third son of **Hugh Bigod**, son of **Roger Bigod**, both Sureties for the Magna Charta and Earls of Norfolk.

Sir Hugh, Earl of Stafford, and Lady Philippa had:

Lady Margaret de Stafford, *d.* 1370, who *m.*, as his first wife, Ralph de Nevill, K.G., created Earl of Westmoreland and great marshal of England, *d.* 1425, and had:

Lady Philippa de Nevill, who *m.* Thomas, Baron de Dacre, of Gillesland, *d.* 1457, and had:

Thomas de Dacre, eldest son, who *d. v. p.* He *m.* Lady Elizabeth, daughter and heiress of Sir William Bowet, of Cumberland, *d.* 1423, and his wife, Lady Amy, daughter and coheiress of Sir Robert d'Ufford, *d.* 1400, eldest son of Sir Edmund d'Ufford, of Horsford, *d.* 1374, youngest son of Sir Ralph d'Ufford, justice of Ireland, *d.* 1346, and his second wife, Lady Eve, only daughter and heiress of John de Clavering, lord of Horsford, Norfolk, second Baron by summons, 1299–1331, *d.* 1332, eldest son of Robert Fitz-Roger, lord of Warkworth and Clavering, summoned to Parliament, 1295, *d.* 1311, eldest son of Roger Fitz-John, feudal Baron of Warkworth and Clavering, *d.* 1249, eldest son of **John Fitz-Robert,** one of the Sureties for the Magna Charta.

Thomas de Dacre had by the Lady Elizabeth Bowet:

Lady Joan de Dacre, *b.* 1432; will proved June 14, 1486. She *m. ante* 1457, Sir Richard Fienes, who was declared Baron Dacre, in right of his wife, heir-general to her grandfather, by Edward IV. He was constable of the Tower of London and lord chamberlain to the household of King Edward IV., and *d.* 1484–5. He was the son of Sir Roger, treasurer to the household to Henry VI., the son of Sir William, high sheriff of Surrey and Sussex, 1297, the son of Sir William Fynes, and his wife, Lady Joan, daughter of Sir Geoffrey, second Baron de Say, admiral of the king's fleet, *d.* 1359, by his wife, Lady Maud, a daughter of the above Guy, Earl of Warwick, a descendant of **Roger Bigod** and **Hugh Bigod,** both Sureties for the Magna Charta. He was the eldest son of Geoffrey, *d.* 1322, son of William, *d.* 1295, son of William, *d.* 1272, the son of **Geoffrey de Say,** one of the Sureties for the Magna Charta.

Sir Richard Fienes, Baron Dacre, and Lady Joan had:
Sir John Fienes, who *m.* Lady Alice Fitz-Hugh, and had:

12. SIR THOMAS FIENES, *b.* 1470, who, as heir to his grandfather, succeeded as Baron Dacre of the South, and was made a Knight of the Bath by Henry VII. in 1495, *d.* 1534. He *m.* Lady Anne, daughter of Sir Humphrey Bourchier, who was *k. v. p.* at Barnetfield, fighting under the banner of Edward IV., eldest son of "John Bourchier de Berners, Chevalier," K.G., *d.* 1474, and his wife, Lady Margery, daughter and heiress of Richard Berners, of West Horsley, Surrey. He was the fourth son of William de Bourchier, Earl of Ewe, and his wife, Lady Anne Plantagenet, widow of both Thomas and Edmund, Earls of Stafford, and a daughter of Thomas, Duke of Gloucester, *d.* 1397, (youngest son of EDWARD III., KING OF ENGLAND), by his wife, Alianore de Bohun, a daughter and coheiress of Humphrey, the last Earl of Hereford and Essex and second Earl of Northampton, *d.* 1372, and his wife, Lady Joan, a daughter of Richard Fitz-Alan, K.G., Earl of Arundel (by his second wife, Lady Eleanor Plantagenet, daughter of Henry, third Earl of Lancaster, a grandson of HENRY III., KING OF ENGLAND, and his wife, Lady Maud de Chaworth, aforesaid, a descendant of **Hugh Bigod** and **Roger Bigod**, both Sureties for the Magna Charta), who was a descendant of **Saber de Quincey** and **Robert de Vere**, both Sureties for the Magna Charta.

Humphrey, the last Earl of Hereford and Essex, was the only son of William de Bohun, K.G., one of the gallant heroes of Cressy, created, in 1337, Earl of Northampton, *d.* 1360, the fourth son of Humphrey de Bohun, Earl of Hereford and Essex, constable of England, who was slain in the battle of Boroughbridge (and his wife, Lady Elizabeth Plantagenet, widow of John, Earl of Holland, and daughter of EDWARD I., KING OF ENGLAND, and his wife, Eleanor of Castile), the son of Humphrey de Bohun, Earl of Hereford and Essex and lord high constable, *d.* in 1297, the eldest son of Humphrey de Bohun, *d. v. p.*, who was taken prisoner at Evesham with his father, also named Humphrey, who was the eldest son of **Henry de Bohun**, one of the Sureties for the Magna Charta, Earl of Hereford and lord high constable of England.

Sir Thomas Fienes, K.B., and Lady Anne had:

13. LADY CATHERINE FIENES, second daughter, who *m.* Richard Loudenoys, of Briade, or Breame, in Sussex, and had:

14. MARY LOUDENOYS, only child, *m.* Thomas Harlakenden, of Worthorn, Kent, will proved in 1564, and had:

15. ROGER HARLAKENDEN, of Kenardiston and Woodchurch, Kent, third son, *b.* 1535, *d.* 1603. He purchased the manor of Earle's Colne, Essex, in 1583, and *m.* first, Elizabeth, daughter of Thomas Hardres and widow of George Harlakenden, of Woodchurch, and had by her:

16. RICHARD HARLAKENDEN, of Kenardiston, Earl's Colne, and Staple's Inn, *b.* 1565, *d.* August 24, 1631, who *m.* Mary (or Margaret), daughter of Edward Hubbart, or Hobart, of Stanstead-Montfichet, and had:

17. MABEL HARLAKENDEN, seventh daughter, *b.* at Earl's Colne, September 27, 1614. In 1635 she came with her brother, Roger Harlakenden, to New England, and *m.* first, in 1636, as his second wife, John Haynes, of Cambridge, Massachusetts, *b.* Copford Hall, Essex, May 1, 1594, arrived at Boston September 4, 1633; made freeman at Boston, May 14, 1634; elected an assistant in 1634 and 1636, and governor of the Massachusetts Bay Colony in 1635. He was colonel of the Second Regiment Massachusetts Militia in 1636. In 1637 he removed to Hartford, Connecticut, and was elected the first governor of that colony in April, 1639, and every second year afterwards until his death, March 1, 1654. He had by his wife, Mabel Harlakenden:

18. RUTH HAYNES, *b.* at Hartford, 1639, *m.* in 1655, Samuel Wyllys, *b.* February 19, 1631-2, *d.* 1709, assistant gov-

ernor of the Connecticut Colony, son of George Wyllys, governor of the Connecticut Colony in 1642, and had:

19. RUTH WYLLYS, *b.* 1656–7, *d.* 1729, who *m.* 1692, Rev. Edward Taylor, *b.* 1642, *d.* 1729, and had:

20. ELDAD TAYLOR, *b.* 1708, *d.* 1777, who *m.* Thankful Day, *b.* 1721, *d.* 1803, and had:

21. REV. JOHN TAYLOR, *b.* December 23, 1762, *d.* December 24, 1840, who *m.* 1789, Elizabeth Terry, *b.* September 10, 1766, *d.* September 17, 1843, and had:

22. HARRIET TAYLOR, *b.* May 18, 1794, *d.* February 7, 1841, who *m.* October 11, 1814, Roderick Terry, *b.* March 2, 1788, *d.* February 9, 1849, and had:

23. EDMUND TERRY, *b.* May 23, 1817, who *m.* March 8, 1855, Anna Prentice, *b.* January 17, 1834, and had:

24. GEORGE DAVIS TERRY, of Brooklyn, New York, *b.* February 5, 1870, one of the founders of the Order of Runnemede, a member of the Society of Colonial Wars, the Society Sons of the American Revolution, the Society of *Mayflower* Descendants, and the Society of Founders and Patriots.

Philip H. Waddell Smith

*

DESCENT from the Sureties for the observance of the Magna Charta:

William d'Albini,	John de Lacie,
Hugh Bigod,	William de Malet,
Roger Bigod,	William de Mowbray,
Henry de Bohun,	Saher de Quincey,
Gilbert de Clare,	Robert de Ros,
Richard de Clare,	Geoffrey de Say,
John Fitz-Robert,	Robert de Vere.

1. **William de Mowbray,** one of the Sureties for the Magna Charta, was the son of Nigel de Mowbray, a crusader, who *d.* on the road to the Holy Land, 3 Richard I., by his wife, Lady Mabel, daughter of Richard de Clare, Earl of Hertford, *k.* 1139, son of Gilbert de Tonsburg, Kent, and his wife, Lady Adeliza, daughter of Hugh, Count de Cleremont, and his wife, Lady Margaret, daughter of Hildwin IV., Count de Montdider and de Rouci, and his wife, Lady Adela, Countess de Rouci, daughter of Eblo I., Count de Rouci and de Reimes, and his wife, Lady Beatrix, daughter of Rynerius IV., Count of Hainault, and his wife Havide, daughter of HUGH CAPET, KING OF FRANCE.

William de Mowbray was a brother of Roger de Mowbray, also one of the Magna Charta Sureties, and *m.* Lady Agnes, daughter of William d'Albini, second Earl of Arundel and Sussex, whose mother was Adeliza of Lorraine, Queen Dowager of England, the second wife and widow of King Henry I., and, dying in 1222, had issue:

2. ROGER DE MOWBRAY, second son, who took part in the

Scottish wars of Henry III., and, dying in 1266, had issue by his wife, Lady Maud, daughter of William de Beauchamp, of Bedford:

3. ROGER DE MOWBRAY, who served in the wars of Wales and Gascony, and was the first of this family summoned to Parliament as Baron Mowbray of Axholme, writ dated June 23, 1295. He *m.* Lady Rose, "a descendant of Richard de Clare," and, dying in 1298, had issue:

4. JOHN DE MOWBRAY, second Baron, who, in consideration of his distinguished services in the Scottish wars of Edward I., had livery of the lands of his inheritance before he attained his majority. In 6 Edward II. he was sheriff of Yorkshire and governor of the city of York, and in the next year, being in an expedition to Scotland, he was constituted one of the wardens of the marshes adjoining that kingdom. But subsequently taking a prominent part in the insurrection of the Earl of Lancaster, and being captured at the battle of Boroughbridge, he was hanged at York in 1321, and his family imprisoned for a time in the Tower of London. He *m.* Lady Aliva, daughter of William de Braose, of Gower, whose grandmother was Princess Margaret, daughter of LLEWELLYN THE GREAT, PRINCE OF NORTH WALES, and had:

5. JOHN DE MOWBRAY, third Baron, who was summoned to Parliament from 1327. He was a favorite of Edward III., who accepted his homage, and gave him the lands of his father, for which he attended the king through his memorable French campaign. He *m.* Lady Joan Plantagenet, daughter of Henry, third Earl of Lancaster (a grandson of HENRY III., KING OF ENGLAND), *d.* 1345, and his wife, Lady Maud, daughter of Patrick de Chaworth, by his wife, Lady Isabel, daughter of William de Beauchamp, created Earl of Warwick, *d.* 1298 (and his wife, Lady Maud Fitz-John, widow of Gerard de Furnival, of Sheffield), whose

mother, Lady Isabel, was a daughter of William de Mauduit and his wife, Lady Alice, granddaughter of Roger de Newburgh, second Earl of Warwick, *d.* 1153, and his wife, Lady Gundred de Warren, daughter of William, second Earl of Surrey, and his wife, Lady Isabel, or Elizabeth, de Vermandois, daughter of Hugh the Great, son of HENRY I., KING OF FRANCE.

Lady Maud Fitz-John, aforesaid, was the daughter of John Fitz-John, chief justice of Ireland, 1258, the eldest son of John Fitz-Geoffrey (son of Geoffrey Fitz-Piers, Baron de Mandeville, Earl of Essex, lord justice of England, *d.* 1212), chief justice of Ireland, 1246, and his wife, Lady Isabel, daughter of Sir Ralph, third son of **Hugh Bigod**, one of the Sureties for the observance of the Magna Charta, second Earl of Norfolk, *d.* 1225 (and his wife, Lady Maud Marshall, sister of William Marshall, Jr., one of the Magna Charta Sureties, and daughter of William, Earl of Pembroke, the adviser of King John, and Protector of England during the minority of Henry III.), son of **Roger Bigod**, one of the Sureties for the observance of the Magna Charta, Earl of Norfolk, and lord high steward of England.

John de Mowbray, of the Isle of Axholme, *d.* in 1361, having issue by his wife, Lady Joan Plantagenet:

6. JOHN DE MOWBRAY, of Axholme, fourth Baron. He was a crusader, and was killed in a battle with the Turks, 1368. He *m.* Lady Elizabeth, only daughter of John, Baron de Segrave, *d. s. p. m.* 1353, and his wife Margaret, Duchess of Norfolk, *d.* 1399, daughter of Thomas de Brotherton, Earl of Norfolk, earl marshal of England, son of EDWARD I., KING OF ENGLAND, and his second wife, Princess Margaret, daughter of PHILIP III., KING OF FRANCE. John de Mowbray and the Lady Elizabeth had:

7. LADY JANE DE MOWBRAY, who *m.* Sir Thomas de Grey, of Berwyke, constable of Norham Castle, 1390, and had:

MEMBERS OF THE ORDER OF RUNNEMEDE 359

8. SIR THOMAS DE GREY, of Heton, second son, who was beheaded for political reasons, August 5, 1415, having *m.* Lady Alice, daughter of Ralph de Nevill, K.G., of Raby, created, in 1399, Earl of Westmoreland and earl marshal of England for life, *d.* 1425 (and his first wife, Lady Margaret, daughter of Hugh de Stafford, K.G., second Earl of Stafford, *d.* 1386, and his wife, Lady Philippa de Beauchamp*), the son of John de Nevill, K.G., of Raby, admiral of the king's fleet, son of Ralph de Nevill, of Raby, son of Ralph, first Baron Nevill, of Raby, and his first wife, Lady Euphemia, daughter of Robert Fitz-Roger, of Clavering, the son of Roger Fitz-John, of Clavering, *d.* 1249, son of **John Fitz-Robert**, one of the Sureties for the observance of the Magna Charta.

Hugh, Earl of Stafford, aforesaid, was the son of Ralph de Stafford, K.G., created, in 1351, Earl of Stafford, one of the original members of the Order of Knights of the Garter, and his wife, Lady Margaret, daughter of Hugh d'Audley, created, in 1337, Earl of Gloucester, and his wife, Lady Margaret, widow of Piers de Gaveston, Earl of Cornwall, beheaded in 1210, and daughter of Gilbert de Clare, Earl of Hertford and Gloucester, *d.* 1295 (and his second wife, Princess Joan d'Acre, *d.* 1305, daughter of EDWARD I., KING OF ENGLAND, and his first wife, Princess Eleanor, daughter of FERDINAND III., KING OF CASTILE AND LEON), son of Richard, Earl of Hertford and Gloucester, *d.* 1262 (by his second wife, Lady Maud, daughter of **John de Lacie**, one

---

* Lady Philippa de Beauchamp was the daughter of Sir Thomas, K.G., third Earl of Warwick, chamberlain of the exchequer, one of the original Knights of the Garter, *d.* 1369 (and his wife, Lady Catherine, daughter of Roger de Mortimer, created Earl of March, executed in 1330), son of Guy, second Earl of Warwick, 1275-1315, son of William de Beauchamp, Earl of Warwick, *d.* 1298, and his wife, Lady Maud Fitz-John, aforesaid, a descendant of **Roger Bigod** and **Hugh Bigod**, both Sureties for the Magna Charta.

of the Sureties for the observance of the Magna Charta, Earl of Lincoln, and his second wife, Lady Margeret, daughter of Robert, *d. v. p.*, eldest son of **Saber de Quincey**, one of the Sureties for the observance of the Magna Charta), son of **Gilbert de Clare**, Earl of Hertford, one of the Sureties for the observance of the Magna Charta (and his wife, Lady Isabel Marshall, daughter of William, Earl of Pembroke, Protector of England, and sister of William Marshall, Jr., a Surety for the Magna Charta), eldest son of **Richard de Clare**, one of the Sureties for the observance of the Magna Charta.

Sir Thomas de Grey and Lady Alice de Nevill had:

9. LADY ELIZABETH DE GREY, who *m.* Sir Philip, fourth Baron d'Arcy, admiral of the royal navy, 1386, *d.* 1398, who was the son of Sir John, second Baron d'Arcy, 1317-1356, and his wife, Lady Elizabeth, a daughter of Nicholas de Meinill, of Wherlton, Yorkshire, *d.* 1342, by his wife, Lady Alice, daughter of William de Ros, of Hamelake, one of the competitors for the crown of Scotland, *d.* 1317, son of Robert de Ros, of Hamelake, *d.* 1285 (and his wife, *m.* 1244, Lady Isabel, daughter of William, *d.* 1285, son of **William d'Albini**, one of the Sureties for the Magna Charta), the son of William de Ros, of Hamelake, who *d.* 1258, eldest son of **Robert de Ros**, of Furfan, fourth Baron Ros, of Hamelake, one of the Sureties for the Magna Charta.

Admiral Sir Philip d'Arcy and Lady Elizabeth had:

10. JOHN D'ARCY, fifth Baron, 1377-1411, who *m.* Lady Margaret, who *d.* 144-, daughter of Sir Henry, fifth Baron de Grey, of Wilton, *d.* 1394, and his wife, Lady Elizabeth, daughter of Thomas, Lord Talbot, *d. v. p.* in France, 145-, eldest son of the celebrated general, John de Talbot, K.G., lord of Furnival, created, in 1448, Earl of Shrewsbury, lord lieutenant and lord chancellor of Ireland, Earl of Waterford and Wexford, in the peerage of Ireland, *k.* in France, 1453,

THE PEDIGREE OF PH

		Henry de Bohun.	Robert de Vere.	
		Humphrey de Bohun.	Hugh de Vere.	
		Humphrey de Bohun.	Robert de Vere.	William de Mowbray
William de Malet.	Geoffrey de Say.	Humphrey de Bohun.	Joan de Vere.	Roger de Mowbray.
Helewise de Malet.	William de Say.	Humphrey de Bohun.	Alice de Warren.	Roger de Mowbray.
John de Muscegros.	William de Say.	Alianore de Bohun.	Richard Fitz-Alan.	John de Mowbray.
Robert de Muscegros.	Lady de Say.	Petronella Butler.	Mary Fitz-Alan.	John de Mowbr
Hawise de Muscegros.	John de Sudley.	Richard de Talbot=Ankaret le Strange.		John de Mowbr
Robert de Ferrers.	Joan de Sudley.		John de Talbot.	Jane de Mowbr
Robert de Ferrers=Elizabeth Boteler.			Thomas de Talbot.	
	Robert de Ferrers.		Elizabeth de Talbot=Henry de Grey.	
	Elizabeth de Ferrers=John de Greystock.			Margaret de Gr

Joan de G
Joa
William, Baron D
James Daubeney
Giles Daubeney, of
John Daubeney, of
George Daubeney, of
Henry Daubeney, of
George Daubeney, of
Andrew Daubeney, of
George Daubeney, of
Lloyd Daubeney, o
Lloyd Daubeney, of New Y
Eliza Martin
William Coventry Henry Waddell, of N
Susan Alice
Philip Henry W

P H. WADDELL SMITH.

Roger Bigod.
Hugh Bigod.
Ralph Bigod.   Saher de Quincey.
Isabel Bigod.   Richard de Clare.   Robert de Quincey.
John Fitz-John.   John Fitz-Robert. Gilbert de Clare.   John de Lacie—Margaret de Quincey.
Maud Fitz-John.   Roger Fitz-John.   Richard de Clare—Maud de Lacie.
Isabel de Beauchamp. Robert Fitz-Roger. Gilbert de Clare.   William d'Albini.   Robert de Ros.
Maud de Chaworth.   Eupheme Fitz-Roger. Margaret de Clare.   William d'Albini.   William de Ros.
Joan Plantagenet.   Ralph de Nevill.   Margaret d'Audley.   Isabel d'Albini—Robert de Ros.
                     John de Nevill.   Hugh de Stafford.   William de Ros.
Thomas de Grey.   Ralph de Nevill—Margaret de Stafford.   Alice de Ros.
     Thomas de Grey—Alice de Nevill.   Elizabeth de Meinill.
     Elizabeth de Grey—Philip d'Arcy.
John d'Arcy.
ock—John d'Arcy.
rcy—Giles, Baron Daubeney.
ey,—Alice de Stourton.
on,—Elizabeth Pauncefote.
rd,————— Coles.
ell,—Alice Penny.
ell,—Elizabeth Coker.
ell,—Edith Symonds.
ell,—Judith Bryant.
am,—Sarah Blackall.
ol,—Jane Lloyd.
tol,—Ducibella Saxbury.
ty,—Mary Coventry.
ney—Henry Waddell, of New York City.
rk,—Julia Anna Cobb.
dell—George Washington Smith, of Parsippany, N. J.
ll Smith, of Pittsburgh, Pa.

MEMBERS OF THE ORDER OF RUNNEMEDE 361

aged eighty years,* the second son of Sir Richard, fourth Baron Talbot, of Goodrich Castle, 1361-1396, Baron le Strange in right of his wife, Lady Ankaret, daughter of John, fourth Baron le Strange, of Blackmere, *d.* 1361, and his wife, Lady Mary, daughter of Sir Richard Fitz-Alan, K.G., Earl of Arundel and Surrey,† *d.* 1375, the son of Edmund, eighth Earl Arundel, K.B., beheaded 1326, and his wife, Lady Alice, daughter of William de Warren, *d.* 1285, and his wife Joan, daughter of Robert de Vere, fifth Earl of Oxford and sixth great chamberlain of England, son of Hugh, Earl of Oxford and great chamberlain (and his wife Hawise, daughter of **Saber de Quincey**, one of the Sureties for the observance of the Magna Charta), son of **Robert de Vere**, Earl of Oxford and great chamberlain, one of the Sureties for the observance of the Magna Charta.

Sir Richard, fourth Baron Talbot aforesaid, was the son of Gilbert, Baron Talbot, of Goodrich Castle, 1332-1387, by his first wife, Lady Petronella, daughter of James Butler, second Earl of Carrick, created, in 1328, Earl of Ormond, Lord Butler of Ireland, and his wife, Lady Alianore, sister of three Earls of Hereford and of William, Earl of Northampton, daughter of Humphrey de Bohun, fourth Earl of Hereford and Essex, lord high constable of England, *k.* 1321 (and his wife Elizabeth, widow of John, Earl of Holland,

---

* His wife was Lady Maud, daughter of Thomas Nevill, Baron Furnival, *d.* 1416 (brother of Sir Ralph, first Earl of Westmoreland), and his wife, Lady Joan, only child of William de Furnival, *d.* 1383, son of Thomas, *d.* 1339, son of Thomas, *d.* 1332, the son of Gerard de Furnival, *d.* 1280, and his wife, Lady Maud, daughter of John Fitz-John, chief justice of Ireland, 1258, *d.* 42 Henry II., aforesaid, a descendant of **Roger Bigod** and **Hugh Bigod**, both Sureties for the Magna Charta.

† His wife was Lady Eleanor, daughter of Henry Plantagenet, third Earl of Lancaster, *d.* 1345, and his wife, Lady Maud de Chaworth, aforesaid, a descendant of **Hugh Bigod** and **Roger Bigod**, both Sureties for the Magna Charta.

and daughter of EDWARD I., KING OF ENGLAND, and his first wife, Eleanor of Castile), son of Humphrey, Earl of Hereford and Essex, *d.* 1297, son of Humphrey de Bohun, *d. v. p.*, eldest son of Humphrey, Earl of Hereford and Essex, *d.* 1274, the son of **Henry de Bohun,** one of the Sureties for the observance of the Magna Charta, by his wife, Lady Maud, a sister of Geoffrey de Mandeville, one of the Sureties for the Magna Charta.

John, Baron d'Arcy, and Lady Margaret had:

11. SIR JOHN D'ARCY, second son, *d.* 1454. He *m.* Lady Joan, daughter of John, Baron de Greystock,* and his wife Elizabeth, daughter of Sir Robert, second Baron Ferrers, of Wemme (and his wife, Lady Joan, daughter of John of Gaunt, Earl of Lancaster, son of EDWARD III., KING OF ENGLAND), who was the son of Sir Robert, first Baron Ferrers, of Wemme, by his wife, Lady Elizabeth, only daughter of William, second Baron Boteler, of Wemme, *d.* 1369, by his wife, Lady Joan, daughter of John, son of John de Sudley, lord chamberlain to Edward I., by his wife, a daughter of William, Baron Say, *d.* 1295, son of William de Say, governor of Rochester Castle, *d.* 1272, the son of **Geoffrey de Say,** one of the Sureties for the observance of the Magna Charta.

Sir Robert Ferrers, of Wemme, was the son of Robert,

---

* He was the son of Robert, fifth Baron Greystock, *d.* 1417, by his wife Catherine, daughter of Roger, Lord Clifford, *d.* 1390 (whose wife Maud was daughter of Thomas de Beauchamp, third Earl of Warwick, aforesaid, and a descendant of **Richard de Clare** and **Gilbert de Clare,** both Sureties for the observance of the Magna Charta), son of Robert, Lord de Clifford, sheriff of Westmoreland County, *d.* 1340, by his wife, Lady Maud, daughter of Thomas, son of Richard de Clare, aforesaid, Earl of Hertford and Gloucester, *d.* 1226 (and Lady Maud de Lacie, his wife, daughter of **John de Lacie,** one of the twenty-five Sureties for the observance of the Magna Charta), a descendant of **Richard de Clare, Gilbert de Clare,** and **Saber de Quincey,** Sureties for the observance of the Magna Charta.

second Baron Ferrers, of Chartley,* son of John, Baron Ferrers, of Chartley, seneschal of Aquitaine, *d.* 1324,† by his wife, Lady Hawyse, daughter of Sir Robert de Muscegros, of Charleton, County Somerset, son of John de Muscegros, of Charleton, the son of Sir Robert de Muscegros, of Berwain, and his wife, Lady Helewise, daughter of William de Malet, one of the Sureties for the observance of the Magna Charta.

Sir John d'Arcy and his wife, Lady Joan Greystock, had:

12. LADY JOAN D'ARCY, widow of John de Beaumont, *m.* Giles, fourth Baron Daubeney, sheriff of Bedfordshire and Bucks, 10 Henry VI., *b.* Kempstead, County Bedford, October 20, 1393, *d.* January 11, 1445–6, buried South Petherton, who was the son of Giles, third Baron Daubeney, *d.* August 22, 1403, will dated June 1, 1400, buried Kempstead Church (and Margery, daughter of Sir John Beauchamp), son of Giles Daubeney, enfeoffed in the lifetime of his father in the manor of South Petherton, *d.* at Barrington, County Somerset, June 24, 1386 (and Eleanor, daughter of Henry de Willington), son of Ralph d'Albini, or Daubeney, K.B., *b.* March 3, 1304–5, summoned to Parliament February 28, 1342 (and Alice, daughter of Lord Montacute), son of Elias d'Albini, or Daubeney, first Baron, summoned to Parliament by writ of Edward I., November 2, 1295, son of Ralph d'Albini, of South Petherton, County Somerset, *d.* 1291, son of Ralph d'Albini, who *d.* Acre, Syria, 1190, a brother of

---

* His wife was Agnes, daughter of Humphrey de Bohun, aforesaid, Earl of Hereford, a descendant of Henry de Bohun, one of the twenty-five Sureties for the observance of the Magna Charta.

† He was the son of Robert de Ferrers, eighth Earl of Derby, *d.* 7 Edward I. (and Eleanor, daughter and heiress of Ralph, Lord Basset), the son of William de Ferrers, seventh Earl of Derby, *k.* 1254, and his second wife, Margaret, daughter of Roger de Quincey, Earl of Winchester, son of Saber de Quincey, one of the Sureties for the observance of the Magna Charta.

William d'Albini, who was one of the Sureties for the observance of the Magna Charta.

Lady Joan d'Arcy and Giles, Lord Daubeney, had:

13. WILLIAM DAUBENEY, fifth Baron, lord of South Petherton, *b.* June 11, 1424, *d.* January 2, 1460. He *m.* Lady Alice, daughter of John de Stourton, of Preston (his sister, Edith de Beauchamp, was the mother of Margaret de Beaufort, grandmother of King Henry VII.), son of John de Stourton, of Preston, *d.* 1364, by his wife, Lady Jane, daughter of Sir Ralph, third Baron Basset, of Drayton, K.B., *d.* 1343, and his wife, Lady Joan, daughter of Thomas de Beauchamp, K.G., third Earl of Warwick, *d.* 1369, aforesaid, a descendant of **Roger Bigod** and **Hugh Bigod,** Sureties for the Magna Charta.

William, fifth Baron Daubeney, and Lady Alice had:

14. JAMES DAUBENEY, second son (brother of Giles, sixth Baron, K.G., one of the esquires for the body of Henry VII., appointed of his council, constable of Bristol Castle and master of the mint, and created Lord Daubeney by patent, dated March 12, 1485-6, also governor of Calais and lord chamberlain of the household, *d.* London, May 28, 1508, will dated May 19, 1508, buried St. Paul's Chapel, Westminster Abbey, where a monument was erected to his memory and that of his wife Katherine, daughter of Sir John Arundel, by whom he left an only son, Henry, seventh Baron by writ of summons, but second Baron under the new creation, aged fourteen at the death of his father, and who was created Earl of Bridgewater by patent, July 19, 1538, *d.* April 8, 1548, when the barony of Daubeney, created in 1486, and the earldom of Bridgewater became extinct, but the barony created by writ, Edward I., *anno* 1295, should have passed to his sister Cecily, Countess of Bath, but upon failure of descendants of that lady it became vested and is now in heirs-general of Elias, first Baron Daubeney), and

eventual heir of Elias, first Baron, aforesaid, *d.* October 1, 1528 (Ex. 20 Henry VIII., No. 158), having issue by his wife Elizabeth, daughter and heiress of Robert Pauncefote:

15. GILES DAUBENEY, of Wayford, Somersetshire, eldest son and heir, aged forty-six at the death of his mother, *d.* at Wayford, March 22, 1558-9 (Ex. September 5, 1 Elizabeth, No. 36), who by his wife, daughter of —— Coles, of Somersetshire, had:

16. JOHN DAUBENEY, of Gorwell, in the parish of Litton Cheyney, Dorsetshire, fourth son, but next heir in remainder after the issue of James (who *d.* 1528) in the settlement of 1546. He *m.* Alice, daughter of Giles Penny, of East Coker, Somersetshire, and *d.* 1570, his will dated August 1, 1570, proved November 25, 1570, and had:

17. GEORGE DAUBENEY, of Gorwell, *d.* September 6, 1612, aged fifty-four years, buried at Litton Cheyney, who *m.* Elizabeth, daughter of Thomas Coker, of Maypowder, Dorsetshire, buried Litton Cheyney, July 23, 1639, and had:

18. HENRY DAUBENEY, of Gorwell, eldest son, will dated December 23, 1655, proved May 19, 1656, buried at Litton Cheyney, who *m.* Edith Symonds, also buried at Litton Cheyney, January 24, 1650, and had:

19. GEORGE DAUBENEY, of Gorwell, eldest son, *bapt.* at Litton Cheyney, December 16, 1616, will dated October 3, 1689, proved October 17, 1690, who *m.* Judith Bryant, of Litton Cheyney, buried there June 29, 1655, and had:

20. ANDREW DAUBENEY, of Pulham, Dorsetshire, *bapt.* at Litton Cheyney, April 14, 1653, buried at Pulham, September 12, 1734, who *m.* Sarah, daughter of Richard Blackall, of Britwell, Oxfordshire, and widow of Charles Revett, of the University of Oxford, clerk, and had:

21. GEORGE DAUBENEY, eldest son, *b.* Buckshaw Hill, Holwell, Somersetshire, buried St. James Church, Bristol, February 28, 1740, will dated February 22, 1730-1, proved May

23, 1741, who *m.* Jane Lloyd, of Bristol, buried St. James, September 15, 1761, and had:

22. LLOYD DAUBENEY, of Bristol, *bapt.* St. Nicholas Church there, November 9, 1718, buried St. James, Bristol, December 22, 1754, administration granted January 16, 1755, who *m.* Ducibella Saxbury, at St. James Church, Bristol, February 4, 1742, and had:

23. LLOYD DAUBENEY, only surviving son, nineteenth in direct male descent from Robert de Todeni, standard-bearer to William the Conqueror and founder of Belvoir Castle, and fifteenth in direct male descent from Elias, first Baron d'Albini, or Daubeney, whose honors, created by writ of summons, November 2, 1295, are now dormant in his heirs-general, believed to be in this line. He was *b.* Bristol, November 22, 1746, and was a resident of New York City before 1768, and owner of large landed estates in St. Lawrence and Otsego Counties, Schuyler's and other patents, New York, and *m.* January 24, 1770, Mary Coventry, *b.* New York City, July 15, 1743, and *d.* New York City, October 6, 1813 (widow of James Calder, of New York City), daughter of Hon. William Coventry (and Elizabeth Hart, *b.* January 29, 1722 (O.S.), *m.* at St. Kitts, West Indies, August 28, 1739, *d.* New York City, August 22, 1803), *b.* in England, April 10, 1715 (O.S.), and removed to the island of St. Christopher, West Indies, and thence to New York City, before 1756, where, as a resident and property-holder in Dock Street, he was for many years one of the magistrates of the city, and *d.* St. Kitts, West Indies, April 25, 1774; son of Thomas Coventry, third son (brother of Walter Coventry, eldest son, who *d.* 1717, and William Coventry, Esquire, second son, who, in 1719, as eldest male descendant of Walter, brother of Thomas Coventry, first Baron and lord keeper of the Great Seal, and in accordance with the limitations of the patent, upon failure of issue of Gilbert,

fourth Earl of Coventry, the last direct male descendant of Thomas Coventry, the lord keeper aforesaid, succeeded as fifth Earl of Coventry and Viscount Deerhurst, and was in turn succeeded, March 18, 1750, by his eldest son, George William, sixth Earl of Coventry and Viscount Deerhurst, who *m.* the very celebrated beauty Maria Gunning, daughter of John Gunning, Esq., of Roscommon) of Walter Coventry, brother of Thomas, first Baron Coventry, of Aylesborough, attorney-general to the crown and lord keeper of the Great Seal in 1625, sons of Thomas Coventry, chief justice of the Court of Common Pleas, 1606, a lineal male descendant of John Coventry, who filled the offices of sheriff and lord mayor of the city of London in 1416 and 1425.

Lloyd Daubeney and Mary Coventry, aforesaid, had:

24. ELIZA MARTIN DAUBENEY, third child, but eventual heiress (others *d. s. p.*), *b.* October 25, 1779, New York City, *bapt.* November 10, 1779, by Rev. Mr. Inglis, rector Holy Trinity Church, New York, *d.* New York City and buried Waddell vault; *m.* November 8, 1800 (by Rev. Dr. Benjamin Moore), Captain Henry Waddell, of New York City, *b.* New York City, March 31, 1767, will dated May 9, 1815, *d.* New York City, July 13, 1819, buried Waddell vault, eldest and only surviving son of Lieutenant-Colonel William Waddell, of New York City, and his wife, Geesie Filkin, *m.* at her father's residence, Pearl Street, New York, April 5, 1761.

Lieutenant-Colonel William Waddell, aforesaid, was *b.* New York City, July 26, 1737 (O.S.), and was one of the aldermen and magistrats of the same prior to the Revolution, during which he served as lieutenant-colonel of a loyalist regiment in New York City, commission dated October 23, 1776, and thereafter removing to London, *d.* there July 27, 1813, and there buried. He was eldest son of Captain John Waddell, *b.* Dover, Kent, England, October 3, 1714, and removed to New York City about 1735, *d.* there May 29, 1762, in his home on Dock Street (purchased from William Coventry, aforesaid), and buried Waddell vault, Holy Trinity Church, New York City, will dated October 9, 1760 (and his wife Anne, daughter of William Kirten, of New York City), eldest son of Lieutenant William Waddell, of the British navy, who lost his right arm in the service in burning the Spanish fleet at Vigo, Spain, *b.* Edinburgh, North Britain, and *d.* Dover, England, son of Captain John Waddell, "of Stebenheath in ye County of Middlesex, Esq., now Captn. of ye Rainbowe, a principall Ship of his ma'ties Navie Royall," who had arms granted to "him and his posteritie, with their due differences, forever," May 3, 1627 (copy of original grant on file Herald's College, London), for great naval victories in the Persian Gulf and Straits of Ormus, *temp.* 1622. It is notable that this same vessel was one of the fleet (and third in point of size) which repelled the Spanish Armada, *temp.* 1588, and that in the engagement, in which Captain Waddell commanded against Kishm and Ormus, the great navigator Baffin was one of the Englishmen to lose their lives.

Geesie Filkin, aforesaid, was *b.* Poughkeepsie, New York, March 25, 1740 (O.S.), *d.* New York City, January 19, 1773, and buried Waddell vault, Holy Trinity Church, daughter of Francis Filkin, of New York City [and his wife Catherine, daughter of Colonel Leonard Lewis, of the colonial wars, a resident of New York City and Dutchess County, New York (and his wife, Elizabeth Hardenburg), son of Thomas Lewis, of English descent, and of New York City before 1668], son of Lieutenant-Colonel Henry Filkin, of the colonial wars, and of New York City as early as 1684, of English descent.

Eliza Martin Daubeney and Captain Waddell, aforesaid, had:

25. WILLIAM COVENTRY HENRY WADDELL, of Murray Hill, New York City, eldest son and heir, and only surviving descendant of Lloyd Daubeney, of Bristol, aforesaid, *b.* New York City, corner Broadway and Wall Street, May 28, 1802, *d.* New York City, June 1, 1884, financial agent of department of state and United States marshal for the Southern District of the State of New York under the administration of Andrew Jackson, official and general assignee in bankruptcy from 1841 to 1884; one of the principals in the important suits to determine the rights of the boards of proprietors of East and West New Jersey to land under water; in 1842, built his home on Murray Hill, northwest corner Fifth Avenue and Thirty-seventh Street, sometimes known as "Waddell Castle," famous in its day as the most imposing residence upon Manhattan Island; *m.* Julia Anna Cobb, January, 1828 (*m.* secondly, Charlotte Augusta Southwick, widow of William McMurray, and had several children, all of whom *d. s. p. v. p.*), *b.* Parsippany, April 29, 1802, *d.* there June 20, 1841, and there buried, daughter of Lieutenant-Colonel Lemuel Cobb, of Parsippany, New Jersey, *b.* May 15, 1762, lieutenant-colonel Fourth Regiment New Jersey Militia, 1809–1815, county judge, 1813–18, 1822–27, 1827–30, surveyor-general board of proprietors of East New Jersey, *d.* April 1, 1830, buried at Parsippany (and his second wife, Susan Farrand, *b.* January 28, 1764, *m.* February 1, 1796, *d.* August 2, 1816, descended from Nathaniel Farrand, who was of Milford, Connecticut, in 1645), son of Edward Cobb, of Parsippany, New Jersey, son of Ebenezer Cobb, *b.* Wales, May 13, 1696.

William Coventry Henry Waddell and Julia Anna Cobb had:

26. SUSAN ALICE WADDELL, *b.* September 26, 1834, Parsippany, New Jersey, *m.* April 8, 1868, New York City, George Washington Smith, *b.* Troy (now Troy Hills),

Morris County, New Jersey, October 2, 1832, removed, 1856, to Monee, Illinois, thence, in 1868, to Madison, New Jersey, and finally, in 1885, to Parsippany, New Jersey, son of Hiram Smith, of Troy, New Jersey, *b.* there August 25, 1799, and there *d.* September 14, 1865, buried Parsippany (and his wife, Mary Allen Osborne, of Parsippany, *b.* April 25, 1802, at Parsippany, *m.* September 19, 1822, *d.* Troy, April 16, 1872, buried at Parsippany, of whom presently), son of Lieutenant-Colonel Hiram Smith, of Troy, *b.* Troy, New Jersey, December 22, 1756, *d.* April 27, 1833, buried Parsippany, served in the war of the Revolution as private, sergeant, and lieutenant in the third regiment of "Jersey Line," Continental army, served also in the eastern battalion, New Jersey Militia, and was major and lieutenant-colonel of the Fourth, or "lower" regiment of militia of Morris County, 1793–1801, high sheriff of Morris County, 1794–97, member of assembly, 1791–2, and county judge, 1800–1805 [and his wife Eleanor Parrett, daughter of Samuel Parrett, of Troy (whose father, Samuel Parrett, was in Elizabethtown as early as 1704), and his wife, Eleanor Alling, only child of Joseph Alling, of Elizabethtown, New Jersey, later of Troy, New Jersey, and one of the earliest settlers and proprietors of that place], eldest son of Benjamin Smith, of Troy, *b.* 1725 (and his wife, Hannah Dod, daughter of Lieutenant Samuel Dod, of Orange, New Jersey, son of Samuel Dod, of Newark, son of Daniel and Mary Dod, both of Brantford, Connecticut, as early as 1646–7), son of Richard Smith, of Troy, one of the earliest settlers of that place.

Mary Allen Osborne, aforesaid, was the only child of Lieutenant Thomas Osborne, Jr., of Parsippany, *b.* October 12, 1753, *d.* July 27, 1818, buried Parsippany, served in the Revolutionary War as lieutenant in Captain Baldwin's company, Eastern Battalion, New Jersey troops (son of Thomas

Osborne, Sr., Parsippany), and his second wife, Hannah Howell, daughter of Gideon Howell, son of Edward Howell, son of Richard Howell, of Southampton, Long Island, son of Richard Howell, Southampton, son of Edward Howell, of Southampton, Long Island, one of the patentees of that place, made "freeman," Boston, March 14, 1639, son of Henry Howell, of Marsh Gibbon, Bucks, England, son of William Howell, who purchased, in 1536, from Sir Robert Dormer, Knight, the manor of Westbury, in the parish of Marsh Gibbon, Bucks County, England.

Susan Alice Waddell and George Washington Smith had:

27. PHILIP HENRY WADDELL SMITH, of Pittsburgh, *b.* January 5, 1869, Madison, Morris County, New Jersey, a member of the Society of Colonial Wars, and Society Sons of the Revolution, and a founder of the Order of Runnemede.

THE PEDIGREE OF CHARLES E. CADWALADER, M.D.

			Roger Bigod.	Richard de Clare.
			Hugh Bigod.	Joan de Clare.
		Saher de	Ralph Bigod.	Rhys-mechyllt.
Henry de Bohun.	Robert de Vere.	Quincey.	Isabel Bigod.	Rhys-vaughn.
Humphrey de Bohun.	Hugh de Vere—Hawise de Quincey.		John Fitz-John.	Rhys-gloff.
Humphrey de Bohun.	Robert de Vere.		Maud Fitz-John.	Madoc ap Rhys.
Humphrey de Bohun.	Joan de Vere.		Isabel de Beauchamp.	Trahairn-goch.
Humphrey de Bohun.	Alice de Warren.		Maud de Chaworth—	David-goch.
William de Bohun.	Richard Fitz-Alan—Eleanor Plantagenet.			Ievan ap David.
Elizabeth de Bohun—Richard Fitz-Alan.				Madoc ap Ievan.
a quibus Col. Clement Biddle, of Philadelphia,—Rebecca Cornell.				Deikws-ddu
		Mary Biddle—Gen. Thomas Cadwalader. *a quo*		
	Henrietta Maria McIlvaine—Judge John Cadwalader.			
	Charles Evert Cadwalader, M.D., of Philadelphia.			

Charles Evert Cadwalader, M.D.

DESCENT from the Sureties for the observance of the Magna Charta:

Hugh Bigod,	Richard de Clare,
Roger Bigod,	Saher de Quincey,
Henry de Bohun,	Robert de Vere.

1. **Richard de Clare,** Earl of Hertford, one of the Sureties for the Magna Charta, *d.* 1218, had by his wife, Lady Amicia, sister of King John's divorced wife and daughter of William, second Earl of Gloucester, *d.* 1183:

2. LADY JOAN DE CLARE (sister to Gilbert de Clare, one of the Sureties for the Magna Charta), who *m.* Rhys-gryd, lord of Yestradtywy, son of Rhys ap Gryffyth, lord of Rhys, Prince and chief justice of South Wales, *d.* 1197, and had:

3. RHYS-MECHYLLT, lord of Llandovery Castle, *d.* 1242-3, who had:

4. RHYS-VAUGHN, lord of Yestradtywy, who *m.* Lady Gwladys, daughter of Griffith, lord of Cymcydmaen, and had:

5. RHYS-GLOFF, lord of Cymcydmaen, who *m.* Gwyrryl, daughter of Maelywn ap Cadwalader, and had:

6. MADOC AP RHYS-GLOFF, who *m.* Tanglwyst, daughter of Gronowy ap Einion, and had:

7. TRAHAIRN GOCH AP MADOC, lord of Llyngnainianoc and Penllech, who *m.* Gwyrryl, daughter of Madoc ap Meirig, and had:

8. DAVID-GOCH AP TRAHAIRN-GOCH, lord of Penllech, *temp.* 1314, who *m.* Lady Maud, daughter of David Lloyd ap Cynveloe ap Llewellyn, a natural son of David, Prince of Wales, son of Llewellyn the Great, Prince of Wales, and his wife, Joan, a natural daughter of King John of England, and had:

9. IEVAN AP DAVID-GOCH, lord of Penllech and Grainoc, *temp.* 1352, who *m.* Eva, daughter of Einion ap Celynnin, lord of Llwydiarth, and had:

10. MADOC AP IEVAN, lord of Grainoc, who had:

11. DEIKWS-DDU AP MADOC, who *m.* Gwen, daughter of Ievan-ddu, and had:

12. EINION AP DEIKWS-DDU, who *m.* Morvydd, daughter of Matw ap Llowasch, and had:

13. HOWEL AP EINION, who *m.* Mali, daughter of Llewellyn ap Ievan, and had:

14. GRYFFYTH AP HOWEL, who *m.* Gwenlian, daughter of Einion ap Ievan Lloyd, and had:

15. LEWIS AP GRYFFYTH, lord of Yshute, who *m.* Ethli, or Ellen, daughter of Edward ap Ievan Llanoddyn, by his wife Catherine, daughter of Gryffyth ap Llewellyn ap Einion ap David, which latter David was lord of Cryniarth, in Edermon, and was the son and heir of David ap Ievan ap Einion, captain of Harlech Castle in 1468, by his wife Margaret, daughter of John Puleston, of Emral, Flintshire, whose mother, Lowry, was a sister of Tudor-Vaughn and Owen Glendower, the celebrated Welsh chieftain, and daughter of Gryffyth-vaughn, fourth lord of Glyndwrdwyn, or Glyndyfrdwy, in Merionethshire, by his wife, *m.* 1343, Eleanor, sister of Margaret, mother of Sir Owen Tudor, the grandfather of King Henry VII. of England. Gryffyth-vaughn was the son of Gryffyth, lord of Rushalt, representative of the sovereign princes of Powys, by his wife Elizabeth, daughter of John, second Baron le Strange, of Knockyn.

Lady Eleanor vch. Thomas, who *m.*, in 1343, Gryffyth-vaughn, was a daughter and coheiress of Thomas ap Llewellyn, lord of South Wales (by his wife Eleanor, daughter of Philip ap Ievan, or Yevor, lord of Iscoed, in Cardiganshire, and Princess Unica, or Catherine, daughter of Llewellyn ap Gryffyth, Prince of North Wales, by his first wife), son of Llewellyn ap Owen, lord of South Wales, by his wife Eleanor, daughter of Henri, Count de Barr, and his wife, the Princess Eleanor Plantagenet, widow of Alphonso, King of Arragon, and daughter of EDWARD I., KING OF ENGLAND, by his first wife, Princess Eleanor, daughter of FERDINAND III., KING OF CASTILE.

Lewis ap Gryffyth, lord of Yshute, had by Ethli, his wife:

16. ROBERT AP LEWIS, who *m.* Gwyrryl, daughter of Llewellyn ap David, lord of Llan Rwst, in Denbigshire, and had:

17. IEVAN AP ROBERT, lord of Rhiwlas and Vron Goch, in Merionethshire, who had by his wife, Jane, but of what family she was is unknown:

18. OWEN AP IEVAN, lord of Vron Goch, who *d.* in 1669, having issue by his wife, Gainor vch. John, a daughter:

19. ELLEN VCH. OWEN, *b.* 1660, *d.* 169–, who *m.* before May 16, 1675, Cadwalader Thomas ap Hugh, of Kiltalgarth, Llanvawr, in Merionethshire, *d.* before February 9, 1682–3, and had:

20. JOHN CADWALADER, *b.* before 1682, who came to Pennsylvania, and was admitted a freeman in Philadelphia in July, 1705. He was elected to the common council, 1718–33; member of the provincial assembly, 1729–34; *d.* July 23, 1734. He *m.* at Friends' meeting, Lower Merion, Pennsylvania, December 29, 1699, Martha, daughter of Dr. Edward Jones, of Merion, Pennsylvania, *d.* 1737 (and his wife Mary, daughter of Dr. Thomas Wynne, of Philadelphia, *b.* 1630, at Bron-vadog, near Caerwys, Flintshire, who came

to Pennsylvania with William Penn in the *Welcome*, in 1682, and was a member and speaker of the first Pennsylvania Assembly), and had:

21. THOMAS CADWALADER, M.D., of Philadelphia, member of the provincial council of Pennsylvania, 1755; medical director in the Continental army, who *d.* at his seat, "Greenwood," near Trenton, New Jersey, November 14, 1779, aged seventy-two. He *m.* June 18, 1737-8, Hannah, *b.* 1711, *d.* 1786, daughter of Thomas Lambert, *b.* 1677, and his second wife, *m.* 1710, Anne, daughter of William Wood, member of Pennsylvania Assembly from Bucks County.

Thomas Lambert, who was justice of the peace for Nottingham Township, 1699, and represented Burlington County, New Jersey, in the New Jersey Assemblies of 1703-10 and in 1721, was the third son of Thomas Lambert IV., *b.* 1621, *d.* 1694, who joined the Yorkshire company of Friends which bought the proprietary rights of Carteret in West Jersey. He came to New Jersey in December, 1678, and settled finally on a tract of eight hundred and eighty-nine acres of land, named "Lamberton," now located in the Sixth Ward of the city of Trenton, and subsequently bought two tracts, eight hundred and eight hundred and fifty-one acres, adjacent to this one. He became member of the New Jersey Assemblies of 1681-85, justice of the peace and commissioner of lands in Nottingham Township, lay-judge of quarter sessions, special and common pleas and general courts, and also held many minor offices of trust; member of the "West Jersey Society," 1691.

Thomas Cadwalader, M.D., of Philadelphia, had by his wife, Hannah Lambert:

22. MAJOR-GENERAL JOHN CADWALADER, of Philadelphia, *b.* January 10, 1742, *d.* February 10, 1786, who had by his second wife, *m.* January 30, 1779, Williamina, *b.* February 23, 1753, *d.* September 9, 1837, daughter of Dr. Phineas

Bond, of Philadelphia, 1717-1773, by his wife Williamina, daughter of Judge William Moore, of "Moore Hall," Chester County, Pennsylvania, 1699-1783:

23. MAJOR-GENERAL THOMAS CADWALADER, of Philadelphia, *b.* October 29, 1779, *d.* October 31, 1841, who *m.* June 25, 1804, Mary, *b.* January 12, 1781, daughter of Colonel Clement Biddle, of Philadelphia, United States marshal for Pennsylvania, and his second wife, Rebekah, only daughter of Gideon Cornell, lieutenant-governor and chief justice of Rhode Island.

Colonel Clement Biddle, *b.* May 10, 1740, *d.* July 10, 1814, was the second son of John Biddle (son of William Biddle, of Mount Hope, in New Jersey), and his wife, *m.* March 3, 1736, Sarah, eldest daughter of Owen Owen, high sheriff in 1726, and coroner of Philadelphia County (and his wife, Anne Wood, *m.* 1714), who was descended as follows from Sureties for the Magna Charta:

Henry de Bohun, a Magna Charta Surety, created, in 1199, Earl of Hereford, lord high constable of England, Earl of Essex, *d.* 1220. He *m.* Lady Maud, daughter of Geoffrey Fitz-Piers, Earl of Essex, lord high justice of England, and sister of Geoffrey de Mandeville, one of the Sureties for the Magna Charta, and had:

Humphrey de Bohun, Earl of Hereford and Essex, *d.* 1274, who *m.* first, Lady Maud, daughter of Henry, Baron d'Eue, and had:

Humphrey de Bohun, governor of Goodrich and Winchester Castles, eldest son, *d. v. p.*, who *m.* Lady Eleanor, daughter of William de Braose, of Brecknock, and had:

Humphrey de Bohun, Earl of Hereford and Essex, lord high constable, *d.* 1297, who *m.* Maud de Fienes, and had:

Humphrey de Bohun, Earl of Hereford and Essex, lord high constable, *k.* 1321, who *m.* November 14, 1302, Princess Elizabeth, widow of Sir John, Earl of Holland, and daughter of EDWARD I., KING OF ENGLAND, and his first wife, Princess Eleanor of Castile, and had:

William de Bohun, K.G., fifth son, created, in 1337, Earl of Northampton, *d.* 1360, who *m.* Lady Elizabeth, daughter of Bartholomew de Badlesmere, executed in 1322, and widow of Edmund de Mortimer, and had:

Lady Elizabeth de Bohun, who *m.* Richard Fitz-Alan, K.G., tenth Earl of Arundel, beheaded in 1398. He was the son of Richard, K.G., Earl of Arundel and Surrey, *d.* 1375 (and his second wife, Lady Eleanor Plantagenet), the son of Edmund, K.G., Earl of Arundel, beheaded in 1326, and his wife, Lady Alice, daughter of William de Warren, *d.* 1286, and his wife, Lady Joan, daughter of Robert de Vere, fifth Earl of Oxford, great high chamberlain, *d.* 1296, the son of Hugh de Vere, Earl of Oxford, great high chamberlain, *d.* 1203 (and his wife, Lady Hawise, daughter of **Saber de Quincey**, a Magna Charta Surety, Earl of Winchester, *d.* 1219), the son of **Robert de Vere**, a Magna Charta Surety, Earl of Oxford, *d.* 1221.

Lady Eleanor Plantagenet, aforesaid, was the daughter of Henry, sixth Earl of Lancaster, *d.* 1345 (a grandson of HENRY III., KING OF ENGLAND), and his wife, Lady Maud, daughter of Patrick de Chaworth, by his wife Lady Isabel, daughter of William de Beauchamp, first Earl of Warwick, *d.* 1298, and his wife, Lady Maud, daughter of John Fitz-John, chief justice of Ireland, 1258, son of John Fitz-Geoffrey, chief justice of Ireland, 1246, and his wife, Lady Isabel, daughter of Sir Ralph, third son of **Hugh Bigod**, son of **Roger Bigod**, both Sureties for the Magna Charta and Earls of Norfolk.

Lady Elizabeth de Bohun and Sir Richard, Earl of Arundel, aforesaid, had:

Lady Elizabeth Fitz-Alan, *d.* 1425, who *m.* thirdly, Sir Robert Goushill, of Hault-Hucknall, Derbyshire, an esquire to Thomas Mowbray, Duke of Norfolk, Lady Elizabeth's first husband, and had:

Lady Joan Goushill, who *m.* Thomas, Baron Stanley, K.G., lord chamberlain, *d.* January 12, 1458–9, and had:

Lady Margaret Stanley, who *m.* secondly, Sir William Troutbeck, of Prynes Castle, Cheshire, *k.* at Bloreheath, and had:

Lady Jane Troutbeck, who *m.* secondly, William Griffith, K.B., of Penrhyn Castle, Carnarvonshire, chamberlain of North Wales, and had:

Sir William Griffith, of Penrhyn Castle, chamberlain of North Wales, who *m.* secondly, Jane, daughter of John Puleston, of Carnarvon, and had:

Sibil Griffith, who *m.* Owen ap Hugh, of Bodeon, high sheriff of Anglesea in 1563 and 1580, *d.* 1613, and had:

Jane Owen, who *m.* Hugh Gwyn, of Penrath, high sheriff of Carnarvonshire, in 1600, and had:

Sibil Gwyn, who *m.* John Powel, of Llanwddwn Township, Montgomeryshire, Wales, and had:

Elizabeth Powel, who *m.* Humphrey ap Hugh ap David ap Howel ap Grono ap Einion, of Merionethshire, and had:

Owen ap Humphrey, of Llwyn-du, Llwyngwrill Township, Merionethshire, a justice in 1678, who had by Jane ——:

Rebecca Humphrey, who *m.* 1678, Robert Owen, of Vron Goch, Merionethshire, *b.* 1657, removed to Pennsylvania in 1690, became a justice of the peace for Merion Township, then in Philadelphia County, and a member of the provincial assembly, *d.* 1697, and had:

Owen Owen, of Philadelphia, 1690–1741, aforesaid, grandfather of Colonel Clement Biddle, whose daughter Mary *m.* June 25, 1804, General Thomas Cadwalader, and had:

24. JUDGE JOHN CADWALADER, LL.D., of Philadelphia, *b.* April 1, 1804; *d.* January 26, 1879; member of Congress and judge of United States District Court of Pennsylvania.

He had by his second wife, Henrietta Maria, widow of Bloomfield McIlvaine and daughter of Charles N. Bancker, of Philadelphia:

25. CHARLES EVERT CADWALADER, M.D., of Philadelphia, *b.* November 5, 1839, eldest son by second marriage. Dr. Cadwalader was a member of the First Troop, Philadelphia City Cavalry, when the American Civil War began, and became first lieutenant in the Sixth Pennsylvania Cavalry; was promoted to captaincy, and in 1862 was brevetted major in the United States Volunteers, and for his gallantry in the battle of Gettysburg was promoted to lieutenant-colonel, being in this celebrated battle an aide-de-camp on the staff of General Meade. Dr. Cadwalader *m.*, at St. Paul's Protestant Episcopal Church, Philadelphia, July 15, 1897, Miss Bridget Mary Ryan. He is a member of the Society of Colonial Wars and a founder of the Order of Runnemede.

Arms.—*Gu, a lion rampant, ar., armed and langued, az.*

GEORGE PERKINS LAWTON.

George Perkins Lawton

DESCENT from the Sureties for the observance of the Magna Charta:

William d'Albini,	John de Lacie,
Hugh Bigod,	William de Mowbray,
Roger Bigod,	Saher de Quincey,
Henry de Bohun,	Robert de Ros,
Gilbert de Clare,	Robert de Vere,
Richard de Clare,	Eustace de Vesci.
John Fitz-Robert,	

1. **Henry de Bohun,** one of the Sureties for the Magna Charta, Earl of Hereford, lord high constable of England, *d.* 1220, *m.* Lady Maud, daughter of Geoffrey Fitz-Piers de Mandeville, first Earl of Essex, lord high justice of England, and sister of Geoffrey de Mandeville, one of the Sureties for the Magna Charta, and had by her:

2. HUMPHREY DE BOHUN, Earl of Hereford and Essex. He was a very distinguished person among the rebellious Barons in the time of Henry III., and was taken prisoner at Evesham, fighting under the baronial banner. In 47 Henry III. he and other Barons were excommunicated for plundering churches in time of war, and he was one of the commanders at the battle of Lewes, and served as governor of Goodrich and Winchester Castles. He *d.* 1274, having issue by his first wife, Lady Maud, daughter of Raoul d' Eue:

3. HUMPHREY DE BOHUN, eldest son, who was taken prisoner with his father at Evesham, and *d. v. p.* He com-

manded a party of infantry at the battle of Evesham, and died in Beeston Castle soon after his capture and imprisonment. He *m.* Lady Eleanor, daughter and coheiress of William, sixth Baron de Braose, of Brecknock, and coheiress of her mother, Lady Eve, one of the daughters and coheiresses of William Marshall, Earl of Pembroke, the friend and adviser of King John, and sister of William Marshall, the younger, one of the Sureties for the Magna Charta, and had:

4. HUMPHREY DE BOHUN, who succeeded as Earl of Hereford and Essex, and was lord high constable. He attended Edward I. on his expedition into Scotland, and took a prominent part in the great battle near Roxborough. He *m.* Lady Maud, daughter of Ingelram de Fienes, or of William, Baron de Fienes, and, dying in 1297–8, had:

5. HUMPHREY DE BOHUN, Earl of Hereford and Essex, lord high constable. He was taken prisoner in the Scottish wars and was exchanged for the wife of Robert Bruce, then a captive-hostage in England. Subsequently he joined the banner of the insurrectionary Barons, under the Earl of Lancaster, and was killed in the battle of Boroughbridge, March 16, 1321–2. He *m.* November 14, 1302, Princess Elizabeth Plantagenet, *b.* 1282, *d.* 1316, widow of Sir John, Earl of Holland, and daughter of EDWARD I., KING OF ENGLAND (by his first wife, Lady Eleanor, daughter of FERDINAND III., KING OF CASTILE AND LEON), the son of KING HENRY III., and grandson of KING JOHN, OF ENGLAND, and had:

6. LADY ALIANORE DE BOHUN, sister of three Earls of Hereford and of William, Earl of Northampton. She *m.* first, 1327, James Butler, second Earl of Carrick, created, in 1328, Earl of Ormond, seventh Lord Butler, of Ireland. He was the son of Sir Edmund Butler, Earl of Carrick (and his wife, *m.* 1302, Lady Joan, daughter of John Fitz-Gerald,

first Earl of Kildare, crowned "King of Ireland"), son of Theobald, the fourth Lord Butler, of Ireland, *d.* 1285, by his wife, Lady Joan de Baronis, daughter of John Fitz-Piers Fitz-Geoffrey, lord of Berkhampstead and Kirtling, sheriff of Yorkshire, 1234, lord justice of Ireland, 1246 (son of Geoffrey de Mandeville, first Earl of Essex, justiciary of England, *d.* 1212), by his wife, Lady Isabel, widow of Gilbert de Lacie, lord of Meath, in Ireland, and daughter of Sir Ralph Bigod, Knight, third son of **Hugh Bigod**, one of the Sureties for the Magna Charta, Earl of Norfolk, *d.* 1225 (by his wife, Lady Maud Marshall, sister of William Marshall, Jr., one of the Sureties for the Magna Charta, and daughter of William, Earl of Pembroke), eldest son of **Roger Bigod**, one of the Sureties for the Magna Charta, Earl of Norfolk, and lord high steward of England, *d.* 1220.

Lady Alianore and James, Earl of Carrick, had :

7. LADY PETRONELLA BUTLER, who *m*., as his first wife, Gilbert, third Baron Talbot, of Goodrich Castle, *b.* 1332, *d.* 1387, who served under the Black Prince in the French wars, son of Richard de Talbot, of Goodrich Castle, in Hereford, a banneret, who headed an invasion of Scotland, on his own account, to recover certain lands, which he claimed in right of his wife, Elizabeth Comyn, and defeated the Scotch at Gleddesmore, but was subsequently taken prisoner and ransomed, and had :

8. SIR RICHARD TALBOT, eldest son, Baron Talbot, of Goodrich and of Blackmere. He was in the wars in Scotland and attained the rank of banneret, and, dying in 1396, had issue by his wife, Lady Ankaret, daughter of John, fourth Baron le Strange, of Blackmere, *d.* 1361, who served in the Scottish wars and attained the rank of banneret, and his wife, Lady Mary, daughter of Richard Fitz-Alan, K.G., Earl of Arundel and Surrey, *d.* 1375, and his second wife, Lady Eleanor Plantagenet, widow of John de Beaumont, *d.*

1342, and daughter of Henry, Earl of Lancaster (by his wife, Lady Maud de Chaworth*), son of Edmund, Earl of Leicester, lord high steward, *d.* 1295 (by his second wife, Lady Blanche, widow of Henry I, King of Navarre, and daughter of Robert, Earl of Artois, son of LOUIS VIII., KING OF FRANCE, by his wife, Princess Blanche, daughter of ALPHONSO VIII., KING OF CASTILE, and his wife, Princess Eleanor Plantagenet, sister of King John, and daughter of HENRY II., KING OF ENGLAND), brother of Edward I., and son of HENRY III., KING OF ENGLAND.

Robert de Vere, a Surety for the Magna Charta, third Earl of Oxford, had by his wife, Lady Isabel de Bolebec: Hugh, fourth Earl, great high chamberlain, *d.* 1263, who had by his wife, Lady Hawise, daughter of **Saher de Quincey,** a Magna Charta Surety: Robert, fifth Earl, *d.* 1296, who *m.* Lady Alice, daughter of Gilbert, Baron de Saundford, and had: Lady Joan, *m.* William de Warren, *d. v. p.* 1286, eldest son of John, seventh Earl of Surrey, and had: Lady Alice, *m.* 1305, Edmund Fitz-Alan, K.B., Earl of Arundel, beheaded in 1326, and had: Sir Richard Fitz-Alan, Earl of Arundel and Surrey, aforesaid.

Sir Richard, Baron Talbot, and Lady Ankaret had:

9. GENERAL JOHN DE TALBOT, K.G., sixth Baron, lord of Furnival, second son, first Earl of Shrewsbury and Earl of Waterford and Wexford, in Ireland. He was one of the most illustrious characters in the whole range of English history. In 1412 he was appointed chief justice of Ireland, and afterwards constituted lord lieutenant. He subse-

---

* Lady Maud, *b.* 1280, was the daughter of Patrick de Chaworth, 1253–1282, by his wife, Lady Isabel, daughter of William de Beauchamp, created Earl of Warwick, *d.* 1298, and his wife, Lady Maud, daughter of John Fitz-John, justiciary of Ireland, 1258, son of John Fitz-Geoffrey, justiciary of Ireland, 1246, and his wife, Lady Isabel Bigod, aforesaid, a descendant of **Roger Bigod** and **Hugh Bigod,** both Sureties for the Magna Charta.

THE PEDIGREE OF GEO

			Roger Bigod.	
			Hugh Bigod.	
Henry de Bohun.	Robert de Vere.		Ralph Bigod.	
Humphrey de Bohun.	Hugh de Vere.		Isabel Bigod.	
Humphrey de Bohun.	Robert de Vere.	William de Mowbray.	John Fitz-John.	John Fi
Humphrey de Bohun.	Joan de Vere.	Roger de Mowbray.	Maud Fitz-John.	Roger Fi
Humphrey de Bohun.	Alice de Warren.	Roger de Mowbray.	Isabel de Beauchamp.	Robert Fi
Alianore de Bohun.	Richard Fitz-Alan.	John de Mowbray.	Maud de Chaworth.	Eupheme
Petronella Butler.	Mary Fitz-Alan.	John de Mowbray—Joan Plantagenet.		Ralph de
Richard de Talbot—Ankaret le Strange.		John de Mowbray.		John de I
	John de Talbot.	Jane de Mowbray—Thomas de Grey.		R
	Thomas de Talbot.		Thomas de Grey—Alice de I
	Elizabeth de Talbot—Henry de Grey.			Eli
			Margaret de Grey—
			Philip d'Arcy—
			Margaret d'Arcy—
			Richard Conyers, of Horden, Durham,—
			Robert Conyers, of Horden,—
			Christopher Conyers, of Horden,—
			Richard Conyers, of Horden,—
			Christopher Conyers, of Horden,—
			Mary Conyers—
			Lawrence Wilkinson, of Providence, R. I.; d. 1692,—
			Samuel Wilkinson, of Providence,—
			Joseph Wilkinson, of Scituate,—
			Joseph Wilkinson, of Scituate,—
			Joseph Wilkinson, of Scituate,—
			Almadus Wilkinson, of Scituate,—
			Mary Ann Wilkinson—
			George Perkins Lawton, of

GE PERKINS LAWTON

				Saher de Quincey.	Eustace de Vesci.
	Richard de Clare.			Robert de Quincey.	William de Vesci.
Robert.	Gilbert de Clare.		John de Lacie—Margaret de Quincey.	William de Vesci.
ohn,		Richard de Clare—Maud de Lacie.		Isabel de Vesci.
Roger.	Gilbert de Clare.	William d'Albini.	Robert de Ros.	Adam de Welles.
z-Roger.	Margaret de Clare.	William d'Albini.	William de Ros.	Adam de Welles.
vill.	Margaret d'Audley.	Isabel d'Albini—Robert de Ros.	John de Welles.
ill.	Hugh de Stafford.		William de Ros.	John de Welles.
h de Nevill—Margaret de Stafford.			Alice de Ros.	Margery de Welles.
ill.			Elizabeth de Meinill.	Henry le Scrope.
th de Grey—Philip d'Arcy.				Joan le Scrope.
n d'Arcy.				Henry Fitz-Hugh.

anor Fitz-Hugh.
John Conyers, of Hornby, Yorkshire.
zabeth Claxton.
argaret Bamforth.
zabeth Jackson.
bel Lumley.
ne Hedsworth.
illiam Wilkinson, of Lanchester, Durham.
annah Smith.
.n Wickenden.
rtha Pray.
ce Jenckes.
zabeth (Brownell) Peckham.
argaret Magee.
thony Lawton, of Newport, R. I.
ratoga Springs, N. Y.

quently distinguished himself in the wars of Henry V., but his splendid reputation as a soldier was acquired under the regent, John, Duke of Bedford, *temp*. Henry VI., but finally, after achieving many victories over the French, his army suffered a disastrous defeat at the hands of the Maid of Orleans, near Patay, in 1429, when he became a prisoner to this enthusiastic amazon and was detained in captivity four years. Again taking the field, he once more became renowned for his triumphs, and was created, in 1442, Earl of Shrewsbury, was again lord lieutenant of Ireland, and made a peer of that kingdom in 1446, receiving many valuable grants. Although now far advanced in life, he was the second time placed in command of the army in France, gaining fresh laurels, and was appointed lieutenant of Aquitaine, which he attempted to subdue, but was defeated and slain by a cannon-ball, in his eightieth year, July 20, 1453. His body was brought to England and interred at Whitechurch, in Salop County.

The Earl of Shrewsbury *m*. first, in 1408, Lady Maud de Nevill, heiress of Furnival,* and had by her:

10. THOMAS DE TALBOT, Lord Talbot, eldest son, who was with his father in the wars in France, where he was slain, *v. p.*, in 1453, having had issue by his wife, whose name has not been preserved:

11. LADY ELIZABETH DE TALBOT, who *m*. Sir Henry, fifth

---

* She was the daughter of Thomas, Baron de Nevill, of Halumshire (brother of Ralph, first Earl of Westmoreland), and lord of Furnival, in right of his wife Joan, daughter of William, fourth Baron de Furnival, *d.* 1383, second son of Thomas de Furnival, Jr., a feudal Baron (by his wife Joan, daughter and coheiress of Theobald de Verdon and widow of William de Montacute, Jr.), *d.* 1339, whose father, Thomas de Furnival, a prominent Baron and military commander in the time of King Edward I., was the eldest son of Gerard de Furnival, *d. ante* 1280, whose wife was Lady Maud, daughter of John Fitz-John, chief justice of Ireland, 1258, aforesaid, a descendant of Roger Bigod and Hugh Bigod, both Sureties for the Magna Charta.

Baron de Grey, of Wilton, *d.* 1394-5, son of Reginald, fourth Baron, son of Henry, third Baron, *d.* 1342, son of John, second Baron de Grey, of Ruthyn, *d.* 1323, by his first wife, Lady Anne, daughter of William de Ferrers, lord of Groby, *d.* 1287 (by his wife, Lady Joan Despencer, sister of Hugh, Earl of Winchester, executed in 1326), second son of William, seventh Earl of Derby, *d.* 1254, by his second wife, Lady Margaret de Quincey, daughter of Roger, second Earl of Winchester, constable of Scotland, *d.* 1264 (by his wife, Lady Helen, daughter of Alan Macdonald, lord of Galloway), the second son of **Saber de Quincey**, Earl of Winchester, one of the Sureties for the Magna Charta.

Henry de Grey and the Lady Elizabeth had:

12. LADY MARGARET DE GREY, who *m.* first, John, fifth Baron d'Arcy, *b.* 1377, *d.* 1411, son of Sir Philip, fourth Baron d'Arcy, admiral of the royal navy, 1356, *d.* 1398, by his wife, Lady Elizabeth, daughter of Sir Thomas de Grey, of Heton, beheaded, August 5, 1415, for political reasons, and his wife, Lady Alice de Nevill.

Admiral Sir Philip d'Arcy was the second son of Sir John, second Baron d'Arcy, 1317-1356, constable of the Tower of London, and his wife, Lady Elizabeth, daughter of Nicholas, Baron de Meinill, of Wherlton, York, *d. s. p. m.* 1342, and his wife, Lady Alice, daughter of William, seventh Baron Ros, of Hamlake, *d.* 1317, son of Robert, sixth Baron Ros, of Hamlake, *d.* 1285 (and his wife, *m.* 1244, Lady Isabel, daughter of William, fourth Baron d'Albini, *d. s. p. m.* 1285, son of **William d'Albini**, one of the Sureties for the Magna Charta), son of William, fifth Baron Ros, of Hamlake, *d.* 1258, the son of **Robert de Ros**, one of the Sureties for the Magna Charta.

Sir Thomas de Grey, aforesaid, was the second son of Sir Thomas de Grey, of Berwyke, constable of Norham Castle, 1390, by his wife, Lady Jane, daughter of John, fourth Baron

MEMBERS OF THE ORDER OF RUNNEMEDE   387

de Mowbray, of Axholme, *k.* 1368, by his wife, *m.* 1353, Lady Elizabeth, only child of John, third Baron de Segrave, *d. s. p. m.* 1353, and his wife Margaret, Duchess of Norfolk, *d.* 1399, daughter of Thomas Plantagenet, Earl of Norfolk and marshal of England, a son of EDWARD I., KING OF ENGLAND, and his second wife, the Princess Margaret, daughter of PHILIP III., THE HARDY, KING OF FRANCE, and his first wife, the Princess Isabella, daughter of JAMES I., KING OF ARRAGON.

John, fourth Baron de Mowbray, aforesaid, who was killed by Turks in June, 1368, was the son of John, third Baron, of Axholme, *d.* October 4, 1361 (by his wife, Lady Joan Plantagenet*), eldest son of John, second Baron, *d.* 1321 (and his wife, Lady Aliva, daughter of William, Baron Braose, of Gower, *d. s. p. m.* 1322), son of Roger, Baron de Mowbray, Lord of the Isle of Axholme, first Baron by writ, *d.* 1298 (and his wife, Lady Rose de Clare, "a granddaughter of the Earl of Clare"), whose father, Roger, *d.* 1266, was the second son of **William de Mowbray**, one of the Sureties for the Magna Charta.

Lady Alice de Nevill, aforesaid, was the daughter of Ralph, Baron de Nevill, K.G., of Raby, created, in 1399, Earl of Westmoreland and earl marshal for life, *d.* 1425, by his first wife, Lady Margaret, daughter of Hugh de Stafford, K.G., second Earl of Stafford, *d.* 1386 (and his wife, Lady Philippa de Beauchamp†), son of Ralph, K.G., created, in 1351, Earl

---

* She was the sister of Henry of Gresmont, Duke of Lancaster, and daughter of Henry, Earl of Lancaster (son of Edmund, Earl of Lancaster, a son of HENRY III., KING OF ENGLAND), by his wife, Lady Maud de Chaworth, aforesaid, a descendant of **Roger Bigod** and **Hugh Bigod**, Sureties for the Magna Charta.

† She was the daughter of Thomas de Beauchamp, third Earl of Warwick, one of the original members of the Order of Knights of the Garter, *d.* 1369 (and his wife, Lady Catherine de Mortimer, daughter of Roger, first Earl of March, executed in 1330), son of Guy, second Earl of Warwick, *d.* 1315,

of Stafford, one of the original members of the Order of Knights of the Garter, *d.* 1372, and his wife, Lady Margaret, daughter of Hugh d'Audley, created, in 1337, Earl of Gloucester, *d.* 1347-9, and his wife, Lady Margaret, widow of Piers de Gaveston, Earl of Cornwall, beheaded in 1310, and daughter of Gilbert de Clare, Earl of Hertford and Gloucester, *d.* 1295, by his second wife, the Princess Joan d'Acre, *d.* 1305, a daughter of EDWARD I., KING OF ENGLAND, and his first wife, Princess Eleanor, daughter of FERDINAND III., KING OF CASTILE AND LEON.

John Fitz-Robert, a Magna Charta Surety, lord of Clavering, had by his wife, Lady Ada de Baliol: Roger Fitz-John, lord of Warkworth and Clavering, *d.* 1249, father of Robert Fitz-Roger, lord of Clavering, first Baron by writ, *d.* 1311, who *m.* Lady Margaret de la Zouche, and had: Lady Eupheme (or Anastasia), heir to her brother, John Fitz-Robert de Clavering, who *m.* Ralph de Nevill, first Baron by writ, *d.* 1331, and had: Ralph, second son and second Baron Nevill, of Raby, *d.* 1367, who *m.* Lady Alice, daughter of Sir Hugh d'Audley, governor of Montgomery Castle in 1310, sister of Hugh, Earl of Gloucester, and widow of Ralph, Baron de Greystock, and had: John de Nevill, K.G., third Baron, *d.* October 17, 1389, who had by his first wife, Lady Maud, daughter of Henry, Baron Percy, of Alnwick: Ralph Nevill, K.G., first Earl of Westmoreland, aforesaid.

Gilbert, Earl of Hertford and Gloucester, aforesaid, was the eldest son of Richard, Earl of Hertford and Gloucester, *d.* 1262 (and his wife, Lady Maud, daughter of **John de Lacie,** Earl of Lincoln, one of the Sureties for the Magna Charta, and his second wife, Lady Margaret, daughter of

---

eldest son of William de Beauchamp, created Earl of Warwick, *d.* 1298, and his wife, Lady Maud Fitz-John, aforesaid, a descendant of **Roger Bigod** and **Hugh Bigod,** Sureties for the Magna Charta.

Robert, eldest son of **Saber de Quincey,** Earl of Winchester, one of the Sureties for the Magna Charta), eldest son of **Gilbert de Clare,** Earl of Hertford and Gloucester (and his wife, Lady Isabel Marshall, daughter of William, Earl of Pembroke, King John's chief councillor, and sister of William Marshall, Jr., one of the Sureties for the Magna Charta), the son of **Richard de Clare,** Earl of Hertford, one of the Sureties for the Magna Charta.

Lady Margaret de Grey had by John d'Arcy:

13. PHILIP D'ARCY, sixth Baron, who *d.* in 1418, before he had attained his majority, when the barony of d'Arcy fell into abeyance between his two daughters. He *m.* Lady Eleanor, daughter of Henry, third Baron Fitz-Hugh, K.G., *d.* 1424, a crusader, who attained great eminence in the reigns of Henry IV. and V., and was appointed constable of England, and was afterwards lord chamberlain to Henry V., and assisted at the council of Constance.

Eustace de Vesci, a Surety for the Magna Charta, had: William de Vesci, *d.* 1253, who had by his second wife, Lady Agnes, daughter of William de Ferrers, Earl of Derby: William de Vesci, second son, *d.* 1297, who *m.* Lady Isabel, widow of Robert de Welles and daughter of Adam de Periton, and had: Lady Isabel de Vesci, who *m.* William de Welles, of Alford and Gremesby, Lincolnshire, *temp.* 11 Edward I., and had: Adam, *d.* 1311, who had: Adam, second son, *d.* 1345, who had: John, *d.* 1361, who had: John, *d.* 1421, who had: Lady Margery, widow of John, son of Sir William de Huntingfield, who *m.* Sir Stephen le Scrope, second Baron, *d.* 1406, and had: Henry, third Baron, of Masham, beheaded in 1415, father of Lady Joan, who *m.* Henry Fitz-Hugh, second Baron, *d.* 1386, and had: Sir Henry Fitz-Hugh, K.G., third Baron, whose daughter, Lady Eleanor, *m.* Philip, Baron d'Arcy, aforesaid, and had:

14. LADY MARGARET D'ARCY, second daughter and co-

heiress, who *m.* Sir John Conyers, of Hornby Castle, Yorkshire, and had:

15. RICHARD CONYERS, lord of Horden Manor, in County Durham, in right of his wife (younger brother of Sir John Conyers, K.G.), who *m.* Elizabeth, daughter and heiress of Sir Richard Claxton, of Horden, and had:

16. ROBERT CONYERS, of Horden Manor, who *m.* Margaret Bamforth, of Seham, in County Durham, and had:

17. CHRISTOPHER CONYERS, of Horden Manor, who *m.* Elizabeth, daughter of John Jackson, of Bedale, and had:

18. RICHARD CONYERS, of Horden Manor, who *m.* Isabel, daughter of Robert Lumley, of Ludworth, and had:

19. CHRISTOPHER CONYERS, of Horden Manor, who *m.* secondly, 1586, Anne, daughter of Sir John Hedsworth, of Harraton, County Durham, and had by her:

20. MARY CONYERS, who *m.* William Wilkinson, of Lanchester, County Durham, son of Lawrence Wilkinson, of Harpley House, County Durham, and had:

21. "LAWRENCE WILKINSON, of Lanchester, officer in arms, went to New England," see Sequestrations in County Durham, 1645-7.* He was a lieutenant in the army of King

---

* Authorities consulted in deducing this pedigree: The Visitation of Yorkshire, Harleian Societies' Publications, vol. xvi. pp. 73, 90, 91, 92, 306, and 307; the Visitations of Worcestershire, Harleian Soc. Pub., xxvii. p. 133; Flower's Visitation of Durham (Mary Conyers' descent); O'Hart's "Irish Pedigrees," pp. 318, etc., and 325, etc.; Catton's "English Peerage," vol. i. pp. 120-122, vol. ii. pp. 25 and 86, and vol. ii. Appendix, "Extinct Peerages," p. 126; Foster's "Noble and Gentle Families of Royal Descent," p. 443; Burke's "Royal Families of England" (1851), vol. ii. ped. xxvi.; Browning's "Americans of Royal Descent," 4th ed., pp. 159, 854-5, 598-9, and "Bulletin," p. xxvi.; Burke's "Extinct and Dormant Baronetcies," 2d ed., p. 128; American Heraldic Journal, vol. i. p. 85; Somerby's "Family of Wilkinson;" Wilkinson's "Memoirs of the Wilkinson Family;" Austin's "Genealogical Dictionary of Rhode Island," pp. 112, 424-5; Chad Brown Memorial, pp. 14, 27; Savage's "Genealogical Dictionary of New England," vol. ii. p. 99; Arnold's "Vital Records of Rhode Island," vols. ii.-iii. p. 278; Births and Deaths

Charles I., and was taken prisoner at the surrender of Newcastle, October 22, 1644; his estates having been sequestered and sold by the Long Parliament, he came with his wife and a son to the Providence Plantations, Rhode Island, in 1645, and settled there January 19, 1646. He was deputy to the Assembly of Rhode Island 1667–1673, and, dying August 9, 1692, had issue by his wife Susannah, *d.* about 1692, daughter of Christopher Smith:

22. CAPTAIN SAMUEL WILKINSON, of Providence, Rhode Island, eldest child, a Quaker, deputy to the Assembly, 1693–1723, *d.* August 27, 1727, having issue by his wife Plain, daughter of Rev. William Wickenden, of Providence:

23. JOSEPH WILKINSON, of Scituate, Rhode Island, *b.* January 22, 1682–3, deputy to the Assembly, 1731, *d.* April 24, 1740, having issue by his wife Martha, *b.* 1689, *d.* 1786, daughter of John and Sarah (Brown) Pray, of Smithfield, Rhode Island:

24. JOSEPH WILKINSON, the younger, of Scituate, Rhode Island, eighth child, *b.* 1721, *d.* September 28, 1755. He *m.* December 6, 1741, Alice, daughter of Obadiah Jenckes, of Gloucester, Rhode Island, and had:

25. JOSEPH WILKINSON, 3D, of Scituate, Rhode Island, *b.* March 11, 1750, *d.* July 5, 1814. He served in the Continental army, and had issue by his wife Elizabeth, *b.* July 27, 1749, *d.* October 30, 1841, widow of Peleg Peckham and daughter of Jonathan Brownell, of Westport, Massachusetts:

---

in Providence, p. 257, vols. ii.–iii. p. 51; Births and Deaths in Scituate, vols. ii.–iii. p. 41; Marriages in Gloucester, vols. ii.–iii., p. 65; Marriages in Providence, vols. ii.–iii. p. 34; Marriages in Scituate; Petition of Elizabeth Wilkinson for Pension, dated July 24, 1838, O. W. & N. Division, Revolutionary Bureau of Pensions, U.S.A.; Records of Births and Marriages in Dartmouth, Mass.; Will of Mary A. Lawton, Bk. Wills, No. 112, p. 252; Will of Anthony Lawton, Bk. Wills, No. 151, p. 35, Surrogate's office, Troy, N. Y.; Omerod's " History of Cheshire," vol. iii. p. 16; the Visitations of Cheshire, Harl. Soc. Pub., etc.

26. ALMADUS WILKINSON, of Scituate, Rhode Island, *b.* August 20, 1787, *d.* October 25, 1837. He *m.* Margaret, *b.* February 12, 1789, *d.* June 13, 1885, daughter of George Magee, of Foster, Rhode Island, and had:

27. MARY ANN WILKINSON, *b.* February 14, 1812, *d.* January 5, 1885, who *m.* August 31, 1846, Anthony Lawton, of Newport and Johnston, Rhode Island, and of Troy, New York, *b.* March 4, 1816, *d.* August 13, 1893, and had:

28. GEORGE PERKINS LAWTON, of Saratoga Springs, New York, *b.* August 19, 1847, a member of the Society of Colonial Wars, one of the founders of the Order of Runnemede, who *m.* November 5, 1885, Jeannie Monteath Wilson, daughter of Daniel Lathrop, of Albany, New York, and had: Daniel Lathrop Lawton, *b.* December 28, 1886.

> Arms.—*Ar., on a fesse between three cross-crosslets fitché, sa., a cinque-foil of the first, pierced of the second.*
>
> Crest.—*A demi-wolf salient regardant, ar., vulned in the back, gu., and licking the wound.*

George S. Marsh

DESCENT from the Sureties for the observance of the Magna Charta:

Hugh Bigod,   Roger Bigod.

1. **Roger Bigod,** one of the Sureties for the Magna Charta, Earl of Norfolk, lord high steward of England, *d.* 1220, *m.* first, before 1195, Lady Isabel de Warren, daughter of Hameline Plantagenet, fifth Earl of Warren and Surrey, *jure uxoris*, who bore one of the three swords at the second coronation of Richard I., and was with that king in the army in Normandy, and *d.* 1202, and his wife Isabella, Countess of Surrey, widow of William de Blois, and only daughter and heiress of William, third Earl of Warren and Surrey, who zealously espoused the cause of King Stephen and had a chief command in his army, son of William, second Earl of Warren and Surrey, and his wife, Lady Isabel, daughter of Hugh the Great, Count of Vermandois, son of HENRY I., KING OF FRANCE, and his wife, Anne of Russia.

Roger Bigod had by his first wife, Lady Isabel:

2. **Hugh Bigod,** eldest son, also one of the Sureties for the Magna Charta, second Earl of Norfolk, *d.* 1225. He *m.*, as her first husband, Lady Maud (or Matilda) Marshall, a sister of William Marshall, one of the Sureties for the Magna Charta, and daughter of William Marshall, created Earl of Pembroke, Protector of England during the minority of Henry III., and his first wife, Lady Isabel de Clare, daughter of Richard the Strongbow, second Earl of Pembroke, lord justice of Ireland, by his wife, Princess Eva, daughter of DERMOT MACMURCHA, KING OF LEINSTER.

Hugh Bigod and Lady Maud had:

3. SIR RALPH BIGOD, third son (brother of Roger, the last Earl of Norfolk), who *m.* Lady Berta, daughter of the Baron Furnival, and had:

4. LADY ISABEL BIGOD, widow of Gilbert de Lacy, lord of Meath, Ireland, who *m.* secondly, John Fitz-Piers Fitz-Geoffrey, lord of Berkhampstead and Kirkling, sheriff of Yorkshire, 1234, chief justice of Ireland, 30 Henry III., half-brother of Geoffrey de Mandeville, a Surety for the Magna Charta, and son of Geoffrey Fitz-Piers, Baron de Mandeville, created, in 1199, Earl of Essex, justiciary of England, *d.* 1212, and his second wife, Lady Aveline, and had:

5. JOHN FITZ-JOHN, chief justice of Ireland, 42 Henry III., and *d.* 1258, leaving issue by his wife, whose name has not been preserved:

6. LADY MAUD FITZ-JOHN, widow of Gerard de Furnival, *d. ante* 1280, who *m.* secondly, William, sixth Baron de Beauchamp, of Elmley Castle, Earl of Warwick, in right of his mother, Lady Isabel, daughter of William, fourth Baron Mauduit, of Hanslape, County Bucks, heritable chamberlain of the exchequer, *d.* 1256, and sister and heiress of William Mauduit, seventh Earl of Warwick. William de Beauchamp was a distinguished captain in Welsh and Scottish wars of Edward I., and *d.* 1298. The mother of Lady Isabel Mauduit was Lady Alice, daughter of Waleran de Newburgh, fourth Earl of Warwick, *d.* 1205 (by his second wife, Lady Alice de Harcourt), son of Roger, second Earl of Warwick, *d.* 1153, by his wife, Lady Gundred de Warren, daughter of the aforesaid William, second Earl of Warren and Surrey, and his wife, Lady Isabel de Vermandois, widow of Robert, Earl of Mellent, and a descendant of HUGH CAPET, KING OF FRANCE.

William de Beauchamp and Lady Maud had:

7. LADY SARAH DE BEAUCHAMP, sister of Guy, Earl of Warwick, who *m.* Richard, sixth Baron Talbot, of Goodrich

Castle, who served in the wars in Wales and in Gascony, and was constituted governor of Cardiff Castle, 25 Edward I. He was a member of the great council held at Lincoln, 29 Edward I., which asserted the right of Edward to the realm of Scotland. His mother was Princess Gwenllian, daughter and heiress of RHESE AP GRIFFITH, PRINCE OF SOUTH WALES, *d.* 1136. Richard, Baron de Talbot, *d.* 1306, and Lady Sarah had:

8. LADY GWENLLIAN TALBOT, sister of Sir Gilbert, seventh Baron Talbot, lord justice of South Wales, who *m.* Sir Payne de Turberville, custos of Glamorganshire, 134-, and had:

9. SARAH DE TURBERVILLE, fourth daughter, and coheiress of her brother, who *m.* William de Gamage, high sheriff of Gloucestershire, 1325, and had:

10. GILBERT DE GAMAGE, lord of Rogiad, who *m.* Lettice, daughter of Sir William Seymour, of Penhow, and had:

11. SIR WILLIAM GAMAGE, lord of Rogiad and Coyty, who *m.* Mary, daughter of Thomas de Rodburg, Knight, and had:

12. SIR THOMAS GAMAGE, lord of Rogiad and Coyty, who *m.* Matilda, daughter of John Dennis, Knight, and had:

13. JANE GAMAGE, who *m.* Roger Arnold, of Llanthony, Monmouthshire, Wales, son of Arnold ap Arnholt Vychan and his wife Sybil, daughter of Madoc ap Einion ap Thomas (*N. E. His. Gen. Reg.*, October, 1879), and had:

14. THOMAS ARNOLD, of Llanthony, who *m.* Agnes, daughter of Richard Warnstead, Knight, and had:

15. RICHARD ARNOLD, of Street parish, Somersetshire, who *m.* Emmote, daughter of Pearce Young, of Damerham, Wilts, and had:

16. RICHARD ARNOLD, of Bagbree, Dorsetshire, *d.* 1595, who had by his wife, name unknown:

17. THOMAS ARNOLD, of Melcomb-Horsey, Cheselbourne, Dorsetshire, who had by his first wife, Alice, daughter of John Gully, of Northover, Tolpuddle parish, Dorsetshire:

18. WILLIAM ARNOLD, *b.* June 24, 1587, who brought his family to New England, May 1, 1635, and settled at Pawtuxet, Rhode Island, in 1638. He was one of the thirteen original proprietors of Providence Plantations, and signed an agreement for a form of civil government, January 27, 1640, was the delegate for Providence to the court of commissioners, 1661, and *d.* 1676, having issue by his wife Christian, *b.* 1583, daughter of Thomas Peake:

19. ELIZABETH ARNOLD, *b.* November 23, 1611, *d.* 1683, who *m.* William Carpenter, of Pawtuxet, *b.* Amesbury, Wiltshire, *d.* September 7, 1685, son of Richard and Christiana Carpenter, was one of the signers to compact for good civil government in the Rhode Island Colony, July 27, 1640; commissioner, 1658-63; deputy, 1664-79; assistant, 1665-72; will proved October 1, 1685, and had:

20. PRISCILLA CARPENTER, sixth child, named in her father's will; *b.* about 1648; *d.* after November 15, 1690. She *m.* May 31, 1670, her cousin, William Vincent (his first wife), *b.* at Amesbury, England, about 1644, *d.* Providence, Rhode Island, will proved March 3, 1695-6, a son of Rev. John Vincent and Fridgswith Carpenter, sister of the aforesaid William Carpenter,[*] and had:

21. NICHOLAS VINCENT, second son by first wife, *d.* at Westerly, Rhode Island, 1749. He *m.* before September 6, 1724, Elizabeth ———, who *d.* 1791, and had:

22. JOSEPH VINCENT, *b.* Westerly, 1737; *d.* February 2, 1823, in Vermont. He *m.* June 15, 1770, Anna Dunbar, of Stonington, Connecticut, and had:

23. TEMPERANCE VINCENT, *b.* Stonington, January 7, 1777, *m.* in May, 1805, Riverius Burt, *b.* Westmoreland, New Hampshire, October 13, 1779, *d.* in Kirby, Vermont, November 19, 1813, and had:

24. LUCY JOSEPHINE BURT, *b.* Kirby, Vermont, September

---

[*] See Austin's "Genealogical Dictionary of Rhode Island."

25, 1812, *d.* Natick, Massachusetts, May 23, 1887, who *m.*, in 1830, George Damon, *b.* Kirby, December 13, 1807, *d.* Barnet, Vermont, October 20, 1862, grandson of Joseph Damon and great-grandson of David Damon, and grandson of Pardon Sheldon, all three Revolutionary War soldiers, and had:

25. CAROLINE RHOBE DAMON, *b.* Barnston, Province of Quebec, February 8, 1833, *d.* Minneapolis, Minnesota, April 21, 1874, *m.* December 19, 1854, Charles A. J. Marsh, *b.* Craftsbury, Vermont, March 13, 1830, son of Charles Marsh (sixth in descent from John Marsh, first of the name in America, who came to Salem, Massachusetts, in ship *Mary and John*, 1633, *d.* 1674, and *m.* Susanna, daughter of Rev. Samuel Skelton, first pastor of the Puritans in America, who was, in 1629, appointed in London a member of the King's Council for the Massachusetts Bay Company) and his wife, Martha Wade, daughter of Amos Smith, Jr., of Greensboro, Vermont (son of Amos Smith, Sr., a Revolutionary War soldier), and his wife Sally, daughter of Benjamin St. Clair, of Meredith, Vermont, son of Thomas St. Clair, both Revolutionary War soldiers, son of Joseph, son of James St. Clair, a soldier in King Philip's war, son of John St. Clair, who came to New England in 1656. Charles A. J. and Caroline Rhobe Marsh had:

26. GEORGE SAMUEL MARSH, of Chicago, *b.* Craftsbury, Vermont, October 13, 1855, a founder of the Order of Runnemede. He *m.* at Evanston, Illinois, July 14, 1880, Emma, *b.* at Steubenville, Ohio, May 17, 1850, great-granddaughter of Benjamin Power, a Revolutionary soldier from Virginia, and daughter of Benjamin Power and Maria J. (Benson) Drennen, and had: Alice Damon, *b.* Minneapolis, April 25, 1881; Charles Drennen, *b.* Milwaukee, October 13, 1883; Everett Thomas, *b.* St. Paul, April 5, 1885; Robert Bridgman, *b.* St. Paul, December 25, 1886.

THE PEDIGREE OF CHARLES WILLIAM DARLING.

	Saher de Quincey.	Roger Bigod.				Robert de Vere.	Henry de Bohun.
	Robert de Quincey.	Hugh Bigod.				Hugh de Vere.	Humphrey de Bohun.
Richard de Clare.	Margaret de Quincey.	Ralph Bigod.	John Fitz-Robert.			Robert de Vere.	Humphrey de Bohun.
Gilbert de Clare.	John de Lacie.	Isabel Bigod.	Roger Fitz-John.	Geoffrey de Say.		Joan de Vere.	Humphrey de Bohun.
Richard de Clare.	Maud de Lacie.	John Fitz-John.	Robert Fitz-Roger.	William de Say.		Alice de Warren.	William de Bohun.
Gilbert de Clare.		Maud Fitz-John.	John de Clavering.	William de Say.		Richard Fitz-Alan.	Humphrey de Bohun.
Margaret de Clare.		Guy de Beauchamp.	Eve de Clavering.	Geoffrey de Say.		Alice Fitz-Alan.	Allanore de Bohun.
Margaret d'Audley.		Thomas de Beauchamp.	Edmund d'Ufford.	Geoffrey de Say.		Eleanor de Holland.	Anne Plantagenet.
Hugh de Stafford=Philippa Beauchamp.			Robert d'Ufford.	Joan de Say.		Alice de Montacute.	John Bourchier.
Margaret de Stafford.				William Fienes.		Alice de Nevill.	Humphrey Bourchier.
Philippa de Nevill.	William Bowet=Amy d'Ufford.			Roger Fienes.			
Thomas de Dacre=Elizabeth Bowet.							

Joan de Dacre=Richard Fienes.
John Fienes=Alice Fitz-Hugh.
Thomas Fienes=Anne Bourchier.

Catherine Fienes=Richard Loudenoys, of Briade, Sussex.
Mary Loudenoys=Thomas Harlakenden, of Worthorn, Kent.
Roger Harlakenden, of Kenardiston, Kent,=Elizabeth Hardres.
Richard Harlakenden, of Kenardiston, Kent,=Mary Hubbart.
Mabel Harlakenden=John Haynes, Governor of Massachusetts and Connecticut.
Rev. Joseph Haynes, of Hartford, Conn.,=Sarah Lord.
Sarah Haynes=Rev. James Pierpont, of New Haven, Conn.
Abigail Pierpont,=Rev. Joseph Noyes, of New Haven, Conn.
Abigail Noyes=Judge Thomas Darling, of New Haven, Conn.
Samuel Darling, M.D., of New Haven, Conn.,=Clarinda Ely.
Rev. Charles Chauncey Darling, of Utica, N. Y.,=Adeline Eliza Dana.
Charles William Darling, of Utica, N. Y.

Charles W. Darling

DESCENT from the Sureties for the observance of the Magna Charta:

Hugh Bigod,	John Fitz-Robert,
Roger Bigod,	John de Lacie,
Henry de Bohun,	Saher de Quincey,
Gilbert de Clare,	Geoffrey de Say,
Richard de Clare,	Robert de Vere.

1. **Geoffrey de Say,** one of the Sureties for the observance of the Magna Charta, *d.* 1230, had by his wife Alice, daughter of John de Cheyney:

2. WILLIAM DE SAY, eldest son, *d.* 1272, who was on the King's side in the battle of Lewes, and had:

3. WILLIAM DE SAY, eldest son, *d.* 1295, who served in the army with Edward I. in Gascony, and had:

4. GEOFFREY DE SAY, eldest son, *d.* 1322, first Baron by writ, 1313. He *m.* Idonea, daughter of William de Leyburne, an admiral of the fleet, first Baron by writ, 1299, *d.* 1309, and had:

5. SIR GEOFFREY DE SAY, second Baron, an admiral of the fleet, *d.* 1359. He *m.* Lady Maud, daughter of Guy de Beauchamp, Earl of Warwick, a descendant of **Roger Bigod** and **Hugh Bigod**, both Sureties for the Magna Charta, and had:

6. LADY JOAN DE SAY, *m.* Sir William Fynes, and had:

7. SIR WILLIAM FIENES, sheriff of Surrey and Sussex, 1297, who had:

8. Sir Roger Fienes, treasurer to the household to Henry VI., who had:

9. Sir Richard Fienes, Baron Dacre, *jure uxoris*, constable of the Tower of London and chamberlain to Edward IV., *d.* 1484. He *m.* Lady Joan, *d.* 1486, daughter of Thomas, Baron de Dacre, and his wife, Lady Elizabeth Bowet. They were descended as follows from the Sureties for the Magna Charta:

Richard de Clare, one of the Sureties for the Magna Charta, Earl of Hertford, had by his wife, Lady Amicia, daughter of William, Earl of Gloucester:

Gilbert de Clare, one of the Sureties for the Magna Charta, Earl of Hertford, who had by his wife, Lady Isabel, sister of William Marshall, a Surety for the Magna Charta:

Richard de Clare, Earl of Hertford and Gloucester, who *m.* secondly, Lady Maud, daughter of **John de Lacie,** one of the Sureties for the Magna Charta, Earl of Lincoln, by his second wife, Margaret, daughter of Robert de Quincey, *d. v. p.*, second son of **Saber de Quincey,** one of the Sureties for the Magna Charta, Earl of Winchester, and had:

Sir Gilbert de Clare, Earl of Hertford and Gloucester, *d.* 1295, who had by his second wife, *m.* May 2, 1290, Princess Joan Plantagenet, *d.* 1305, a daughter of Edward I., King of England, by his wife, Eleanor of Castile:

Lady Margaret de Clare, who *m.* secondly, Hugh d'Audley, Earl of Gloucester, and had:

Lady Margaret d'Audley, who *m.* Ralph de Stafford, K.G., one of the original Knights of the Garter, a commander at Cressy, first Earl of Stafford, and had:

Hugh, second Earl of Stafford, K.G., a crusader, *m.* Lady Philippa, daughter of Thomas de Beauchamp, K.G., Earl of Warwick, one of the original Knights of the Garter, a commander at Cressy and Poictiers, and a crusader, son of Guy,

Earl of Warwick, the son of William, first Earl of Warwick, by his wife Maud, daughter of John Fitz-John, chief justice of Ireland, 1258, son of John Fitz-Geoffrey, chief justice of Ireland, 1246, and his wife Isabel, daughter of Sir Ralph, son of **Hugh Bigod**, son of **Roger Bigod**, both Sureties for the Magna Charta and Earls of Norfolk.

Hugh, second Earl of Stafford, and Lady Philippa had:
Lady Margaret de Stafford, who *m.* Ralph de Nevill, K.G., Earl of Westmoreland and marshal of England,* and had:
Lady Philippa de Nevill, who *m.* Thomas, Baron de Dacre, of Gillesland, *d.* 1457, and had:
Thomas de Dacre, eldest son, who *d. v. p.* He *m.* Lady Elizabeth, daughter of Sir William Bowet, *d.* 1423, and his wife, Lady Amy, daughter of Sir Robert d'Ufford, *d.* 1400, son of Sir Edmund d'Ufford, of Horsford, *d.* 1374, son of Sir Ralph d'Ufford, justiciary of Ireland, *d.* 1346, and his second wife, Lady Eve, daughter of John de Clavering, second Baron, *d.* 1332, eldest son of Robert Fitz-Roger de Clavering, first Baron, *d.* 1311, eldest son of Roger Fitz-John, feudal Baron of Warkworth and Clavering, *d.* 1249, eldest son of **John Fitz-Robert,** one of the Sureties for the Magna Charta.

Thomas de Dacre had by the Lady Elizabeth Bowet:
Lady Joan de Dacre, heir-general to her grandfather. Her will was proved June 14, 1486. She *m.* Sir Richard Fienes, aforesaid, and had:
10. SIR JOHN FIENES, eldest son, who *d. v. p.* He *m.* Lady Alice, daughter of Henry, Baron Fitz-Hugh, of Ravensworth, and his wife, Lady Alice, daughter of Richard Nevill,

---

* He was the son of John, third Baron de Nevill, of Raby, K.G., admiral of the fleet, *d.* 1385, the son of Ralph, second Baron, *d.* 1367, son of Ralph, first Baron, and his first wife, Lady Euphemia, daughter of Robert Fitz-Roger de Clavering, son of Roger Fitz-John, the son of **John Fitz-Robert,** one of the Sureties for the Magna Charta.

K.G., Earl of Salisbury,* by his wife, Lady Alice Montacute, daughter of Thomas, Earl of Salisbury, and his first wife, Lady Eleanor, daughter of Thomas de Holland, second Earl of Kent, and his wife, Lady Alice, daughter of Richard Fitz-Alan, K.G., Earl of Arundel and Surrey, by his second wife, Lady Eleanor Plantagenet.† He was the son of Edmund, K.B., eighth Earl of Arundel, who fell a victim to the ill will of Mortimer and the queen, and was executed at Hereford in 1326, and his wife Alice, daughter of William de Warren by his wife, Lady Joan de Vere, daughter of Robert, Earl of Oxford, lord great chamberlain, the son of Hugh, Earl of Oxford, lord great chamberlain (by his wife, Lady Hawyse, daughter of Saber de Quincey, one of the Sureties for the Magna Charta, Earl of Winchester) the son of Robert de Vere, Earl of Oxford and lord great chamberlain, one of the Sureties for the Magna Charta.

Sir John Fienes and Lady Alice Fitz-Hugh had:

11. THOMAS FIENES, K.B., who succeeded as Baron Dacre of the South. His wife was Lady Anne, daughter of Sir Humphrey Bourchier, who was *k. v. p.* at Barnetfield, eldest son of John Bourchier, K.G., the fourth son of William de Bourchier, Earl of Ewe, and his wife, Lady Anne Plantagenet, widow of both Thomas and Edmund, Earls of Stafford, a daughter of Thomas, Duke of Gloucester (youngest son of EDWARD III., KING OF ENGLAND), by his wife, Lady Alianore, a daughter of Humphrey, the last Earl of Hereford

---

* He was the eldest son of Ralph de Nevill, K.G., first Earl of Westmoreland, by his second wife, Lady Joan de Beaufort, daughter of John, Duke of Lancaster, son of EDWARD III., KING OF ENGLAND.

† She was the daughter of Henry, Earl of Lancaster (son of Edmund, Earl of Lancaster, son of HENRY III., KING OF ENGLAND, and his wife, Eleanor of Provence), by his wife, Lady Maud, daughter of Patrick de Chaworth and his wife, Lady Isabel, daughter of William de Beauchamp, first Earl of Warwick, by his wife, Lady Maud Fitz-John, aforesaid, descended from Hugh Bigod and Roger Bigod, both Sureties for the Magna Charta.

and Essex and second Earl of Northampton (and his wife, Lady Joan Fitz-Alan*), the only son of Sir William de Bohun, K.G., Earl of Northampton, the fourth son of Humphrey, Earl of Hereford and Essex, constable of England, who was slain in the battle of Boroughbridge (and his wife, Princess Elizabeth, daughter of EDWARD I., KING OF ENGLAND, and his wife, Eleanor of Castile), son of Humphrey, Earl of Hereford and Essex, and constable, the son of Humphrey de Bohun, *d. v. p.*, son of Humphrey, Earl of Hereford and Essex, the son of **Henry de Bohun,** one of the Sureties for the Magna Charta, Earl of Hereford.

Thomas Fienes, K.B., Baron Dacre, and Lady Anne had:

12. LADY CATHERINE FIENES, who *m.* Richard Loudenoys, or Londenoys, of Briade, Sussex, and had:

13. MARY LOUDENOYS, who *m.* Thomas Harlakenden, of Worthorn, Kent, his will proved in 1564, and had:

14. ROGER HARLAKENDEN, of Kenardiston and Woodchurch, Kent, and Earl's Colne, Essex, third son, *b.* 1535, *d.* 1603. He *m.* first, Elizabeth, daughter of Thomas Hardres and widow of George Harlakenden, of Woodchurch, and had:

15. RICHARD HARLAKENDEN, of Kenardiston, Earl's Colne, and Staple's Inn, *b.* 1565, *d.* 1631, who *m.* Mary, daughter of Edward Hubbart, of Stanstead-Montfichet, and had:

16. MABEL HARLAKENDEN, *b.* at Earl's Colne, September 27, 1614. In 1635 she came with her brother Roger to New England, and *m.* first, in 1636, as his second wife, John Haynes, of Cambridge, Massachusetts, *b.* Copford Hall, Es-

---

* She was a daughter of Richard Fitz-Alan, K.G., Earl of Arundel (by his second wife, Lady Eleanor Plantagenet, daughter of Henry, Earl of Lancaster, a grandson of HENRY III., KING OF ENGLAND, and his wife, Lady Maud de Chaworth, aforesaid, a descendant of **Hugh Bigod** and **Roger Bigod,** both Sureties for the Magna Charta), who was, as before stated, a descendant of **Saher de Quincey** and **Robert de Vere,** both Sureties for the Magna Charta.

sex, May 1, 1594; arrived at Boston September 4, 1633; made freeman "at a General Court holden at Boston," May 14, 1634; elected an assistant in 1634 and 1636, and governor of the Bay Colony in 1635; colonel of the Second Regiment Massachusetts Militia in 1636. In 1637 he removed to Hartford, and was elected the first governor of the Connecticut Colony in April, 1639, and every second year afterwards until his death, March 1, 1654. He had by his wife, Mabel Harlakenden:

17. REV. JOSEPH HAYNES, of Hartford, *b.* 1641, who *m.* 1668, Sarah, daughter of Richard Lord, of Hartford, and, dying in 1679, had issue:

18. SARAH HAYNES, *b.* 1673, *d.* 1696, who *m.* May 30, 1694, as his second wife, Rev. James Pierpont, of New Haven, one of the founders of Yale College, *b.* 1659, *d.* 1714, and had:

19. ABIGAIL PIERPONT, only child, *b.* 1696, *d.* 1768, who *m.* November 6, 1716, Rev. Joseph Noyes, of New Haven, *b.* 1688, *d.* 1761, and had:

20. ABIGAIL NOYES, *b.* 1724, *d.* 1797, who *m.* July 23, 1745, Judge Thomas Darling, of New Haven, Connecticut, *b.* 1719, *d.* 1789, and had:

21. SAMUEL DARLING, M.D., of New Haven, *b.* 1751, *d.* 1842, who *m.* December 22, 1779, Clarinda, *d.* 1847, daughter of Rev. Richard Ely, of Saybrook, Connecticut, *b.* 1759, and had:

22. REV. CHARLES CHAUNCEY DARLING, of New Haven, Connecticut, *b.* 1799, *d.* 1887, who *m.* July 28, 1829, Adeline Eliza, *b.* 1798, *d.* 1882, daughter of William and Eliza (Davis) Dana, of Boston, Massachusetts, and had:

23. BRIGADIER-GENERAL CHARLES WILLIAM DARLING, of Utica, New York, *b.* 1830, New Haven, Connecticut. He is a founder of the Order of Runnemede and a member of the Society Sons of the Revolution, by right of his descent from

Major Robert Davis, of the Continental army, his maternal great-grandfather. When Mr. Morgan was elected governor of New York he appointed Mr. Darling a member of his staff, with the rank of colonel. During the draft riots in New York City in 1863, Colonel Darling performed the difficult and dangerous duties of a staff-officer on that memorable occasion with such distinction that he received the most cordial approbation of both the military and civil authorities. In 1864 Colonel Darling was appointed a volunteer aide-de-camp on the staff of Major-General Butler, and next year was assigned to duty in the paymaster-general's department, New York. In 1866 he was commissioned as commissary-general of subsistence, New York, and in 1867 was appointed by Governor Fenton military engineer-in-chief of New York State, with the rank of brigadier-general. He *m.* December 21, 1857, Angeline Eliza, daughter of Jacob A. Robertson, of New York City. No issue.

Arms.—*Ar., on a bend, gu., three escollopes, or, bend-coitesed, vert, two five-point mullets of the second.*

Crest.—*An esquire's helmet, pp., surmounted by a lion's head, erased, or.*

THE PEDIGREE OF CHARLES COOLIDGE POMEROY.

```
Saher de Quincey.    Roger Bigod.                    Robert de Vere.    Henry de Bohun.
Robert de Quincey.   Hugh Bigod.                                         Humphrey de Bohun.
Margaret de Quincey. Ralph Bigod.                    Hugh de Vere.       Humphrey de Bohun.
John de Lacie.       Isabel Bigod.   John Fitz-Robert. Robert de Vere.   Humphrey de Bohun.
Maud de Lacie.       John Fitz-John.  Roger Fitz-John. Joan de Vere.     Humphrey de Bohun.
Richard de Clare.    Maud Fitz-John.  Robert Fitz-Roger. Alice de Warren. William de Bohun.
Gilbert de Clare.    Guy de Beauchamp. John de Clavering. Richard Fitz-Alan. Humphrey de Bohun.
Richard de Clare.    Thomas de Beauchamp. Eve de Clavering. Alice Fitz-Alan. Altanore de Bohun.
Gilbert de Clare.                    Edmund d'Ufford. Eleanor de Holland. Ame Plantagenet.
Margaret de Clare.                   Robert d'Ufford.  Alice de Montacute. John Bourchier.
Margaret d'Audley.   Philippa Beauchamp.              Alice de Nevill.   Humphrey Bourchier.
Hugh de Stafford—Philippa Beauchamp.
Margaret de Stafford.
Phillippa de Nevill. William Bowet—Amy d'Ufford.
Thomas de Dacre—Elizabeth Bowet.
                                     Geoffrey de Say.
                                     William de Say.
                                     William de Say.
                                     Geoffrey de Say.
                                     Geoffrey de Say.
                                     Joan de Say.
                                     William Fienes.
                                     Roger Fienes.
                   Joan de Dacre—Richard Fienes.
                         John Fienes—Alice Fitz-Hugh.
                         Thomas Fienes—Anne Bourchier.
                   Catherine Fienes—Richard Loudsoye, of Briade, Sussex.
                   Mary Loudsoye—Thomas Harlakenden, of Worthorn, Kent.
                   Roger Harlakenden, of Kenardiston, Kent,—Elizabeth Hardres.
                   Richard Harlakenden, of Kenardiston, Kent,—Mary Hubbart.
                   Mabel Harlakenden—John Haynes, Governor of Massachusetts and Connecticut.
                          Ruth Haynes—Samuel Wyllys.
                   Hezekiah Wyllys, of Hartford, Conn.,—Elizabeth Hobart.
                   Col. George Wyllys, of Hartford, Conn.,—Mary Woodbridge.
                          Mary Wyllys—Eleazar Pomeroy, of Middletown, Conn.
                   Samuel Wyllys Pomeroy, of Pomeroy, Ohio,—Clarissa Alsop.
                   Samuel Wyllys Pomeroy, of Pomeroy, Ohio,—Catherine Boyer Coolidge.
                          Charles Coolidge Pomeroy, of New York City.
```

Charles C. Pomeroy

DESCENT from the Sureties for the observance of the Magna Charta:

 Hugh Bigod,   John Fitz-Robert,
 Roger Bigod,   John de Lacie,
 Henry de Bohun,   Saher de Quincey,
 Gilbert de Clare,   Geoffrey de Say,
 Richard de Clare,   Robert de Vere.

1. **John Fitz-Robert,** one of the Sureties for the Magna Charta, lord of Warkworth Castle and Manor, and Clavering Manor, d. 1240, had by his wife, Ada de Baliol:

2. ROGER FITZ-JOHN, feudal lord of Warkworth and Clavering, d. 1249, who had:

3. ROBERT FITZ-ROGER, lord of Warkworth and Clavering, first Baron by writ, 1295, d. 1311, who had by his wife, Margaret de la Zouche:

4. JOHN DE CLAVERING, lord of Horsford, in Norfolk, second Baron, d. 1332, who had by his wife, Hawyse de Tibetot:

5. LADY EVE DE CLAVERING, only daughter and heiress, who m. first, as his second wife, Sir Ralph d'Ufford, justiciary of Ireland, d. 1346, brother of Robert, first Earl of Suffolk, K.G., and had:

6. SIR EDMUND D'UFFORD, of Horsford, youngest son, d. 1374, who m. Sybil, daughter of Sir Simon Pierpont, of Hensted, Suffolk, and had:

7. SIR ROBERT D'UFFORD, eldest son, d. 1400, who m. Helen, daughter of Sir Thomas Felton, and had:

8. AMY D'UFFORD (her name appears sometimes as Joan), who *m.* Sir William Bowet, of Cumberland, *d.* 1423, and had:

9. ELIZABETH BOWET, *m.* Thomas de Dacre, *d. v. p.*, eldest son of Thomas, Baron de Dacre, of Gillesland, *d.* 1457, and his wife, Lady Philippa Nevill, who was descended as follows:

Richard de Clare, one of the Sureties for the Magna Charta, Earl of Hertford, had by his wife, Lady Amicia, daughter of William, Earl of Gloucester:

Gilbert de Clare, one of the Sureties for the Magna Charta, Earl of Hertford, who had by his wife, Lady Isabel, daughter of William Marshall, Earl of Pembroke:

Richard de Clare, Earl of Hertford and Gloucester, who *m.* secondly, Lady Maud, daughter of **John de Lacie,** a Surety for the Magna Charta, Earl of Lincoln, and had:

Sir Gilbert de Clare, Earl of Hertford and Gloucester, *d.* 1295, who had, by his second wife, *m.* May 2, 1290, Princess Joan Plantagenet, *d.* 1305, a daughter of EDWARD I., KING OF ENGLAND, by his wife, Eleanor of Castile:

Lady Margaret de Clare, widow of Piers de Gaveston, Earl of Cornwall, who *m.* secondly, Hugh d'Audley, first Earl of Gloucester, and had by him, who *d.* 1347-9:

Lady Margaret d'Audley, only child, who *m.* Ralph de Stafford, one of the original members of the Order of Knights of the Garter, seneschal and captain-general of Aquitaine, first Earl of Stafford, *d.* 1372, and had:

Hugh de Stafford, K.G., second Earl of Stafford, *d.* 1386. He *m.* Lady Philippa, daughter of Thomas de Beauchamp, third Earl of Warwick, one of the original members of the Order of Knights of the Garter, a commander at Cressy and Poictiers, and a crusader; *d.* 1369. His father was Guy, second Earl of Warwick, *d.* 1315, the son of William de Beauchamp, first Earl of Warwick, by his wife,

Lady Maud, widow of Gerard de Furnival, and daughter of John Fitz-John, chief justice of Ireland, 1258, son of John Fitz-Piers Fitz-Geoffrey, chief justice of Ireland, 1246, and his wife, Lady Isabel, widow of Gilbert de Lacie, and daughter of Sir Ralph, third son of **Hugh Bigod**, son of **Roger Bigod**, both Sureties for the Magna Charta and Earls of Norfolk. Sir Hugh, Earl of Stafford, and Lady Philippa had:

Lady Margaret de Stafford, *d*. 1370, who *m*., as his first wife, Ralph de Nevill, K.G., created Earl of Westmoreland and marshal of England, who took a leading part in the political drama of his day, *d*. 1425, and had: Lady Philippa de Nevill, aforesaid.

Thomas de Dacre had by the Lady Elizabeth Bowet:

10. LADY JOAN DE DACRE, will proved June 14, 1486. She *m. ante* 1457, Sir Richard Fienes, Baron Dacre of the South in right of his wife. He was constable of the Tower of London and lord chamberlain to the household of King Edward IV., and *d*. 1484-5. He was the son of Sir Roger, treasurer of the household to Henry VI., the son of Sir William, high sheriff of Surrey and Sussex, 1297, the son of Sir William Fynes, and his wife, Lady Joan, daughter of Sir Geoffrey, second Baron de Say, admiral of the king's fleet, *d*. 1359 (by his wife, Lady Maud, a daughter of the above Guy, Earl of Warwick, a descendant of **Roger Bigod** and **Hugh Bigod**, both Sureties for the Magna Charta), the eldest son of Geoffrey, *d*. 1322, son of William, *d*. 1295, son of William, *d*. 1272, the son of **Geoffrey de Say**, one of the Sureties for the Magna Charta.

Sir Richard Fienes, Baron Dacre, and Lady Joan had:

11. SIR JOHN FIENES, eldest son, who *d. v. p.* He (some peerage-books give his name as Thomas) *m*. Lady Alice, daughter of Henry, Baron Fitz-Hugh, of Ravensworth, *d*. 1472, and his wife, Lady Alice, daughter of Richard Nevill,

K.G., Earl of Salisbury, by his wife, Lady Alice Montacute, daughter of Thomas, Earl of Salisbury, and his first wife, Lady Eleanor, daughter of Thomas de Holland, second Earl of Kent, marshal of England, and his wife, Lady Alice, daughter of Richard Fitz-Alan, K.G., Earl of Arundel and Surrey, *d.* 1375, the son of Edmund, K.B., eighth Earl of Arundel, executed in 1326, and his wife, Lady Alice, daughter of William de Warren, *d.* 1286, by his wife, Lady Joan de Vere, daughter of Robert, Earl of Oxford, lord great chamberlain, *d.* 1296, the son of Hugh, Earl of Oxford, lord great chamberlain, *d.* 1203 (by his wife, Lady Hawyse, daughter of **Saber de Quincey**, one of the Sureties for the Magna Charta, Earl of Winchester), the son of **Robert de Vere**, Earl of Oxford and lord great chamberlain, one of the Sureties for the Magna Charta.

Sir John Fienes and Lady Alice Fitz-Hugh had:

12. THOMAS FIENES, Baron Dacre of the South, made a Knight of the Bath by Henry VII., *d.* 1534. He *m.* Lady Anne, daughter of Sir Humphrey Bourchier, who was *k. v. p.* at Barnetfield, fighting under the royal banner, eldest son of John Bourchier, K.G., the fourth son of William, Earl of Eue, and his wife, Lady Anne Plantagenet, widow of both Thomas and Edmund, Earls of Stafford, and a daughter of Thomas, Duke of Gloucester, *d.* 1397, youngest son of EDWARD III., KING OF ENGLAND.

The wife of the Earl of Eue was Lady Alianore de Bohun, a daughter of Humphrey, the last Earl of Hereford and Essex and second Earl of Northampton, *d.* 1372. He was the only son of Sir William de Bohun, K.G., Earl of Northampton, *d.* 1360, the fourth son of Humphrey de Bohun, Earl of Hereford and Essex, constable of England, who was slain in the battle of Boroughbridge, March 16, 1321–2 (and his wife, *m.* November 14, 1302, Lady Elizabeth Plantagenet, widow of John, Earl of Holland, and daughter of EDWARD I., KING OF ENGLAND), the son of Humphrey de Bohun, Earl of Hereford and Essex and constable of England, *d*. 1297, the eldest son of Humphrey de Bohun, *d. v. p.*, the son of Humphrey, Earl of Hereford and Essex and constable of England, the son of 𝕳𝖊𝖓𝖗𝖞 𝖉𝖊 𝕭𝖔𝖇𝖚𝖓, one of the Sureties for the Magna Charta, Earl of Hereford.

Thomas Fienes, K.B., Baron Dacre, and Lady Anne had:

13. LADY CATHERINE FIENES, second daughter, who *m*. Richard Loudenoys, of Breame, in Sussex, and had:

14. MARY LOUDENOYS, only child, *m*. Thomas Harlakenden, of Warhorn, Kent, his will proved in 1564, and had:

15. ROGER HARLAKENDEN, of Earl's Colne, Essex, Kenardiston and Woodchurch, Kent, third son, *b*. 1535, *d*. 1603. He *m*. first, Elizabeth, daughter of Thomas Hardres and widow of George Harlakenden, of Woodchurch, and had:

16. RICHARD HARLAKENDEN, of Earl's Colne, *b*. 1565, *d*. August 24, 1631, who *m*. Mary (or Margaret), daughter of Edward Hubbart, of Stanstead-Montfichet, and had:

17. MABEL HARLAKENDEN, seventh daughter, *b*. at Earl's Colne, September 27, 1614. In 1635 she came with her brother Roger to New England, and *m*. first, in 1636, as his second wife, John Haynes, of Cambridge, Massachusetts, *b*. 1594, *d*. 1653, who was elected an assistant in 1634 and 1636, and governor of Massachusetts Colony in 1635; colonel of the Second Regiment Massachusetts Militia in 1636. In 1637 he removed to Hartford, Connecticut, and was elected the first governor of that colony in April, 1639, and every second year afterwards until his death, March 1, 1653–4. He had by his wife, Mabel Harlakenden:

18. RUTH HAYNES, *b*. 1639, *m*. in 1655, Samuel Wyllys, *b*. February 19, 1631–2, *d*. 1709, assistant governor of the Con-

necticut Colony, son of George Wyllys, who came to Hartford in 1638, and became governor of the Connecticut Colony in 1642, and had:

19. HEZEKIAH WYLLYS, *b.* April 3, 1672, *d.* December 24, 1741. He held many municipal offices in Hartford, Connecticut, and was secretary of the colony, 1712-34. He *m.* May 2, 1704, Elizabeth, daughter of Rev. Jonathan and Elizabeth (Whiting) Hobart, of East Haddam, Connecticut, and had by her, who died in 1762:

20. COLONEL GEORGE WYLLYS, of Hartford, *b.* 1710, *d.* 1796, who was for over sixty years secretary of Connecticut. He *m.* his cousin Mary, *b.* 1715, *d.* 1774, daughter of Rev. Timothy Woodbridge, of Simsbury, *d.* August 28, 1742, son of Rev. Timothy Woodbridge, of Hartford, *d.* April 30, 1732 (by his wife, her third husband, Mehitable, *b.* 1658, *d.* 1697, daughter of the aforesaid Samuel Wyllys and his wife, Ruth Haynes), one of the founders of Yale College, son of Rev. John Woodbridge, of Newbury, Massachusetts, assistant of the Massachusetts Colony, *d.* 1694, and his wife Mercy, daughter of Thomas Dudley, governor of Massachusetts Colony. Colonel George Wyllys had by his wife, Mary Woodbridge:

21. MARY WYLLYS, *b.* 1742, who *m.* March 8, 1764, Eleazer Pomeroy, of Middletown, Connecticut, *d.* 1738, son of Rev. Benjamin and Abigail Pomeroy, of Hartford, and had:

22. SAMUEL WYLLYS POMEROY, *b.* 1764, *d.* 1841. He removed to Ohio and founded the city of Pomeroy, having *m.* 1793, Clarissa, daughter of Richard and Mary (Wright) Alsop, of Middletown, Connecticut, and had:

23. SAMUEL WYLLYS POMEROY, of Pomeroy, Ohio, who *m.* Catherine Boyer Coolidge, of Boston, Massachusetts, and had:

24. CHARLES COOLIDGE POMEROY, of New York City, one of the founders of the Order of Runnemede, who *m.* Edith,

daughter of Robert Wallace and Margaret (Groesbeck) Burnet, of Cincinnati, Ohio, who is also descended, through James Claypoole, of Philadelphia, Pennsylvania, *d.* 1687, from several of the Sureties for the Magna Charta and from blood royal. *Issue:*
1. Margaret B. Pomeroy.
2. Mary S. Pomeroy.

Henry James Hancock

DESCENT from the Sureties for the observance of the Magna Charta:

Hugh Bigod,   Roger Bigod,
       Richard de Clare.

1. **Roger Bigod**, a Surety for the Magna Charta, Earl of Norfolk, steward of England, d. 1220, had by his wife, Lady Isabel de Warren, daughter of Hameline Plantagenet, Earl of Surrey in right of his wife, Lady Isabel, daughter and heiress of William, third Earl of Warren and Surrey:

2. **Hugh Bigod**, a Surety for the Magna Charta, Earl of of Norfolk, d. 1225, who had by his wife, Lady Maud, a daughter of William Marshall, Earl of Pembroke, Protector of England during the minority of Henry III., and sister of William Marshall, a Magna Charta Surety:

3. SIR RALPH BIGOD, third son, who m. Lady Berta de Furnival and had:

4. LADY ISABEL BIGOD, who m. first, Gilbert de Lacy, d. v. p., eldest son of Walter, sixth Baron de Lacy, lord of Trim Castle, in Ireland, d. 1241, and his wife, Lady Margaret, daughter of William, Baron de Braose, of Brecknock, and had:

5. LADY MAUD DE LACY, who m. Geoffrey de Genevill, lord of Trim Castle, first Baron Genevill by writ, 1299, d. 1306–7, and had:

6. PETER DE GENEVILL, second son and second Baron, d. s. p. m. He m. Lady Joan, daughter of Hugh le Brune, Earl of Angoulême, and had:

7. LADY JOAN DE GENEVILL, who *m*. Sir Roger de Mortimer, first Earl of March, executed for treason, and had:

8. LADY MAUD DE MORTIMER, who *m*, John de Cherlton, second Baron, lord of Powys, chamberlain to Edward III., *d.* 1360,* and had:

9. LADY JANE DE CHERLTON, who *m*. John le Strange, sixth Baron, lord of Knockyn, *d.* 1397.† He was a lineal descendant of Sir John le Strange, K.B., first Baron, *d.* 1310, the eldest son of John le Strange, lord of Knockyn, *d.* 1276, and his wife, Lady Joan, daughter of Roger de Somerei, lord of Dudley, and his first wife, Lady Nicola, daughter of William d'Albini, second Earl of Arundel and Sussex, son of William, first Earl, and his wife Adeliza, queen dowager of England, the second wife and widow of Henry I. and daughter of Godfrey, Duke of Lorraine, and his wife, Lady Ida of Namur, both descendants of the EMPEROR CHARLEMAGNE.

Roger de Somerei, aforesaid, was the son of William Percival de Somerei, lord of Dudley, *d.* 1221, a great-grandson of Gervaise Paganel, lord of Dudley, the son of Robert, second Earl, son of Robert de Beaumont, first Earl of Leicester and Earl of Mellent, and his wife, Lady Isabel de Vermandois, daughter of Hugh Magnus, the son of HENRY I., KING OF FRANCE.

John, Baron le Strange, and Lady Jane had:

10. LADY ELIZABETH LE STRANGE, who *m*. Gruffydd ap Madoc Vychan, of Rhuddalt, third Baron of Glyndyfrdwy,‡ the son of Madoc Vychan, son of Griffyth Vychan, son of Griffyth ap Madoc, lord of Bromefield, Wales, and his wife Emme, daughter of Henry d'Alditheley, or Audley, *d.* 1236, a powerful feudal Baron, who remained loyal to King John

---

* See Jones's "Feudal Barons of Powys."
† See Lloyd's "History of Powys Fadog," iv. 118.
‡ See Lloyd's "History of Powys Fadog," iv. 118, and Burke's "Royal Families," Chart Pedigree, vol. ii. p. lxi.

in the baronial insurrection, and his wife, Lady Bertred, daughter of Ralph de Meisnilwarin, and had:

11. GRUFFYDD VYCHAN, fourth Baron of Glyndyfrdwy, who *m.* Lady Eleanor, daughter and coheiress of Thomas ap Llewellyn, of Trefgarned, lord of South Wales, and his wife, Eleanor vch. Philip ap Yevor, and his wife, Catherine vch. Llewellyn, or Leoline ap Gryffyth, prince of North Wales, and his wife, Lady Eleanor, daughter of Simon de Montfort, second Earl of Leicester, *k.* 1264, and his wife, Princess Eleanor Plantagenet, a daughter of KING JOHN OF ENGLAND, and his wife, Isabel of Angoulême.

Simon, second Earl of Leicester, was the son of Simon de Montfort, first Earl, and high steward of England, by his wife, Lady Amicia, daughter of Robert, third Earl, son of Robert, second Earl, son of Robert de Beaumont, Earl of Mellent and first Earl of Leicester, aforesaid.

Simon, first Earl of Leicester, aforesaid, was a descendant of ROBERT THE PIOUS, KING OF FRANCE, through his son, Almaric de Montfort, father of Simon, father of Almaric, father of Simon de Montfort, created Earl of Leicester.

Thomas ap Llewellyn was the son of Llewellyn ap Owen and his wife, Lady Eleanor, daughter of Henry, Count de Barre, by his wife, Princess Eleanor Plantagenet, a daughter of EDWARD I., KING OF ENGLAND, and his first wife, Eleanor of Castile.

Gruffydd Vychan and Lady Eleanor had:

12. TUDOR AP GRUFFYDD VYCHAN, lord of Gwyddelwern (a brother of the celebrated Owen Glendower), *k.* 3 mo. 15, 1405. He *m.* Maud vch. Ieuf ap Howel ap Ada, and had:

13. LOWRY V. TUDOR, heiress, who *m.* Gruffydd ap Einion, of Corsygedol, Merionethshire, and had:

14. ELLISSAU AP GRUFFYDD, who *m.* Margaret vch. Jenkin ap Ievan and his wife, Leiki vch. Llewellyn ap Edneyfed, of Sonby, in Maelor.

Richard de Clare, Earl of Hertford, one of the Sureties for the Magna Charta, *d.* 1218, had by his wife, Lady Amicia, daughter of William, second Earl of Gloucester.

Lady Joan de Clare (sister to Gilbert de Clare, one of the Sureties for the Magna Charta), who *m.* Rhys-gryd, lord of Yestradtywy, son of Rhys ap Gryffyth, lord of Rhys, Prince and chief justice of South Wales, *d.* 1197, and had:

Rhys-mechyllt, lord of Llandowery castle, *d.* 1242-3, who had by his wife, Ellen vch. Madoc ap Meredith:

Rhys-vaughan, lord of Yestradtywy, *m.* Lady Gwladys, daughter of Griffith, lord of Cymcydmaen, and had:

Margaret, who *m.* Griffith ap Iorwerth, of Lluynon, a descendant of Tudor Trevor, and had:

Margaret, who *m.* Llewellyn ap Yugr O'Ial, lord of Gelligynon, and had:

Meredith, who *m.* Efa, daughter of Kerric Sais ap Itel-Vychan, and had:

Griffith Lloyd ap Meredith ap Llewellyn, who had:

Llewellyn, who *m.* Margaret, daughter of Llewellyn ap David Vychan, and had:

Ievan, who *m.* Mabli, daughter of Grono ap Tudor, and had:

Jenkin, whose daughter Margaret *m.* Ellissau ap Gruffydd, aforesaid, and had:

15. LOWRY V. ELLISSAU, who *m.* Reinault ap Gruffydd ap Rhys, of Branas Uchaf Llan Drillo Plas Ynghrogen,* and had:

16. MARY V. REINAULT, who *m.* Robert Lloydd ap David Lloydd ap Ievan Vychan, of Gwern y Brychdwyn and Glanllyn, and had:

17. THOMAS LLOYD, *b.* about 1515-20, *d.* May, 1612, *m.*

---

* See Dwynn's "Visitations of Wales," ii. 126.

Catherine vch. Robert ap Griffyth and Margaret vch. Cadwalader ap Rhys Lloyd, of Cydros, and had:

18. MARY LLOYD, who *m.* Richard, of Tyddyn Tyfod,* and had:

19. RHYS AP RICHARD, who had:

20. GRIFFITH AP RHYS,† and had:

21. RICHARD PRICE, of Llanfawr, Glanllvideogen, will dated January 26, 1685-6, proved in 1686, at St. Asaph Registry, who had:

22. HANNAH PRICE, mentioned in the above will with her children, *b.* about 1656, *d.* 9 mo. 29, 1741, *m.* Rees John William, *d.* 11 mo. 26, 1697, and had:

23. LOWRY JONES, *b.* about 1680, *d.* 11 mo. 25, 1762, *m.* at Merion Monthly Meeting, Pennsylvania, 8 mo. 11, 1698, Robert Lloyd, of Philadelphia, *b.* about 1669, in Merionethshire, Wales, *d.* 3 mo. 29, 1714, and had:

24. HANNAH LLOYD, *b.* 9 mo. 21, 1699, *d.* 1 mo. 15, 1763, *m.* secondly, 9 mo. 22, 1722, William Paschall, of Chester County, Pennsylvania,‡ *b.* 1 mo. 8, 1699, *d.* 8 mo. 1732 (adm. issued in Chester County, 8 mo. 11, 1732), and had:

25. JOANNA PASCHALL, *b.* 1725, *m.* at Goshen Monthly Meeting, Pennsylvania, 4 mo. 5, 1746, Samuel James, of Chester County, Pennsylvania, *b.* 1720, *d.* 1754, who conveyed land, 5 mo. 2, 1752, as heir-at-law of William Paschall, deceased, a grandson of Morgan James, of Narbeth, Wales, and had:

26. JESSE JAMES, *b.* 1750, *d.* 4 mo. 18, 1816, *m.* at Abington Monthly Meeting, Pennsylvania, 11 mo. 17, 1779, Phœbe Townsend, *b.* 1 mo. 20, 1761, *d.* 9 mo. 25, 1832, fourth in descent from John Townsend, of Oyster Bay, Long Island,

---

* See Glenn's "Merion in the Welsh Tract," p. 95.

† See Glenn's "Merion in the Welsh Tract," Pennsylvania, and authorities there cited, pp. 79, 80.

‡ See Glenn's "Merion in the Welsh Tract," pp. 79, 81.

and from Captain John Seaman, of Long Island, and had:

27. JESSE JAMES, *b.* 6 mo. 1, 1789, *d.* 1 mo. 23, 1880, *m.* 10 mo. 16, 1822, Martha Walmsley, *b.* 11 mo. 24, 1799, *d.* 2 mo. 1, 1887, fifth in descent from Thomas Walmsley, who came to Pennsylvania in the ship *Welcome*, and third in descent from Evan ap Thomas, of Llanykeven, and had:

28. ELIZABETH JAMES, *b.* 7 mo. 6, 1840, *m.* 5 mo. 7, 1862, George W. Hancock, of Philadelphia, *b.* 3 mo. 2, 1839, of royal descent, and a descendant of Marchweithian, lord of Issalet, through John ap Thomas, son of Thomas ap Hugh, of Wern Fawr,* and had:

29. HENRY JAMES HANCOCK, of Philadelphia, a founder of the Order of Runnemede. He *m.* at Philadelphia, 6 mo. 1, 1892, Eliza Penn-Gaskell, daughter of Major Peter Penn-Gaskell Hall, United States army (retired), a descendant of ROBERT BRUCE, KING OF SCOTLAND (see Browning's "Americans of Royal Descent," third edition), and also of William Penn, proprietary of Pennsylvania, and Robert Barclay, proprietary governor of East New Jersey, and had:

Jean Barclay Penn-Gaskell Hancock, *b.* 3 mo. 24, 1893.

---

* Mr. Hancock is also seventh in descent from Nathaniel Allen, one of William Penn's commission of three to execute the Conditions and Concessions; sixth in descent from Marmaduke Coate, secretary to William Penn; seventh in descent from William Cooper, of New Jersey, land commissioner, member of the Assembly, justice of Gloucester County in 1682; sixth in descent from Edward Bradway, of New Jersey, justice, etc., signer of "Conces. and Agree.," March, 1676; sixth in descent from John Pancoast, of New Jersey, signer of "Conces. and Agree.," March 3, 1676; seventh in descent from Christopher White, of New Jersey, signer of "Conces. and Agree.," March 3, 1676, and member of council, May, 1684, etc.; eighth in descent from Richard Burden, of Rhode Island, general treasurer, 1654, commissioner for Portsmouth, and assistant for Portsmouth.

THE PEDIGREE OF JOHN J. RIKER.

```
                                                                    Roger Bigod.
                                                                    Hugh Bigod.
                                                                    Ralph Bigod.                              Saher de Quincey.
                                                                    Isabel Bigod.                             Robert de Quincey.
                                                                    John Fitz-John.                           Margaret de Quincey.
                                                                    Maud Fitz-John.           John de Lacie—Maud de Lacie.            Eustace de Vesci.
                                                                    Guy de Beauchamp.                                                 William de Vesci.
                                        Robert de Vere.             Thomas de Beauchamp.     Richard de Clare.                        William de Vesci.
                                        Hugh de Vere.               Maud de Beauchamp—Roger de Clifford.                              Isabel de Vesci.
                                        Robert de Vere.             Catherine de Clifford—Ralph de Greystock.   Richard de Clare—Maud de Lacie.   Adam de Welles.
                                        Joan de Vere.                                                           Thomas de Clare.                  Adam de Welles.
                                        Alice de Warren.                                       Maud de Greystock—Eudo de Welles.      Thomas de Clare.   John de Welles.
                       John Fitz-Robert. Euphemia de Clavering.                                                 Mary de Welles.
                       Roger Fitz-John.  Richard Fitz-Alan.                                                     Margaret Lawrence.    William de Mowbray.
                       Robert Fitz-Roger. Ralph de Nevill.                                                      William Lawrence.     Roger de Mowbray.
                                          Alice Fitz-Alan.                                                      Edmund Lawrence.      Roger de Mowbray.
                                          John de Nevill.                                                       John Lawrence.        John de Mowbray.
                                          Eleanor de Holland. Ralph de Nevill.                                  William Lawrence.     John de Mowbray.
                                          Alice de Montacute—Richard de Nevill.                                 John Lawrence.        John de Mowbray.
Robert de Ros.                            Alice de Nevill.                                                      Thomas Lawrence.      Margery de Mowbray.
Robert de Ros.                            William Parr—Elizabeth Fitz-Hugh.                                     Thomas Lawrence.
William de Ros.                           William Parr.
William de Ros.                           Elizabeth Parr.
Thomas de Ros.                            Fulke Woodhull.
Thomas de Ros.                            Lawrence Woodhull.
Elizabeth de Ros.                         Richard Woodhull.
John Parr.                                                      Deborah Woodhull—John Lawrence.
Thomas Parr.                                                                    John Lawrence—Patience Sackett.
                                                                                Joseph Lawrence—Patience Moore.
                                                                                Anna Lawrence—Samuel Riker.
                                                                                John Lawrence Riker—Lavinia Smith.
                                                                                John Lawrence Riker—Mary A. Jackson.
                                                                                John Jackson Riker, of New York City.
```

John J. Riker

DESCENT from the Sureties for the observance of the Magna Charta:

Hugh Bigod,
Roger Bigod,
Gilbert de Clare,
Richard de Clare,
John Fitz-Robert,
John de Lacie,

William de Mowbray,
Saher de Quincey,
Robert de Ros,
Robert de Vere,
Eustace de Vesci.

1. **Saber de Quincey,** a Surety for the Magna Charta, Earl of Winchester, *m.* Lady Margaret, daughter of Robert, Earl of Leicester, lord high steward of England, and had:

2. ROBERT DE QUINCEY, eldest son, *d. v. p.* in the Holy Land, leaving issue by Lady Hawyse de Meschines, daughter of Hugh, fifth earl palatine of Chester, *d.* 1181:

3. LADY MARGARET DE QUINCEY, only child, who *m.*, as his second wife, **John de Lacie,** one of the Sureties for the Magna Charta, first Earl of Lincoln, *d.* 1240, and had:

4. LADY MAUD DE LACIE, who *m.*, as his second wife, Richard de Clare, Earl of Hertford and Gloucester, *d.* 1262, son of **Gilbert de Clare** and grandson of **Richard de Clare,** both Sureties for the Magna Charta and Earls of Hertford, and had:

5. THOMAS DE CLARE, second son, constable of Gloucester Castle, 1266, was constituted governor of the city of London by Edward I. upon his accession, and *d.* 1287, in Ireland, having issue by his wife, Lady Amy, daughter of Sir Maurice Fitz-Maurice, of Mallahuffe Castle, Desmond:

6. THOMAS DE CLARE, third son, father of:

7. LADY MAUD DE CLARE, who *m.* Robert de Clifford, of

Appleby, first Baron by writ, 1299, who was slain at the battle of Bannockburn, 1313, and had:

8. ROGER DE CLIFFORD, second Baron of Appleby, lord of Westmoreland, *d.* 1390, who *m.* Lady Maud, daughter of Thomas de Beauchamp, K.G., third Earl of Warwick,* the eldest son of Guy, second Earl of Warwick, *d.* 1315, son of William, sixth Baron de Beauchamp, of Elmly, created Earl of Warwick, *d.* 1298, and his wife, Lady Maud, daughter of John Fitz-John, chief justice of Ireland, 1258, son of John Fitz-Piers Fitz-Geoffrey, chief justice of Ireland, 1246, by his wife, Lady Isabel, daughter of Sir Ralph Bigod, third son of **Hugh Bigod**, and grandson of **Roger Bigod**, both Sureties for the Magna Charta.

Roger, second Baron Clifford, and Lady Maud had:

9. LADY CATHERINE DE CLIFFORD, who *m.* Ralph, fifth Baron de Greystock, *d.* 1417, and had:

10. LADY MAUD DE GREYSTOCK, who *m.* Eudo de Welles, *d. v. p.*, eldest son of Sir John, fifth Baron de Welles, of Gainsby, *d.* 1421, and his wife, Lady Margery, daughter of John, fourth Baron de Mowbray, *k.* 1368.†

---

* His wife was Lady Catherine, daughter of Sir Roger de Mortimer, Earl of March, who was convicted of treason and executed. He was the son of Sir Edmund Mortimer, of Wigmore Castle, the son of Roger de Mortimer, captain-general of the king's forces in Wales, *d.* 1282, and his wife, Lady Maud, a daughter of William, sixth Baron de Braose, of Brecknock, by his wife, Lady Eva Marshall, sister of William Marshall, one of the Sureties for the Magna Charta, and daughter of William, Earl of Pembroke, and his first wife, Lady Isabel de Clare, daughter of Richard the Strongbow, Earl of Pembroke, lord justice of Ireland, son of Gilbert, Earl of Pembroke, and his wife, Lady Elizabeth de Beaumont, daughter of Robert, Earl of Mellent and Leicester, *d.* 1118, by Lady Isabel, daughter of Hugh Magnus, Count de Vermandois, a son of HENRY I., KING OF FRANCE.

† His wife was Lady Elizabeth, daughter of John, third Baron de Segrave, *d.* 1353, and his wife Margaret, Duchess of Norfolk, daughter of Thomas Plantagenet, Earl of Norfolk, *d.* 1338, son of EDWARD I., KING OF ENGLAND, by his second wife, Princess Margaret, daughter of PHILIP III., KING OF FRANCE.

William de Mowbray, a Surety for the Magna Charta, had by his wife, Lady Agnes, daughter of William d'Albini, Earl of Arundel and Sussex: Roger de Mowbray, second son, *d.* 1266, *m.* Lady Maud, daughter of William de Beauchamp, of Bedford, and had: Roger de Mowbray, *d.* 1298, *m.* Lady Rose de Clare, and had: John de Mowbray, who took part in the insurrection of Thomas of Lancaster, was taken prisoner and executed at York in 1321; he *m.* Lady Aliva, daughter of William de Braose, of Gower, and had: John de Mowbray, third Baron, *d.* 1361,* who had: John de Mowbray, *k.* 1368, aforesaid.

Eustace de Vesci, a Magna Charta Surety, had by his wife, Lady Margaret, a daughter of William the Lion, King of Scotland: William de Vesci, who had by his second wife, Lady Agnes, daughter of William de Ferrers, Earl of Derby: William de Vesci, second son, first Baron by writ, *m.* Lady Isabel, daughter of Adam de Periton, and widow of Robert de Welles, and had: Lady Isabel, *m.* William de Welles, of Alford, and had: Adam, first Baron by writ, 1299, whose second son, Sir Adam, third Baron, had: John, fourth Baron, *d.* 1361, who had: John, fifth Baron, *d.* 1421, *m.* Lady Margery de Mowbray, and had: Eudo de Welles, who *m.* as aforesaid, Lady Maud de Greystock, and had:

11. LADY MARY DE WELLES, who *m.* John Laurence, of Rixton Manor, Lancastershire, returned to Parliament for Lancaster County, October 16, 1419, and had:

---

* His wife was Lady Joan Plantagenet, daughter of Henry, third Earl of Lancaster, *d.* 1345 (and his wife, Lady Maud, daughter of Patrick de Chaworth, and his wife, Lady Isabel de Beauchamp, daughter of William, first Earl of Warwick, and his wife, Lady Maud Fitz-John, aforesaid, a descendant of **Hugh Bigod** and **Roger Bigod,** Sureties for the Magna Charta), eldest son of Edmund, Earl of Leicester, Lancaster, and Chester, high steward of England, *d.* 1295 (a son of HENRY III., KING OF ENGLAND), and his second wife, Lady Blanche, widow of Henry I., King of Navarre, and daughter of Robert of Artois, a son of LOUIS VIII., KING OF FRANCE.

12. MARGARET LAURENCE, who *m.* Robert Laurence, son of Sir Robert Laurence, of Ashton Hall, Lancastershire, and had:

13. WILLIAM LAWRENCE, of Withington, and Sevenhampton, in Gloucestershire, which he bought; will proved in 1559. He *m.* before 1518, Isabel, daughter of John Molineaux, of Sefton Manor and Chorly, in Lancashire, and had:

14. EDMUND LAWRENCE, of Withington parish, Gloucestershire, fourth son; will proved January 10, 1559. He had by his wife Eleanor:

15. JOHN LAWRENCE, of St. Albans, in Hertfordshire. He was chief burgess in 1553, and mayor of St. Albans in 1567 and 1575, and had:

16. WILLIAM LAWRENCE, of St. Albans, who *m.* November 25, 1559, Catherine Beamond, or Beaumont, and had:

17. JOHN LAWRENCE, *bapt.* at Abbey Church, St. Albans, January 12, 1561–2, who had by his second wife, *m.* January 25, 1586–7, Margaret Roberts:

18. THOMAS LAWRENCE, of St. Albans, second son, *bapt.* at St. Albans, February 2, 1588–9, *d.* March 20, 1624–5. He was an assistant of the borough of St. Albans, 1622, and *m.* October 23, 1609, Joan, daughter of Walter and Joan Antrobus, of St. Albans, and had:

19. MAJOR THOMAS LAWRENCE, *bapt.* at St. Albans, March 8, 1619–20. He came to Long Island some time after the settlement there of his brothers John and William, and was a patentee of Middleboro, or Newtown, Long Island, and resided in New York City in 1645, and appears as "Captain Tho. Lawrence" on the tax-list, 1678. He was very prominent in colonial affairs, and received the commission of major of horse in Queens County, New York, dated December 24, 1689. His will was proved April 25, 1703. He had by his wife Mary, whose surname has not been preserved:

20. CAPTAIN JOHN LAWRENCE, of Newtown, Long Island, high sheriff of Queens County. He *d.* December 17, 1729, having issue by his wife Deborah, 1659-1742, daughter of Richard Woodhull, who was *b.* at Thenford, in Northumberland, September 13, 1620, and came to Long Island in 1646-7, where he purchased, in 1665, over one hundred thousand acres of land, now the site of Brookhaven, and was a justice in 1666, and *d.* in 1690.

Richard Woodhull, aforesaid, was the son of Lawrence, of Thenford, the son of Fulke, of Thenford, Northumberland, the son of Sir Nicholas Woodhull, and his second wife, Lady Elizabeth, daughter of William, Baron Parr, of Horton, Northamptonshire, chamberlain to the queen, *d.* 1546 (uncle of Queen Catherine Parr, last wife of Henry VIII.), second son of Sir William Parr, K.G., constable of England, who had a principal command at Barnet Field, whose wife was Lady Elizabeth, daughter of Henry, fifth Baron Fitz-Hugh, *d.* 1472, by his wife, Lady Alice de Nevill, daughter of Richard, Earl of Salisbury, by his wife, Lady Alice Montacute. He was the eldest son of Ralph de Nevill, first Earl of Westmoreland, and his second wife, Lady Joan de Beaufort, widow of Robert de Ferrers, and a daughter of John of Gaunt, Duke of Lancaster, a son of EDWARD III., KING OF ENGLAND.

Sir Ralph, first Earl of Westmoreland, earl marshal of England, was the son of John, third Baron de Nevill, of Raby (and his wife, Lady Maud Percy*), the son of Ralph, second Baron, the son of Ralph, first Baron de Nevill, of Raby, by writ, and his first wife, Lady Euphemia, daughter of Robert Fitz-Roger, lord of Warkworth, Eure, and Claver-

---

* She was the daughter of Henry, Baron Percy, of Alnwick, and his wife, Lady Ida, or Imania, daughter of Robert, Baron de Clifford, of Appleby, and his wife, Lady Maud, daughter of Thomas, son of Thomas, son of Richard, Earl of Hertford and Gloucester, son of Gilbert de Clare and grandson of Richard de Clare, both Sureties for the Magna Charta.

ing, son of Roger Fitz-John, lord of Clavering, son of **John Fitz-Robert**, a Magna Charta Surety.

Robert de Ros, of Farfan and Hamlake, one of the Sureties for the Magna Charta, had by his wife, Lady Isabel, a daughter of WILLIAM THE LION, KING OF SCOTLAND: Robert, Baron de Ros, of Werke Castle, Northumberland, who *m.* Lady Margaret, daughter of Peter de Brus, of Skelton, by his wife Helewise,* sister of William de Lancaster, and had: William Ros, of Kendal, whose grandson, Sir Thomas de Ros, of Kendal, was the grandfather of Lady Elizabeth de Ros, who *m.* Sir William Parr, *d.* 1405, and had: John, *d.* 1408, father of Sir Thomas, *d.* 1465, who was the father of the aforesaid Sir William Parr. K.G.

Lady Alice de Montacute, aforesaid, was the daughter of Thomas, Earl of Salisbury, and his first wife, Lady Eleanor, daughter of Thomas de Holland, second Earl of Kent, marshal of England, *d.* 1397, and his wife, Lady Alice Fitz-Alan, daughter of Sir Richard, Earl of Arundel and Surrey, K.G.,† the son of Sir Edmund, Earl of Arundel, K.B., beheaded in 1326, and his wife, Lady Alice, daughter of William de Warren, *d.* 1286, and his wife, Lady Joan de Vere, daughter of Robert, fifth Earl of Oxford, lord chamberlain, son of Hugh, fourth Earl of Oxford (and his wife, Lady Hawyse, daughter of **Saber de Quincey**, a Magna Charta Surety,

---

* Lady Helewise was the daughter of Gilbert Fitz-Reinfred and his wife, Lady Helewise, daughter of William de Lancaster, steward to Henry II., the son of William, governor of Lancaster Castle, and his wife, Lady Gundred, widow of Roger, second Earl of Warwick, and daughter of William de Warren, second Earl of Surrey, *d.* 1135, and his wife, Lady Isabel de Vermandois, daughter of Hugh the Great, a son of HENRY I., KING OF FRANCE.

† His second wife, the mother of Lady Alice, was Lady Eleanor Plantagenet, daughter of Henry, Earl of Lancaster, a grandson of HENRY III., KING OF ENGLAND, and his wife, Lady Maud, daughter of Patrick de Chaworth, by his wife, Lady Isabel, daughter of William de Beauchamp, first Earl of Warwick, and his wife, Lady Maud Fitz-John, aforesaid, a descendant of **Hugh Bigod** and **Roger Bigod**, both Sureties for the Magna Charta.

Earl of Winchester), the son of **Robert de Vere,** a Surety for the Magna Charta, third Earl of Oxford.

Captain John Lawrence had by his wife Deborah:

21. JOHN LAWRENCE, of Newtown, Long Island, *b.* September 9, 1695, *d.* May 7, 1765, who *m.* December 8, 1720, Patience, daughter of Joseph Sackett, and had:

22. JOSEPH LAWRENCE, who *m.* Patience Moore, and had:

23. ANNA LAWRENCE, *b.* November 27, 1749, who *m.* January 17, 1769, Samuel Riker, of Newtown, Long Island, *b.* April 8, 1743, *d.* May 19, 1823, and had:

24. JOHN LAWRENCE RIKER, of Newtown, *b.* April 9, 1787, *d.* May 11, 1861, who *m.* February 9, 1830, Lavinia Smith, *b.* October 21, 1796, *d.* December 15, 1875, and had:

25. JOHN LAWRENCE RIKER, of Newtown, Long Island, *b.* November 23, 1830, who *m.* June 17, 1857, Mary A., *b.* December 16, 1835, daughter of John C. Jackson, 1809–1889, and his wife, *m.* November 18, 1834, Martha M., 1811–1889, daughter of Andrew Riker, 1771–1817, son of the aforesaid Samuel Riker, of Newtown, 1743–1823, and had:

26. JOHN JACKSON RIKER, of New York City, *b.* April 6, 1858, a founder of the Order of Runnemede, and a member of the Society of the Cincinnati and the Society of Colonial Wars. Mr. Riker enlisted in the Seventh Regiment, N. G. S. N. Y., May 26, 1878; was appointed first lieutenant and aide-de-camp on the staff of the First Brigade, August 7, 1879; captain and aide-de-camp April 1, 1880; major I. R. P., May 19, 1880; resigned February 18, 1881; appointed captain and ordinance officer February 18, 1881; major and inspector, October 27, 1882; honorably discharged October 25, 1883; elected major of Twelfth Infantry, N. G. S. N. Y., January 9, 1884; resigned January 14, 1889. He *m.* April 20, 1881, Edith M., daughter of Samuel B. Bartow. No issue.

Arms.—*Az., a rose, ar., between three six-point mullets, or.*
Crest.—*A rose, ar., between two proboscedes, ar. and az.*

Richard Henry Greene

DESCENT from the Sureties for the observance of the Magna Charta:

Henry de Bohun, Saher de Quincey, Robert de Vere.

1. **Robert de Vere,** a Surety for the Magna Charta, Earl of Oxford, lord great chamberlain, had by his wife, Lady Isabel de Bolebec:

2. SIR HUGH DE VERE, Earl of Oxford, lord great chamberlain, *d.* 1263, had by his wife, Lady Hawyse, daughter of **Saber de Quincey,** a Magna Charta Surety, Earl of Winchester:

3. LADY ISABEL DE VERE, who *m.* John de Courtenay, lord of Oakhampton, Devonshire, and had:

4. SIR HUGH DE COURTENAY, lord of Oakhampton, who *m.* Lady Alianore, sister of Hugh, Earl of Winchester, and daughter of Hugh, Baron le Despencer, justiciary of England, *k.* at Evesham, and had:

5. SIR HUGH DE COURTENAY, Lord Oakhampton, 1299, created Earl of Devon in 1335, who *m.* Agnes, daughter of Sir John St. John and sister of Baron St. John, of Basing, and had:

6. HUGH DE COURTENAY, K.G., second Earl of Devon, second son, *d.* 1377, who *m.* 1325, Lady Margaret de Bohun, *d.* 1392, whose descent was:

Henry de Bohun, one of the Sureties for the Magna Charta, Earl of Hereford, constable of England, *d.* 1220, *m.*

MEMBERS OF THE ORDER OF RUNNEMEDE 429

Lady Maud, sister of Geoffrey de Mandeville, one of the Sureties for the Magna Charta, and had:

Humphrey de Bohun, Earl of Hereford and Essex, and constable of England, *d.* 1274–5. He *m.* first, Lady Maud, daughter of Raoul, Baron d'Eue, *d. s. p. m.*, and had:

Humphrey de Bohun, *d. v. p.* He *m.* Lady Eleanor, daughter of William, sixth Baron de Braose, of Brecknock, and Lady Eva, sister of William Marshall, one of the Sureties for the Magna Charta, and had:

Humphrey de Bohun, Earl of Hereford and Essex, and constable of England, *d.* 1298. He *m.* Maud de Fienes and had:

Humphrey de Bohun, Earl of Hereford and Essex, and constable of England, *k.* at Boroughbridge. He *m.* May 20, 1302, Princess Elizabeth, *b.* 1282, *d.* 1316, widow of Sir John, Earl of Holland, and daughter of EDWARD I., KING OF ENGLAND, by his first wife, Eleanor of Castile, and had:

Lady Margaret de Bohun, aforesaid, who *m.* Sir Hugh, Earl of Devon, and had:

7. EDWARD COURTENAY, of Godrington, Devon, second son, who *d. v. p.*, having issue by his wife, Lady Emeline, daughter and heiress of Sir John d'Auney, of Modeford Terry, Somerset, and Cheviock, Cornwall:

8. SIR HUGH COURTENAY, of Haccomb, Devonshire, and Boconnock, Cornwall, second son, brother of Edward, third Earl of Devon; he *m.*, as his third wife, Maud, daughter of Sir John Beaumont, of Sherwell, Dorset, and had by her:

9. MARGARET COURTENAY, who *m.* Sir Theobald Grenville, Knight, of Stowe, Cornwall, and had:

10. SIR WILLIAM GRENVILLE, Knight, of Bideford, who *m.* Lady Philippa, daughter of Sir William Bonville, K.G., Lord Bonville, of Chuton, and had:

11. THOMAS GRENVILLE, of Stowe, Cornwall, high sheriff

of Gloucestershire, who *m.* Elizabeth, daughter of Sir Theobald Gorges, Knight, of Devonshire, and had :

12. SIR THOMAS GRENVILLE, Knight, of Stowe, Cornwall, who *m.* Elizabeth, daughter of Sir Otis Gilbert, of Compton, Devon, high sheriff of Devonshire, 1474, *d.* 1494, and had :

13. SIR ROGER GRENVILLE, of Stowe and Bideford, high sheriff of Cornwall, who *m.* Margaret, daughter of Richard Whitleigh, of Efford, Devon, and had :

14. AMY GRENVILLE, *d.* 1579, who *m.* John Drake, of Ashe and Exmouth, Devon, high sheriff of Devonshire, 1561-2, *d.* 1558, and had :

15. ROBERT DRAKE, of Wiscombe Park, Devon, who *m.* Elizabeth, daughter of Humphrey Prideaux, of Thewborough, Devon, *d.* 1550, and had :

16. WILLIAM DRAKE, of Wiscombe Park, who *m.* Philippa, daughter of Sir Robert Dennys, of Holcombe, Devon, who *d.* 1592, and had :

17. JOHN DRAKE, *b.* 1600, who came to New England in 1630 and settled, in 1635, at Windsor, Connecticut, and, dying August 17, 1659, had issue by his wife, Elizabeth Rogers, who *d.* October 7, 1681 :

18. JOB DRAKE, *d.* Windsor, Connecticut, August 6, 1689, who had by his wife, Mary Wolcott, *m.* June 25, 1646 :

19. MARY DRAKE, *b.* December 12, 1649, *d.* December 2, 1728 ; *m.* March 3, 1686, Thomas Marshall (1664-1735), son of Captain Samuel Marshall, who was slain in the " Swamp Fight," December 19, 1675, and had :

20. JOHN MARSHALL, *b.* April 3, 1701, *d.* May, 1772, who had by his wife, Elizabeth Winslow :

21. RUTH MARSHALL, *b.* April 6, 1737, *d.* November 27, 1816; *m.* February 13, 1754, Captain James Greene, of the Second Connecticut Light Horse, *b.* September 17, 1728, *d.* March 11, 1809, and had :

22. CAPTAIN RICHARD GREENE, of East Haddam, Con-

necticut, *b.* March 10, 1765, *d.* February 8, 1848; *m.* May 1, 1803, Sally Webb, *b.* July 9, 1779, *d.* June 5, 1858, and had:

23. WILLIAM WEBB GREENE, *b.* March 29, 1807, *m.* August 10, 1836, Sarah Ann, *b.* June 21, 1813, *d.* March 8, 1883, daughter of Colonel William W. Todd, and had:

24. RICHARD HENRY GREENE, of New York City, one of the founders of the Order of Runnemede, a member of the New York Historical Society, New York Genealogical and Biographical Society, Society of *Mayflower* Descendants, Society Sons of the Revolution, Society of the War of 1812, and Society of Colonial Wars; graduated Yale College, 1862, LL.B.; Columbia, 1865; served in the Civil War as captain of New York Volunteers, 1862–4; *b.* June 12, 1839; *m.* June 20, 1867, Mary Gertrude Munson, and had issue six children, of whom survive Marshall Winslow and Edna Munson.

THE PEDIGREE OF DANDRIDGE SPOTSWOOD.

Saher de Quincey.
Robert de Quincey.
Margaret de Quincey=William de Mowbray.
Roger de Mowbray.
Roger de Mowbray.
John de Mowbray.
John de Mowbray.
John de Lacie=Maud de Lacie.
Richard de Clare=Eleanor de Mowbray.
Joan de la Warr.
Reginald de West.
Richard de West.
Thomas de West.
George West.
William West.
John West.
William Dandridge=Unity West.

Richard de Clare.
Gilbert de Clare.
Thomas de Clare.
Thomas de Clare.
Margaret de Clare.
William de Roe=Margaret Badlesmere.

Eustace de Vesci.
William de Vesci.
William de Vesci.
Isabel de Vesci.
Adam de Welles.
Adam de Welles.
John de Welles=Maud de Roe.

Roger Bigod.
Hugh Bigod.
Ralph Bigod.
Isabel Bigod.
Joan Fitz-John.
Edmund Butler.
Alianore de Bohun=James Butler.
Elizabeth d'Arcy=James Butler.

Henry de Bohun.
Humphrey de Bohun.
Humphrey de Bohun.
Humphrey de Bohun.
Humphrey de Bohun.

William de Lanvallei.
Hawyse de Lanvallei.
John de Burgh.
Margaret de Burgh.
Joan de Burgh.

Robert de Ros.
William de Ros.
Robert de Ros=Isabel d'Albini.
William de Ros.
William d'Albini.
William d'Albini.

John de Welles=Margaret de Mowbray.
James Butler=Anne de Welles.
Richard Butler.
Pierce Butler.
James Butler.
John Butler.
Walter Butler.
Margaret Butler.
Edward Bryan.
Anne Butler Bryan=Alexander Spotswood.
John Spotswood=Mary Dandridge.
Alexander Spotswood=Elizabeth Washington.
John Spotswood=Sally Rowsie.
Dandridge Spotswood=Catharine Brooke Francisco.
Isabella Matoaca Dunlop=William Francisco Spotswood.
Dandridge Spotswood, of Petersburg, Va.

Richard de Clare.
Gilbert de Clare a quo Alexander Lindsey.
David Lindsay.
Rachel Lindsay.
Robert Spottiswood.
Robert Spotswood.

Robert de Vere a quo Thomas d'Echyngham.
Margaret Echyngham.
Elizabeth de Blount.
Edith Wyndsore.
Thomas Ludlow.
Gabriel Ludlow.
Sarah Ludlow.
Robert Carter.
Ann Carter.
Nathaniel Harrison.
Robert Maitland=Susannah Harrison.
James Dunlop=Isabella Lenor Maitland.

Dandridge Spotswood

DESCENT from the Sureties for the observance of the Magna Charta:

William d'Albini,
Hugh Bigod,
Roger Bigod,
Henry de Bohun,
Gilbert de Clare,
Richard de Clare,
John de Lacie,

William de Lanvallei,
William de Mowbray,
Saher de Quincey,
Robert de Ros,
Robert de Vere,
Eustace de Vesci.

1. **Richard de Clare**, a Magna Charta Surety, Earl of Hertford, had by his wife, Lady Amicia, daughter of William, Earl of Gloucester:

2. **Gilbert de Clare**, a Magna Charta Surety, Earl of Hertford and Gloucester, *m.* Lady Isabel, daughter of William Marshall, Earl of Pembroke, and sister of William Marshall, a Magna Charta Surety, and had:

3. LADY ISABELLA DE CLARE, who *m.* Robert de Bruce, or Brus, fifth Earl of Annandale, 1210–1295, and had:

4. ROBERT DE BRUCE, Earl of Annandale and Carrick, 1245–1304, who *m.* 1271, Margaret, Countess of Carrick, *d.* before October, 1292, widow of Adam de Kilconeath, *d.* 1270, and daughter and heiress of Neil, second Earl of Carrick, a regent of Scotland, 1255, *d.* 1256, and his wife, Lady Margaret, daughter of Walter, steward of Scotland, and had:

5. LADY ISABEL DE BRUCE, sister of Robert I., King of

Scotland, who *m.* first,* Sir Thomas Randolph, of Strathwith, chamberlain of Scotland, 1296, and had:

6. THOMAS RANDOLPH, created, in 1314, Earl of Moray, regent of Scotland, who *m.* Lady Isabel, daughter of Sir John Stewart, of Bonkyl, 1246–1305, second son of Alexander, steward of Scotland, and had:

7. LADY AGNES RANDOLPH, who, during the absence of her husband, defended Dunbar Castle for five months against the English in 1337–8. She was the sister and heiress of John, Earl of Moray, and *m.* Patrick Dunbar, ninth Earl of Dunbar and March, Earl of Moray in right of his wife, 1285–1369, son of Patrick, eighth Earl, *d.* 1309, son of Patrick, seventh Earl, *d.* 1289, by his wife, Lady Christiana Bruce,† and had:

8. GEORGE DUNBAR, tenth Earl of Dunbar and March, 1338–1420, who *m.* Christiana, daughter of Sir William de Seton, and had:

9. SIR DAVID DUNBAR, of Cockburn, sixth son.‡ He was the first to come to the assistance of King James I. when he was attacked by assassins in 1437. He had by his wife, whose name has not been preserved:

10. MARIOTA DUNBAR, heiress, who *m.* Alexander Lindsay, second Earl of Crawford,§ *k.* January 13, 1445–6, and had:

---

* Wood's " Douglas's Peerage of Scotland," i. 65 ; ii. 249.

† She was the daughter of Robert, Earl of Annandale, and Isabella de Clare, aforesaid, and a descendant of Richard de Clare and Gilbert de Clare, Sureties for the Magna Charta.

‡ Wood's " Douglas's Peerage," ii. 170.

§ He was the son of Sir David Lindsay, of Glenesk, created, in 1389, Earl of Crawford, *d.* before 1412, and his wife, Princess Catherine Stewart, daughter of ROBERT II., KING OF SCOTLAND (and his first wife, Lady Elizabeth Mure), son of Walter, steward of Scotland, 1293–1326, and his second wife, Princess Marjory Bruce, daughter of ROBERT BRUCE, KING OF SCOTLAND (and his first wife, Lady Isabel Marr), son of Robert, sixth Earl of Annandale, aforesaid, a

MEMBERS OF THE ORDER OF RUNNEMEDE   435

11. SIR WALTER LINDSAY, laird of Edzell, Kidblethmont, and Bewfort, third son,* who *m.* either Isabel, daughter of William, Lord Livingston, or Sophie, daughter of Livingston of Saltcoats, and had:

12. SIR DAVID LINDSAY, of Edzell and Bewfort, *d.* 1527, who had by his first wife, Catherine Fotheringham, of Powrie:

13. WALTER LINDSAY, of Edzell, eldest son, slain at Flodden,† who had by his wife, a daughter of Erskine, of Dun:

14. ALEXANDER LINDSAY (younger brother of Sir David Lindsay, eighth Earl of Crawford), who had by his wife, a daughter of Barclay, of Mathers:

15. RT. REV. DAVID LINDSAY, D.D., of Leith, 1531–1613, chaplain to James I. of England, and Bishop of Ross in 1600, father of:

16. RACHEL LINDSAY (her mother's name has not been preserved), who *m.* the Most Rev. John Spottiswoode, laird of that ilk, *b.* 1565, *d.* London, December 2, 1639, buried, by the king's command, in Westminster Abbey. He was archbishop of St. Andrew's, 1615, chancellor of Scotland, 1635, and crowned Charles I. of England. He was the son of Rev. John Spottiswoode, D.D., the son of William Spottiswoode, of that ilk, *k.* at Flodden. Archbishop Spottiswoode sold the barony of Spottiswoode in 1620.‡ His second son by Rachel Lindsay:

17. SIR ROBERT SPOTTISWOODE, of New Abbey, *b.* 1596, was a member of the privy council to James VI. of Scot-

---

descendant of 𝕽𝖎𝖈𝖍𝖆𝖗𝖉 𝖉𝖊 𝕮𝖑𝖆𝖗𝖊 and 𝕲𝖎𝖑𝖇𝖊𝖗𝖙 𝖉𝖊 𝕮𝖑𝖆𝖗𝖊, Sureties for the Magna Charta.

* Wood's "Douglas's Peerage," i. 164 and 376.

† See Lindsay's "Lives of the Lindsays" and "The Lindsays of America."

‡ See Douglas's "Baronage of Scotland;" Playfair's "British Family Antiquity," viii. 305; Campbell's "Spottswood Genealogy;" "The Spottiswoode Miscellany," published by the Spottiswoode Society, 1844.

land, and was appointed in 1634, by Charles I., lord president of the College of Justice and secretary for Scotland. He was knighted in 1624, and was put to death by the Covenanters, at St. Andrew's, January 20, 1646. In 1629 he *m.* Bethia, daughter of Sir Alexander Morrison, of Prestongrange, a senator of the College of Justice, and his wife, Eleanor Maule, who was a descendant of ROBERT BRUCE, KING OF SCOTLAND, through Lord Panmure and the Lindsays, Lords Crawford, and had:

18. ROBERT SPOTTSWOOD, M.D., third son.* He was appointed physician to the governor and garrison of Tangiers, and *d.* there in 1680. In 1673 he published a work on "Plants within the Fortifications of Tangiers." He *m.* Catherine Elliot, widow, and had an only child:

19. MAJOR-GENERAL ALEXANDER SPOTTSWOOD, of "Porto Bello," James City County, Virginia, *b.* at Tangiers, 1676, *d.* June 7, 1740. He was an aide-de-camp to the Duke of Marlborough, and subsequently lieutenant-governor and commander-in-chief of the Virginia Colony, 1710–1723, and deputy postmaster-general for the American Colonies, 1739. He *m.* in 1724, Anne Butler Bryan, who *m.* secondly, Rev. John Thompson, of Culpeper County, Virginia.

Mrs. Anne Spottswood was the daughter of Edward Bryan, of Westminster, London, second son of Bryan FitzPatrick, fifth lord of Upper Ossory, and his wife, Lady Margaret Butler, sister of Thomas Butler, Lord Thurles, father of James Butler, created Duke of Ormond,† and daughter of Sir Walter Butler, of Kilcash, who succeeded as eleventh Earl of Ormond, *d.* 1632, and his wife, Lady Helena, *d.* 1631, daughter of Edmund Butler, Viscount Montgarret.

Henry de Bohun, a Surety for the Magna Charta, Earl

---

* See Sir Robert Douglas's "Baronage of Scotland," 1798.
† See Lodge's "Peerage of Ireland," 1789.

of Hereford, constable of England, *m*. Lady Maud, daughter of Geoffrey Fitz-Piers de Mandeville, first Earl of Essex, justiciary of England, and sister of Geoffrey de Mandeville, a Surety for the Magna Charta, and had :

Humphrey de Bohun, Earl of Hereford and Essex, *d*. 1274–5, who had by his first wife, Lady Maud d'Eue:

Humphrey de Bohun, eldest son, *d. v. p.** He commanded the infantry at the battle of Evesham, was taken prisoner, and died in Beeston Castle. He *m*. Lady Eleanor, daughter of William, Baron de Braose, of Brecknock, and Lady Eva Marshall, sister of William Marshall, a Surety for the Magna Charta, and had:

Humphrey de Bohun, Earl of Hereford and Essex and constable of England, *d*. 1298, who *m*. Maud de Fienes and had:

Humphrey de Bohun, Earl of Hereford and Essex, constable of England, *k*. at Boroughbridge. He *m*. November 14, 1302, Princess Elizabeth, widow of Sir John, Earl of Holland, and daughter of EDWARD I., KING OF ENGLAND, by his first wife, Eleanor of Castile, and had:

Lady Alianore de Bohun, who *m*. James Butler, second Earl of Carrick and first Earl of Ormond, the son of Sir Edmund, Earl of Carrick (and his wife, Lady Joan, daughter of John Fitz-Gerald, first Earl of Kildare, crowned "King of Ireland"), son of Theobald, the fourth Lord Butler, of Ireland, *d*. 1285, by his wife, Lady Joan, daughter of John Fitz-Piers Fitz-Geoffrey, sheriff of Yorkshire, 1234, lord justice of Ireland, 1246, by his wife, Lady Isabel, widow of Gilbert de Lacie, and daughter of Sir Ralph, third son of 𝔥𝔲𝔤𝔥 𝔅𝔦𝔤𝔬𝔡, a Surety for the Magna Charta, Earl of Nor-

---

* See American Historical Review, April and July, 1896, "Bohun Wills" and authorities there cited, by Melville M. Bigelow, and Doyle's "Official Baronage."

folk (by his wife, Lady Maud Marshall, sister of William Marshall, Jr., a Surety for the Magna Charta), son of **Roger Bigod**, a Surety for the Magna Charta, Earl of Norfolk and steward of England.

James Butler, Earl of Carrick, and Lady Alianore had:

James Butler, second Earl of Ormond, justiciary of Ireland, *m.* Lady Elizabeth d'Arcy (see below), and had:

James Butler, Earl of Ormond and Gowran, *m.* Lady Anne de Welles (see below), and had:

Sir Richard Butler, of Polestown, Kilkenny, *m.* Catherine, daughter of Gildas O'Riley, lord of Cavan, and had:

Sir Pierce Butler, who succeeded, in 1516, as eighth Earl of Ormond, lord high treasurer of Ireland in 1524, created, in 1527, Earl of Ossory, *m.* in 1485, Lady Margaret, daughter of Gerard Fitz-Gerald, eighth Earl of Kildare, and had:

James Butler, Earl of Ormond and Viscount Thurles, lord high treasurer of Ireland and admiral of the kingdom, *m.* Lady Joan, daughter of James Fitz-Gerald, eleventh Earl of Desmond, and had:

The Hon. John Butler, of Kilcash, *d.* 1570, who *m.* Catherine, daughter of Cormac MacCarthy-reagh, and had:

Sir Walter Butler, Earl of Ormond, aforesaid.

William de Lanvallei, a Surety for the Magna Charta, had by his wife, a daughter of Alan Basset, of Wycombe:

Lady Hawyse de Lanvallei, who *m.* Sir John de Burgh, eldest son of Hubert de Burgh, Earl of Kent, justiciary of England, guardian of King Henry III., and had:

John de Burgh, only son and heir, Baron of Lanvallei. He *d.* 1279, having issue by his wife, probably Cicily, daughter of Hugh de Baliol:

Margaret de Burgh, who *m.* Richard de Burgh, second Earl of Ulster, justiciary of Ireland, 1296, and had:

Lady Joan de Burgh, widow of Thomas, second Earl of Kildare, who *m.* July 3, 1329 (his second wife), Sir John, first Baron d'Arcy by writ, sheriff of Yorkshire, Derby, etc., constable of the Tower of London, steward of England, justiciary and governor of Ireland, *d.* 1347, and had: Lady Elizabeth d'Arcy, aforesaid.

Eustace de Vesci, a Surety for the Magna Charta, had by his wife, Lady Margaret, a natural daughter of William the Lion, King of Scotland:

William de Vesci, *d.* 1253, *m.* secondly, Lady Agnes, daughter of William de Ferrers, Earl of Derby, and had:

William de Vesci, first Baron by writ, *d.* 1297, *m.* Isabel, daughter of Adam de Periton, and had:

Lady Isabel de Vesci, who *m.* William de Welles, lord of Alford, 1274, and had:

Sir Adam de Welles, first Baron by writ, *d.* 1311, *m.* Lady Joan, daughter of John, Baron d'Engaine, of Gainsby, and had:

Sir Adam de Welles, third Baron, second son, *d.* 1345, *m.* Lady Margaret, daughter of John, Baron Bardolf, and had:

John de Welles, fourth Baron, *d.* 1361, *m.* Lady Maud de Roos, or Ros (see below), and had:

John de Welles, fifth Baron, *d.* 1421-2, *m.* Lady Margaret de Mowbray (see below), and had: Lady Anne de Welles, aforesaid.

Robert de Ros, a Magna Charta Surety, had by his wife, Lady Isabel, a natural daughter of William the Lion, King of Scotland:

William de Ros, of Hamlake, *d.* 1258, *m.* Lucia, daughter of Reginald Fitz-Piers, of Blewleveny, Wales, and had:

Robert de Ros, of Hamlake, *d.* 1285, *m.* Lady Isabel, daughter of William, eldest son of **William d'Albini,** a Magna Charta Surety, and had:

William de Ros, of Hamlake, *d.* 1316, *m.* Lady Maud, daughter of John de Vaux, of Feston, and had:

William de Ros, of Hamlake, *d.* 1342, *m.* Margaret de Badlesmere, and had: Lady Maud de Ros, aforesaid.

Lady Margaret Badlesmere, aforesaid, was the daughter of Bartholomew, Baron Badlesmere, of Leeds Castle, and his wife Margaret, daughter of Thomas, son of Thomas, son of Richard de Clare, Earl of Gloucester (and his wife Maud, daughter of **John de Lacie**, a Magna Charta Surety, by Margaret, daughter of Robert, son of **Saber de Quincey**, Earl of Winchester, a Magna Charta Surety), the son of **Gilbert de Clare**, son of **Richard de Clare**, both Sureties for the Magna Charta and Earls of Hertford.

William de Mowbray, a Magna Charta Surety, had by his wife, Lady Agnes, daughter of William d'Albini, Earl of Arundel and Sussex:

Roger de Mowbray, *d.* 1266, *m.* Lady Maud, daughter of William de Beauchamp, of Bedford, and had:

Roger de Mowbray, first Baron by writ, *d.* 1298, *m.* Rose de Clare, a granddaughter of Richard de Clare, and had:

John de Mowbray, second Baron, executed in 1321, *m.* Lady Aliva, daughter of William de Braose, of Gower, and had:

John de Mowbray, third Baron, *d.* 1361, *m.* Lady Joan Plantagenet,* and had:

John de Mowbray, fourth Baron, *d.* 1368, *m.* Lady Elizabeth, daughter of John de Segrave and Margaret, Duchess of Norfolk, a granddaughter of EDWARD I., KING OF ENGLAND, and had: Lady Margaret de Mowbray, aforesaid.

General Alexander Spottswood and Anne Bryan had:

20. JOHN SPOTSWOOD, eldest son, *d.* 1759. He *m.* in 1745, Mary, daughter of Captain William Dandridge, R.N.,

---

* She was the sister of Henry of Gresmont, Duke of Lancaster, and daughter of Henry, Earl of Lancaster (son of Edmund, Earl of Lancaster, a son of HENRY III., KING OF ENGLAND), by his wife, Lady Maud de Chaworth, a descendant of **Roger Bigod** and **Hugh Bigod**, Sureties for the Magna Charta.

of "Elsen Green," King William County, Virginia, and his wife Unity, daughter of Colonel John West, governor of Virginia, 1635,* whose descent was as follows:

William de Mowbray, a Surety for the Magna Charta, had: Roger, *d.* 1266, who had: Roger, first Baron by writ, *d.* 1298, who had: John, second Baron, executed in 1321, who had: John, third Baron, *d.* 1361, who had: John, fourth Baron, *d.* 1368, who had:

Lady Eleanor de Mowbray, who *m.* Sir Roger, Baron de la Warr, will dated April 28, 1368,† and had:

Lady Joan de la Warr, who *m.* Sir Thomas, third Baron de West, and had:

Reginald de West, second son, *b. ante* 1396, fifth Baron, and Lord de la Warr, *d.* 1451,‡ *m.* Margaret, daughter of Robert Thorley, and had by her:

Sir Richard de West, Lord de la Warr, *b.* 1432, *d.* 1475-6, *m.* Catherine, daughter of Robert Hungerford, and had:

Sir Thomas de West, K.B., K.G., Lord de la Warr, *d.* 1524, will dated October 8, 1524,§ *m.* secondly, Elizabeth, daughter of Sir Roger Coply, of Gatton, and had:

Sir George West, *m.* Elizabeth, daughter of Sir Anthony Moreton, of Lechdale, and had:

Sir William West, created, in 1568, Lord de la Warr, *m.* Elizabeth, daughter of Thomas Strange, of Chesterton, and had: Governor John West, of Virginia,‖ aforesaid.

John Spotswood and Mary Dandridge had:

21. GENERAL ALEXANDER SPOTSWOOD, of Orange County, Virginia, eldest son, who *m.* Elizabeth, daughter of General

---

* See Brown's "Genesis of the United States," p. 1045.
† See Nicolas's "Testamenta Vetusta," pp. 75 and 605.
‡ See Doyle's "Official Baronage."
§ See Nicolas's "Testamenta Vetusta," pp. 75 and 605.
‖ See Neill's "Virginia Carolorum," p. 15.

William Augustine Washington, half-brother of President Washington,* and had :

22. CAPTAIN JOHN SPOTSWOOD, of Virginia, who *m.* Sally Rowzee, of Essex County, Virginia,† and had :

23. DANDRIDGE SPOTTSWOOD, of Virginia, who *m.* Catherine Brooke, daughter of Peter Francisco and his wife Catherine, daughter of Robert Brooke, and had :

24. WILLIAM FRANCISCO SPOTSWOOD, of Petersburg, Virginia, *m.* Isabella Matoaca, daughter of James Dunlop, of "Mont View," Petersburg, and his wife Isabella Lenox, daughter of Robert Maitland, of New York City, and his wife, Susannah Harrison. (See below.)

James Dunlop was the son of John Dunlop, of London, England (and his wife, Mary Ruffin Gilliam, of Virginia), son of James and Marian (Buchanan) Dunlop, son of Colin and Martha (Bogle) Dunlop. Colin Dunlop, *b.* January 7, 1706, was the thirteenth child of James Dunlop, second laird of Garnkirke, who bore for arms : *Ar., an eagle displayed, with two heads, gu., a mullet for difference.* Crest, *a rose, ppr.* Motto, *E spinis.* These were, with the exception of the mullet, the arms of Dunlop of Dunlop, whose crest was *a dexter hand holding a dagger, ppr.*, and motto, *Merito.*

The original name of the Dunlop family was de Morville, from the barony of Morville, in Normandy. When Prince David, lord of Cumberland, succeeded, in 1100, his brother as King of Scotland, Hugh, Baron de Morville, went with him and was created feudal lord of Cuningham and constable of Scotland, and conferred on his younger brother the lands and barony of Dunlop, in Cuningham, and the office of huntsman, from whence Dunlop was called Hunthall. Another younger branch of de Morville remained in

---

* See Welles's "Washington Family" and Brock's "Spotswood Papers."
† See Hayden's "Virginia Genealogies," p. 498.

Cumberland, and of this was Hugh de Morville, one of the four lords in waiting to Henry II. He had only one daughter, who, by marriage, carried his baronies into her husband's family. The elder branch of Cuningham also became extinct in the male line after three generations. Hugh was succeeded by his son Richard, who was succeeded by his son William, whose daughter and heiress married Alan, lord of Galloway, and through her daughter the lordship of Cuningham came to the royal family of Baliol, and after to the royal family of Stuart, and is now part of the principality of Scotland.

The only male line of de Morville now remaining is in the line of William de Dunlop, lord of Dunlop in 1260. His son Robert had: Nigel, who had: John, who had: James de Dunlop, who forfeited the barony of Dunlop for adhering to the royal family of Baliol, and it was granted to the Earls of Douglas, but was afterwards restored to the family of Dunlop. In 1407 John de Dunlop succeeded in the barony, and in 1424 his son Alexander succeeded, who in 1471 was succeeded by his son Constantine, and in 1476 was succeeded by his son Constantine de Dunlop, of Dunlop, who was succeeded in 1489 by his son Constantine (whose daughter Jane married James Stuart, lord of Bute, grandson of King Robert II. and ancestor to the Earls of Bute), whose son, John de Dunlop, succeeded in 1507. He *m.* Lady Marion, daughter of the Earl of Douglas, in 1492, and was succeeded by his son Alexander, who *m.* Lady Helen Cuningham, daughter of the Earl of Glencairn. In 1549 his son James succeeded. He *m.* Isabel Hamilton, of Orbuston, and had James and Alan. Alan was a rich merchant and the provost of Irvine, Ayrshire, whose daughter Bessie married, first, John Maxwell, a merchant of Glasgow, who bequeathed her all his property, with which the lands and barony of Garnkirke were bought from the archbishop of

Glasgow on her marriage to her cousin, John Dunlop, her second husband, by whom she had an only son, James Dunlop, laird of Garnkirke, who *m.*, during his father's lifetime, Elizabeth, daughter of James Roberton, of Bedlay. He was trained to the law, and is alluded to as a writer in Glasgow in some of the old papers. Of this marriage there were six sons and three daughters. James Dunlop, aforesaid, was his eldest son and the second laird of Garnkirke, succeeded in 1697. He was also a lawyer, and *m.* in 1689, Lilias Campbell, only daughter of Robert Campbell, of Northwoodside. They had sixteen children.

Susannah Harrison, aforesaid, wife of Robert Maitland, was the daughter of Nathaniel Harrison, member and speaker of the Virginia State Senate, sheriff of Prince George County in 1779, and his first wife, Anne, daughter of William Gilliam. He was a brother of Brigadier-General Charles Harrison and Benjamin Harrison, governor of Virginia and a signer of the Declaration of Independence, father of President William Henry Harrison, who was the grandfather of President Benjamin Harrison. Nathaniel Harrison, aforesaid, was the son of Benjamin Harrison, of "Berkeley," member of the Virginia House of Burgesses, *d.* 1744,* and his wife Anne, daughter of Colonel Robert Carter, called "King Carter," of "Carotoman," Lancaster County, Virginia,† 1663–1732 (and his first wife, Judith, daughter of John Armistead), president of His Majesty's council in Virginia, whose descent was as follows:

Robert de Vere, a Magna Charta Surety, Earl of Oxford, *d.* 1221, had by his wife, Lady Isabel, daughter of Hugh de Bolebec:

Hugh de Vere, Earl of Oxford and chamberlain of Eng-

---

* See Keith's "Ancestry of Benjamin Harrison," p. 52.
† Ibid.

land, *m*. Lady Hawyse, daughter of 𝕾𝖆𝖇𝖊𝖗 𝖉𝖊 𝕼𝖚𝖎𝖓𝖈𝖊𝖞, a Magna Charta Surety, Earl of Winchester, and had:

Robert de Vere, Earl of Oxford and chamberlain of England, *m*. Lady Alice, daughter of Gilbert de Saundford, and had:

Lady Joan de Vere, who *m*. William de Warren, eldest son of John, Earl of Warren and Surrey, son of Earl William and his wife, Lady Maud, widow of Hugh Bigod and sister of William Marshall, Sureties for the Magna Charta, and had:

Lady Alice de Warren, who *m*. 1305, Edmond Fitz-Alan, K.B., Earl of Arundel, beheaded in 1326,* and had:

Richard Fitz-Alan, K.G., Earl of Arundel and Surrey, *d*. 1375–6, *m*. secondly, Lady Eleanor Plantagenet, *d*. 1372, widow, a daughter of Henry, Earl of Lancaster,† a grandson of HENRY III., KING OF ENGLAND, and had:

John Fitz-Alan, second son, Baron Maltravers and marshal of England, *d*. December 15, 1379.‡ He *m*. Lady Eleanor Maltravers, *d*. January 10, 1404–5, granddaughter and heiress of Baron Maltravers, and had:

Lady Joan Fitz-Alan, *d*. 1404, widow of Sir William de Brien, of Kemsyng, *d*. 1397, who *m*. secondly, about 1401, Sir William d'Echyngham, *d*. March 20, 1412,§ and had:

Sir Thomas d'Echyngham, *d*. October 15, 1444, *m*. Margaret, widow of Sir Thomas Marny, who *d*. 1414, and had:

Thomas d'Echyngham, *d*. January 20, 1482–3, *m*. Lady

---

* See Tierney's " History and Antiquities of the Castle and Town of Arundel."

† His wife was Lady Maud, daughter of Patrick de Chaworth, 1253–1282, and his wife, Lady Isabel de Beauchamp, daughter of William, first Earl of Warwick, and his wife, Lady Maud Fitz-John, a descendant of 𝕽𝖔𝖌𝖊𝖗 𝕭𝖎𝖌𝖔𝖉 and 𝕳𝖚𝖌𝖍 𝕭𝖎𝖌𝖔𝖉, Sureties for the Magna Charta.

‡ His will dated November 26, 1379, and that of his wife, September 26, 1404. See Nicolas's " Testamenta Vetusta."

§ See Betham's " Genealogical Tables of the Sovereigns of the World."

Margaret, daughter of Reginald de West, Lord de la Warr, aforesaid, and had:

Margaret d'Echyngham,* who *m.* William le Blount, *d. v. p.*, eldest son of Walter le Blount, K.G., first Baron Montjoy, and had:

Lady Elizabeth le Blount, *d.* before March 26, 1543, who *m.* Sir Andrews, Baron Wyndsore, of Stamwell and Bardsley Abbey, will proved July 31, 1543,† and had:

Lady Edith de Wyndsore, who *m.* before March 26, 1543, George Ludlowe, of Hill Deverill, Wilts, sheriff of Wiltshire, 1567, will proved February 4, 1580, and had:

Thomas Ludlowe, of Dinton and Baycliffe; buried at Dinton, November 25, 1607; will proved June, 1608. He *m.* Jane (her will proved July 6, 1650), daughter of Thomas Pyle, of Bopton, Wilts, and his wife Elizabeth, daughter of Ralph Langrish, of Borden, and had:

Gabriel Ludlow, *bapt.* at Dinton, February 10, 1587; called to the bar in 1620; *d.* after June 28, 1639. He had by his wife Phyllis, whose surname has not been preserved:

Sarah Ludlow, *d.* before 1669, who *m.* before 1663, as his

---

* See Hall's "Echynghams of Echyngham" and Sussex Archæological Collections, "Echyngham Church."

† He was the son of Thomas de Wyndsore and Elizabeth, daughter of John Andrews, of Stoke and Baytham, Suffolk, and Elizabeth, daughter of John Stratton, of Weston sur Mare, Norfolk, and Elizabeth, widow of William Harleston, and daughter of Sir Hugh Luttrell, M.P., lord of Dunster Castle, Somerset, steward to Queen Catherine, 1420 (and his wife, *m.* 1396, Catherine, widow of John Streech and daughter of John Beaumont, of Shirwell, Devon), son of Sir Andrew Luttrell, of Chilton (son of Sir John Luttrell, of the Isle of Lundy, by his wife Joan, daughter of Sir John, first Baron de Mohun, son of John, *d.* 1278, son of Reginald, *d.* 1256, and his wife, a sister of Henry de Bohun, a Magna Charta Surety), and his wife, Lady Elizabeth de Courtenay, widow, a daughter of Sir Hugh, second Earl of Devon, *d.* 1377, and his wife, Lady Margaret, daughter of Humphrey de Bohun, Earl of Hereford and Essex, *k.* 1321, a descendant of 𝕳𝖊𝖓𝖗𝖞 𝖉𝖊 𝕭𝖔𝖍𝖚𝖓, a Magna Charta Surety.

third wife, Colonel John Carter, a member of the Virginia House of Burgesses, *d.* June 10, 1669,* and had:

Colonel Robert Carter, of Virginia, 1663–1732, aforesaid.

William F. and Isabella Spotswood, of Petersburg, Virginia, had:

25. DANDRIDGE SPOTSWOOD, of Petersburg, Virginia, a founder of the Order of Runnemede.

Arms.—*Ar., on a chevron, gu., between three oak-trees, eradicated, vert, a boar's head, couped, of the first.*

Crest.—*An eagle rising, gu, looking to the sun in splendor.*

Motto.—*Patior ut Potior.*

---

* See Keith's "Ancestry of Benjamin Harrison."

Index

Abberbury, 200, 203.
Abbot, 144.
Adams, 209, 258.
William d'Albini, 25, 26, 27, 61, 71, 174, 189, 195, 198, 201, 278, 289, 308, 360, 364, 386, 439.
Albini, 181, 225, 243, 306, 331, 339, 356, 363, 366, 415, 423.
Alden, 285.
Alexander, 140, 264.
Allen, 209, 263, 419.
Allerton, 208.
Alling, 370.
Alsop, 412.
Andrews, 133, 134, 441.
Anthony, 284.
Antrobus, 183, 245, 341, 424.
Ario, 202.
Armistead, 444.
Arnold, 283, 395, 396.
Arundel, 175, 289, 364.
Asheton, 148.
Aton, 172.
Audley, 149, 172, 175, 192, 230, 250, 288, 297, 310, 351, 359, 388, 400, 408, 415.
Aufrère, 167.
Aylmer, 278, 279.

Bache, 219.
Badlesmere, 169, 174, 195, 197, 225, 250, 289, 290, 307, 308, 378, 435.
Baillie, 213, 322.
Baker, 347.
Baliol, 171, 177, 259, 310, 388, 407, 433.
Ball, 202.
Esek S. Ballord, 205-209.
Bamforth, 390.
Banastre, 292.
Bancker, 380.

Barclay, 137, 167, 218, 219, 325, 326, 419, 430.
Bardolf, 175, 205, 434.
Barnes, 202.
Barre, 170, 416.
Barrington, 143.
Bartow, 427.
Baskerville, 170, 171.
Basset, 135, 205, 211, 291, 310, 311, 321, 345, 363, 364, 433.
Bates, 208.
Bayard, 154.
Beach, 252.
Beamond, 183, 245, 340, 424.
Beare, 314, 315.
Beauchamp, 134, 135, 151, 152, 153, 157, 172, 181, 190, 191, 192, 193, 214, 222, 223, 225, 230, 233, 240, 242, 243, 253, 268, 277, 282, 298, 306, 309, 310, 316, 317, 323, 329, 338, 339, 351, 357, 359, 362, 364, 378, 384, 387, 394, 399, 402, 408, 422, 423, 435, 440.
Beaufort, 152, 163, 164, 165, 197, 214, 215, 217, 232, 269, 277, 310, 323, 324, 402.
Beaumont, 168, 177, 242, 245, 259, 305, 338, 340, 345, 415, 422, 441.
Beck, 291.
Bedles, 200.
Beke, 291.
Belknap, 171.
Bellomont, 239, 291.
Bennet, 333.
Benson, 397.
Bereford, 199.
Berkeley, 152, 309.
Bermingham, 279.
Berners, 234, 307, 353.
Besford, 199.

Frederic H. Betts, 228, 229–237.
Beverley, 150.
Biddle, 377, 379.
Melville M. Bigelow, 343–347, 437.
Hugh Bigod, 26, 61, 74, 135, 169, 191,
 193, 194, 195, 196, 197, 198, 201, 215,
 217, 223, 225, 230, 232, 233, 234, 242,
 243, 249, 253, 255, 266, 268, 277, 281,
 289, 298, 299, 309, 317, 323, 324, 330,
 339, 351, 352, 353, 358, 359, 361, 364,
 378, 383, 384, 385, 387, 388, 393, 399,
 401, 403, 409, 414, 422, 423, 426, 437,
 440, 445.
Roger Bigod, 17, 26, 61, 77, 135, 169, 191,
 193, 194, 195, 196, 197, 198, 201, 215,
 217, 223, 225, 230, 232, 233, 234, 242,
 243, 249, 253, 255, 266, 268, 277, 281,
 289, 298, 299, 309, 317, 323, 324, 330,
 339, 351, 352, 353, 358, 359, 361, 364,
 378, 383, 384, 385, 387, 388, 393, 399,
 401, 403, 409, 414, 422, 423, 425, 438,
 440, 445.
Bigod, 166, 345.
David S. Bispham, 220, 221–227.
Blackall, 365.
Bladen, 150.
Blair, 165.
Blaket, 171.
Anthony J. Bleecker, 210, 211–219.
Bloomfield, 380.
Blount, 160, 440, 446.
Bogle, 437.
Henry de Bohun, 28, 61, 80, 133, 134, 169,
 194, 196, 198, 226, 235, 278, 300, 306,
 311, 332, 343, 354, 262, 363, 377, 381,
 403, 411, 428, 436, 446.
Bolebec, 267, 349, 384, 439.
Bond, 377.
Bonville, 345, 429.
Bostwick, 142.
Bosum, 199, 204.
Boteler, 196, 197, 279, 311, 362.
Bothe, 148, 317, 318.
Bourchier, 179, 234, 300, 306, 307, 353,
 402, 410.
Bowet, 178, 179, 231, 298, 352, 400, 401,
 408.

Bowne, 341.
Boyce, 256.
Boyd, 155.
Boyer, 412.
Bradford, 292, 302.
Bradish, 254, 327.
Bradway, 419.
Bragg, 347.
Brampton, 308.
Braose, 169, 181, 191, 225, 241, 243, 306,
 307, 338, 339, 343, 357, 377, 382, 387,
 414, 422, 423, 432, 435.
Bray, 153, 180.
Brereton, 291.
Breynton, 171.
Brien, 313, 440.
Briggs, 258.
Brock, 209.
Brockburn, 173.
Brockett, 183.
Bromley, 292.
Bromsall, 200.
Brooke, 134, 224, 331, 442.
Brown, 284, 391.
Browne, 157, 165, 333.
Brownell, 391.
Charles H. Browning, 277, 280.
Browning, 333.
Bruce, 136–139, 140, 141, 144–147, 154–
 156, 166, 206, 211, 212, 213, 216, 259,
 269, 270, 271, 272, 273, 321, 428, 429.
Bruen, 318.
Brugge, 170.
Brune, 414.
Bryan, 147, 436.
Bryant, 365.
Buchanan, 437.
Bulfinch, 155.
Morgan G. Bulkeley, 255–258.
Burden, 419.
Burgh, 143, 153, 154, 155, 156, 157, 171,
 172, 197, 198, 205, 211, 215, 269, 270,
 272, 278, 311, 312, 321, 433.
Burk, 263.
Burling, 341.
Burlingame, 284.
Burnet, 144, 255, 413.

INDEX

Burnham, 184.
Burrington, 326.
Burt, 396.
Butler, 194, 278, 361, 382, 431, 432, 433.
Byrd, 151.

Charles E. Cadwalader, 372, 373-380.
Calder, 366.
Calthorpe, 150.
Calvert, 164.
Campbell, 136, 139, 144, 156, 272, 273, 274, 280, 444.
Carey, 134.
Carnegy, 140.
Carpenter, 292, 396.
Carter, 133, 184, 444, 447.
Carteret, 246.
Cary, 164.
Cecil, 183.
Chamberlain, 206.
Chamberlin, 347.
Champernon, 180.
Chaucombe, 291.
Chauncy, 256-257.
Chaworth, 191, 193, 197, 214, 222, 225, 233, 243, 253, 268, 323, 330, 339, 353, 357, 361, 378, 384, 423, 440.
Chedworth, 306.
Cheever, 278.
Cheney, 172, 316.
Cherleton, 149, 151, 415.
Chetwood, 257.
Cheyney, 399.
Chichester, 202, 203.
Cholmoneley, 154.
Gilbert de Clare, 26, 28, 62, 83, 136-149, 166, 168, 186, 192, 195, 196, 197, 198, 201, 212, 213, 214, 216, 217, 218, 221, 229, 239, 250, 253, 266, 270, 271, 272, 273, 274, 275, 277, 289, 297, 308, 321, 322, 324, 325, 327, 329, 337, 350, 360, 362, 389, 400, 408, 421, 433, 434, 440.
Richard de Clare, 26, 62, 85, 136-149, 166, 168, 186, 193, 195, 196, 197, 198, 201, 212, 213, 214, 216, 217, 218, 221, 229, 239, 250, 253, 266, 270, 271, 272, 273, 274, 275, 277, 289, 297, 308, 321,
322, 324, 325, 327, 329, 337, 350, 360, 362, 373, 389, 400, 408, 417, 421, 433, 434, 440.
Clare, 151-154, 172, 181, 243, 281, 306, 312, 339, 356, 387, 393.
Clark, 252.
Clarke, 134, 162.
Clarkson, 219, 247.
Clavering, 178, 196, 231, 298, 310, 352, 359, 388, 401.
Claxton, 390.
Claypoole, 162, 413.
Cleremont, 356.
Clifford, 148, 154, 172, 173, 240, 242, 253, 308, 309, 337, 338, 362, 422.
Clinton, 163, 164, 317.
Clute, 295.
Coate, 419.
Cobb, 369.
Cockercraft, 160.
Codding, 264.
Coffin, 155.
Coker, 173, 365.
Colden, 326.
Cole, 346.
Coles, 365.
Colle, 136.
Collier, 292.
Colville, 198.
Comyn, 260, 261, 271, 334.
Converse, 162.
Conway, 202.
Conyers, 162, 195, 198, 313, 390.
Cooke, 200.
Coolidge, 412.
Cooper, 134, 165, 419.
Coply, 441.
Cornell, 377.
Cornwall, 183, 257.
Cotes, 206.
Courtenay, 133, 166, 344, 345, 429, 446.
Cousins, 226.
Coventry, 366, 368.
Craik, 136.
Cream, 280.
Crocheron, 319.
Crophull, 170.

Cummings, 183, 185.
Cunyngham, 142.
Curzon, 206.
Cusack, 152.
Custis, 164.
Cutting, 247.

Dacre, 179, 230, 231, 298, 350, 351, 352, 400, 401, 408, 409.
Damon, 397.
Dana, 404.
Dandridge, 440.
Dangerfield, 202, 246.
Charles W. Darling, 398, 399-404.
Darrell, 173.
Daubeney, 363-367.
Davis, 184, 185, 226, 227, 355, 404.
Day, 355.
Deincourt, 175, 176.
Dennis, 283, 395.
Dennys, 346, 430.
Despencer, 151, 152, 329, 345, 386.
Devereux, 169, 170, 171.
Digby, 207.
Digges, 138, 153.
Dod, 370.
Douglas, 140, 145, 147, 156, 163, 166, 215, 217, 271, 324.
Downes, 280.
Downing, 161.
Doyle, 141.
Drake, 346, 430.
Drallyer, 219, 325.
Drennen, 397.
Dudley, 179, 276, 291, 314, 412, 415.
Dunbar, 145, 146, 147, 212, 216, 217, 271, 273, 322, 396, 429.
Dundas, 145, 148.
Dunlop, 442-444.
Dutton, 288, 317, 318.
Dymoke, 158, 201.
d'Arcy, 190, 193, 194, 198, 278, 314, 360, 362, 386, 389, 432, 433.
d'Auney, 345, 429.
d'Engaine, 175, 431.
d'Ergadia, 156.
d'Espec, 262.

d'Esturmé, 173.
d'Eu, d'Eue, d'Ewe, 169, 307, 343, 377, 431.
de Lancey, 326.
Delafield, 152.
de la Field, 278.
Delaplaine, 342.
de la Roche, 170.
de la Spine, 199, 204.
de la Vergne, 219.
de la Warr, 159, 160, 206, 436.

Ferdinand P. Earle, 316-319.
Earle, 285.
Eaton, 236.
Echyngham, 160, 175, 445.
Edwards, 137.
Elderkin, 346, 347.
Eliot, 236, 237.
Elliot, 431.
Ellis, 152, 207.
Elmedon, 334.
Ely, 404.
Enos, 347.
Ergadia, 215, 269, 272.
Erskine, 141, 217, 327, 430.
Etherstone, 334.
Everard, 143.
Evert, 380.
Ewell, 136.
Eyre, 257.

Fairfax, 150, 154, 202.
Farrand, 369.
Farwell, 180, 181, 182, 183.
Fauntleroy, 136.
Featherstonehaugh, 334.
Felbrigge, 166.
Fellows, 263.
Felton, 178, 231, 407.
Ferrers, 161, 170, 171, 172, 174, 176, 195, 196, 244, 253, 277-279, 310, 311, 312, 340, 362, 363, 386, 389, 423, 434.
Fienes, 170, 179, 231, 232, 233, 235, 299, 300, 307, 344, 350, 352, 353, 377, 382, 399, 400, 401, 402, 409, 410, 432.
Filkin, 367, 368.

INDEX

Fillol, 175.
Flagg, 184, 185.
Fleete, 202.
Alexander F. Fleete, 328, 329, 334.
Fletcher, 183.
Flower, 313.
Foliot, 169.
Forbes, 137.
Ford, 263.
Forrest, 315.
William de Fortibus, 27, 63, 95.
Foster, 264, 333, 334.
Fotheringham, 430.
Fowke, 202.
Fowler, 346.
Fox, 318.
Francisco, 442.
Fraser, 137, 145, 213, 274, 275.
Freeman, 293.
Fuller, 208.
Furnival, 169, 191, 193, 213, 230, 249, 268, 282, 309, 351, 361, 385, 394, 414.
Fitz-Alan, 161-165, 193, 214, 215, 223, 225, 233, 234, 268, 277, 299, 305, 307, 323, 330, 332, 349, 353, 361, 378, 383, 384, 402, 403, 410, 440.
Fitz-Geoffrey, 194, 214, 223, 230, 242, 253, 282, 298, 309, 317, 330, 338, 409, 422, 432, 433.
Fitz-Gerald, 157, 278, 382.
Fitz-Henry, 240.
Fitzhugh, 146, 167, 179, 194, 198, 232, 299, 313, 350, 389, 491, 409.
Fitz-John, 135, 191, 193, 214, 223, 225, 230, 233, 242, 243, 253, 268, 282, 298, 309, 317, 323, 330, 338, 339, 351, 357, 359, 361, 378, 385, 388, 394, 401, 402, 409, 422, 440.
Fitz-Maurice, 168, 240, 309, 337, 421.
Fitz-Osborne, 262.
Fitz-Patrick, 436.
Fitz-Piers, 169, 174, 189, 191, 289, 298, 308, 377, 383, 435.
Fitz-Reinfred, 426.
John Fitz-Robert, 63, 89, 177, 196, 197, 198, 201, 231, 278, 298, 310, 352, 359, 388, 401, 407, 426.
Robert Fitz-Walter, 11, 21, 25, 26, 28, 63, 91, 113, 121, 136, 149, 176.
Fitz-William, 240, 309.

Gamage, 282, 395.
Gardiner, 149, 258.
Gardner, 347.
Garrard, 276.
Gascoigne, 135, 195, 197, 201, 311, 312, 313.
Gaskell, 137, 419.
Gaveston, 192, 229, 297, 359.
Geneva, 249.
Genevill, 169, 170, 249, 289, 414.
Gerard, 262, 290, 292.
Gifford, 256.
Gilbert, 346, 430.
Gilliam, 439, 444.
Gilman, 209, 219.
Godolphin, 346.
Gooche, 208.
Gordon, 137, 145, 213, 218, 275, 322, 324.
Gorges, 346, 430.
Gotherson, 226.
Goushill, 162, 378, 379.
Gower, 224, 330.
Graeme, 137, 138.
Graff, 342.
Graham, 215, 324.
Grandison, 170.
Grant, 274.
Grantemaisnill, 239.
Graves, 263.
Gray, 165, 347.
Richard H. Greene, 428-431.
Greene, 263.
Greenleaf, 148.
Greilly, 206.
Grenville, 345, 346, 429.
Greslei, 206.
Grey, 143, 149, 151, 161, 176, 178, 190-194, 201, 207, 278, 358, 359, 360, 386.
Greystock, 148, 182, 242, 244, 253, 278, 339, 362, 422.
Griffin, 140, 206, 207.
Griffith, 379.
William H. Griffith, 286, 287-295.

Groesbeck, 412.
Grover, 276.
Gully, 395.
Gunning, 367.
Gurdon, 135, 308.
Guyon, 319.
Gwyn, 379.

Hagar, 182.
Hall, 419.
Hallett, 152.
Hamilton, 145-148, 216, 217, 438.
Hampden, 276.
Henry J. Hancock, 414, 419.
Hanford, 252.
Hanlon, 280.
Harby, 153, 160.
Harcourt, 282, 307, 394.
William de Hardell, 63, 97.
Hardenbrook, 219.
Hardenburg, 368.
Hardres, 235, 301, 354, 403, 411.
Harlakenden, 235, 236, 301, 354, 403, 411.
Harrison, 315, 442, 444.
Hassylden, 150.
Hastings, 291.
Hatch, 346.
Hawthorn, 347.
Haynes, 236, 301, 354, 403, 404, 411, 412.
Hedsworth, 390.
Henley, 144.
Henlon, 280.
Henry, 156.
Hepburn, 163.
Hering, 160.
Heron, 201.
Herrick, 295.
Hesilrigge, 144.
Hews, 276.
Hicks, 246.
Higgins, 279.
Hill, 219, 333, 346.
Hoadley, 237.
Hobart, 236, 354, 412.
Hobby, 208.
Hogben, 226.
Holbrook, 237.

Holford, 318.
Holland, 162-165, 214, 233, 250, 268, 277, 288, 299, 323, 350, 402, 410.
Hollyman, 158.
Home, 217.
Hoo, 183.
Hooe, 202.
Hopkins, 293.
Horsmanden, 151.
Hosie, 326.
Houghton, 258, 291.
Howard, 177, 183, 224, 306, 307, 331.
Howell, 151, 371.
Hubbard, 302.
Hubbart, 236, 301, 354, 403, 411.
Hudson, 314.
Humberston, 257.
Hume, 148.
Humphrey, 164, 379.
Hungerford, 161, 441.
Hunter, 315.
William de Huntingfield, 47, 63, 98, 150, 180.
Huntingfield, 312.
Hutchings, 319.
Hyde, 134, 262.

Innes, 275.
Isaac, 156, 215, 269, 272.
Ismay, 342.

Jackson, 390, 427.
James, 418.
Jenckes, 391.
Johnson, 254, 327.
Jones, 149, 264, 319, 333, 375, 418.

Kaye, 135, 198, 309, 313.
Keith, 137, 145, 213, 216, 274, 325.
Kempe, 224, 331.
Kendall, 183.
Ker, 155.
Kilconeath, 269, 428.
Kirten, 368.
Knapp, 327.
Knatchbull, 226.
Knolleys, 164.
Knowlton, 294.

INDEX 455

Knox, 138.
Knyvett, 307, 308.
Kynaston, 149, 151.

La Forge, 247.
La Touche, 279.
le Brune, 170, 249.
le Despencer, 153, 222, 223.
John de Lacie, 26, 27, 64, 100, 122, 151, 152, 153, 168, 192, 195, 196, 197, 198, 201, 221, 229, 239, 250, 253, 277, 289, 297, 309, 329, 337, 359, 362, 388, 400, 408, 421, 440.
Lacy, 169, 288, 414.
Lambert, 261, 262, 265, 376.
Lancaster, 291, 426.
Langrish, 446.
Langton, 290.
William de Lanvallei, 64, 104, 154, 155, 156, 157, 171, 198, 201, 205, 211, 215, 266, 270, 272, 274, 278, 311, 321, 324, 438.
Lathrop, 392.
Latimer, 206.
Lawrence, 182-184, 199, 252, 318, 340, 423.
Robert C. Lawrence, 238, 239-247.
George P. Lawton, 381-392.
Lay, 319.
Lea, 292.
Learned, 182.
Lechmere, 161.
Edward C. Lee, 281-285.
Lee, 164, 285.
Leete, 237.
Leighton, 164.
Lenox, 442.
Lesley, 156.
Leslie, 155.
Leventhorp, 256.
Leverett, 302.
Lewis, 293, 303, 368.
Lewright, 280.
Leyburne, 172, 316, 317, 399.
Lindsay, 139, 140, 146, 147, 280, 434, 435.
Lippincott, 227.
Lispenard, 219.

Livingston, 141, 166, 326, 327, 430.
Lloyd, 149, 292, 366, 417, 418.
Locke, 319.
Lockhart, 167.
Loftus, 150.
Logan, 148, 203.
Londenoys, 235.
Longespee, 287.
Longford, 244.
Lord, 404.
Lothrop, 285.
Loudenoys, 235, 300, 354, 403, 411.
Lovat, 274.
Lovel, 176, 177.
Ludlow, 133, 446.
Lumley, 390.
Luqueer, 246.
Luttrell, 133, 134, 446.
George A. Lyman, 259-264.
Lynde, 207, 208.

McCarty, 202, 203.
McIlvaine, 380.
McIntosh, 275, 276.
McKay, 341.
McKinney, 318.
McMurray, 369.
Macalester, 156.
Mac Carthy, 157, 438.
Macdonald, 213, 259, 287, 322, 386.
Mac Donnell, 141.
Macintosh, 275, 276.
Mackenzie, 274, 275.
Mac Williams, 173.
Maddox, 163.
Madison, 347.
Magee, 392.
Mainwaring, 333.
Maitland, 442, 444.
William Malet, 26, 64, 105, 157, 171, 197, 201, 279, 310, 363.
Maltravers, 445.
Geoffrey de Mandeville, 26, 27, 46, 64, 82, 107, 194, 362, 377, 381, 394, 431.
Mandeville, 306, 343, 358, 383.
Manning, 184.
Mansfield, 256.

Markenfield, 135, 195, 198, 312, 313.
Marny, 440.
Marr, 141, 429.
Marrow, 199.
George S. Marsh, 393–397.
William Marshall, Jr., 27, 65, 96, 106, 110, 117, 191, 192, 221, 241, 253, 255, 281, 358, 360, 382, 383, 389, 393, 400, 414, 422, 433, 438, 445.
Marshall, 168, 169, 229, 249, 267, 297, 308, 329, 338, 344, 350, 430.
Marston, 314.
Martian, 200.
Martin, 367.
Mason, 202, 203.
Mattison, 347.
Mauduit, 223, 230, 261, 282, 351, 358, 394.
Mauleverer, 135, 198, 309, 313.
Maynard, 144.
Meade, 143.
Meinill, 190, 198, 278, 360, 386.
Melville, 347.
Menteth, 141.
Menzies, 139.
Merces, 162.
Merriman, 263.
Meschines, 239, 337, 421.
Mickle, 314, 315.
Middleton, 160.
Milbourne, 170, 171.
Milligan, 142.
Minshall, 288.
Mohun, 441.
Molineaux, 183, 245, 340.
Montacute, 233, 250, 290, 299, 350, 363, 402, 410.
Montagne, 318.
Montague, 207.
Roger de Montbegon, 26, 27, 65, 111, 114.
Montdider, 356.
Monteath, 247, 392.
Richard de Montfichet, 28, 65, 96, 113.
Montfort, 261, 317, 416.
Montgomery, 144, 156, 166, 167, 273, 317.
Moore, 145, 377, 427.
Moreton, 441.
Morgan, 176, 258.

Morrison, 430.
Mortimer, 143, 154, 170, 172, 197, 240, 249, 288, 290, 310, 312, 338, 359, 387, 415, 422.
Morville, 442.
Roger de Mowbray, 27, 67, 111, 114, 190.
William de Mowbray, 26, 28, 66, 110, 114, 115, 158, 159, 160, 181, 190, 195, 198, 201, 225, 243, 253, 278, 306, 331, 339, 356, 387, 423, 440, 441.
Mulineaux, 424.
Multon, 176.
Mumbezon, 112.
Mumbray, 116.
Munson, 431.
Mure, 271, 429.
Murray, 163.
Muscegros, 196, 279, 310, 311, 363.
Mynne, 292.

Napier, 136.
Nephew, 276.
Nevill, 134, 151, 153, 160, 162, 176, 179, 181, 183, 192, 195, 197, 201, 224, 230, 232, 278, 298, 299, 310, 312, 331, 350, 359, 361, 385, 387, 401, 408.
Newburgh, 282, 358, 394.
Newdigate, 208.
Newkirk, 207.
Newmarch, 311.
Norman, 263.
Norris, 177, 179, 180.
Norton, 161.
Norville, 161.
Norwich, 150, 181.
Noyes, 404.

O'Crean, 280.
O'Hanlon, 280.
O'Riley, 438.
O'Sullivan, 157.
Ogle, 201.
Olney, 199, 203, 204.
Opie, 146.
Osborne, 263, 265, 370.
Owen, 377, 379.
Oxenbridge, 153, 160.

INDEX 457

Paine, 293.
Pancoast, 419.
Pardoe, 251.
Parkhurst, 185, 284.
Parr, 167, 425.
Parrett, 370.
Parry, 251, 308.
Schuyler L. Parsons, 320, 321-327.
Parton, 182.
Paschall, 418.
Pashley, 224, 330.
Pauncefote, 365.
Peake, 396.
Peche, 317.
Peckham, 391.
Peirce, 184.
Pelham, 159.
Pendleton, 202.
Penn, 137, 419.
Penn-Gaskell, 419.
Penny, 365.
Richard de Percy, 26, 27, 66, 118.
Percy, 143, 154, 172, 176, 195, 197, 201, 310, 312, 388, 425.
Periton, 174, 244, 312, 340, 389, 423, 434.
Perkins, 392.
Perry, 247.
Perwich, 207.
Peyton, 150.
Philler, 285.
Pickering, 198, 199.
Pierpont, 178, 231, 404, 407.
Pinney, 318.
Pinto, 318.
Pitt, 318.
Plantagenet, 143, 153, 169, 172, 181, 191, 193, 214, 225, 233, 235, 243, 249, 253, 268-281, 297, 300, 305, 309, 312, 323, 331, 339, 349, 351, 353, 357, 316, 375, 378, 383, 387, 393, 402, 410, 414, 416, 423, 435, 440.
Platt, 294.
Plunket, 278, 279.
Pole, 143, 150.
Pollard, 185.
Charles C. Pomeroy, 406, 407-412.
Poole, 184.

Poultney, 207.
Powel, 379.
Powell, 246.
Power, 397.
Poynings, 312.
Pray, 391.
Preis, 251.
Prentice, 258, 355.
Preston, 335.
Prestwith, 207.
Prevost, 140.
Price, 418.
Prideaux, 346, 430.
Proffit, 256.
Puleston, 374, 379.
Pyle, 446.
Pympe, 224, 330.

Saher de Quincey, 11, 26, 28, 46, 66, 102, 106, 110, 120, 160, 161, 162, 163, 168, 192, 194, 195, 196, 197, 198, 201, 215, 217, 221, 224, 229, 233, 234, 239, 250, 253, 259, 266, 267, 277, 287, 290, 299, 305, 323, 324, 330, 334, 337, 345, 349, 351, 353, 360, 361, 362, 363, 378, 389, 400, 402, 403, 410, 421, 427, 428, 439, 440.

Randolph, 146, 147, 212, 216, 272, 322, 428.
Read, 148.
Reade, 182, 200.
Redvers, 345.
Reed, 184.
Reeves, 276.
Reynolds, 182.
Richardson, 209.
Marmaduke Richardson, 277-280.
John J. Riker, 420, 421-427.
Roach, 251.
Roberdeau, 142.
Roberts, 183, 245, 251, 341, 424.
Robertson, 156, 295, 404, 439.
Robinson, 182.
Rochford, 134.
Rochfort, 279.
Rodam, 261, 334.

Rodburg, 283, 395.
Rodney, 158.
Rogers, 346, 430.
Roosevelt, 219.
Roper, 207.
Robert de Ros, 26, 27, 66, 119, 123, 174, 189, 195, 198, 201, 278, 289, 308, 360, 386, 426, 439.
Ros, or Roos, 262, 288.
Rose, 145, 146.
Rosewell, 314.
Rositer, 237.
Rouci, 356.
Rowe, 293.
Rowzee, 442.
Ruckman, 285.
Ruffin, 437.
Ruggles, 263.
Russell, 227, 237, 301.
Rutgers, 326.
Ryan, 380.
Rysse, 209.

St. Clair, 154, 397.
St. John, 134, 164, 172, 344.
St. Lawrence, 152, 278.
St. Leger, 151, 153.
St. Liz, 180.
St. Maur, 172.
Sackett, 427.
Saltonstall, 135.
Andrew H. M. Saltonstall, 305–314.
Sampson, 156.
Saundford, 169, 267, 305, 349, 384, 439.
Savage, 288, 291.
Saxbury, 366.
Geoffrey de Say, 66, 126, 163, 172, 197, 201, 232, 279, 299, 311, 316, 352, 362, 399, 409.
Scales, 166.
George R. Schieffelin, 336, 337–342.
Schuyler, 326.
Scott, 165, 224, 226, 263, 330, 331, 332.
Scoville, 237.
Scrope, 167, 181, 182, 194, 195, 313, 389.
Scull, 227.
Seaman, 419.

Seddon, 335.
Sedgwick, 303.
Sedley, 308.
Segrave, 182, 191, 225, 242, 288, 291, 306, 331, 358, 387, 422, 435.
Sergeant, 177.
Sergeaux, 224, 330.
Seton, 137, 145, 166, 213, 216, 273, 429.
Seymour, 157, 172, 175, 180, 276, 283, 395.
Sheffield, 149, 150.
Sheldon, 397.
Sheppard, 148.
Sidney, 280.
Sinclair, 155, 271, 275.
Skelton, 397.
Skidmore, 252.
Skinner, 264.
Skipwith, 158.
Philip H. Waddell Smith, 356–371.
Smith, 158, 165, 246, 251, 284, 319, 341, 391, 397, 427.
Snow, 293.
Someri, 291, 415.
Southwick, 369.
Southworth, 290, 292.
Spencer, 153, 164, 170, 222.
Spotswood, 147.
Dandridge Spotswood, 432, 433, 447.
Spottiswood, 147, 435.
Spottswood, 436.
Sprott, 140.
Stafford, 135, 149, 151, 170, 174, 192, 196, 230, 284, 289, 291, 297, 308, 310, 351, 359, 387, 400, 408.
Stanley, 290, 291, 379.
Stapylton, 150.
Steere, 209.
Stevens, 392.
Still, 257.
Stoneham, 183.
Story, 149.
Stourton, 135, 136, 364.
Strange, 193, 361, 374, 383, 415, 441.
Strangeways, 198.
Stratton, 133, 134, 446.
Striker, 319.

INDEX

Stuart and Stewart, 137-141, 156, 163-166, 215-217, 269, 271-274, 275, 314, 324, 327, 429.
Sudley, 197, 279, 311, 362.
Summers, 315.
Sutherland, 154, 155, 212, 213, 271, 322.
Sutton, 179.
Suydam, 252.
Swynnerton, 291.
Syme, 156.
Symes, 202.
Symonds, 365.

Taggart, 304.
Taintor, 258.
Talbot, 193, 194, 276, 283, 360, 361, 383-385, 394.
Talboys, 201.
Tarrent, 146.
Taylor, 183, 355.
Terry, 285.
George D. Terry, 348, 349-355.
Thompson, 431.
Thorley, 441.
Thornton, 288.
Throckmorton, 153, 160.
Charles W. Throckmorton, 189-203.
Tibetot, 178, 181, 407.
Tilney, 307.
Tiptoft, 181.
Tirwhitt, 198.
Todd, 431.
Todeni, 366.
Tomlin, 333.
Toni, 134, 261, 262, 310, 317.
Touchett, 175, 250, 288, 289, 290.
Townley, 246, 341.
Townsend, 418.
Treadcroft, 276.
Treat, 293.
Tregoz, 206.
Trethewy, 262.
Trevor, 342.
Troutbeck, 379.
Tudor, 374.
Tuke, 331.
Turberville, 283, 395.

Tuthill, 245, 341.
Tutt, 202.
Tuttell, 245.
Tuttle, 304, 319, 341.
Tyndale, 166.

Ufford, 178, 231, 298, 352, 401, 407.
Umfraville, 174, 260, 261, 289, 334.

Valentine, 208.
Valonies, 176.
Vaughn, 251.
Vaun, 251.
Vaux, 174, 190, 289, 308, 435.
Verdon, 277, 385.
Robert de Vere, 26, 67, 127, 164, 165, 166, 168, 194, 198, 215, 217, 224, 233, 234, 266, 267, 277, 300, 305, 324, 330, 345, 349, 353, 361, 378, 384, 402, 403, 410, 427, 428, 439.
Vere, 149, 161-163, 176, 177.
Vermandois, 358, 415.
Vernon, 317.
Eustace de Vesci, 11, 26, 27, 67, 129, 167, 174, 195, 198, 201, 243, 254, 278, 312, 340, 389, 423, 439.
Vincent, 165, 396.
Vivonia, 157, 171, 172.
Van Benthuysen, 219.
Van Cortlandt, 326.
Van Schaick, 219, 325.
Van Zant, 246.
Von Rydingsvärd, 168-185.

Wacker, 334.
Waddell, 367, 369.
Wade, 397.
Waer, 291.
Waimstead, 283.
Walker, 154, 184, 276, 332, 333.
Wallace, 163, 412.
Waller, 144.
Walmsley, 419.
Ward, 237, 314.
Charles S. Ward, 297-304.
Warne, 251.
Warnstead, 395.

INDEX

Warren, 148, 161–165, 193, 205, 215, 223, 233, 255, 267, 277, 279, 280, 282, 291, 299, 305, 323, 330, 349, 358, 361, 378, 384, 393, 394, 402, 410, 414, 440.
Washburn, 182, 285.
Washington, 202, 442.
Webb, 209, 431.
Welch, 138.
Welles, 158, 167, 175, 182, 195, 201, 242, 244, 252, 253, 278, 312, 339, 340, 389, 422, 423, 433, 434.
Welsh, 257.
Wentworth, 173, 309.
West, 159, 160, 441.
Wheathill, 207.
Whettles, 207.
White, 419.
Whitehead, 303.
Whiting, 134, 412.
Whitleigh, 346, 430.
Whitney, 171, 176, 180–183.
Stephen Whitney, 248, 249–254.
Whittlesey, 303.
Wickenden, 391.
Wickliffe, 203.
Wildey, 333.
Wilkins, 227.
Wilkinson, 390–392.
Willington, 363.
Wilson, 392.
Windebank, 201.
Windsor, 133, 134, 160.
Wingfield, 162, 175.
Winslow, 430.
Winston, 156.
Frederick H. Winston, 266, 267–276.
Winthrop, 161, 166, 219, 314.
Wishart, 167.
Witherspoon, 138.
Wolcott, 430.
Wood, 376, 377.
Woodbridge, 412.
Woodhull, 167, 425.
Woodruffe, 309.
Wright, 263, 412.
Wyatt, 224, 331.
Wye, 171.

Wyke, 204.
Wyllys, 236, 301, 354, 355, 411, 412.
Wyman, 184.
Wyndham, 182.
Wyndsore, 446.
Wynne, 375.

Young, 283, 395.
Youngs, 165.

Zouche, 160, 161, 178, 287, 310, 388, 407.

EARLS.

Abercorn, 186.
Albemarle, 76, 95, 110.
Angus, 217, 261, 334.
Annandale, 84, 136, 147, 166, 186, 212, 216, 269, 270, 272, 321, 322, 323, 327, 428, 429.
Argyle, 144, 156, 272, 274.
Arran, 186.
Arundel, 87, 117, 161–165, 181, 190, 193, 214, 215, 223, 225, 233, 234, 243, 268, 299, 305, 306, 323, 330, 331, 332, 339, 349, 353, 356, 361, 378, 383, 384, 402, 410, 423, 435, 440.
Athol, 156, 165, 215, 216, 271, 275, 324.
Bothwell, 163, 217.
Buchan, 122, 260, 271, 334.
Buckingham, 86, 87.
Caithness, 154, 271.
Cambridge, 121, 143, 291.
Carrick, 136–142, 144, 146, 147, 166, 186, 211, 212, 269, 322, 361, 382, 428, 432.
Chester, 87, 100, 102, 122, 239, 243, 268, 337, 339, 349–421.
Clare, 85, 86, 116, 221, 239, 250, 387.
Comyn, 129.
Cornwall, 83, 192–230.
Crawford, 139, 140, 146, 147, 186, 429.
Cumberland, 154.
Derby, 106, 122, 161, 172, 174, 176, 196, 244, 253, 312, 340, 363, 386, 389, 423, 434.
Desmond, 433.
Devon, 84, 133, 344.

INDEX 461

Douglas, 215, 324, 345.
Dunbar, 145, 146, 212, 216, 217, 271, 273, 322, 429.
Eglington, 144, 166.
Erroll, 216, 324.
Essex, 82, 83, 94, 95, 101, 107, 108, 133, 169, 170, 191, 194, 226, 234, 235, 300, 306, 332, 343, 353, 358, 361, 377, 381, 383, 394, 410, 431.
Exeter, 183.
Fife, 139.
Gloucester, 83, 87, 88, 103, 108, 143, 148, 149, 151, 152, 153, 168, 172, 192, 195, 221, 229, 230, 239, 250, 270, 297, 308, 329, 337, 350, 351, 359, 373, 388.
Hereford, 80, 81, 85, 122, 133, 169, 170, 226, 234, 235, 300, 306, 311, 332, 343, 344, 353, 361, 362, 363, 377, 381, 402, 410, 432.
Hertford, 76, 83, 88, 116, 127, 143, 148, 149, 151, 152, 153, 168, 190, 192, 194, 198, 221, 229, 239, 250, 253, 270, 297, 308, 312, 321, 329, 337, 350, 356, 359, 373, 388, 389, 421, 428.
Holland, 226.
Huntingdon, 81, 91, 120, 122, 212, 260, 270, 334.
Huntly, 137, 145, 213, 216, 217, 218, 322, 325.
Kent, 143, 162, 163, 164, 165, 171, 205, 211, 214, 233, 268, 270, 299, 311, 321, 323, 350, 402, 410, 433.
Kildare, 157, 383, 432, 433.
Kilmarnock, 155.
Kyme, 261.
Lancaster, 172, 181, 193, 197, 214, 225, 233, 234, 243, 253, 268, 305, 306, 312, 323, 339, 349, 353, 361, 362, 378, 384, 387, 403, 423, 435, 440.
Lennox, 216, 273, 272, 324.
Leicester, 88, 121, 168, 239, 242, 259, 267, 287, 312, 337, 338, 349, 384, 421, 422.
Lincoln, 84, 101, 103, 122, 164, 168, 192, 221, 229, 239, 297, 309, 329, 337, 350, 360, 388, 400, 421.
Linlithgow, 166.

Lothian, 155.
Marr, 141, 142, 217, 271, 327.
Marsh, 143, 145, 146, 147, 154, 170, 172, 197, 212, 216, 217, 241, 250, 273, 288, 310, 312, 322, 338, 359, 387, 422, 429.
Mellent, 242, 259, 338, 345.
Moray, 146, 147, 212, 216, 217, 271, 272, 322, 429.
Moreton, 91, 163, 166.
Morton, 156, 216.
Mulgrave, 150.
Norfolk, 74, 76, 78, 85, 121, 169, 191, 215, 223, 225, 230, 243, 249, 255, 268, 291, 298, 317, 323, 330, 331, 339, 345, 351, 358, 378, 383, 389, 393, 409, 414, 422.
Northampton, 81, 120, 194, 225, 234, 260, 300, 306, 307, 332, 344, 353, 378, 403, 410.
Northumberland, 81, 113, 120, 143, 154, 197, 201, 260, 270, 312.
Nottingham, 225, 306, 331.
Orkney, 154, 155, 271.
Ormond, 194, 361, 382, 431, 432, 433.
Oxford, 78, 79, 108, 127, 128, 149, 161, 162, 163, 164, 165, 166, 168, 169, 176, 177, 194, 215, 223, 224, 233, 267, 299, 323, 330, 345, 349, 361, 378, 384, 402, 410, 439.
Pembroke, 74, 75, 76, 102, 110, 122, 168, 169, 191, 192, 221, 229, 242, 249, 253, 255, 281, 282, 297, 308, 309, 329, 338, 344, 350, 358, 360, 382, 383, 389, 393, 414, 422, 428.
Richmond, 81.
Ross, 213, 216, 322.
Rothes, 155, 156.
Salisbury, 233, 250, 287, 299, 350, 402, 410.
Shrewsbury, 193, 360, 384.
Somerset, 163, 164, 165, 214, 269, 323.
Southesk, 140.
Stafford, 135, 149, 151, 170, 174, 192, 196, 197, 230, 234, 291, 297, 308, 310, 351, 359, 387, 400.
Sterling, 186.
Strathern, 215, 324.
Suffolk, 85, 121, 150, 231, 291.

Surrey, 79, 81, 116, 161, 162, 163, 164, 165, 169, 193, 205, 214, 223, 225, 233, 249, 255, 267, 305, 309, 323, 330, 349, 358, 361, 378, 384, 393, 410.
Sussex, 117, 190, 225, 243, 306, 331, 339, 356.
Sutherland, 137, 154, 155, 212, 213, 216, 271, 321, 322.
Tankerville, 149, 151.
Traquier, 140.
Ulster, 143, 153, 154, 155, 156, 157, 171, 197, 198, 270, 312, 321, 433.
Warren, 205, 223, 255, 267, 281, 282, 305, 330, 349, 393, 394, 440.
Warwick, 82, 118, 135, 152, 172, 191, 214, 223, 225, 230, 233, 240, 242, 243, 253, 268, 298, 299, 309, 310, 316, 323, 330, 338, 339, 351, 352, 357, 358, 359, 362, 364, 378, 384, 387, 394, 399, 402, 422, 423, 440.
Waterford, 193, 360, 384.
Westmoreland, 135, 162, 181, 192, 196, 197, 201, 230, 232, 298, 310, 312, 350, 359, 387, 401, 409.
Wexford, 193, 360, 384.
Winchester, 102, 120, 122, 161, 168, 215, 222, 229, 239, 259, 267, 287, 299, 305, 329, 330, 334, 337, 345, 349, 351, 363, 378, 386, 400, 421.
Worcester, 151, 153.
York, 95.

DUKES.

Albany, 138, 139, 217, 273, 327.
Chatelherault, 186.
Clarence, 143, 153, 197, 269, 312.
Gloucester, 234, 300, 307, 353, 402, 410.
Guildres, 216.
Lancaster, 214, 232, 269, 323, 350, 435.
Norfolk, 224, 225, 242, 305, 331.
Somerset, 152, 164, 175.
Suffolk, 178.
Touraine, 215, 324.
York, 143.

MONARCHS.

Alfred the Great, 334.
Alphonso VIII. of Castile, 384.
Charlemagne, 290, 415.
David I. of Scotland, 81, 213, 260, 270, 287, 322, 334.
David II. of Scotland, 269.
Dermot, of Ireland, 76, 282, 393.
Edmund Ironsides, 213, 260, 270.
Edward I. of England, 170, 191, 192, 194, 198, 214, 222, 225, 226, 229, 235, 243, 269, 297, 300, 307, 312, 323, 329, 331, 332, 339, 344, 350, 351, 353, 358, 359, 362, 375, 378, 382, 387, 388, 400, 403, 408, 411, 416, 422, 429, 437, 440.
Edward III. of England, 172, 196, 197, 214, 232, 234, 269, 300, 307, 310, 312, 323, 350, 353, 362, 402, 410, 425.
Ferdinand III. of Castile, 192, 359, 375, 382, 388.
Henry I. of England, 190.
Henry II. of England, 243, 384.
Henry III. of England, 96, 110, 214, 243, 305, 306, 312, 323, 339, 353, 357, 378, 382, 384, 387, 402, 403, 423, 426, 440, 445.
Henry IV. of England, 269.
Henry I. of France, 79, 81, 88, 191, 223, 242, 259, 281, 290, 291, 338, 358, 393, 415, 422, 426.
Hugh Capet, 86, 282, 356, 394.
James I. of Scotland, 166, 186, 214, 216, 217, 218, 269, 322, 325.
James II. of Scotland, 186, 215, 216, 217, 269, 271.
James III. of Scotland, 216.
James I. of Arragon, 243, 387.
John, of England, 83, 110, 221, 374, 382, 416.
Llewellyn, of Wales, 241, 557, 374.
Louis IV. of France, 290.
Louis VII. of France, 211, 270.
Louis VIII. of France, 243, 339, 384, 423.
Malcolm III. of Scotland, 260, 270.
Otto I. of Saxony, 86.

INDEX

Philip III. of France, 192, 214, 225, 243, 269, 323, 331, 339, 350, 358, 387, 422.

Robert I. of Scotland, 137, 138, 139, 140, 141, 155, 156, 166, 186, 211, 212, 214, 215, 260, 269, 271, 272, 273, 274, 275, 321, 327, 419, 434, 436.

Robert II. of Scotland, 137, 138, 139, 140, 166, 186, 214, 215, 217, 271, 272, 324, 327, 434.

Robert III. of Scotland, 137, 166, 186, 214, 217, 272.

Robert I. of France, 79, 261, 416.

William I. of England, 116, 118, 129.

William the Lion, of Scotland, 174, 212, 125, 130, 243, 271, 289, 308, 312, 434, 439.

THE END

www.ingramcontent.com/pod-product-compliance
Lightning Source LLC
Chambersburg PA
CBHW031540300426
44111CB00006BA/121